The Talented Women of the Zhang Family

A

Philip E. Lilienthal (signature)

■   ■   ■

B O O K

The Philip E. Lilienthal imprint
honors special books
in commemoration of a man whose work
at the University of California Press
from 1954 to 1979
was marked by dedication to young authors
and to high standards in the field of Asian Studies.
Friends, family, authors, and foundations have together
endowed the Lilienthal Fund, which enables the Press
to publish under this imprint selected books
in a way that reflects the taste and judgment
of a great and beloved editor.

The Talented Women
of the Zhang Family

SUSAN MANN

UNIVERSITY OF CALIFORNIA PRESS
BERKELEY   LOS ANGELES   LONDON

University of California Press, one of the most distinguished university presses in the United States, enriches
lives around the world by advancing scholarship in the
humanities, social sciences, and natural sciences. Its
activities are supported by the UC Press Foundation and
by philanthropic contributions from individuals and
institutions. For more information, visit www.ucpress.edu.

University of California Press
Berkeley and Los Angeles, California

University of California Press, Ltd.
London, England

Library of Congress Cataloging-in-Publication Data

Mann, Susan, 1943–.
   The talented women of the Zhang family / Susan Mann.
      p.   cm. — (Philip E. Lilienthal Asian studies
imprint)
   Includes bibliographical references and index.
   ISBN 978-0-520-25089-5 (cloth : alk. paper)
   ISBN 978-0-520-25090-1 (pbk. : alk. paper)
      1. Women authors, Chinese—Biography.   2. Chinese
literature—Qing dynasty, 1644–1912—History and
criticism.   3. Chang family.   I. Title.

PL2277.M355   2007
895.1'093522—dc22   2006036294

Manufactured in the United States of America

15   14   13   12   11   10   09   08   07
10   9   8   7   6   5   4   3   2   1

The paper used in this publication meets the minimum
requirements of ANSI/NISO z39.48-1992 (R 1997)
(*Permanence of Paper*).

To my own grand family

MANN * JONES * SKINNER

CONTENTS

ILLUSTRATIONS

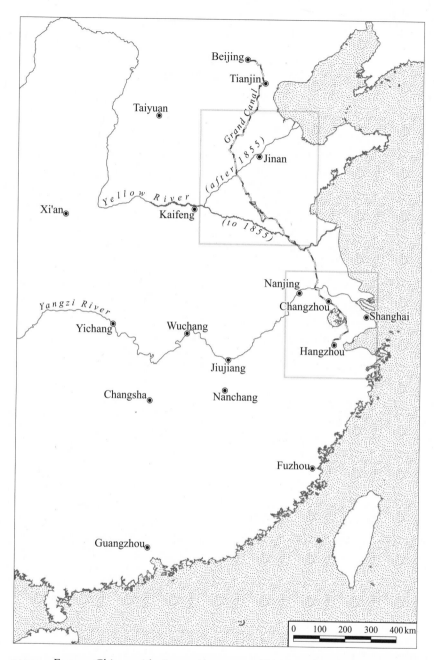

MAP I. Eastern China, mid-nineteenth century. (Cartography by Mark Henderson and G. William Skinner, University of California, Davis. Base map from the China Historical GIS project, Harvard University, www.fas.harvard.edu/~chgis.)

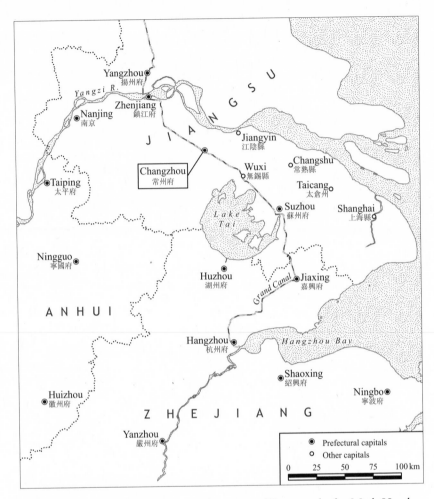

MAP 2. Lower Yangzi, mid-nineteenth century. (Cartography by Mark Henderson and G. William Skinner, University of California, Davis. Base map from the China Historical GIS project, Harvard University, www.fas.harvard.edu/~chgis.)

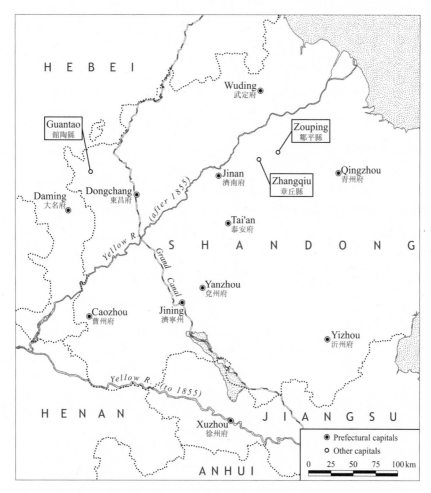

MAP 3. Western Shandong, mid-nineteenth century. (Cartography by Mark Henderson and G. William Skinner, University of California, Davis. Base map from the China Historical GIS project, Harvard University, www.fas.harvard.edu/~chgis.)

GENEALOGICAL CHART OF THE ZHANG FAMILY
AND THEIR COLLATERAL KIN

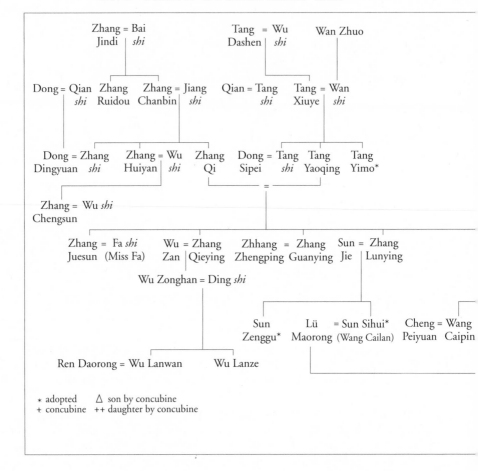

* adopted   △ son by concubine
+ concubine ++ daughter by concubine

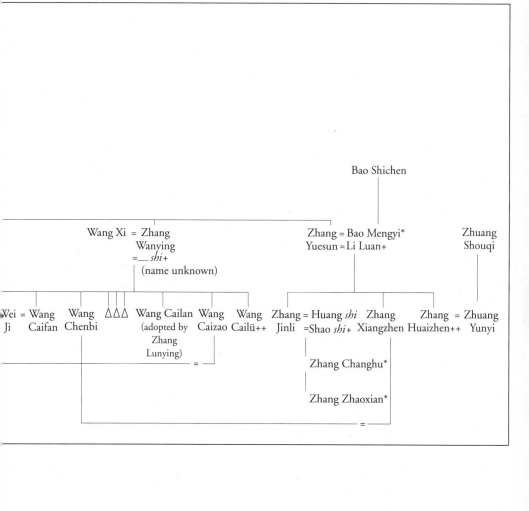

Bao Shichen

Wang Xi = Zhang Wanying
=__ *shi*+
(name unknown)

Zhang Yuesun = Bao Mengyi*
=Li Luan+

Zhuang Shouqi

Wei = Wang Caifan
Ji

Wang Chenbi

△△△

Wang Cailan
(adopted by Zhang Lunying)

Wang Caizao

Wang Cailü++

Zhang Jinli =Shao *shi*+ = Huang *shi*

Zhang Xiangzhen

Zhang Huaizhen++ = Zhuang Yunyi

Zhang Changhu*

Zhang Zhaoxian*

=

=

PROLOGUE

THE PEOPLE YOU ARE ABOUT TO MEET lived and died a long time ago, but they left behind a treasure: beautiful copies of their own writings in woodblock print. They did not want to be forgotten. I have reconstructed their lives from those writings, using anything else I could find that might help to unlock the secrets they chose to keep to themselves. I have also asked some questions about their lives that they themselves would not have thought to ask, much less answer.

The phrase "talented women" is a direct translation of the Chinese word *cainü,* which was widely used during the eighteenth and nineteenth centuries, often with reference to the women in this book. On the other hand, although this book is about the Zhang family's talented women, my subjects do not all share the Zhang surname, and my use of the term "family" is therefore loose, by Chinese standards. In late imperial China, a woman kept the surname of her natal family's patriline after marriage. Thus, Zhang Qi's wife's surname was Tang, while his four daughters bore his surname, Zhang, and his youngest daughter's daughters took the surname Wang, after their own father's line. The genealogical chart on pages xii–xiii should help keep all of this straight. Further complicating my use of the term "family" is the fact that, strictly speaking, after marriage a Chinese woman kept her surname but left her natal family to join the patriline of her husband, moving into his home. As the stories that follow make clear, the Zhang over three generations managed to ignore this conventional family practice on several fronts. Their ingenuity in doing so supplies some of the plot line for their family history.

Finally, the Zhang history as recorded here is somewhat unconventional. In Chinese it would be called a *waishi,* meaning a history that is slightly outré or out of bounds. A *waishi* records things that *might* have happened, based on invented or unauthenticated sources, or on gossip. Although most of the stories in this book come directly from the Zhang family records, some of what you will read is my own conjecture and invention. Here I have followed a central tenet of Chinese historical writing, which strives to bring to life people from the past with their feelings, words, and deeds intact. My comments as the historian, which follow each section and fill the notes as well as the epilogue that concludes the book, feebly attempt to honor both the style and the critical standards set nearly two millennia ago by the great Han historian Sima Qian, who kept his lively historical narratives and his personal judgments separate. In search of a narrative style that would suit this purpose, I followed advice from the writer Erie Vitiello: "To write a good story," she told me one day, "you have to learn to set a scene."[1] She might have taken the words right out of the mouth of Sima Qian, whose finest historical prose features scenes that make great movies[2] and even better reading.

In setting out to write a book that my readers would enjoy half as much as I enjoy the work of the Grand Historian, I was skeptical. I thought setting scenes would be a slippery slope toward playing fast and loose with my evidence. To my great surprise, however, recreating historical moments in my mind invited me to pull together disparate pieces of evidence I might otherwise never have connected. For example, in setting the scene where Tang Yaoqing reads about Miss Fa's declared intention, I found myself tracing a ripple of consequences through both the Fa and the Zhang families, a ripple I could not have seen even in a strict, close reading of my evidence. The scene and the consequences are invented, to be sure, insofar as they are not described in any historical source. But their veracity can be documented in countless Zhang family records. Similarly, in imagining Zhang Wanying's trip to bury her husband's body, I had to link the history of Wang Xi's grand family to Wanying's prolonged search for a gravesite, and then ask the reason for her anomalous reception at the Wang home in Taicang. This led to new insights into the interfamily dynamics of uxorilocal marriage. Finally, in reinventing Xu Zhenyi's act of composing the preface to Wang Caipin's poems, I came face to face with his marginal position as an official whose charge was no longer important to the empire he had loyally served. These were not insights I could have arrived at simply by reading the documents. It took a scene to show me the full picture. Evidence can tell us only what we are able to hear, and setting a scene makes it talk louder.

PLATE 1. Hong Zhang, *Linking Verse across Adjoining Rooms*, 2005. Ink and color on silk, 1′ × 7′. Hong Zhang, born in China, has exhibited her work in Asia, North America, and Europe. She received her B.F.A. in Chinese painting from the Beijing Central Academy of Fine Arts in 1994 and M.F.A. from the University of California, Davis, in 2004. She currently resides in Lawrence, Kansas.

PLATE 2. Zhang Yuesun and Bao Mengyi. Detail (right panel) from Zhang, *Linking Verse across Adjoining Rooms.*

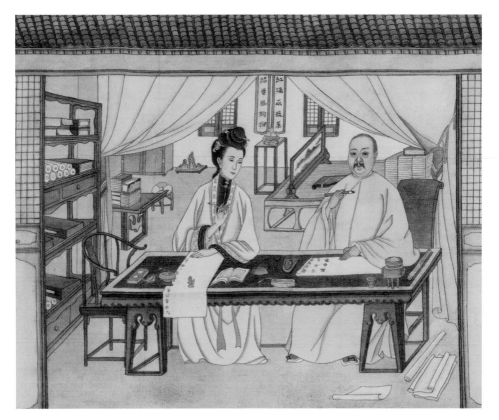

PLATE 3. Zhang Lunying and Sun Jie. Detail (center panel) from Zhang, *Linking Verse across Adjoining Rooms.*

PLATE 4. Zhang Wanying and Wang Xi. Detail (left panel) from Zhang, *Linking Verse across Adjoining Rooms.*

ONE

Jining, Shandong

(1893–1895)

THE DIRECTOR-GENERAL OF THE GRAND CANAL sat at his writing table, his inkstone and brushes buried under a pile of poems. Near the edge of the table lay a long narrow box of faded brocade, fraying at the corners and recently dusted. One of its ivory fastenings was broken. He did not know where the box came from, but he recognized the poems. Over the past several months, he had read them all, line by line, discarding pages he felt were incomplete or written too hastily, saving the margin notes wherever he found them. The poems that survived his scrutiny were the ones now stacked before him, arranged in chronological order. He rifled through them briefly just to reassure himself.

He had resolved in the autumn to publish the poems to honor their author, his children's late governess. She had been in his employ since his brief stint in Henan, where he met her through friends.[1] At the time, she was a widow in the worst possible circumstance: the in-laws to whom she had devoted herself were dead, and her late husband's only heir had not survived. She was utterly alone. It so happened that he needed a governess for his children, born to his young concubine and living with him at the time. But it took some care on his part to extend an offer of employment to a woman of Wang Caipin's upbringing. She had never worked outside her home, nor felt the need to do so, although he was told that she had received pupils in a special room set aside for that purpose in the home of her parents-in-law and by this means had earned a modest income. Facing destitution as she was at the time he met her, however, she needed a respectable place to live. The widows' homes that had sprung up throughout the country in the wake of the Taiping Rebellion were decidedly not to her liking.

So they had reached a genteel agreement, based on the eminence of her family and her distinction as a poet, calligrapher, and painter, as well as his own dignified position and timely need. In the years that followed, he had grown attached to her. Her elegy for his beloved concubine, composed just a few years before her own death, had sealed their friendship. It was time to repay her.

Her poems were ready. His own last task, composing the preface, stared up at him from the tabletop. Moving the sheets of paper to one side, he carefully dropped water onto the massive inkstone and ground the ink with measured force. Then he selected a favorite brush and wrote. He began with a flourish: a series of grand allusions to the difficulties facing women writers who wished to remain virtuous and above reproach, particularly as widows, and to the many female writers and scholars who had preceded Wang Caipin's own fame as a learned woman. The examples he selected fell nicely into parallel prose as his brush sped over the paper. This prepared him to introduce the author herself: "Wang Caipin was the granddaughter of Zhang Qi and the grandniece of Zhang Huiyan. She was heir to the long tradition of women who transmit classical learning. She grew up in the home of her maternal uncle at Wuchang, where she lived with her mother and her maternal aunt."[2]

Here Xu Zhenyi embellished his preface with some allusions to other famous learned women of literati families. He knew them all. He pointed out that Wang Caipin had "studied under the tutelage of her aunts: the poet Zhang Qieying and the calligrapher Zhang Lunying." He then supplied appropriate details of the marital connections of these ladies and described the illustrious reputations of all concerned. He dropped the names of the ladies' two most illustrious admirers: the legendary leaders of the victory over the Taiping rebels, Zeng Guofan (1811–1872) and Hu Linyi (1812–1861). Then he began to narrate the life of the author of the poems.

Despite the grand prose in which he chose to celebrate Wang Caipin's work, Xu considered his late governess a modest and understated person. She had lived quietly in her private quarters near his comfortable office in Jining. She enjoyed the company of his concubine, and up until the time of the concubine's death, they all spent an evening together every ten days or so, following the lunar cycle.[3] After the concubine died, however, the governess withdrew into her privacy, and he rarely saw her.

The Director-General reflected that he and Wang Caipin were born at nearly the same time. They had lived through the mid-century Taiping Rebellion. They had idolized the same heroes. They had both expected a "restoration" of the grand empire they had known in their youth, led by those very heroes, particularly Zeng Guofan and Hu Linyi.[4] Xu Zhenyi himself did not acknowledge that the Restoration program was a failure.[5] But in his present post, there was no denying that dramatic changes had been transforming the polity beyond recognition ever since the Taiping Rebellion.

Xu Zhenyi's official position was close to the top of the imperial bureaucracy: as Director-General of the Grand Canal, his formal rank was 2a.[6] But the shifting economy and ecology of the 1870s and 1880s had combined to make his title an empty one. The Grand Canal was no longer the lifeline of the capital's food supply, and the crucial Yellow River crossing that had blocked the Canal with silt since the river's change of course in 1855— the area that was his particular charge—had been nearly erased from the priorities of an imperial government whose concerns now focused on foreign trade along the coast and the growing treaty port sector of the economy.[7] The governors of Henan and Shandong were now in charge of the political economy of his region, and his own office—he had to face it— was superfluous.[8]

Wang Caipin, he knew, had grown skeptical about the country's future. She began her life as a talented prodigy, celebrated as one of the brilliant *cainü,* or "talented women," of her time.[9] She made an excellent marriage in 1850 to an equally talented young man, and even though the marriage took her far from her home and the extended family where she had grown up, the match was a good one. This recollection inspired him to add some conventional phrases on connubial harmony to his description of her married life: "On her dressing table beside her inkstone case were scattered poems, and copies of the *Book of Changes, Zhuangzi,* and Qu Yuan's 'Encountering Sorrow.'" The Director-General wanted to make sure his readers knew that Wang Caipin had married into a scholarly family where the highest standards in women's learning were honored. It was the best way to praise her learned family's choice of a spouse.

Soon after the marriage came the Taiping Rebellion. Wang Caipin's husband had died early in the course of the fighting. She contemplated suicide but realized that she must dedicate herself to caring for her husband's parents and rearing his heir. Her brilliance as a poet had faded somewhat in the pedestrian labor of tutoring and caregiving that followed, although Xu Zhenyi thought many of her late poems were quite fine. Her writing also changed over the years. Her joyful embrace of life as a young woman gave way to grief following her husband's early death. She then achieved a state of graceful resignation during her years of widowhood, as one by one the members of her extended family scattered and died. At the same time, many of her poems showed flashes of anger and frustration at the country's military weakness. This surprised the Director-General only slightly, given what he knew of her close correspondence with her maternal aunt and her uncle during the years when the Taiping Rebellion raged.

Xu Zhenyi turned back to his preface, in search of the right words to conclude it. A story about the death of the Han official Fan Pang came to mind. Fan Pang's parting words to his mother were: "Life and death, each has its proper place. Do not grieve over this farewell."[10] Pleased with the effect of this final allusion, and relieved that the printing could now proceed, Xu Zhenyi called for his clerk to deliver the manuscript to a scribe. This was only the first stage in a publication process that would yield handsome woodblock editions of Wang Caipin's poetry that he planned to send as gifts to friends, relatives, and admirers of the Zhang family. He congratulated himself for repaying his debt to Wang Caipin in such a satisfying way.

The Director-General had one thing left to do. He turned to the box at the edge of his table, fumbled with the clasps—the broken one gave way easily—and lifted the lid. Inside was a handscroll, tightly rolled and carefully wrapped in fine gauze. He realized at once what it must be. Surely this was the famous painting he had heard so much about from the elderly governess, who loved to recount how the scroll's odd combination of subjects and settings had caused so much comment when it was first painted. This was the original work commissioned by Wang Caipin's maternal uncle, Zhang Yuesun, to celebrate his unique joint family household: one where a brother and his two sisters and their respective spouses and children all lived together under one roof.

Xu Zhenyi called a servant and ordered a low table placed near one wall of his study. He dismissed the servant, settled himself on a mat beside the table, and carefully untied the handscroll, revealing copious inscriptions copied onto the margins at the beginning. Then he began to view it, unrolling it carefully in sections, from right to left. The painting, in ink and color on silk, featured three couples "linking verse in adjoining rooms," as the title had it. Xu wondered briefly how he would be able to identify the subjects, but he quickly saw that the painter had left little to the imagination. The first to come into view were clearly Zhang Yuesun himself and his demure wife, Bao Mengyi. The refinement of their faces, the elegant placement of the objects in their chamber, and their primacy in the order of the handscroll made it plain that this was a portrait of the family head, heir of the paterfamilias, Zhang Qi. The middle section of the scroll showed a separate but adjoining chamber, in which appeared a dignified woman writing calligraphy in the company of a slightly pudgy man. Surely this was Caipin's bumbling Uncle Sun, seated beside his spouse, the renowned woman calligrapher Zhang Lunying. Xu Zhenyi tried to read more into the painter's rendering of this improbable couple, but he failed to discern even a hint of irony. Of course, he thought to himself, for a family portrait anything less than idealism would have been unthinkable, a gross affront to the family, and a telling indictment of the artist's failure to put duty ahead of feelings.

The final panel in the handscroll showed Wang Caipin's own parents, her father, Wang Xi, and her mother, Zhang Wanying, captured by the painter in an interaction of such subtle amity and intimacy that Xu Zhenyi caught his breath. When he called the servant to rearrange the room, his voice was husky and his manner brusque. Poems and painting together had shown him the hearts and minds of people long dead. He rose and left his study to meditate in the garden.

In the fall of 1893, when the copying of Wang Caipin's manuscript was nearly finished, Xu Zhenyi composed an afterword. His words cast a foreboding light on the history of the Zhang family's learning: "This lady," he wrote, "was the last surviving person to carry on the teachings of her great-uncle, Zhang Huiyan, and her grandfather, Zhang Qi."[11] The woodblocks for printing Wang Caipin's collected poems, titled *Duxuan lou chugao*, were finished by the spring of 1894 and published with Xu Zhenyi's own dedication on the frontispiece. Written in an ancient calligraphic style, the dedication was embossed with two of Xu's finest seals.

Later that same year, the Japanese navy routed and sank China's finest warships in a brief battle lasting barely six hours. In 1895 China signed the humiliating Treaty of Shimonoseki, marking the failure of the Restoration's "self-strengthening" movement, and Xu Zhenyi was inspired to compose a letter of remonstrance to the throne. His letter placed his former mentor and Wang Caipin's patron, Zeng Guofan, and his colleague Hu Linyi— their heroes of the Restoration—in a new light:

> In days gone by, officials like Zeng Guofan and Hu Linyi had theories that were unsurpassed, and talents that made them indispensable. A true heart was the basis for their actions, and love of the people was their primary concern. Of Western learning (*yangxue*) they said virtually nothing. And they never purchased weapons from abroad. In the end, they were able to pacify a massive rebellion and restore the rule of the imperial government, but only by recourse to the *lijin* commercial tax, which sapped the energy of the people. For the sake of expediency, they stole the people's resources, although— feeling uneasy about this—they planned to halt the *lijin* as soon as the mil-

itary crisis subsided. Their experience should be a cautionary mirror on our time. Because now the entire world is in a state of such turmoil that a man who does not have Western learning cannot be called talented, and a policy that does not address reform cannot be called useful.[12]

The elderly governess Wang Caipin had died just in time. She was not the last of imperial China's cultivated ladies *(guixiu).*[13] But her family learning had suddenly become obsolete.

The historian says:

Wang Caipin's life, like that of her employer, Xu Zhenyi, was framed by the millenarian movement known as the Taiping Rebellion. From its modest stirrings in 1851 far to the south of Caipin's home, the movement swept into the Lower Yangzi region and occupied it for more than a decade. The Taiping were not fully defeated until 1866, when their self-proclaimed "Heavenly Kingdom" collapsed. The rebellion shocked people like Wang Caipin for reasons beyond the sheer loss of life. Unlike other mass movements of the Qing period, the Taiping movement was not confined to distant borderlands or remote hill areas. Instead, against all odds and despite the presence of powerful Manchu and Han Chinese garrisons deployed to stop them, the ragtag Taiping rebels seized towns and cities of the Lower Yangzi heartland one after the other. At the peak of their power, they controlled all of China's economic heartland, the homeland of governing-class families like Wang Caipin's. As shocking as their improbable military success was the Taiping ideology. Taiping leaders preached a messianic communitarian doctrine derived from readings of the Biblical Old Testament. Their apocalyptic vision rejected Confucian family and social relationships outright. Inspired by Christian missionary tracts that circulated on the streets of Canton, Taiping preachers won converts in the rural hills of Guangxi province, where hundreds of thousands of marginal people packed up their families and joined the quest for a heavenly kingdom in this world. To cap the horrifying spectre of a seditious attack on civilization, the Taiping advocated the overthrow of the ruling Manchu house and the enthroning of their own leader, whom they regarded as Jehovah's second son. For all of these reasons, the movement spelled ruin for the lives of elite families like Wang Caipin's, who faced the choice of fleeing and becoming refugees or standing firm in a walled city to face almost certain death at the hands of the rebels or by suicide.

It is unclear how much people like Wang Caipin knew about the Taiping following. The Taiping core leadership and initial converts comprised large numbers of Hakka people, a subethnic group whose social practices set them apart from the Han majority. Among themselves, Taiping followers were considered children of the God Jehovah, each one equal in his eyes. Taiping believers attacked the Chinese family system and family relationships, singling out women for special attention, perhaps because of Hakka opposition to Han customs such as footbinding and female seclusion. Taiping armies included battalions of female soldiers with female generals in command, and in occupied areas the Taiping leadership created a civil service examination track to recruit female officials. These policies promoted and preserved the strict segregation of the sexes enforced in the earliest Taiping communities, where men and women were housed separately in dormitories. Moreover, because the original Taiping movement was dominated by Hakkas who did not practice footbinding, Hakka female leaders forcibly unbound the feet of captive Han Chinese women in newly occupied territories.[14]

What was well publicized by anti-Taiping leaders like Zeng Guofan was the Taiping program promoting "brotherhood and sisterhood" among all living creatures. Zeng's announcements and writings to the public about the Taiping underscored the inflammatory language in Taiping documents, which referred to all men as *xiongdi* (brothers) and all women as *jiemei* (sisters) and declared that "we are all God's children, created equal by God." To elite families like the Zhang, this was a repulsive attack on values that lay at the core of their civilization. As one anti-Taiping tract put it: "They defy the orderly hierarchy of the cosmos, in complete ignorance of the proper relationship between elders and youth, between persons of honor and persons who are lowly" *(ni tian bei li buzhi zhangyou zunbei zhi xu)*. Rallying local leaders to the war effort, Zeng Guofan called on "all those who can read" to heed and fight the teachings of the Taiping movement. His "Call to Purge the Guangdong Rebels" ("Tao Yuefei xi") described with disgust the Taiping "perversion of normative moral relationships" *(mingjiao zhi qibian)*. "How," he demanded, "can any educated person possibly fold his hands in his sleeves and do nothing?"[15] Wang Caipin and other members of her family recorded their own visceral reactions to the Taiping movement, as the reader will later learn.

For obvious reasons, revulsion against the Taiping sparked a will to "restore," not reform, imperial China's values and institutions. Reacting to the empire's obvious military weakness, underscored by the signing of two humiliating treaties with Western powers in 1842 and 1861, the Qing government launched a vigorous program for "self-strengthening," led by men who were closely associated with Wang Caipin's family. Self-strengthening, with its emphasis on shipyards, arsenals, translation bureaus, and restoring the agrarian economy, required no change in women's roles. If anything, the self-strengthening program made talented women like Wang Caipin even more valuable and important as widows and survivors who would rear and educate the next generation. Not until 1895, the crucial turning point in Xu Zhenyi's own consciousness of his country's plight, was self-strengthening acknowledged as a failure. Increasingly radical reforms, then revolution, followed within a decade. With them came a condemnation of the *guixiu* of Wang Caipin's generation, who were dismissed as frivolous and ignorant dependents upon men whose bound feet and fancy poetry were an embarrassment to an emerging nation.

The talented women of the Zhang family led lives that later reformers in China and elsewhere dismissed as benighted and backward. But hearing their stories now makes us ask: what was "new" about the "new woman" of the twentieth century?

TWO

Tang Yaoqing, *Guixiu*

(1763–1831)

GIRLHOOD

"To study and then constantly put into practice what you have learned—how delightful it is!" Tang Yaoqing sat on a stool at her grandfather's feet, chanting. She was learning the first lines of the *Analects* of Confucius.[1] Around her sat her elder sister and five male cousins, waiting to be called on. Her grandfather placed a light hand on her head, smiled broadly, and turned to the next grandchild.

As her sister began to read, Yaoqing's eyes wandered around the study where she had taken her lessons for the past four years. Behind her grandfather's chair, on the north wall, hung an elegant scroll celebrating his seventieth birthday. She could not read every word in the inscription, but a cousin had pointed out the characters for Grand Secretary, her grandfather's exalted title at the court. The scroll specifically mentioned the honors graciously bestowed upon his parents and grandparents by the Qianlong Emperor.[2] On another wall, inscribed in Han-style archaic calligraphy, was a poem her grandfather had written for an old friend, the great physician Fa Qianyi, patriarch of the local lineage of medical practitioners.[3] Her grandfather's desk held treasures he had brought home from his travels: a red carved lacquer box shaped like a lotus, a small, elongated, milky jade pig—which he sometimes hung from his belt—and an immense inkstone embellished with designs from the studio of a fine local artist.

The next pupil had barely begun to recite when Yaoqing's father stepped softly into the room. "Is he not a man of highest virtue who feels no discomfort even if others take no note of him?" asked her cousin Yiyan rhetorically.[4] Seeing her father, her grandfather's face fell. He rose abruptly, praised the children for their recitations, and dismissed them, closing the door behind them. As Yaoqing moved quickly toward the back of the house, eager to escape to her mother's rooms, she heard her grandfather boom a question, and her father's answering murmur. The voices of father and son rose and faded, following her down the courtyard.[5]

A few years later Yaoqing's lessons with her grandfather came to an end. She had entered her twelfth year and was ordered to spend all of her leisure time with the women of the house in the inner quarters, at the back of the flowered courtyard that separated the heart of the household from the guest areas where her grandfather presided. She had only her older sister and a few female cousins to set examples for her or to keep her company, and she lost touch with her male cousins, who had been able to help her understand the emotions that erupted in the outer part of the house. The tensions there could be felt by the women in the inner quarters, but Yaoqing was unable to learn what caused them.

In that same year, as if to mark an end to Yaoqing's childhood, Grandfather Tang died. Yaoqing's father, who was constantly traveling in search of work, immediately moved his wife and children out of the large Tang family compound over which his father and uncles had presided. In their new lodgings, where Tang Yaoqing would spend the rest of her youth, she and her parents and siblings—now two sisters and an adopted brother, her cousin Yimo—occupied a single wing in a sprawling mansion owned by the Qian family. This was the marital home of Yaoqing's father's elder sister. That lady had wanted more daughters, and she was thrilled at the prospect of her niece's company. Yaoqing quickly saw that she need not mourn the loss of her grandfather's instruction. Aunt Tang was ready to ply her with books and writing assignments.

Meanwhile, Yaoqing's father commenced the mourning period for Grandfather Tang. He followed the rituals precisely and with obsessive attention to detail. For twenty-seven months, Yaoqing's father dressed in coarse white hemp. He slept alone and not with her mother. When he woke, he sat upright, staring straight ahead. He ate only vegetarian food.[6] Yaoqing was embarrassed to hear people talking about him. It seemed that these kinds of practices were specified in the *Book of Rites,* but in the present day few people took them that seriously.

Yaoqing wanted to support her father, but the gossip gave her pause. She saw that her aunt felt his ritual devotions were excessive and that her aunt likewise did not want to encourage him. Instead, Aunt Tang urged Yaoqing's father to take her grandfather's place as her formal tutor. He agreed. He broke the silence of his mourning regimen once each day to study classics and histories with his daughter. In the brief hours of their daily interaction, usually over a book, Yaoqing's father's unhappiness slowly came out. He told her how he had struggled and worked to establish his name, as he knew he must, and how his plans seemed always to fail. His brothers were all successful, with many sons, flourishing careers, and high ambitions. Recounting his disappointments filled him with gloom.

Yaoqing spent many hours of their study time trying vainly to cheer her father up. She knew that he loved history. His nickname was "Changzhou Encyclopedia," meaning that he was a living, breathing authority on every possible bit of local historical knowledge.[7] Yaoqing could always draw her father out if she could make him talk about a famous personality or a renowned figure from the past. She longed for him to find an outlet for his special talent.

Yaoqing's father's views on women's conduct were far stricter than her aunt's, and she began to understand those strict views as simply one aspect of her father's personality, related to his rigid and literal reading of the classics. Aunt Tang began to indulge her niece, relieving Yaoqing of all household duties so she could devote her full attention to reading and writing. At the same time, as Yaoqing's brilliance became apparent, her father grew increasingly ambitious for her education. She constructed a careful balancing act. In her father's company she was grave and serious; with her affectionate aunt, she relaxed.

In the early stages of her education, Yaoqing memorized her texts mechanically. She liked the sound of her own voice reciting, but she did not dwell on the meaning of the words. With her grandfather and her cousins she had mastered the *Three Character Classic* and begun to study the *Analects*.[8] Now her father expanded her curriculum to include the entire *Four Books—Analects, Mencius, Great Learning,* and *Doctrine of the Mean.* He also began reading with her the "Er nan" sections from the *Book of Odes,* which he thought offered the finest role models for womanly virtue in the entire classical repertoire.[9]

The women's classics were the inevitable next step. Her father started out with Ban Zhao's *Instructions for Women,* which Yaoqing found rather tedious. (She much preferred Ban Zhao's prose-poems, which she read with her aunt.) The *Instructions* was the first of the *Four Books for Women,* which her father presented to her in an elegant edition with an imperial court endorsement on the frontispiece.[10] With her father she also read the lives of famous women from an illustrated and annotated version of Liu Xiang's original classic, *Biographies of Exemplary Women.* These her father liked to compare with the versions of the same stories compiled with a more recent commentary by the Ming scholar Lü Kun in his *Gui fan.*[11]

Yaoqing's father enjoyed biographies of women, but he did not like to dwell on plots. Instead he lectured her on the moral lessons in women's lives, repeatedly stressing the "four quintessential attributes" *(side)* of a gentle-woman, reminding her that she was a *guixiu*—a young woman whose moral character and classical learning had been cultivated in the inner apartments of an elite household. Yaoqing had been able to recite the four attributes of a respectable woman from the time she could memorize. They were personal virtue *(de)*, proper speech *(yan)*, proper comportment *(rong)*, and diligent work *(gong)*. She did not mind drawing these lessons from the lives she was reading, but she loved the pictures and the plots more than she was willing to acknowledge to her father. She developed a fondness for some of the characters in the stories, as Liu Xiang's cryptic and ironic style caught her imagination. The short dialogues and pithy plots inspired her to flesh out the characters in her mind. The fancy illustrations, capturing the most dramatic moments, helped.[12] She was particularly fond of the story of the "woman of Lu from Qishi," who delivered tongue-lashings defending her womanly interest in the king's business, and also the story of the "rustic" woman of Chu, who thwarted an advance from a bullying, arrogant diplomat with a humiliating virtuous riposte.[13]

In addition to the classics, Yaoqing's father liked her to study advice books. He selected two for his daughter's education as a future wife: Lan Dingyuan's *Women's Learning (Nüxue)*, and Chen Hongmou's *Bequeathed Guidelines for the Education of Women (Jiaonü yigui)*.[14] Most of the rules for manners and the moral examples in these readings were too obvious and too heavy-handed to appeal to Yaoqing. But some of the historical material was fascinating because it talked about life in large joint families like her own, and it focused on the difficulties women faced in such complex domestic settings, offering tips on how to handle servants and how to cope with in-law conflicts.[15] Yaoqing had begun to develop her own views on such matters, particularly in light of what she had seen of her mother's fate after their move to the Qian household. Aunt Tang, as her father's elder sister and the senior woman in her generation, presided over their new home with a sure hand, which had the immediate effect of pushing Yaoqing's mother to the margins of the household's management. Yaoqing's mother's position was weakened further by the fact that she had not borne a son. The adoption of her little cousin Yimo, now her brother, was merely testimony to that fact.[16] Yaoqing knew without being told that her mother's position in the Qian household was weak. She was also quite sure that her father was unable and perhaps even unwilling to do anything about it. He was fond of his sister, and he was greatly in her debt for taking them in.

The Tang and the Qian families, as residents of Changzhou, lived in one of the preeminent cultural centers for talented women poets. Yaoqing's aunt and many of her female Tang cousins moved in some of the liveliest circles of Changzhou's notable *guixiu,* and Yaoqing's aunt was eager to develop her niece's poetic gifts. For her first assignment, she asked Yaoqing to compose a single couplet in either five- or seven-word rhyme. She suggested as a topic "flower." Yaoqing wanted to describe a flower blooming in the courtyard outside her bedroom window. The flower opened in the evening and closed as the sun rose, so she could juxtapose evening and morning, moonlight and blossom, sunrise and a spent flower. It took her two days to work this out, using seven-word lines in a moderately difficult rhyming pattern.[17] Quite satisfied with the results, she brought the poem to her next lesson and boldly showed it to her father. He barely looked at the page. Instead, his eyes blazing and fixed on his daughter's suddenly downcast face, he spoke through clenched teeth: "For a woman to be without talent is itself a virtue! Women's words do not pass beyond the women's quarters!" *(nüzi wu cai bian shi de; neiyan buchu kunwai!)* Seeing his daughter's dismay, and recalling that his own sister had probably encouraged her poetic experiments, he began to speak more calmly, though still rapidly. He warned Yaoqing that poetry written by women carried risks too grave for a family like theirs to contemplate. She risked having her poetry used by others to speculate about her private life. She risked winning fame that might turn her head and ruin her chaste personality. She risked coming into contact with men or women whose reputations might not be suitable.

Yaoqing's father paused to consider the impact of his lecture on his brilliant second-born child. Standing very straight, she took the couplet away from her father, bowed, and backed out of the room. She walked to her bedroom, where she crushed the poem in her hand. Later that night she held it over a candle and burned it up.[18]

Yaoqing understood her father's views. She knew he was proud to oppose what he regarded disdainfully as current fashion, and she wanted him to be proud of *her.* She also knew that her Aunt Tang would be furious with him when she found out about his anger over her poems. But she could not weigh her aunt's praise more heavily than her father's blame. And because she understood so well her father's complete dedication to ritual correctness, and because she admired his strength of conviction, she accepted his judgments and defended him fiercely when anyone—even Aunt Tang—criticized him. To please him, she decided before she turned twenty that she would keep poetry and the women who wrote it at a distance, at least outside her family's own circle. Throughout her girlhood, and even after her father's death ten years following her marriage, Tang Yaoqing did not write a single poem.

She could not stop learning, however. She had access to all the finest classical books she ever wanted to read, and she memorized volumes of poetry, the great poets and the lesser writers. She picked her favorites and chanted them to herself until she felt like a walking library. Meanwhile, she expressed herself in the one aesthetic pursuit her father found acceptable for a genteel young lady: silk embroidery and piecework. She started making simple flowers, butterflies, and birds, using patterns of her mother's and appliquéing these on a backing of silk or satin stiffened with a kind of starch (for hanging) or left soft (for pillow covers). She advanced to dragons, phoenixes, elaborate cloud and wave patterns, and stylized calligraphy: words like "long life," "good fortune," "wealth," "happiness." Soon she was inventing entire landscapes filled with mountains, overrun with streams, dotted with huts and pagodas and temples, and laced with paths and trails along which moved donkeys, carts, and people. Before long there were fish swimming in the water, rabbits running through the meadow, cranes soaring through the air, and (once) an immortal flying through the heavens on her way to meet the Queen Mother of the West.[19] Her family members, groaning under the weight of her silken gifts, gave them to friends, and soon even the maids were able to take home some of her lesser pieces.

Sometimes as she sat embroidering Tang Yaoqing would glance in the mirror on her boudoir table. What she saw there always surprised her: a delicate face with pale glowing skin, classic brows shaped like the feathery antennae of a fluttering moth, and eyes that danced and shone as if concealing a secret pleasure. It was vain, she thought, to regard oneself that way, and she tried to keep that mirror out of sight. Only under her aunt's doting gaze, as she dressed for a gathering of women for tea or presented herself at a formal family gathering in her finest silk jacket and embroidered skirt, did she permit herself to consider that she might be beautiful.

MARRIAGE

Her parents loved her very much. She was certain of this, and certain too that this was the reason for her father's strictness. He did not look forward to her marriage, knowing that marriage would take her away from him and into her husband's family. For the same reason, her parents had to take their time about arranging for her betrothal, to be sure that her marriage was a good one. Unlike the parents of many young women she knew, including those in her own family circle, her parents did not rush to marry her off. Yaoqing was betrothed, as was proper, just after her hairpinning ceremony at the age of fifteen. The fiancé her parents chose for her was a man named Zhang Qi, selected (she was certain) because of his family's exceptional reputation for moral and ethical conduct and his own scholarly promise.[20]

The wisdom of their decision was confirmed in the years that followed the engagement in 1780, as Zhang Qi's elder brother, Huiyan, moved steadily ahead in his ambitious scholarly career. In 1786, Huiyan won the *juren* degree, the gateway to the highest civil service examination degree and the critical mark of high status for people of his family's class. His first appointment, in the school for bannermen at the palace, placed him in the inner circles of capital politics.[21]

News of the Zhang family's triumph arrived at almost the same time that the Tang family suffered a great blow: the tragic death of Yaoqing's great-uncle Dakui and his son, slain fighting a rebellion in Taiwan. Dakui's posthumous title, awarded to him as a martyr to the imperial cause, was shared by his descendants through the hereditary *yin* privilege, with the comic result that Yaoqing's uncle Tang Yifen, who became a famous painter in Nanjing, was sometimes addressed as "General."[22]

Tang Yaoqing and Zhang Qi did not marry until she was twenty-seven years old—far past the time considered proper even among the upper classes of Changzhou, who liked to keep their daughters at home as long as possible. The marriage was delayed because her husband-to-be made much slower progress in his career than her parents had expected when they arranged the match. Yaoqing welcomed the delay because she did not know what to expect from a wedding. Yet while she waited for the betrothal period to end, she also brooded about her advancing age, about meeting her future husband and his family, and about leaving the comfortable life she had enjoyed under her aunt's care. Her younger sister died before she was betrothed. Her elder sister, to whom she had never been close, had long since married. Yaoqing had a favorite maid who liked to entertain all the girls in the women's quarters with sex toys that she got from the market, including some tiny walnut shells that cleverly encased even tinier naked figures that lay entwined with each other's moving body parts.[23] She found these shell games embarrassing. They did nothing to ease her premarital anxieties.

Her aunt came to her rescue one afternoon shortly before the day of her marriage ceremony. Lying back on the cushions in her aunt's boudoir, together they looked through a book with watercolored illustrations that Aunt Tang had purchased through a friend. The pictures were far more beautiful and refined than the images in the maid's walnut shells, though to Yaoqing's dismay they conveyed much the same message about sexual intercourse. Turning the pages with a strange feeling of agitation, she cast her eyes downward as her aunt matter-of-factly explained how tiny fetuses grow inside women's bodies and how important a woman's body is to the future of her baby: her posture, her comportment, her reading matter, her very thoughts—all had a direct effect on the development of the *tai* (fetus).[24] Her aunt described orgasm and stressed how important female pleasure was to a successful conception, especially of a healthy male baby.[25] Aunt Tang also pointed out that some men know as little about these matters as women do at marriage, and that Yaoqing might need to give her husband an education. In another book, which Yaoqing had actually seen before in her father's library, her aunt showed her the descriptions of blood and life-energy—blood from the woman, life-energy from the man—that made possible the conception of a new human being. Curiosity and a growing sense of anticipation, coupled with the stirrings of emotion and physical desire that she had been trying to ignore for some time, now began to displace Yaoqing's anxieties. She wondered if she could possibly be eager to marry Zhang Qi.

Her first views of him gave little reassurance of either physical attraction or intellectual compatibility. Zhang Qi was a slight man, shy by nature, modest in bearing, and nervous at the thought of being alone with a woman. His precarious social standing only exacerbated these qualities. In the year of their wedding, he had just achieved the first degree in his examination studies and become a "county student," qualified to sit for the next level of the examinations at the provincial capital. By contrast, Zhang Qi's older brother, Huiyan, who was far more assertive, was by now studying furiously to become a *jinshi*—a metropolitan scholar with a degree bestowed at the capital, where winners were presented to the emperor. At the same time, Zhang Qi's shyness made Tang Yaoqing feel more confident. She was, after all, slightly older than her new husband, and she came from far more comfortable circumstances. She found herself unconsciously putting him at ease: flattering him about the poems he showed her, moving quickly to serve his mother so that he would feel proud of her, and—to her own amazement—introducing him to the rituals of the bedchamber illustrated in her books.

At the time Yaoqing became engaged to Zhang Qi, her father gave her a lecture on the Zhang family and its reputation. For generation after generation, rich or poor, he told her, the Zhang never wavered in their devotion to study. She could expect that her own sons would be educated for success in the examinations and government office, the highest honors the emperor could bestow. Her father's stories about Zhang scholarship focused on two widows: her fiancé's paternal grandmother, Lady Bai, who reared three sons on her own, and her fiancé's mother, Lady Jiang, who was also widowed young. The stories gained life as soon as Yaoqing entered the Zhang household and began to serve her new mother-in-law.

In Yaoqing's hearing, Lady Jiang was constantly compared to Lady Bai. Lady Bai, she was told time and again, had educated all three of her fatherless boys, defying the advice of well-meaning friends who suggested that she apprentice them in useful trades. Yaoqing could quote Lady Bai's very words from memory: "For five generations before my father-in-law, this family was a family of scholars. My own husband continued that tradition. If I permit my sons to end it, I will betray my father-in-law's dying wish!" Yaoqing managed to note that however idealistic Lady Bai may have been, she was also very practical. She had used her moral authority to persuade her late husband's uncle to provide a teacher for her sons, for instance.[26]

Lady Bai did indeed sound formidable, but Lady Jiang was not formidable at all, at least not in person. Perhaps Lady Jiang sensed that her new daughter-in-law was sympathetic and admiring. In the years after Yaoqing's marriage, she read and heard more stories that revealed her mother-in-law's dedication to her late husband's line. Lady Jiang was widowed at twenty-eight, with two young children and another on the way—the son Zhang Qi, who grew up to be Yaoqing's husband. She had no living kin who could give her a home. She and her young daughter took in sewing to make ends meet, and to save money she sent the elder son, Huiyan, to live with relatives so he could study alongside his cousins as soon as he was old enough. She kept her youngest, Zhang Qi, with her. After Huiyan's first month of study in town with his cousins, he came home for a short visit. He would barely have time to spend the night with his mother and siblings before setting out at dawn the following day to resume his classes, and he was so eager to see his mother that he did not stop to eat on the way. It was very late when he finally arrived, and he went to bed with an empty stomach. By morning Huiyan felt so weak from hunger that he could not get up. As he lay there moaning weakly his mother came to his bedside, bent over him scornfully, and said: "How pitiful that you are so unaccustomed to going hungry! This is how your sister and brother and I feel all the time!" Huiyan would sometimes tell this story himself, especially the final humiliating scene, in which his sister begged some pennies from a neighbor and bought him a stuffed ricecake to eat.[27]

Huiyan also told another story about his mother to Yaoqing. In the year following his father's death, when Huiyan was only five *sui* and Qi was a newborn, Lady Jiang suffered a nervous breakdown. Weeping constantly day and night for a month, she became increasingly distraught, to the great distress of her two older children. Then suddenly one day she lay down and became very still. Huiyan was playing at the foot of her bed and thought with relief that she must have cried herself to sleep. Only when his grandmother came in and screamed did he realize that his mother had strangled herself with her sash. With frantic effort and a maid's assistance, Huiyan's grandmother was able to revive his mother.[28]

Hearing those stories made it easy to understand Huiyan's drive to excel and his unrelenting pressure on himself. The stories also made Yaoqing realize that her own husband had escaped the stress of those early years. When she married him, he was easy-going and free of the guilt that drove his brother. At the same time, when Tang Yaoqing entered the Zhang household, she saw at once that the family's days of crisis were by no means over. Her husband, still a student, was financially dependent on his elder brother, who was also supporting their mother, then in her fifty-fourth year. Huiyan's new baby, born that same year, added still another mouth to feed. Although the family had barely enough for themselves, crowds of the brothers' male friends were always visiting, and they could not be turned away. Moreover, since Yaoqing's sister-in-law was caring for her baby and recovering from childbirth, it was clear that Yaoqing was supposed to step in and take charge of the kitchen.

Yaoqing realized with a shock, and for the first time, that her girlhood of privilege had spoiled her. She did not even know how to cook rice. Zhang Qi's mother, however, was patient, and Yaoqing was anxious to please her. It was not long after she began her duties that she heard her mother-in-law remark to a friend, "Considering how little the new bride knows about cooking, she shows remarkable aptitude."[29] In the seven years that followed, before Lady Jiang's death, Yaoqing learned countless ways to make her mother-in-law comfortable, washing her face and hands in the morning, serving her tea before anyone else was given food, finding special treats to place on her plate during the evening meal.

Within two years of her marriage, Yaoqing gave birth to a son, Juesun.

The next year came a daughter, Qieying, and after that another girl, Guan-ying. Her happiness in her children was marred slightly by her continuing concern about her aging father and his lifelong disappointments. For years her father had been working on a project led by a leading intellectual, Lu Wenchao, who took up a position teaching in the Longcheng Academy in Changzhou and from there expanded his agenda to include an immense new project: compiling a local gazetteer. On hearing of her father's reputa-tion, Lu put him in charge of all of the biographical material for the project. For months Yaoqing's father traveled around the county conducting inter-views, poring over genealogies, checking old records, and writing new drafts. He had a full manuscript prepared and ready to submit when Lu Wenchao died unexpectedly. With no money to finance the gazetteer project, and no leadership to carry on Lu's cause, the project collapsed. Her father's manu-script, never published, was lost. He was never paid for his work.[30] When her father died three years later, Yaoqing recalled that long-ago moment in her grandfather's studio when her father entered while her cousin was read-ing those fateful lines from the *Analects*. She now saw clearly that her father was like the person Confucius had in mind: a man whose virtue was not given its due. But her father could not rise to Confucius' standard as a gen-tleman. All his life, he cared too much about what people thought of him.

At the time of her mother-in-law's death, just before Guanying was born, Yaoqing and her sister-in-law were part of a close-knit circle of female kin, each with a different surname: Yaoqing's mother-in-law, Lady Jiang; Yao-qing's husband's brother's wife, Lady Wu; Yaoqing herself (a Tang), and Yao-qing's husband's married sister, a Zhang who was part of the Dong house-hold.[31] For almost ten years, they barely passed a day without seeing one another. Yaoqing grew especially attached to her husband's sister, who was terribly fond of Yaoqing's daughters, having none of her own. The two women watched their children move back and forth between the two fam-ilies, studying and playing together. During these early years of her mar-riage, Yaoqing and her children did not have a home of their own; they were always living with relatives. Mindful of their difficulties, when Huiyan received an invitation to work for a distinguished scholar in Anhui, he arranged for his brother's family to come along. It would be a fine living arrangement, he assured them all, and an interesting journey to boot.[32] For the first time, in her thirty-fifth year, Yaoqing had to leave Changzhou.

The invitation to live in Huizhou, Anhui, came from a patron of schol-arship and the arts, Jin Bang, and his elder brother, Jin Yunhuai.[33] The Jin brothers employed the Zhang brothers as tutors to their sons and grand-sons and gave them housing in their own vast compound. Yaoqing was trans-ported from a crowded home where she worked all the time to an immense joint family compound much like the household where she grew up. The Zhang brothers and their wives and children had an entire wing all to them-selves, with servants to wait on them, gardens to explore, and libraries to browse in.

Yaoqing noted an immediate change in her husband, who began avidly studying medicine with Jin Yunhuai and practicing calligraphy under the tutelage of master artists who gravitated to Jin Bang's studios. Zhang Qi was suddenly drawn into networks of prominent scholars. One of his most important acquaintances was the master calligrapher Deng Shiru, who was teaching a new style of writing. The style was based not on silk copies of ancient masters' work but rather on rubbings from stone steles from the Han and Six Dynasties periods. Fine calligraphy should mimic stone tablets, said Deng Shiru. "The open spaces should permit a horse to gallop through; the written areas should be dense enough to block the wind. If one always calculates the white space and then allocates the black, rare results will be achieved."[34]

Yaoqing recognized this as a radical departure from the calligraphy she had studied briefly in her aunt's home. Her teacher had never mentioned the balance of white and black on the page, never asked her to consider the overall design of a finished inscription before she began to write. The fo-cus was entirely on the strokes and the transmission of spiritual energy through the brush onto the paper as ink. Deng Shiru and his disciples had identified a different source of inspiration. The Anhui statecraft scholar Bao Shichen, an admirer of Deng Shiru, also gravitated to the Jin compound in Huizhou.[35] Yaoqing liked what she heard about him, and she would re-member him. She had no way of knowing at the time how deeply he would enter into their lives.

Huizhou was an old merchant center, renowned for its conservative at-titudes toward women.[36] As Yaoqing passed along the streets, peering through the curtains of her sedan chair, she could see row after row of lofty stone arches carved with the names and accolades of faithful widows of Huizhou who had refused to remarry after suffering the early death of a husband. Some arches actually celebrated the suicides of women who died resisting rape or—this she found most shocking of all—killed themselves to "follow a husband in death." Yaoqing believed this kind of martyrdom was an aberrant form of virtue, virtue taken to extremes, as people often

put it. She found herself regarding the Huizhou *guixiu* with something between curiosity and distaste. In any event, her social life there was remarkably constricted. She was not allowed to show herself in front of her husband's friends and associates, and much of the information passed back and
forth among local women arrived as gossip through maids. Often bored,
Yaoqing withdrew into her needlework, passing the days with the children
and her sister-in-law, surrounded by the helping hands of servants and nan-
nies. Her husband, on the other hand, was delighted with the family's location. In addition to his new studies in calligraphy and stone stele inscriptions, he also began working with his brother on a collection of song lyrics
(ci) representing an archaic style they both admired. This meant little to Yaoqing. She did not compose song lyrics. Her children were growing up far
away from her extended family. In spite of herself, she began to long for home.

The year after the move to Huizhou, Yaoqing's third daughter, Lunying,
was born, and the following year her husband's brother went to the capital
to sit for the metropolitan examinations, the highest level possible. His success was immediate and it came at a propitious time. In the same year that
Huiyan won the *jinshi* degree, the Qianlong Emperor died, the patronage
networks centered on his favorite courtier, Heshen, collapsed with Heshen's
fall from power, and the Jiaqing Emperor began housecleaning in the imperial bureaucracy, relying heavily on the advice of a distinguished scholar
and official named Zhu Gui. It happened that Zhu Gui was the chief examiner at the time that Huiyan won his degree. Zhu Gui recognized Huiyan's
brilliance and began aggressively promoting Huiyan's career. Within a short
time, he had been appointed a Compiler in the Hanlin Academy.[37]

As soon as word of Huiyan's *jinshi* degree, with all of the accompanying
flourish and show, reached the Jin residence, Huiyan's wife started packing
for the move to Beijing to join her husband. Yaoqing watched her, knowing that Zhang Qi, in fact, was lucky to have a job at all. Although she knew,
as did her husband, that he had been invited into the Jin entourage because
of the reputation of his brother and on his brother's recommendation, she
was also confident that their patrons would not let Zhang Qi go simply because his brother had moved to the capital. Their life in Huizhou, distant
though it was from Changzhou, was also very comfortable. And, she realized, her husband was extremely happy—happier, in fact, than she had ever
seen him.

Zhang Huiyan's departure brought Zhang Qi out from under the shadow
of his elder brother.[38] He formed a close bond with Bao Shichen, with whom
he shared many interests, especially their common passion for calligraphy.[39]

Calligraphy was an art that Yaoqing had never mastered, although she could write with a passable hand and knew how to compose proper notes and letters. But calligraphy had suddenly become an obsession for her husband. He and Bao Shichen and Scholar Jin studied rubbings from the grand collection taken from steles all over the empire and assembled in the Jin studios. Night after night passed with her husband and his friends bent over a table examining a rare specimen, to be copied and recopied the next day, followed by tea and more conversation. The writing on those tablets was, to the ordinary, untrained eye, crude and rough, with large characters set squarely into the stone by stone carvers. But to Yaoqing's husband and his friends they were precious original images imprinted directly by the brush, carved into stone for eternity—never distorted by a copyist's flourishes or errors. Day after day, her husband and his friends set out over the countryside to look for tablets at the famous places where they could still be found, occasionally ordering rubbings for themselves.

It was during their years in Anhui that Yaoqing and her husband moved into a new stage in their lives. While they sojourned, Yaoqing's father died. She did not learn of his passing until weeks after his body had been received by relatives in Changzhou; he had died many miles from home while teaching. The fact that she could not attend his burial filled her with remorse, guilt, and grief. She saw that now she and her husband were the senior generation in their family, the persons responsible for the future of their children and for the continuation of the ancestral rites. To console herself, Yaoqing began a schedule of sacrifices to the ancestors, starting with her father but also including sacrifices to her husband's deceased mother, Lady Jiang, and to her own father's mother, Lady Wan. To the best of her knowledge, neither of those women's tablets had found a place on anyone else's ancestral altar.[40]

It was a comfort to Yaoqing to see her husband finally developing as a scholar. His expanding horizons gave her more confidence in their family's future. In fact, the friendship he formed with Bao Shichen ultimately led to a wonderful betrothal, though she could not see that far ahead at the time. A year after her brother-in-law's triumph in the capital, Yaoqing gave birth to a fourth daughter, whom they named Wanying.

Just after the celebration of baby Wanying's one-year birthday, a messenger from Beijing arrived breathless at the gate of the Jin compound with shocking news. Zhang Huiyan had died in a plague epidemic at the age of forty-two.[41] The courier had taken three months to reach them. An escort had to be arranged to take the body and Huiyan's family from the capital for mourning and the burial at home in Changzhou. Yaoqing and her husband packed the children and their belongings and left Huizhou for Chang-zhou so quickly that for months afterward she was searching for familiar pieces of clothing and dowry items that she had never managed to tuck into their satchels. For the next several months her husband was in a daze. His brother had always charted their course, set the standards, eased the changes. Now Zhang Qi, too, felt the burden of seniority fall entirely on his shoulders.

Nothing—not even her brother-in-law's tragic death—could dampen Yaoqing's pleasure at their return to Changzhou. She began to think systematically about their new circumstances and how to deal with them. Huiyan's financial success had been assured by his high degree and the certainty of lucrative commissions and appointments. His success had served in her mind as a kind of insurance, a resource she knew they could fall back on if they ran into difficulty. Now Huiyan's widow and young son might instead be requiring her help. Yaoqing hoped that Huiyan's widow would get support from her natal family, the Wu, but she did not know much about their circumstances.

In the midst of these practical plans, Yaoqing tried to set aside her own uneasiness at having only one son. She and her husband could not afford a concubine, and anyway, neither of them cared to introduce another woman into the household. They both adored their children. She had breastfed them all—in fact, she was still nursing Wanying—and all five had developed into strong and healthy children.[42] It was petty to worry about a second son when Yaoqing's widowed sister-in-law had only one child to depend on in her old age. Yaoqing and her husband reveled in the congratulations that flowed their way on their return home with four daughters, for Changzhou people loved baby girls.

Yaoqing threw herself into planning her children's education. The four girls with their elder brother made a lovely picture seated in the studio with the tutor presiding. Little Wanying, alert and happy all the time, was the family's darling and the pacesetter in their daily lessons. When she grew bored, Qieying or Guanying would pick her up and walk her around the courtyard or the corridors of the house, singing her songs or dangling her tiny feet over a railing while the others returned to work. Juesun, who was by then past twelve, had little patience for such fooling around because his own tests for the county school were just a few years away. As Juesun's studies advanced, the tutor became entirely involved in his education, leaving the girls' instruction to Yaoqing. Remembering Aunt Tang's devotion, and her own distress over how to develop her talent, Yaoqing made sure that Qie-ying and her sisters practiced poetry every day, in addition to their formal training in classics. At a very early age both Qieying and Guanying were showing signs of poetic gifts, and when Zhang Qi stopped by the family quarters during a study session, he would make up themes for them to use in short verses. "Poems on a thing" quickly became a favorite family game, with Juesun always in the lead, as Zhang Qi called out "plum blossom!" "sword!" "inkstone!" and Juesun raced to complete his entry first.

Yaoqing and her husband were still in mourning for Huiyan when Juesun became ill. He stopped studying and lay in bed day after day, listless and pale. His temperature rose alarmingly. Zhang Qi summoned the best physicians in Changzhou: doctors from the Fa lineage. For generations the Fa had been the leading practitioners in Changzhou, and both Yaoqing and her husband had special confidence in them because of their close personal ties.[43] There was the special relationship between Yaoqing's grandfather and the great Fa physician known as Master Muting.[44] Moreover, to honor that relationship, Yaoqing had earlier arranged the betrothal of Juesun to the fourth daughter of Fa Ding, who was a descendant in the sixth generation of the founding physician of the Fa line, Fa Zhenglin.[45] Juesun died, with a Fa doctor hovering helplessly over him, at the age of fourteen. Betrothed as a youth, he was just on the cusp of the capping ceremony that marked every young man's entry into adulthood.

For Yaoqing, Juesun's death was a triple blow. Her son was gone; her confidence in the Fa medical practice was destroyed; and her carefully laid plans for her son's marriage lay in ruins, along with the future of Juesun's fiancée, Miss Fa. Struggling with her own desperate grief, she watched her husband with concern. He blamed himself, and he blamed the Fa family. Bitterly, he told anyone who would listen: "My son was killed by a mediocre physician." The man who had bloomed in the Jin compound at Huizhou suddenly shrank back into his shell. He lost heart. He abandoned his studies for the examinations and began to study medicine full-time. He vowed to Yaoqing that he would make himself a master of medicine who would cure and not kill: "Ilness does not kill people; doctors kill people."[46]

Yaoqing loved her girls; they filled her heart with joy and, practically speaking, they also made her life much easier as they grew. All four endured footbinding with little complaint. She did her best to protect them from the worst of the inevitable pain by calling in the seasoned female practitioner who had the most experience in medicating and massaging newly bound feet, by starting at an early age and progressing gradually, and by making sure that her girls received plenty of comfort and warmth and special favors while their feet were being molded into the proper shape.[47] She was pleased to see that all four could walk short distances without assistance and stand for long periods of time without tiring before they were out of their milk-teeth years. Qieying was already quite able to do housework. But fussing over her daughters' care and readying them for their own futures did not relieve Yaoqing of her overriding concern: she knew she had to have another son to carry on the Zhang family line. Her widowed sister-in-law, with an only son, was hardly in a position to give Yaoqing and her husband an adopted heir, which would have been the obvious solution under better circumstances. Past forty when Juesun died, and certain that her child-bearing years were over, Yaoqing nevertheless began to pray. She bowed at Guanyin's altar and promised the Bodhisattva that if she would only send one more son, she would dedicate his life to medicine so that he could save lives and prevent other mothers from suffering the way she had suffered.[48]

It was at this point that Zhang Qi first observed his wife composing a poem.[49] The first one he managed to keep described their journey after Juesun's burial, when he moved the family far southward down the Grand Canal and across the provincial border into Zhejiang to take up a position as a teacher in Jiaxing. Jiaxing was closer to home than Huizhou, and it was more like the Changzhou area, especially in attitudes toward women and their education. Her poem, nevertheless, was a lament of the sort new brides sometimes wrote: a lament on leaving home, a lament for her mother and her widowed sister, who were now living together in Changzhou. What the poem did not say was that she needed to be with her husband during this time because they had to have another son. Even so, her husband spent the next several years traveling, and he was often away at the New Year, enjoying his broad circle of friends in Yangzhou and elsewhere in the area.[50]

Yaoqing became pregnant again at age forty-four, while she and her children were living in Jiaxing. They returned to Changzhou in time for the birth. Guanyin granted Yaoqing's prayers: the baby was a boy, whom they named Yuesun, pronounced to rhyme with the name of their lost first-born. No sooner was Yuesun safely delivered than Yaoqing's husband seemed to feel a new urgency about the future. This time he departed alone, right after the Mid-Autumn Festival, leaving Yaoqing in Changzhou with five children and a single servant.[51] For the next twenty years, Zhang Qi traveled constantly. The money Yaoqing kept hidden with her dowry for emergencies was all she had.[52]

At home in Changzhou with her new son and her daughters, Yaoqing grew obsessed with the baby. Qieying and Guanying, the oldest girls, seeing their mother so preoccupied, began to help. At fifteen, Qieying was quite able to cook, and she took over the kitchen. Guanying, past twelve, took on what Qieying could not manage. The two of them never complained and never even seemed to wonder what to do. At times, when Yaoqing watched them teetering around with dishes in one hand and a book tucked under a sleeve, chanting poems to each other as if they had not a moment in their lives to waste, she forgot to worry about money and joined them in a verse.[53]

For three full years after her husband's departure, Yaoqing received nothing from him: not a single letter, not one message, and no money. Qieying and Guanying went to work embroidering and brought in some bits of income. Out of desperation, Yaoqing took some of their finest pieces of embroidery to a wealthy grain broker's home and made arrangements to supply the broker's family with dowry items on an ongoing basis, in exchange for a regular allowance of rice delivered to her home.[54] She also found time to do some sewing for women in families better off than her own. Lunying, at eleven, and Wanying, who was only nine *sui,* were still too young to produce anything of value.

Yaoqing handled her family's business well, though the humiliation grated on her pride. She insisted that the girls' education continue. She induced her uncle, the artist Tang Yifen, to come and stay in their home for a while and teach her daughters the elementary principles of monochrome landscape painting. All four girls were conscientious pupils, but Lunying, to Yaoqing's great surprise, showed a true aptitude for the brush. Bao Shichen, who traveled to see them while he was living in Shanghai, confirmed her observations. Almost playfully, he showed Lunying how he used the big brushes of the stele style of calligraphy, which was his specialty. That style was not an art for girls, especially diminutive types like Lunying, he allowed. Yaoqing noticed Lunying's interest, but she had no reason to encourage her daughter to pursue it, much less the means to support her.[55]

Yaoqing had a small savings account that she had carefully sequestered from her dowry and that was amplified from time to time by a discreet contribution from her aunt or one of her other female kin. This she set aside from what she had to spend on food, maintenance of the house, and payment for the servant, and she lent it out at interest to relatives and trusted female friends. During the leanest years of her husband's absence, Yaoqing and the children ate gruel at nearly every meal. When a neighbor or a friend came by with a piece of fish or pork, they had meat. Meanwhile, unexpected visitors kept arriving—friends of Zhang Qi's or relatives in need or travelers who had been told to look for her by kinsmen—and they all had to be served proper food. She spent her savings on those things. She also kept a small garden, where the girls tended green vegetables, and she owned a few laying hens. Qieying made herself an expert in planning meals centered on chicken, eggs, and her delicious bean sprouts and "hollow greens" with crisp stems and tender leaves. Qieying had also long since learned to make excellent tiny Shanghai-style dumplings, mostly vegetable, and many other small morsels that Changzhou specialty shops served, so no one ever guessed at how empty their own bowls were most of the time. Still, Yaoqing knew that people talked. She also knew that her artist uncle had spoken of her situation to other members of her natal family. But her married sister and brother-in-law had moved away, and her remaining relatives were little better off than she. In fact, she found herself often being the one to make loans and send small gifts to them when their needs came to her attention.

At last, in 1811, Zhang Qi returned home for a short visit.[56] Their relationship was strained. Yaoqing was exhausted from worry and work. He, on the other hand, seemed hopeful and confident. For the first time, he found his family a decent place to live: he rented Changzhou's famous "Near Garden," a small but elegant old estate dating from the early years of the dynasty.[57] Near Garden had a small lake (perhaps better called a large pond) stocked with flashing gold and silver koi and surrounded by rocky grottoes. Small bridges crossed from rock to rock, with tiny pavilions where the children could sit and read or paint or play chess. Yuesun adored that garden. Yaoqing and her daughters had to watch him constantly as he ran crazily along the stone paths that skirted the water's edge and climbed over the small islands in the middle of the pond, playing hide and seek. A gardener came with the rental of the space. He pruned the trees so they arched and stretched and bent elegantly above the shining surface of the water. He clipped the hibiscus and set out water lilies and lotus. The Near Garden was Yaoqing's home for almost ten years.[58]

Now that her family had a decent home, she began to think about her own relatives. One cousin in particular was on her mind. This was a nephew of her father's named Yunqing. Yunqinq had never amounted to much, but he had a special place in her heart because he had accompanied her father on the last journey of his life, brought him home ill and indisposed, and watched over his deathbed. What was even more important to Yaoqing was Yunqing's exceptional devotion: he had made sure that all of her father's papers were carefully gathered up and preserved, so that when she finally asked her husband to print her father's collected works, the entire corpus was ready and available.[59] This great debt that she owed Yunqing, in her father's name, she now repaid in the best way she knew how: she invited Yunqing to come and live with them in the Near Garden.

At the time she extended the invitation to her cousin, Yaoqing did not consider the gossip that such a move might provoke. Her husband was traveling much of the time and now a man, unmarried and nearly her same age, was living permanently in their home. Many people were of course unaware that he was a cousin, but that probably would not have put a stop to the gossip. Zhang Qi was stung for years afterward by the stain on his wife's name inflicted by her generous nature.[60] Yaoqing, however, was unfazed and her generosity was not dampened. She took an interest in another relative, a boy named Qian Zizhen, the grandson of one of her Aunt Tang's husband's cousins. The boy's father and his uncle had once studied the classics under Zhang Qi's father's tutelage, so Yaoqing's husband knew them both from his youth. When it became clear that Zizhen, as an orphan, had no one to take him in, Yaoqing saw nothing for it but to invite him as well into the Near Garden. His birth mother came with him. Zizhen joined the children at their lessons, and he and his mother were still living with Yaoqing years later when her family moved north to join her husband at his first official post.[61]

Yuesun, meanwhile, was growing up. Yaoqing kept his destiny on her mind, her vows to Guanyin. She made sure that her precious son studied medicine, and she saw to it that father and son cultivated their medical expertise together during her husband's brief visits home. She herself tutored Yuesun in the classics. Zhang Qi presided over Yuesun's introduction to the major literary genres, from the histories to poetry to song lyric. Rather to Yaoqing's dismay, her son did not confine himself to these worthy pursuits, however, and he took an early liking to fiction, especially the new novel *Dream of the Red Chamber,* which was circulating throughout Jiangnan in manuscript copies.[62] Yaoqing assumed the copy that made its way into the Near Garden had come from one of her husband's friends. Whatever the source, her son spent every idle moment reading and rereading it, and when he was not reading it, he was discussing it with anyone else who had the remotest acquaintance with the book and its female characters. His sisters were unrepentantly enthusiastic about this project, having borrowed their brother's copy and devoured it.

The question of Yuesun's future calling hung over them. Yaoqing knew she had dedicated her son's life to medicine, but her husband could not conceal his desire that his son become a scholar official. This unspoken conflict was resolved by chance, when one of Zhang Qi's friends insisted that Yuesun be examined by a physiognomist. A famous practitioner of that art happened to be sojourning in Changzhou as the guest of a family she had known since her childhood, the Dong, relatives of her sister's husband. This gentleman agreed to see Yuesun privately in the Near Garden. When he arrived at the appointed hour, he was ushered into the middle courtyard, where Yaoqing served him tea on a stone table near her finest hibiscus bushes, overlooking the pond. She had asked Yuesun to make himself ready in the study, and after her guest had enjoyed his tea and admired the garden and taken a walk through it, she escorted him to the study, where Yuesun waited. The physiognomist asked the boy to sit very still and look out the moon window facing the courtyard while he carefully examined his face. After what seemed to Yaoqing an interminably long time, the physiognomist declared himself convinced that Yuesun was a master scholar returned to life, and that he should abandon his plans for a career as a doctor and set his sights on an official career.[63] Abandoning her vows to Guanyin with relief, Yaoqing gave her son over completely to a regimen of study for the civil service examinations.

One day only a few years after Yaoqing and her family had moved into the Near Garden, at about the time that Yuesun's future as a civil servant had been reckoned, Yaoqing was listening to Yuesun recite his lessons from the *Analects* when she heard the call of a messenger at the outer gate. Yuesun had just made his way through the first chapter of the first section, about the delights of studying and visits from friends, and he was looking up at her proudly. She was not expecting callers, her husband was away, and she had sent the single servant they managed to maintain off to deliver some of the sewing she had finished the night before. So she had to go to the gate herself. She told Yuesun to recite loudly so she would be able to hear him after she went out the door into the garden. Years later she remembered these details vividly.

The gate of the Near Garden fronted on a narrow side street in a crowded neighborhood. Beyond it she could already hear what sounded like a small crowd gathering outside. She knew what they were doing there: they wanted to peek at the garden and they wanted to find out the caller's business. Their voices grew louder as she approached, and once she got past the spirit wall, she could no longer hear Yuesun. She stood facing the heavy wooden doors and wished her servant would come back. When at last she pulled the heavy gate inward, an elderly man stepped into view. She recognized him at once: he was a servant of the Fa family. In his hand he held a sealed letter, which he gave to her respectfully. Then he bowed and backed away, murmuring that he would return the next day for her response. She shut the gate and walked back into the house. She knew already what the letter would say.

A full ten years had passed since her son Juesun's death. His betrothed was a girl who was still known to Yaoqing only by her surname. Her given name had never been revealed to the family. Yaoqing had arranged for the betrothal herself, around the time of Juesun's first birthday in 1791. She had not thought of the Fa family in some time. They had lived in Changzhou nearly as long as her own family, the Tang, and the Zhang as well. The Fa physicians in the past had used their medical training to benefit society rather than to make money, although those grand philanthropic days seemed to be behind them now.[64] Yaoqing was aware that the most glorious years of the Fa's medical practice had ended with her grandfather's generation, but their illustrious name and the family connection had once made her son's marriage to a Fa girl a highly suitable match.

This was all well and good until Juesun died under the Fa's care. Yaoqing and her husband had their own grief to contend with, but they also knew that Juesun's death represented a tragedy for the Fa. In families like theirs, daughters were taught that "a husband is like heaven to his wife" and "a wife follows only one husband." Certainly Yaoqing herself had been brought up that way: from the time she was betrothed to Zhang Qi, her image of herself and the future centered completely on him and his family. She could never have contemplated a marriage to any other man. Everything she embroidered for her dowry, everything her mother and father told her about her future, everything her sister said to her presumed that Zhang Qi would be her husband. So Yaoqing understood as soon as Juesun's death was announced that his fiancée Miss Fa might as well have become a widow. But Miss Fa was not a widow. She had never been married.

Yaoqing was so grief-stricken at the time Juesun died that she could not think about anyone or anything else, but she knew what the Fa family had to face. They did not have many choices, and the choices they had were not attractive. Miss Fa's parents could try to persuade their daughter to become engaged to someone else, which was a natural inclination of loving parents, and which Yaoqing certainly would have done in their situation. But that depended on Miss Fa's willing cooperation. And, truth be told, whatever Miss Fa decided to do would create problems. If she assented to another betrothal, people would talk. If she refused another betrothal, on the other hand, no matter what that might have said about her virtue, she could not remain unmarried in her parents' home. There was no place on a family's ritual altar for a daughter, who is supposed to marry out into another patriline. Facing such a terrible dilemma, Yaoqing knew that Miss Fa might kill herself, as many such young women did. But she had not heard anything about a suicide, and if Miss Fa had killed herself Yaoqing was certain she would have been told right away.

There was one other choice open to Miss Fa, and that choice was on Yaoqing's mind as she looked at the unopened letter in her hand. It was also a controversial choice, but it did offer a moral solution to an intractable moral problem. People of what Yaoqing considered her class argued all the time about just how "moral" this choice actually was. There was no denying, however, that in the eyes of society at large it was a legitimate choice. In fact, the imperial court bestowed public honors on young women who chose this particular path, and many of them became local or even empire-wide celebrities whose stories were told in the county history and picked up by playwrights and authors. The choice was for a young girl whose fiancé had died to declare herself a "faithful maiden" (zhennü). As a faithful maiden, she could move into the home of her deceased fiancé, serve his parents, and even adopt an heir to carry on his line, just as if she were actually a widow.[65]

From the point of view of many young girls facing tragedy, this moral solution had obvious appeal, and Yaoqing could understand why. It removed the prospect of having to make a second marital commitment, which was emotionally impossible for women like herself, and morally repugnant besides, given their upbringing. It also solved the problem of where to live and where to place ancestral tablets, since a faithful maiden took up her proper place in the home and descent line of her intended husband. Still, because declaring oneself a faithful maiden was such a momentous decision, people who had studied these problems recommended a waiting period of ten years before a young woman's judgment could be trusted. By that time, so the thinking went, a young girl would be ready to make an informed decision, unmoved by romantic notions of heroism, self-sacrifice, imperial honors, or family pressure.

All of this came back to Yaoqing in force as she stood there with that letter in her hand. She opened it and read, inscribed in the careful, regular calligraphy of Miss Fa's father: "Our daughter Miss Fa has declared her intention to enter the household of her deceased fiancé as a zhennü."[66]

What Yaoqing felt, when she read those words, was complicated. First she thought of what the Fa had to gain. Miss Fa's moral resolve would be honored by the emperor himself. Her family would petition the county magistrate's office, the staff would investigate and send a recommendation to the Board of Rites in the capital, and eventually an imperial inscription of merit would be mounted above the gate of the Fa household, bringing glory to her natal family. At the same time, the ritually compromised daughter would be safely removed from her natal family's own sight, her plight assigned to the coping strategies of another household. She would move in with Yaoqing and her children.

Then Yaoqing thought of what she and her own children would lose. Sometimes, in such arrangements, the family of the deceased fiancé actually welcomed a faithful maiden, who could provide necessary help around the house and service to her aging in-laws, and who could also adopt an heir to continue the family line. But Yaoqing had plenty of help at home, with all of her daughters still around her. In fact, she and her husband were anticipating a uxorilocal marriage for at least one of their daughters. She had no need of a daughter-in-law's labor. Moreover, Yuesun would carry on the line, so adoption of an heir for Juesun was unnecessary. Indeed, it was likely that an heir for Juesun would have to be named from among Yuesun's own sons, if he were fortunate enough to have more than one.

While these thoughts raced through her head, Yaoqing understood that her deepest reactions were a step removed from such practical concerns. After a decade of living without Juesun, both she and her husband were at last beginning to be free from the pain of his loss. Miss Fa would bring it all back. But it was worse than that. Miss Fa stood to ruin the plans she and Zhang Qi had made for their precious second son. They had just arranged a wonderful match for Yuesun. The family's dear friend Bao Shichen, just a few years before, had adopted the orphaned daughter of his sister and given her his own surname. And Bao Mengyi, who was now five years old, had just been formally engaged to Yuesun. They had planned for a wedding in another ten to twelve years. Of course, all of those arrangements had been made on the understanding that Mengyi would be the sole daughter-in-law. And since Bao Shichen loved all of the Zhang daughters, he said he would be delighted if any of them continued to live at home with their parents, even after Yuesun and Mengyi married. (This had come up when Yaoqing and her husband explained to Bao Shichen their intention to "bring in a son-in-law" for one or both of the youngest daughters so they could remain at home with their parents after marriage. Often relations between a married-in daughter-in-law and the sisters of her husband could be strained, so the point was important to clarify.) If Miss Fa came to live with the Zhang family, however, the picture would completely change, and Yaoqing knew it. When Yuesun married, Miss Fa would be the senior daughter-in-law and Yuesun's wife would have to bow to her! Yaoqing was sure that Bao Shichen would never have agreed to the engagement had he known about Miss Fa. She herself would have had difficulty with the idea that Bao Mengyi would be placed in a vulnerable position.

Yaoqing's husband was not due home for a week or more, but she already knew what their answer to that letter must be. Miss Fa had been betrothed to their son, and she had refused another betrothal. Her fate was now tied to the Zhang family, and she had placed her fate in their hands. Miss Fa would have to come.

SUCCESS

After the move to the Near Garden, Zhang Qi went back on the road to teach, study, and sit for the examinations, and in the next ten years he returned home only once more.[67] The year was 1814, and the occasion was the Mid-Autumn Festival, which the family celebrated together as a grand reunion of parents and children. Yaoqing's eldest daughter, Qieying, was married by then, and by rights she should have been living with her new husband in the capital. But Yaoqing had managed to persuade Qieying's husband's family to let her stay in her parents' home until the groom was well established in his studies and his future plans were clear.

Yaoqing's husband came home because they had something to celebrate: after eleven attempts, and in his fiftieth year, Zhang Qi had finally won a high degree—not the highest, to be sure, but the *juren*—one step away from the coveted *jinshi* bestowed on his late elder brother.[68] Winning that degree gave Zhang Qi the prestige he needed to join the circles of the most highly educated and the top-ranked official families in Changzhou. As a *juren* degree holder, for the first time Zhang Qi enjoyed a network of influential friends. They were all based in the capital because he sat for the exams under the special quota system created for the area around Beijing. Freed at last from relying on his late brother's connections, he was eager to launch his own literary projects, and when the Mid-Autumn celebrations ended, he promptly returned to Beijing. There he set to work compiling an anthology of ancient-style poetry and publishing a book on the historical geography of the Zhou period. He wrote enthusiastic letters home describing these ventures. Yaoqing, reading his letters, tried to ignore the disappointment she had felt when he arrived home in despair, having left his only copy of three hundred of his early poems at an inn on the way.[69]

Yaoqing was once again in charge of the family. Her second daughter married, then the third, and then the youngest. Because her husband was away, Yaoqing managed the plans for every dowry and trousseau, and for the myriad ceremonial gifts that the bride's family was expected to provide. Fortunately, she and her husband had arranged for the two youngest girls to marry but remain at home by bringing in a son-in-law for each of them. Guanying, the second daughter, was "married out" in the usual fashion, however. Her wedding procession, with its musicians, troops of men to carry the chests, and maids and servants to attend the bride and see her in style to her new home, all cost more money than Yaoqing had dreamed she would need. Arranging for the wedding at a price she could afford was almost impossible. She had to do a lot of sewing for the dowry chests, but in addition there were her customers, who wanted embroidered bits of finery just as nice for their own daughters' weddings, and whose payments she desperately needed. She was up every night for months working in the light of the lamp near her sewing table, piecing silk and working her designs.[70]

Meanwhile, her husband's career unfolded slowly. For seven years he occupied himself with scholarship and calligraphy, publishing two books.[71] At last, in 1820, he was appointed a copyist in the office compiling the Veritable Court Records of the late Jiaqing Emperor. He wrote Yaoqing that many people were impressed with his talent in writing and his conscientious and meticulous performance. Guanying's first child was born in the middle of Zhang Qi's term on the Veritable Records staff, and Yaoqing was preoccupied with news of her daughter's health. She worried about the birth and the wet-nurse and all of the other details that a mother could not do much about when she was unable to attend to her daughter. With one eye on her husband's glowing letters, she kept up her sewing and embroidery. She had barely enough income to feed her family and pay the rent.

In the winter of 1824, Yaoqing received a long letter from her husband. He was sixty years old and he had just returned from a brief visit home to celebrate his birthday. Now he had arrived at a new post as an acting magistrate far to the north, in the county of Zouping, Shandong province. His letter explained that it was impossible for him to take a leave. As a Jiangnan native, Yaoqing knew little of the northern plains, but her husband had obviously studied his new post in some depth. He wrote:

> The magistrates of Shandong depend upon surpluses from the grain transport system for their budgets, so in famine years they have no income, even though their costs remain the same. Complaints about this situation have been severely punished in the past—just this autumn my predecessor flogged

two village elders who came to complain that they were unable to pay the grain levies. When I arrived here to assume my duties, only a day after receiving my credentials, I saw all of the vast fields in the county lying cracked like tortoise shells, unsown.

So the first thing I did was to tour the countryside interviewing local elders. They all told me the same story about the flogging. And they explained to me that even though there are regulations governing disasters like the present one, they do not apply after the ninth month, so no one has any recourse after that.

This is what I said to them: "If taxes are being levied on fallow land, and the strength of the farmers is exhausted, even if the higher authorities press urgently for payments, where will they come from? It will be better simply to state that there has been no rain throughout the autumn and winter and we have been unable to plant grain. I have to travel through four hundred and seventy-two villages and I will be able to return to my official quarters on the day before New Year's Eve. If on that day every village sends one representative to the county seat, I will in the new year lead them to lodge a legal complaint at the provincial capital before the grand authorities there. This will surely win leniency and a reduction in the tax." When I said these words, every one of my listeners began to weep.

On the fourth day of the first month of the New Year (1824), I traveled to pay my New Year respects to the governor, Qishan, and to the lieutenant governor, Zhu Guizhen. Fortunately I had previously met both of these gentlemen. I begged a hearing from Master Zhu and proceeded to give him a detailed account of the bitter conditions I witnessed. Master Zhu informed Qishan. I think we will see some results.[72]

On this confident note, before concluding with his usual formal affection and respect, Zhang Qi added a message to his wife. He wanted her to bring the family north to join him.

Yaoqing put down her husband's letter. She thought first of Guanying. The healthy baby Guanying had delivered two years before had somewhat reduced her concern about her second daughter's marital situation. Yaoqing had briefly believed that things might be going well for Guanying, whom she now rarely saw. A servant had recently intimated, however, that her second daughter's health was failing. Yaoqing kept in regular contact with Guanying's husband's family, but what she could learn under the circumstances was limited. Guanying herself had stopped writing, which heightened Yaoqing's anxiety.[73] Finally, in desperation, Yaoqing gave a silver coin to the woman who came door-to-door selling silk thread and asked her to collect gossip in the neighborhood where Guanying was living. Then she waited.

While Yaoqing waited for news of her daughter, her husband's family matters demanded her attention. She had long urged her husband to buy a spacious plot and build an ancestral hall and cemetery for the members of the Great South Gate branch of the Zhang lineage, whose present burial ground was full. This project had made little headway. There was simply no money for it. Her husband's parents' bodies were encoffined in the finest wood and rested in a nearby temple, a service for which she offered a very nominal donation each month. She worried about leaving Changzhou without better arrangements for them. She had other concerns, even more pressing. Her late mother-in-law, Lady Jiang, who died in 1794, had been singled out in 1798 for imperial commendation as a chaste widow. For more than twenty-five years the money to construct a memorial arch in her honor had been held by the family, allocated for that purpose by the Ministry of Rites.[74] A beautiful stone to be engraved for the memorial had been purchased on the family's behalf by Guanying's husband's father, who kept it in Jiangyin.[75] Over the years, that stone proved troublesome. When a series of epidemics struck Jiangyin, local people said the stone was cursed and sued its owner, who was forced to spend his own money to keep it in his care. Then, just when Yaoqing's family was in the direst financial straits, she got word from Jiangyin that a prospective buyer had offered twice the stone's estimated value. Did she wish to sell? Having fought to keep the stone for all these years, she knew that she must now take action. She had to arrange for it to be hauled to Changzhou. She had to contract with the stonemason, seek a family friend to compose the inscription, appoint the calligrapher, and supervise the engraving, the design, and the final construction of the arch. Yaoqing understood that if she did not see to these things now, her mother-in-law's arch would never be built. She also knew that the precious sum of government silver had long since been spent on daily necessities and wedding and other expenses. Somehow she would have to pay for the arch herself. So she wrote to her husband and told him in no uncertain terms that she would not join him until she was satisfied that she had fulfilled all of her duties at home as his wife.

There was also the matter of her own parents. Her father had died with only an adopted heir to carry on his line. They had buried her father in a temporary grave, next to the grave of her beloved grandfather.[76] She had determined from consulting a geomancer, however, that this particular site was extremely inauspicious and that if she wished to avoid future calamity for her father's descendants, she must locate a suitable permanent grave for her father. When word got around that Tang Yaoqing was looking for a new grave for her father, on top of all the other things she had to do, the reaction of many people was to laugh in disbelief. Yaoqing's dire financial straits were not clearly known to outsiders, but many who purchased the girls' handwork and Yaoqing's own embroidery could guess.[77]

Yaoqing grimly forged ahead. Her mother, Lady Wan, had died some nine years earlier, and her coffin was still in repose in a side room of the Near Garden. She borrowed more money, found and purchased a gravesite, moved her father's coffin, and buried her parents together, with full ritual honors and simple carved gravestones. She watched the memorial arch for Lady Jiang begin its rise at a place near the entrance to the family's old neighborhood in the De'an quarter of the city, replete with an inscription for the facade celebrating her late mother-in-law's purity, fidelity, and faithful service to her own mother-in-law and her husband's line. She could not forget, as the arch was completed, her own mother's final words: "Your elder sister's life has been bitter. Look after her when I'm gone." Yaoqing packed a large bundle of clothing and some articles of value, along with a packet of money she had set aside for her widowed sister's funeral and burial expenses, summoned a trusted courier, and sent these things on their way. Now she was ready to join her husband in Shandong.[78]

Just at that point, a messenger arrived with a letter from the family of Guanying's husband. Inside was a formal announcement inscribed in the ancient language of mourning, and dated the seventh month of the year 1824. Her third child, her second daughter, was dead.

Her husband continued to write. He had been transferred from Zouping to Zhangqiu county. He told her that his new jurisdiction was not so far from Zouping in space, but a world away in culture. It was home to new managerial landlords who were buying up the farms for commercial development in anticipation of a boom up north. These new landlords were rich, like the local elite in most communities. Their money, however, came from real estate development and commercial farming, and they had limited exposure to the values of highly educated officials like Zhang Qi. Community investment, for example, was not a priority for most of them, so a magistrate like himself could not count on their support for public works or philanthropic ventures, let alone famine relief. In fact, he wrote, most of them were hostile to central government authority, except insofar as they could use the courts to advance their own interests. Zhangqiu was a pettifogger's paradise, where litigation was a daily obsession.[79] During his first months in Zhangqiu, with a thousand cases waiting for a hearing, he had worked from dawn until midnight every day, whittling away at that caseload, until finally his desk was clear. True, his work had paid off—not a single plaintiff had appealed his rulings. But the cost . . . !

Yaoqing pondered his letter and wondered about the cost, to both of them. She had no energy to write a comforting reply, much as she sympathized with her husband's plight. Her mind was numb with the news of Guanying's death and exhausted by the strain of the past months. It struck her that everything she had anything to do with now was associated with death and dying. She began to meditate and to read the Chan Buddhist sutra *Lengyan jing* to gather her strength.[80] She did not have much time.

Within a month Tang Yaoqing was leading her household on the journey north.[81] The company was large, including her eldest daughter, now married but staying with her mother while her husband studied in the capital; her son Yuesun; the forlorn cousin Zizhen and *his* mother; the faithful maiden Miss Fa; and, finally, her other two married daughters, along with the uxorilocally married spouse of her youngest; and her first grandchildren, including a babe in arms. But Qieying and Lunying both had beautiful children, and the slow passage up the Grand Canal gave her time to enjoy them. She tried to concentrate on keeping calm. Her son and son-in-law managed the boatmen and the porters. Her daughters sat with her to embroider or read when they stopped en route.

At Jining, they left the boat to travel overland on imperial courier roads through the elegant city of Jinan and from there to her husband's post. They arrived at Zhangqiu exhausted, overcome not only by the strain of the long journey but by the noise of the welcoming parade sent up the road to greet them. Yaoqing, approaching Zhang Qi after descending from her sedan chair, tried to recover from her shock at the sight of him. His black hair had turned almost white.[82] The family's embraces and tears went on for some time before everyone quieted for the evening meal.

Barely a year after the move, Zhang Qi was transferred to another temporary post, as magistrate of Guantao.[83] Guantao was far removed from the central plains of Shandong, where they had begun to settle in. Far to the west, on the very edge of the Shandong border, Guantao was a famously remote and dangerous location. Yaoqing and the rest of the family avoided another arduous move and retreated to Jinan, where they lived for a time in rented quarters. Zhang Qi's appointment to Guantao, after all, was not permanent, and the city of Jinan was a refuge: a beautiful oasis on the vast dry northern plains. The refined mansions and gardens in the city's heart made Yaoqing think of home. Jinan's famous Daming Lake drew them for picnics and outings as often as the weather would permit.

It was the peak of springtime, and the city was overflowing with sightseers. Crowds filled the inns and hotels in the area where Yaoqing's family was staying, and she began to hear ominous reports. Smallpox had broken out in a nearby neighborhood. Yaoqing stopped the outings and they retreated into their quarters, but too late. Several of their servants left work, too sick to continue, and four of Yaoqing's grandchildren came down with diarrhea and fever, then earaches and chills. Then they broke out with the dreaded pustules. Vigils, fasting, prayers, and frantic visits from every doctor they could locate made no difference. In less than two weeks, all four— Qieying's son and daughter, and Lunying's two little girls—lay dead.[84] Yaoqing sent word to Qieying's husband in Beijing. Lunying's spouse, Sun Jie, had traveled to Guantao with his own father, who was ill, to seek help from Zhang Qi. Wanying's husband had gone to take a temporary teaching position not far away. A courier was dispatched to Guantao with the grim news. Through all of this, Wanying's first-born daughter, Caipin, who had managed to fight off the infection, toddled about draped with amulets, the adults watching her every move. Wanying herself, in the last months of another pregnancy, remained in isolation in her room, determined to stay well. Her second child, another baby girl, arrived at about the time they received Zhang Qi's urgent response from Guantao. His appointment in Guantao was now permanent, it said, and they should come at once.

The family's state of mind on reaching Guantao was beyond imagining. Qieying, pale and silent, her eyes dry and lifeless, fixed her gaze on her father's welcoming silhouette. Lunying, distraught and unable to find comfort from her husband, wept uncontrollably. Hours later, with the family settled, Yaoqing sank into a chair opposite her husband in the room where the family had eaten their evening meal. Zhang Qi was so agitated that he could barely sit down, and he leaped up and strode around the room as he began to talk. Exhausted by her journey and by grief, she tried to follow what he was saying. At the time of his arrival in Guantao many months before, with a prolonged drought still taking its toll, three days and nights of fierce wind blew up a dust storm that buried the wheat ripening in the fields, withering the entire crop. The people were in a panic. He knew of the importance of certain shrines in the communities of the North China plain, and so he made a public performance before the local people, praying devoutly at the Dragon King Shrine. To his astonishment, his prayers were followed within a few days by torrential rains.[85] Armed with this stroke of incredible luck, he sought tax relief for the local people, which required him to inspect all of the households on the tax rolls. In neighboring counties other important officials scolded him for making unnecessary trouble, but Zhang Qi was vindicated when imperial orders went out demanding detailed reports on the extent of the famine conditions, which he now had readily at hand. Although all the areas around Guantao were on the brink of disaster, only his county submitted reports that were judged convincing and accurate. As a result, Guantao people had received generous relief. His charismatic reputation as a magistrate was now growing. When locust plagues struck the neighboring counties and darkened the skies near Guantao, they came very close to Guantao's borders, but none actually strayed into the county itself. Rumor spread that the same thing had happened in Zhangqiu during the last locust plague, while Zhang Qi was magistrate there. More apocryphal stories followed, because just this year the heavy rains and hail in autumn had flooded only some fields that were not planted, so the new grain crop was spared. . . .[86] Zhang Qi paused to look at his wife. She was sound asleep, leaning forward on the table, her head resting on her folded arms.

As Yaoqing settled into her time in Guantao, she could see how her husband worked and how, in the face of discouraging conditions, he kept up his intellectual and scholarly interests. His most satisfying pursuit was medicine. He had arrived to find Guantao without a single good physician. With his son Yuesun and his son-in-law Wang Xi, Wanying's husband, on hand, he now moved to establish a community clinic *(huimin ju)*, with the two younger men in charge. They were able to study medicine and practice while working at the clinic, and he was able to use the clinic's income and its charitable endowment to provide them with modest salaries. The girls made themselves at home, supervising Wanying's children and improving the furnishings and services at the magistrate's quarters. Occasional letters arrived from Bao Shichen, who was in Canton at the time with a temporary position in the office of the Guangdong Customs Superintendent (Hoppo). Bao was actively involved now in government policies on coastal affairs. He was publishing essays urging the court to abandon the Grand Canal in favor of shipping tribute grain by sea up to the capital. He was also conferring with the scholars affiliated with Ruan Yuan's Xuehai Academy, who were assessing conditions among China's tributary states in the South China Sea.[87]

During those years Yaoqing was struck by her husband's unique interaction with Lunying. She was not sure if he paid Lunying special attention because of her grief over her babies, but she noticed that the two of them spent long hours in a secluded room inside the *yamen*'s private quarters,[88] a delightfully quiet studio shaded by an immense "scholar's tree." There they singlemindedly practiced calligraphy.[89] One evening her husband, retiring to their room, turned to her and said gravely, "I believe that our daughter's brushwork now surpasses my own." It was not long after this that the queries from the capital began to arrive, and Lunying's fame was assured.[90] Only then did Yaoqing recall Lunying's precocious fascination with the brush as a child.[91]

In the evenings after supper, Zhang Qi regaled his family with stories from his courtroom. Yaoqing and her daughters slipped in and out of the room, checking on the servants who waited on the men at the table and listening. "This afternoon," Zhang Qi said on one occasion, "I heard another case filed by a local degree candidate. Those people love to file lawsuits, and since they don't know the law very well, they always take up far too much of my time. This fellow," he went on, "happens to be a lazy student who I know for a fact has not been submitting his monthly essays on time for the county tests. So he laid out his case until I was very bored, and when finally he stopped to take a breath, I asked him: 'How is it that your essay this month still isn't turned in, but you've found time to file a lawsuit?' He got all embarrassed and left and returned right away with his essay, which I then proceeded to read on the spot. It needed a lot of corrections. After I had finished and given it back to him for rewriting, we went on with the case. The rest of it didn't take much time." Zhang Qi leaned back in his chair with satisfaction. "Scholars around here are careful now," he said, "about what they bring before my court."

This was an invitation to further discussion of the melodramas unfolding daily in Zhang Qi's tribunal. "Father," Yuesun demanded, "tell us again how you conduct your hearings." Expansive now, Zhang Qi described his interrogation techniques. He avoided the technical tricks that magistrates liked to use to entrap their plaintiffs. One in particular, called the "fishhook technique," was supposed to lure a plaintiff, through leading questions, into providing information that would destroy his case. "So today, for example, I was hearing a trial involving a complicated property dispute, where each side was making wild claims about the value of the land. The plaintiff, who said he'd been cheated in a sale, was asking for damages that I thought were excessive. I could have forced his hand by asking him a lot of unrelated questions about other prices: how much is a *mu* of land with a house on it worth? What's the lowest price you'd expect to pay for a *mu* of land? What's the highest? And so on. If I structured my questions in the right order, I could get him to acknowledge that the price he had in mind was outrageous. But actually," said Zhang Qi, "I hate to do that. I'd much rather use my own sense of whether or not a person before me is honest. If he's honest and I think he has a genuine complaint, I pursue it carefully and respectfully. I help him; I don't try to ruin him. And if I have to render a negative judgment, I usually do it in very general terms as a kind of admonition for the future, rather than a penalty in the present, so everyone can learn from the person's mistake."[92]

Zhang Qi's children thought about this. Yaoqing, who was only following part of it while she passed back and forth, saw their serious faces and smiled. Her husband was a challenging role model. Their empty pockets were a direct consequence of his absolute refusal to accept bribes, gifts, or favors from anyone in the *yamen*.[93] She knew that when the time came to leave Guantao, the family would have neither a house nor land. As far as she knew, Zhang Qi had not even tried to set aside money for burial expenses for her or for himself.

As the magistrate's wife, Yaoqing understood that her own conduct, as well as that of her daughters, was part of her husband's reputation. She made it known that she would have neither hairpins nor earrings of the sort magistrates' wives liked to wear. She was extremely careful with her household budget so as to be able to entertain her husband's friends and relatives in style. She became known in the county as a philanthropist, caring for the elderly and the sick, providing donations of clothing and offering comfort and kindness to people who were afflicted.[94] She also won a certain reputation of her own in Guantao as a midwife, particularly in one case where— called to a delivery in the middle of the night—she arrived to find the mother already dead with a living fetus still undelivered. She forced down the mother's throat the medicine she had sent earlier with a maid, and the baby miraculously was delivered and survived.[95] Charity of this kind was not new to her. In the relative opulence of the Guantao *yamen,* however, she enjoyed amenities and services that her married life up to that time had always put beyond her reach. Her largesse grew in response.

The relatives she had left behind in Changzhou remained in her thoughts. There were kinsmen on both sides whom Yaoqing considered her responsibility. One of these was a truant teenager named Zhang Shaozeng, a grandson of her father-in-law's brother Ruidou. Ruidou had once been Yaoqing's husband's tutor for examination essays. At the time Yaoqing left for Guantao, Ruidou and his wife and son had died, leaving this grandson and his birth mother, a concubine. Since Shaozeng was a minor (aged 14) and not yet married, Yaoqing was devastated by the prospect that his branch of the

Zhang line would die out unless he could be located.[96] Twice she sent someone back down south to search for Shaozeng and bring him to see her; twice the messenger returned alone. Finally she gave up. She was somewhat more successful with her own cousin Qian Zizhen. After a great deal of elaborate juggling, she and her husband arranged a plan to finance Zizhen's studies for three years at an examination training school in Baoding, and managed to send him off within six months of their arrival in Guantao.[97]

As for Miss Fa, she kept to her quarters and rarely ventured out. A maid was placed in charge of her needs, which Yaoqing made sure were met. Beyond regular consultations with that maid, there was no call for her to do more.

Yaoqing lived in Guantao for four years. During that time Yuesun married Bao Mengyi, and his first children were born, beginning with the daughter whom they named Xiangzhen.[98] Yaoqing's seventieth birthday was approaching, and the family prepared to celebrate. Her daughters had survived tragedy to savor a new life in a comfortable official compound. By the time of the Mid-Autumn Festival in 1829, Qieying felt secure enough to bid her parents and siblings farewell, and she was sent off to join her husband in the capital.[99] Qieying was still on the road when news reached her that her mother had taken ill.

The illness did not appear to be serious, but Yaoqing could not find the strength to fight it. She lost her appetite and her energy slipped away. She spent more and more time resting quietly in her room, while the family's busy lives carried on around her. Wanying was pregnant again. The babies and toddlers were brought in for visits from time to time, when Yaoqing was feeling up to it, but eventually even this was too much excitement. She began to limit her time with others, even her husband.

Still, she continued to think ahead and plan for the future of her family. One day Yaoqing summoned Yuesun to her bedside. She had to tell him, just once, what she was sure he already knew: he must make a home for his sisters when their parents were gone. By "sisters," they both understood that she referred to Lunying and Wanying. Qieying's spouse, Wu Zan, was so successful that neither of them expected her to need her brother's support. But the other two brothers-in-law had not been so lucky. Sun Jie, Lunying's husband, and Wang Xi, the spouse of Wanying, had never achieved success in the examinations or in any particular business or occupation. Yaoqing knew that when her husband passed away, there would be no one else to look after her two youngest daughters.

When the little family gathered around Yaoqing's deathbed in 1831, it was the seventh month.[100] In just one more lunar cycle, her children would celebrate the Mid-Autumn Festival without her for the first time. Yuesun set off for Changzhou with her coffin, and Zhang Qi returned to his duties as a magistrate. He survived his wife by less than two years.[101]

The historian says:

Tang Yaoqing's life began in the town of Changzhou in southeastern China, one of two flourishing centers for women's learning in the Qing period, and an intellectual hub of the empire.[102] She died far from home, in a remote northern county where her husband was enjoying the ironic rewards of his scholarly struggles. To understand the distance Yaoqing traveled in her lifetime, both physically and culturally, we must begin with Changzhou and its place in the Qing imperial order.

In Yaoqing's day, Changzhou was one of the empire's leading economic and cultural centers. Its population of about 60,000 placed Changzhou in the middle range of cities in the highly urbanized Lower Yangzi region. The walled city itself, the seat of the prefecture of Changzhou, was also divided administratively between two separate counties, Yanghu and Wujin.[103] Located halfway between the old imperial capital at Nanjing and what is now the metropolis of Shanghai, Changzhou was easily reached by boat via the Grand Canal, which could be navigated northward across the Yangzi River all the way to the capital at Beijing, and southward to the coastal city of Hangzhou.

Changzhou's list of famous sons and daughters is long, and today visitors can tour carefully restored old dwellings that honor the memory of Changzhou's distinguished natives. From the modern era, these include the revolutionary intellectual Qu Qiubai (1899–1935), the Communist martyr Zhang Tailei (1898–1927), and the revolutionary heroine Shi Liang (1900–1985),[104] one of the "seven *junzi*" who founded the Society to Resist Japan and Save the Country during the 1930s. Shi Liang went on to serve in the Communist government after 1949. In memory of the city's famous citizens of the Qing era, one can still see the house built by Qianlong official Bi Yuan (1730–1797) to honor the historical geographer and scholar of integrity Hong Liangji (1746–1809),[105] or visit the former residences of Zhao Yi (1727–1814) and Duan Yucai (1735–1815), great scholars whose names are still well remembered in Changzhou's local history office. The home of Sheng Xuanhuai (1844–1916),[106] a pivotal figure in China's late-nineteenth-century self-strengthening movement and a member of the so-called *yangwu pai,* or Western affairs lobby, has also become a national pilgrimage site for tourists. Sheng, as the chief promoter of late Qing dynasty reforms in industry and banking, is a cultural hero of China's current reform era, but his family background emphasized Confucian learning of the sort we see in the Zhang family's records. As Yaoqing's daughters and her granddaughter will show us, the links between Sheng Xuanhuai's interest in Western affairs and his Changzhou intellectual heritage are not as far apart as they might seem.

Changzhou's finest hour came in Tang Yaoqing's day, during what is called in Chinese the Qian-Jia era, meaning the decades from the late Qianlong (1736–1796) through the Jiaqing (1796–1820) reign periods, or—in the vocabulary of the Western calendar—the late eighteenth century and the first decades of the nineteenth. During those years, Changzhou was arguably the intellectual center of China's vibrant Confucian culture: home to the most influential literati, renowned for the most flourishing talent, the most prominent place in the empire. The list of the famous (mostly men) from that era is dazzling, and local history buffs today still like to rattle off their names just to savor the cumulative effect. They include (in addition to Zhao Yi and Hong Liangji and Zhang Qi's elder brother, Zhang Huiyan) Huang Jingren (1749–1783), Sun Xingyan (1753–1818), Yun Jing (1757–1817), Zhao Huaiyu (1747–1823), Zhuang Shuzu (1751–1816), and Li Zhaoluo (1769–1841)—men whose fields of scholarship encompassed every sphere, from classics to philology to philosophy to mathematics, geography, astronomy, and *belles lettres*. This is not to mention the physicians and practitioners of literati medicine (three major families), the calligraphers (three major names), or the painters (three of those as well). To top the list off, the cognoscenti would add two Changzhou scholars who first made the study of "New Text" interpretations of the classics respectable: Zhuang Cunyu (1719–1788) and Liu Fenglu (1776–1829). It was their research that planted the seeds for the radical utopian thought of Kang Youwei (1858–1927) and his followers only a few generations later, on the eve of the Boxer Uprising and the first Chinese revolution.[107] By the beginning of the twentieth century, Changzhou was one of three centers in Jiangsu that served as home to a new generation of scientists, translators, and journalists: "social actors in the field of new learning" who would lead the country on its way to modern nationhood.[108]

In Qing times, Changzhou was second only to Suzhou as a home to female writers: Changzhou boasted 281 women writers and listed 330 separate works by women in its various gazetteers, catalogues, and literary collections.[109] This reputation for talented women got one of its most dramatic charges during one of the Qianlong Emperor's much-touted Southern Tours, when the Empress Dowager threw a banquet for local ladies in her temporary quarters along the Canal, inviting the leading women of the area to join her for an evening of poetry and wine. On that occasion, as the local gazetteer and other sources repeatedly recall, Lady Jin—the wife of the distinguished scholar Qian Weicheng (1720–1772)—rose and with great poise offered a song lyric in tribute to the emperor's mother. The Empress Dowager, delighted, gazed around the room at the assembled lovely ladies and famously observed: "Truly this is the wife of a *zhuangyuan!*"[110] This rare vignette shows us the Qianlong Emperor and his mother bringing the court to the very doorstep of Changzhou's talented women, inviting them to join in the cultural production that was the essence of the Southern Tour's purpose, while the court itself enjoyed the panache of its association with the high culture of the Lower Yangzi elite.[111] In other words, learned women were an essential part of Changzhou's prestige.

As a nurturing environment for women's learning during the Qing period, Changzhou was part of a band of counties and prefectures reaching across the province of Jiangsu, south of the Yangzi River, an area sometimes called Su'nan (Southern Jiangsu). No one is sure precisely what factors combined to produce a local environment so favorable to women's intellectual development and talent. Many features of the cultural landscape help to explain it, starting with the fabulous wealth of the land and its exceptionally high productivity, together with the lucrative salt monopolies also clustered there, which made it a mainstay of the entire empire's tax revenue. Much of this wealth was invested in what contemporaries called "examination culture," that is, in libraries, book publishing, academies, teachers, and all of the things necessary to train successful civil servants—learned men who could test all the way to the top in the imperial examination system, the gateway to appointment in the official bureaucracy and the key to success.

But cornering the market in examination degrees for men does not necessarily point to more opportunities for learned women. Other factors besides wealth and examination ambitions must be considered. One is the transformation of the landed elite in this area during the early Ming dynasty.[112] When the Zhang's ancestors first moved to Changzhou, a minor revolution in land tenure patterns was under way. Lands earlier held by the Song and Yuan courts, abandoned lands left ownerless in the interdynastic war, and massive confiscation of lands held by families who resisted the Ming provided the government with the opportunity to create "official properties" *(guantian)* on an unprecedented scale. These properties became the foundation of the Ming campaign to create a small farm economy in the Jiangnan heartland. As a result, the late Yuan social system dominated by large land-holders and powerful bullies was replaced by an economy of "middle" and "small" tillers. This in turn paved the way for the rise of an entirely new up-wardly mobile group of people based in the richest farmland in the empire. In the late eighteenth century, the Zhang lineage of Changzhou—all thirty-eight branches of it—was a long-term beneficiary of these early Ming trans-formations. The Zhang's modest lives of genteel aspiration, clinging doggedly to the manners of the high-born while working to exhaustion to educate their children, remind us of the fragility of elite status in the mobile society of the late empire, and of women's crucial place in maintaining it.

Local marriage customs in the Su'nan region are another key to the puz-zle of women's learning in Su'nan, and in Changzhou in particular. Chang-zhou's local tradition of "instruction by the mother" *(mujiao)* flourished in the interface between the home and the male heads of household, who were constantly traveling to further their careers or who were preoccupied by their rigorous programs of study while living on the margins. The mothers left behind assumed responsibility for their children's education. Both bride-givers and bride-takers invested heavily in female education, and carrying on "family learning" *(jiaxue)* was a responsibility of both sons and daughters.[113] These local customs affected everything from fer-tility and sex ratios at birth (Changzhou families who "ran to girls" were proud of it) to residence patterns. Virilocal residence—in which a bride moves into the household of her husband—was the norm in China's patri-lineal family system, but it was a minority practice among many of Chang-zhou's grand families, whose members spent their lives rotating through the homes of various maternal kin (mothers, married sisters, grandmothers). Changzhou was also a locality where uxorilocal marriage arrangements—in which the groom moves into the bride's household—were extremely com-mon and widely accepted among the elite.[114] Such marriages were gener-ally arranged by parties of equal rank and status to mutually enhance their interests and privileges; questions about surname, inheritance, and the like were not involved. Changzhou's uxorilocal marriages could be completed in many different ways, including very temporary residence in the house-hold of the bride and a later move to the household of the groom, as in the case of Hong Liangji, perhaps the most famous Changzhou example.[115] The spouses of Yaoqing's two younger daughters spent much of their mar-ried lives in the household of their wives' father (and later, brother), as ux-orilocally married men.

Living as she did in a center for women's learning and high literati culture, Yaoqing might have expected more support for her writing than her father gave her. In her story, her father appears almost a victim of his erudition, bound to a rigid formulaic understanding of the rites that limited his empathy for his daughter yet aligned him firmly with some of the most outspoken critics of women's poetry of his day, particularly the philosopher Zhhang Xuecheng (1738–1801),[116] who wrote a biting attack on literary women, their poems, and their patrons that circulated widely in Yaoqing's father's day.[117] In any case, the Zhang family into which Yaoqing married was famously dedicated to women's learning, as we see from the family's own records of the educated women who kept their men going generation after generation.

The Zhang's native place in Changzhou made them part of a kin-based marriage market spanning the "golden triangle" centered on Lake Tai and the Yangzi River. Far to the east, this territory included Taicang, the native place of Zhang Wanying's husband; it also encompassed Changshu, the native place of Wu Zan, Qieying's husband; and Jiangyin, the native place of Guanying's husband. Wu Ren'an, who has studied the great lineages of this area, traces the origins of this local elite to transformations begun by the first Ming emperor, who sought to unseat or limit the power of the great families that had held sway in the area since the Six Dynasties period and whose power by the end of the Yuan was formidable. Zhu Yuanzhang's campaign against these "old landlords" inspired adroit political maneuvering. Some of their members insinuated themselves in the new tax collection system established by the early Ming central government, serving as tax collectors or tax unit captains *(liangzhang, jiazhang, lizhang)*. Others entered official service at the court. In their new political roles, the old landlord elite merged with incoming settlers whose interests were promoted by the early Ming state as a counterweight, forming what some historians have termed a "new official class" *(xin shihuan jieji)*.[118] It is probably this elite, with origins in the early Ming, to which the Changzhou Zhang belonged. Sitting for the examinations was the preferred strategy for upward mobility among this new local elite, but it was by no means the only option. Enterprising family members sought wealth from farming or from trade and commerce, and medicine was a lucrative occupation. Less profitable but more prestigious callings focused on teaching and taking in pupils, and included strategies to seek honorary titles or to take advantage of the hereditary *yin* privilege.[119] The Zhang family's exclusive and prideful focus on scholarship is the clearest signal we have of their determination to remain in the ranks of the local elite, despite their misfortunes.

If the Changzhou Zhang were in fact descendants of this early Ming "new class," their genealogical record of prolific offspring suggests that they did very well by themselves. On the other hand, the pitifully thin line of descent that traces Zhang Qi and Zhang Huiyan's descendants through the generations that followed their deaths also shows that membership in a huge lineage like that of the Changzhou Zhang—with thirty-eight branches identified by the compilers of the twentieth-century genealogy—was no guarantee of access to the lineage's collective wealth and demographic success. Some lines, like that of Zhang Huiyan, simply died out. Zhang Qi's own line, which ran to girls, brought him and his son a fair share of recognition and respect in Changzhou's local culture, but little to show by way of descendants. The genealogical record is mute testimony to the dependence on civil service examination success and official appointment among literati from even the most notable families at the peak of the empire's local cultural systems.

Zhang Huiyan's brief scholarly career dramatizes the close relationship between individual political experience and scholarly success. Having won his *juren* degree in 1886, he waited more than a decade to attempt the *jinshi*. The reasons for this were never explicitly stated, but they may be surmised from the facts at hand. Famine in Changzhou, plus a convenient political connection through the Jin family, probably first brought Huiyan and his brother to Anhui as members of Jin Bang's entourage of scholars-in-residence *(mufu)* in 1785.[120] Gossip from the capital would have made it clear to men of strong moral convictions, such as the Zhang brothers, that they should keep their distance as long as the Qianlong Emperor and the Heshen clique remained in power. This meant that only with the accession of the Jiaqing Emperor in 1796 was Zhang Huiyan likely to contemplate travel to the capital. Even so, he seems to have waited for the demise of the Qianlong Emperor in 1799 before taking the *jinshi* exam. As most contemporary accounts attest, it was only then that officials could hope the recently enthroned Jiaqing Emperor might move against the corrupt factions that had dominated the late Qianlong court. With Zhu Gui supervising as head examiner, and Ruan Yuan setting the theme for the main essay, Zhang Huiyan tested under two of the most eminent scholars of his time, who were also leaders of the Jiaqing reform movement.[121] Huiyan's first appointment was for a term of study as a probationer *(shujishi)* in the Institute of Advanced Studies (Shuchang Guan) at the prestigious Hanlin Academy at the court, an honor reserved for the top-ranking *jinshi* awardees in any given year.[122] This honor, we are told, he won thanks to Zhu Gui's recommendation. In the Hanlin Academy, Zhu Gui himself was his primary instructor, assisted by the redoubtable Hong Liangji (also of Changzhou). In the same year that Huiyan won his *jinshi,* Hong Liangji submitted his infamous letter criticizing the newly empowered Jiaqing Emperor and detailing the lingering problems of the emperor's late father's reign. When Hong was immediately sentenced to death and then spared by exile to Yili, Chinese Turkestan, Zhang Huiyan was one of the small group who escorted Hong from the capital.[123] These small signs of Zhang Huiyan's personal political connections all hint at the role he might have played at the court had he lived longer.

Scholarly Careers

The careers of Zhang Qi and his brother, Huiyan, show us how irresistible was the government's lure for those with literary talent, and the brothers' legendary devotion to study is displayed in their endless quest for civil service degrees and official titles. Zhang Huiyan's success in the examination system—a system that he nevertheless personally despised—was never matched by his brother, son, or nephew, or indeed, as we shall see, by any of the male progeny in his line. Yet it is clear in the writings of both Zhang Qi and his son Yuesun that each measured himself against Huiyan's high standard, as measured by his *jinshi* degree, and each carried the burden of that duty to excel throughout his life. In his vexed relationship to imperial power Zhang Qi represents the epitome of the struggling literatus of his time. He did, after all, achieve fame in the finest sense of the Confucian scholarly heritage: he won appointment at the court as a secretary for a grand historical project; he was sent out as a magistrate to deeply troubled counties, where he served with honor; and he meanwhile built for himself a formidable reputation as a poet, a scholar, and a medical practitioner. When we see how modestly Zhang Qi's family lived when he was out of office, and how painfully the family suffered because of his long years on the road, it is difficult not to conclude that families like the Zhang belonged not to an elite of the sort we commonly imagine, leisured and lofty, but rather to a kind of professional working class whose driving energy welled up from a deep aversion to manual labor and fear of scholarly failure. Meanwhile, the honor Zhang Qi's modest life won him shows how firmly he was established in the ranks of the scholar class, despite his marginal position.

The travels of Zhang Qi that are well documented all place him securely under the care of a wealthy patron. The patrons on whom Zhang Qi and his brother relied in their early careers made it possible for them to meet leading scholars from all over the realm long before they entered the empire-wide scholarly networks focused on the capital. One of the most striking features of those networks is their social range, which encompassed members of the lower and upper gentry and extended to foreigners as well. Bao Shichen, who is perhaps the best example of this networking in connection with the Zhang's story, never held a formal office and did not even win a civil service degree. Yet his brilliance in both the arts and the study of statecraft made him a sought-after consultant to countless important officials and placed him at the center of lively intellectual circles. Through Bao Shichen the name and reputation of the Zhang spread throughout circles of statecraft reformers in the mid-nineteenth century, with the result that Zeng Guofan, Feng Guifen, Hu Linyi, and other leaders of China's self-strengthening movement knew the names of the Zhang daughters and were among those invited to compose prefaces for their work. Li Zhaoluo and—through Li Zhaoluo and Bao Shichen—Ruan Yuan are among the other scholars of note whose fame attached itself to the Zhang's own records.

We also find Zhang Qi, early on in his career, developing his talent in arenas that allowed him to excel outside the boundaries of the civil service examination. His shockingly long absences from home, which are never explained, appear to represent times when he was pursuing these alternative careers. The first was in calligraphy, the second in medicine. He also became a leader of a song lyric "school" associated closely with his brother, as described in a later chapter.

Calligraphy

In Zhang Qi's day, calligraphers were divided in their aesthetic taste and practice. Adherents of the so-called stele school studied rubbings taken from original stone engravings. The Zhang family's fascination with archaic stele inscriptions from the Northern Wei dynasty (386–534), such as the one shown in figure 1, made them part of a passionate cohort of mid-Qing aesthetes and scholars who prized the purity of characters carved in stone. The stele style in calligraphy *(Wei bei ti)* that they admired was a variation on the standard script *(kaishu)*, distinguished by "a compact structure, slanting strokes, and prominent angular dots."[124] Eighteenth- and nineteenth-century connoisseurs embraced early models of this script, especially favoring the so-called *Twenty Inscriptions from Longmen*, which were carved between 495 and 507.[125] Incised into the stone niches and steles inside the complex of Buddhist caves southwest of Luoyang in North China, these inscriptions were respected for their angular style and for the sense of strength conveyed by the strokes of each character.[126] In their fascination with these very early models, Qing scholars implicitly rejected the judgments of Song dynasty connoisseurs, who had scorned stone steles as crude and criticized them as derivative art forms, one step removed (by the mediation of the stone carver) from the genius of the calligrapher. Song dynasty scholars treasured calligraphy written directly on silk or paper, where the original ink traces could be seen.[127]

Bao Shichen and his circle admired the antique qualities of stone-carved calligraphy, creating special techniques for capturing those qualities in their own brushwork, attempting to "infuse the force of bronze and stone" into their ink strokes.[128] Bao's style, known as *shi gen zhong qian* ("beginning with *gen* and ending with *qian*"), required the calligrapher to sit facing south, beginning and ending each stroke according to positions that corresponded with the eight trigrams in the *Book of Changes*. Zhang Qi's daughter Lunying's success in this rarified world of calligraphic technique and historical scholarship made her especially remarkable, as we shall see.

Bao Shichen's and Zhang Qi's obsessive study of early stone steles was, on one level, simply a continuation of intellectual quests begun in the early Qing period with the rise of practical learning *(shixue)*, which drew scholars to the study of pre-Song dynasty sources. Gu Yanwu, the pioneer in this intellectual shift, was the first Qing scholar to rediscover Northern Wei steles and begin research on their meaning and significance. A further impetus for research on steles came from the Manchu emperors' imperially sponsored compilation projects, especially the *Four Treasuries (Siku quanshu)*.[129] The research methods developed to authenticate texts required scholars working on these projects to compare ancient texts and historical records with stone and bronze inscriptions on steles and vessels. As a result, scholastic studies and calligraphy became, as Yūjirō Nakata once put it, "as closely melded as two sides of a coin."[130] By Zhang Qi's time, the results of this research saw publication in major works that involved close study of Chinese characters, including Duan Yucai's *Shuowen jie zi zhu*. A new travel literature was also born, as scholars made special trips to locate, identify, and study steles at their original sites and reported their findings in such works as the *Huanyu fangbei lu* (Record of visiting steles throughout the realm), published in 1802 by the Changzhou scholar Sun Xingyan.[131] Finally, the new orientation of stele-style calligraphers sparked a growing interest in design, which they came to view as an integral part of the process of producing fine calligraphy.

Much of the theory of stele-style calligraphy was developed by Bao

FIGURE 1. Northern Wei stele rubbing: "Eulogy for Yuan Zhen" (detail). (Source: Wang Jingxian 1986, no. 105.)

Shichen's mentor, Deng Shiru (1743–1805), who is often called the founder of the stele school. For Deng, calligraphic composition required careful preparation with acute attention to the placement of ink on paper and to the overall balance and aesthetics of the finished scroll or hanging. This attention to design is captured in the pair of hanging scrolls by Bao Shichen in figure 2. Deng was initially inspired by his own research on printed editions of Six Dynasties stele rubbings, and his work was deeply influenced by Northern Wei styles. We have already seen his famous comment regarding calligraphic composition: "The open spaces should permit a horse to gallop through; the written areas should be dense enough to block the wind. If one always calculates the white space and then allocates the black, rare results will be achieved."[132] Bao Shichen shared with Deng not only a local identity as an Anhui scholar but also a social identity as a person from a commoner family, and Bao based his own theory of calligraphic technique on Deng's work.[133] His ideal was "vividness," achieved by moving and holding the brush with a "reverse beginning and smooth ending" to embody the pure, "dense" beauty he saw in original stone engravings. Bao Shichen and Deng Shiru, in other words, practiced calligraphy to develop its spiritual and aesthetic possibilities. Their interests were somewhat different from those of researchers like Ruan Yuan, who were preoccupied with the historical and scholastic aspects of stele school work.[134] Yet it is impossible to separate the historical research from the aesthetic pursuits of these nineteenth-century calligraphers.

Critics of the stele school have argued that eighteenth-century stele scholars smothered the creative experiments with bizarre and eccentric calligraphy that had flourished in the seventeenth century.[135] But the material interests of the stele group also led to a broadening and deepening of the range of sources considered worthy of scholarly attention, particularly archeological sources with "ancient inscriptions by unknown and unsung artisans, on bricks, cliffs, and stone and metal objects."[136] It was this sense of historical excitement that animated Zhang Qi and his circle as they pursued their passion for stele-style calligraphy.

Literati Medicine

In Changzhou, local medical practice was dominated by a single lineage, the Fa. But in Zhang Qi's lifetime, medical specialists like the Fa family physicians were encountering competition from self-trained individual literati who acquired patients through their scholarly networks and official positions. Zhang Qi was one of these literati doctors. He increasingly regarded

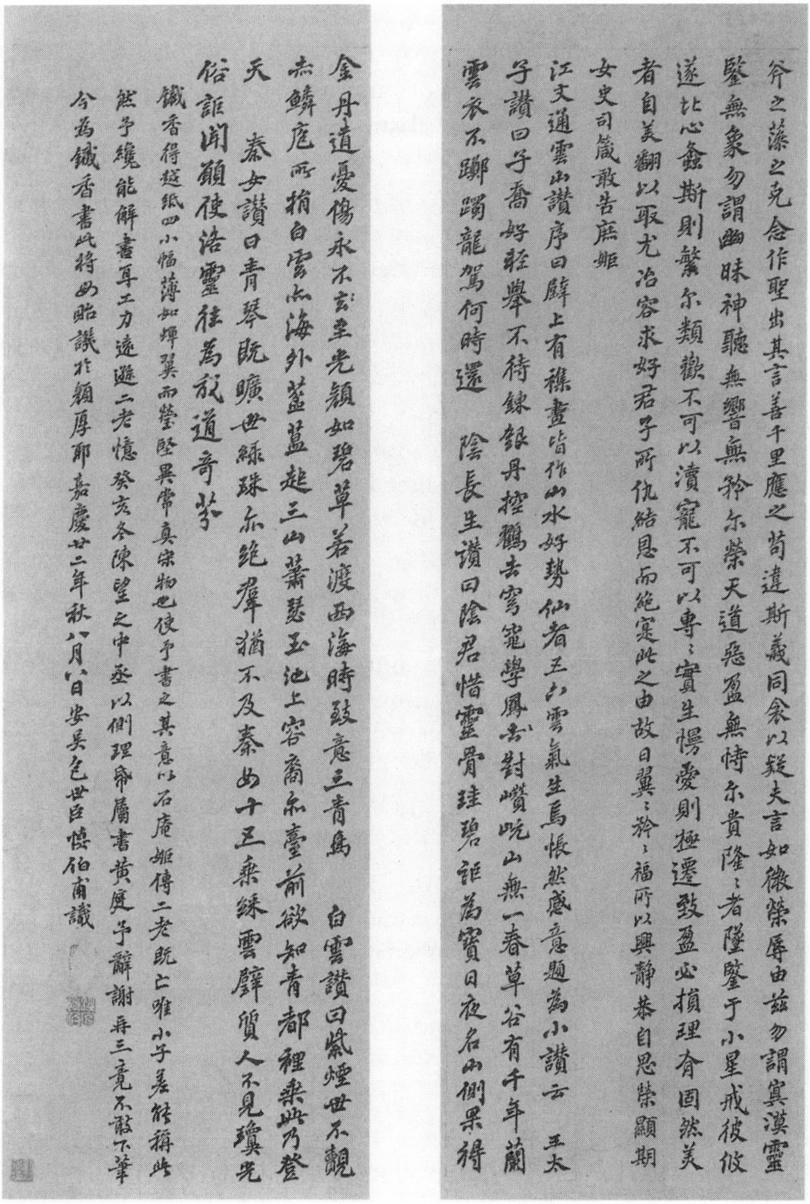

FIGURE 2. Two of a set of four scrolls by Bao Shichen. Nanjing Museum. (Source: Li Lan 1999, p. 43.)

medicine as his second career. Not only was he a medical practitioner and advocate, he also conducted research on medical texts. While Zhang Qi was serving as magistrate in Guantao he completed and published an annotated commentary on the Han medical classic titled *The Yellow Emperor's Inner Classic: Basic Questions (Huang Di nei jing su wen)*.[137] His son Yuesun went on to produce a textbook on gynecology and neonatal care and devoted many years of his life to his own medical practice.[138] The Zhang family's careers in literati medicine represent the culmination of a transition begun in the late Ming print revolution, when medical texts were revised, reprinted, and copied in cheaper and more accessible versions. Wang Ang, best known for his syntheses and concise summaries of the research of other medical scholars, was also a patron of practicing physicians and published medical texts as a charitable undertaking, providing texts to publishers without charge.[139] The Huanduzhai publishing house edition of a book titled *Outline of Gynecology (Jiyin gangmu)*, for example, printed in 1665 with extensive annotations by Wang Qi (c. 1600–after 1668), advertised that "ordinary people will keep a copy at their fingertips and display it as a great treasure of an orderly home."[140]

Literati medical texts were first dominated by old paradigms dating from the Song and earlier, in which physicians were expected to identify systematic correspondences between, on the one hand, the symptoms of disease in their patients and, on the other, the forces of yin and yang and what were called the "Five Phases" *(wu xing)* in nature.[141] In the late Ming and early Qing eras, by contrast, as practical experience and growing numbers of practitioners questioned the old Song schema, practicing physicians began to write handbooks reporting their observed results of various drug therapies. The search for practical applications meshed nicely with the rise of the Han learning movement, since it pushed literati physicians to consult pre-Song medical works and to experiment with diverse theoretical and practical approaches to healing. The late Ming was also the time when scholars versed in medical terminology began to embrace medicine's possibilities for broader social uses. The late Ming scholar Lü Kun, for example, extended medical rhetoric into political discourse, likening magistrates and other local officials to doctors and calling them healers of society who could cure moral ills.[142] And at the local level, gentry leaders invested in private medical charities that displayed their own moral and fiscal stature in the community.[143] In the early Qing period, the growing numbers of specialized physicians maintained close ties with the elite scholar class to which most of them belonged, and research on medical texts was pursued by some of the leading early Qing literati, including Yan Yuan (1635–1704) and Sun Xingyan.[144] Authors of the many pharmaceutical and dietary texts that came into print during the late Ming and early Qing periods were also inspired by the "Han learning" movement to return to the earliest original medical texts, especially the Han classic *Shennong benjing*. The publication of the scholar Lu Fu's reconstruction of this text in 1624 initiated a series of similar publications in 1625, 1647, 1715, 1767, and in the 1780s and 1790s.[145] All this publishing activity points not just to the spread of medical knowledge among the elite but also to the dissemination of that knowledge among literate commoners.

As early Qing medical scholars produced a corpus of diverse and complex new medical texts,[146] Jiangnan became a major center of medical learning, home to the two schools of medicine that dominated the Qing period: the "traditionalists" led by Xu Dachun (1693–1771) of Wujiang (Jiangsu), and the "modernists," whose leading exponent was Ye Gui (1666–1745), a physician from Wu county, also in Jiangsu. Xu Dachun, who was frequently summoned to the imperial court to treat the highest officials, advocated a return to the earliest medical classics, especially the *Yellow Emperor's Inner Classic (Huang Di nei jing)*.[147] A leading member of Xu Dachun's inner circle was the physician Huang Yuanyu (b. 1705), whose edition of eight standard medical works that formed the core of his school of medicine was Zhang Qi's introduction to the field.[148] For one of these texts, *Sisheng xinyuan*, Zhang Qi himself later wrote an afterword. Followers of Xu's school subscribed to the classical view that the primary cause of all disease was "cold damage" resulting from seasonal or seasonally anomalous *qi* throughout the year.[149] Xu's rival Ye Gui pioneered the use of aromatic stimulants to combat epidemic fevers, and his school offered the main alternative for practitioners who did not wish to follow the classical *Nei jing* tradition. However, most of the extant works attributed to him were probably written by disciples or anonymous writers trying to sell books under his name.[150]

Zhang Qi's charge that his elder son, Juesun, died of a fever at the hands of a "mediocre physician" *(yong yi)* leads me to wonder if the physician treating Juesun used the aromatic stimulants advocated by Ye Gui's school. In this case the phrase "mediocre physician" may have served as a code for a physician of the "modern" school, indicating Zhang Qi's own preference for the "traditionalist" learning of Ye's critics. Or perhaps the death of his son drove Zhang into the traditionalist camp because of a disillusionment with the efficacy of "modern" medicine. In any case, Zhang Qi's and his son Yuesun's fascination with medical practice and their engagement in the production of medical texts place them squarely in the local culture of their day, where debates about medical techniques and practices were fierce, the annotation and publication of medical books was vigorous, and being a physician was an integral part of being a nurturing official, a benevolent leader, and an erudite person whose learning could be put to practical use. The line between philanthropy and medical practice, statecraft and healing, was too fine to draw.

Tang Yaoqing's Story

Reading Yaoqing's story, one cannot help but be shocked at the dislocation suffered by "successful" literati families like hers when the honor of an official appointment also meant a traumatic move to a strange part of the country. In the beginning of the nineteenth century, Guantao was not simply a distant post; it was a notorious trouble spot. The land had been stripped of trees and even of brush by a steadily rising population desperate for farmland, building materials, and fuel.[151] As a result, most of western Shandong, crosscut by the dikes of the Grand Canal and the Yellow River—which at the time flowed to the south of the Shandong Peninsula—was waterlogged and leached. Farmers scratching out a living from the unforgiving soil grew mostly dry crops: wheat, soy, and sorghum, some millet and a little cotton. Yet often these were entirely lost when floods washed relentlessly over the flat plains in the rainy season or prolonged drought or locust plagues devastated the area. In this bleak environment few landlords were motivated to invest in the community development projects that sustained social order in more prosperous parts of the province. Bandit gangs, and sometimes political rebels, ruled the local countryside. Their power was enhanced by the fact that Guantao abutted the boundaries of three provinces—Zhili, Shandong, and Henan—creating a free-for-all zone known facetiously to officials as a "not-my-problem" jurisdiction (*san buguan,* literally, "three don't-cares"), because as bandits skipped handily back and forth across provincial boundaries, each governor could declare them out of his territory. The region was also part of a larger zone encompassing two such internal frontiers, variously known to officials as "Huaibei" ("north of the Huai River") and "Huang-Yun" ("the intersection of the Grand Canal and the Yellow River"). During the 1770s, Guantao was home to White Lotus rebels. In the first half of the nineteenth century, marauding *nian* bands made their base in southwestern Shandong, on Guantao's flank. And at the end of the nineteenth century, martial arts clubs from northwestern Shandong sent thousands of young men on a campaign to kill all the foreigners on the North China plain, a movement that became the Boxer Uprising of

1900.[152] Ironically, it was due to her husband's very success that Yaoqing had to move from the cultural center of the empire to its far periphery, where she died.

Tang Yaoqing was reared in an area that nurtured women's learning, and her life displays the burdens that accompanied such a privileged background. Foremost among these was the pressure to sustain her family's reputation for scholarly achievement, a pressure that increased as the competition for civil service examination degrees made it harder for men to win the degrees of *juren* and *jinshi,* the hallmarks of excellence that set the elite apart from the hundreds of thousands of scholars who had to settle for minor degrees or purchased titles. As Zhang Qi's peripatetic career shows, life on the road became a necessity for scholars who failed in the "examination hell," as one historian has dubbed it. But what of the wives and families they left at home?

Tang Yaoqing's story raises many questions about intimate relationships in scholarly families at this time. What was a husband's financial responsibility for his family, and how was it determined and enforced? How did sojourning men look after the families they left behind, particularly in an age of haphazard courier and banking services that depended largely on personal connections? And how did wives handle the inevitable uncertainties of sustaining a family in the absence of a traveling spouse? Nowhere in the record of the Zhang family's history can we find criticism of Zhang Qi for his prolonged absence from home. What we know of it comes only through the detailed descriptions of his wife's travails. So let us begin with those.

Tang Yaoqing's family members left detailed accounts of her conduct and her artistry, especially her compulsive attention to propriety and her absolute dedication to the dignity of her family's reputation. She was indeed a virtuous and generous person. But most of what she accomplished in her lifetime required money, and not just a little money. Where did she get it? How did she manage it? The renting of the Near Garden for so many years represents an investment that no one ever explains, and it seems doubtful that it was financed entirely by a windfall from Zhang Qi's official labors. As for Yaoqing's own assets, something must have enabled her to entertain the housefuls of people and the never-ending parade of guests. Somehow, she also managed to send an immense flow of charity out the door. It seems that Yaoqing's money (let's call it savings) came from three sources: her dowry; her father's sister, the doting Aunt Tang; and her own mother before her mother's death.

Pious allusions to the wife who pawns her dowry jewelry to meet her husband's needs are common in biographies of exemplary women, and accounts of Yaoqing's life are no exception. Using a dowry for the benefit of a husband's family was considered the paradigmatic display of wifely selflessness, because a bride's dowry belonged neither to her husband's patriline nor to her husband's parents, nor even to the conjugal couple. The dowry was the property of the wife alone, to use as she saw fit. From her natal family's point of view, a bride's dowry was a kind of insurance policy or savings account, protecting her from the risk of an impecunious or disabled or deceased provider, and allowing her the means to support herself as a widow should her husband's family be unable or unwilling to do so. True, dowries in the Qing period rarely included land, and for that reason they have sometimes served as evidence of the absence of women's property rights in late imperial law. Instead of land or titles thereto, dowries in Qing times were primarily moveable goods: furniture (especially a fine carved bed), household implements (all kinds of lacquer boxes, basins, bowls, and utensils), clothing, and jewelry. The dowry's contents were supposed to be beautifully boxed in red and gilt chests, then paraded through the streets en route to the husband's home on the day of the wedding, accompanied by a band playing festive music, for all to see and admire.[153]

What makes a dowry of this sort interesting to historians of women, beyond its performative aspects, is that all of it could be pawned, and none of it could be taxed. In other words, dowries, unlike land, were a form of tax-free inheritance, the value of which was not recorded by any government agency or disputed in any court of law.[154] In fact, dowries—although they were sometimes itemized in a fancy book during prenuptial negotiations—were never subject to public quantification or valuation, leaving the bride's actual monetary worth a matter known primarily to herself and her parents, who put together her dowry. The folk term for the cash in a dowry, *sifang qian* (private room money), underscores its restricted use, to be stashed by the bride for her own purposes, notably for the welfare of the children of herself and her spouse.[155] It is also easy to imagine the shared interest of a bride and her parents in understating the amount of that secret stash, to protect her from being pressured to spend it or lend it. With this understanding of dowry, we can make much better sense of Tang Yaoqing's resourcefulness and her seemingly endless capacity for making ends meet while generously entertaining friends and sustaining those in need beyond her immediate family.

Women's dowries could also be saved for their own daughters, nieces, or granddaughters. A possible source of financial support for Yaoqing would have been her widowed mother, Lady Wan, whose dowry was probably substantial, given her own father's status as a *jinshi* degree holder. And Aunt Tang, being a person of means, surely took an interest in Yaoqing's future as the wife of a marginal scholar. It seems reasonable that Aunt Tang might have passed on to Yaoqing some of her personal dowry wealth, since Aunt Tang's own marital family, the Qian, were well off and she would have had no need to draw on it. If a woman like Aunt Tang could use her dowry to benefit another woman of the Tang patriline, we begin to see how in an area like Changzhou, where cross-clan intermarriage was pervasive, dowry might serve as an even broader insurance policy used by women to cover their female kin regardless of the patriline into which they married.

Dowry alone cannot account for all of Yaoqing's resources, of course. We know that Guanying's marital family, the Zhhang, helped her with family finances. The Zhhang, in fact, sent Yuesun the money to bring his father's body back to Changzhou following his death, so the ties between the families survived the death of Guanying. Such ramified networks of financial aid must have helped to fund Yaoqing's generosity; they also suggest why generosity paid off. Many of the guests Yaoqing so lavishly entertained, and many of the needy who received her aid, were surely kinsmen with Tang or Wan or Zhhang connections. As she helped so many people, Tang Yaoqing built a reservoir of goodwill among people indebted to her, upon whom she and the members of her family could call for help.

THREE

Zhang Qieying, Poet

(1792–AFTER 1863)

QIEYING LOOKED AWAY FROM HER BOOK and listened. In the early spring light, green shoots bent around the stonework at her feet. Her eyes traveled to the empty pots that lined the far wall of the garden, waiting for the new season's flowers. Above them was the window of her mother's room. She carefully set her reading aside. Then she rose and crossed the courtyard. Peering through the lattice, she caught the faint glow of incense. The scent drifted out toward the spot where she was standing on tiptoe. Inside the room, her mother, Tang Yaoqing, knelt on a cushion before a small altar where she had placed an image of the Bodhisattva Guanyin, garbed in white and holding a baby. The image, surrounded by fresh fruit, looked down as if with pity on Qieying's mother as she chanted her prayers.

Qieying was in her thirteenth year. She had studied with her older brother, Juesun, until she turned twelve, when she was told she must no longer sit with boys. In the rear quarters of the household (the "women's chambers") her mother had taken over her instruction. But since Juesun's death Qieying had not had a single lesson. Juesun died before he was capped, when he was not yet a man. His burial was painfully simple. Sons who died earlier than their parents received few ritual honors. While Juesun's body lay in its coffin in the great hall, Qieying overheard the servants gossiping about a funeral where the father lost his composure and beat his son's coffin, cursing the departed spirit for being so unfilial. During and after Juesun's funeral, Qieying's own father was extremely quiet. He was angry at himself for selecting an incompetent physician. "Illness doesn't kill people," he cried to Qieying in a rare outburst, "*doctors* kill people."[1] Her father was referring, Qieying knew, to the Fa family practitioners who had treated Juesun and failed to save him. Her father now referred to them as quacks.[2]

As soon as Juesun was buried, Qieying's father announced that the family would move to Jiaxing, many miles to the southeast. An acquaintance had found him a teaching position there. He departed almost at once, leaving his wife and daughters to make arrangements to join him. Qieying had no more time to pay attention to the springtime or to her disappointments. For the first time in her memory, her mother seemed incapable of action, and in her father's absence the house fell into disarray. Instinctively, she tried to take charge. She started with the kitchen, the part of the house she knew best. Her mother had taught her to stuff and steam dumplings; she made dozens every day. She chopped vegetables, pounded rice, brewed tea. She simmered grain for porridge. Each morning she put out the pickles and condiments for breakfast, staring hard at the crock of dried salted pork shreds that Juesun had especially loved. She took money from the secret box her mother kept in the bedroom, sent the servant out to market, served and cleared and washed and began preparing for the next meal.

For the first few days she coped well, but after a week she was exhausted and discouraged, and she turned for help to her ten-year-old sister, Guanying. Guanying was Qieying's soul mate in reading but not a sister one might look to for help with the chores. Qieying showed the squeamish Guanying how to kill and pluck the live chicken that returned home from the market dangling by its neck in the servant's firm grip. She taught her how to draw the water, how to measure the rice, where to put the leftovers for the servant to have as her dinner.

Between the two of them, Qieying and Guanying tried to manage the household. They even mothered their little sisters. But the details were too much for them, and the servant was careless. Mice ate into the bags of rice stocked in the kitchen, the salt supply ran out, the vegetables their mother had planted in the garden outside withered and died when Qieying forgot to water them in an unexpected heat wave. She was relieved when it came time to move to Jiaxing and join her father.

While her elder brother was alive, Qieying's education was taken for granted. Juesun's tutor began preparing him for the examinations when he was barely four years old, and Qieying was allowed to study with him as soon as she could pay attention. Guanying eventually joined them. Now Qieying missed Juesun's serious demeanor; his careful, slightly mocking way of reciting his lessons to her (he was always far ahead); his habit of slipping a sweet into the writing case where she kept her practice books. But she missed her lessons even more. In Jiaxing her father was busy teaching, and her mother was preoccupied with grief. Still, Qieying had begun to study the *Book of Odes* with her father before Juesun died, and she secretly practiced writing poems of her own. This was the one thing she was determined not to give up.[3] She embarked on her own learning program. She took books off the shelf in her father's study. She carried the books to her room and went on studying by herself. She had two methods for learning. One was the simple rote memory method, in which she would practice the lines her father taught her during her lessons. But that process was very slow. On the rare occasions when her father was home and at leisure, he liked to teach both of his older daughters, and the amount they covered was limited because their pace was keyed to Guanying's reading speed, which was still far behind Qieying's.

So Qieying devised another plan. And here she received some unexpected help from her mother. In the wake of Juesun's death, Tang Yaoqing had suddenly taken to writing poems and chanting them aloud to herself. Sometimes she showed the girls her recent work. But Qieying was interested in something else: her mother's obvious love for the great Tang and Song poets, and her nearly encyclopedic mastery of the whole corpus of great works from that period. So Qieying begged her mother to recite her favorite Tang and Song poems, until Qieying had committed them to heart. Then Qieying searched through her father's books, looking for each poem she knew until she found it. (She knew enough characters by that time to be able to identify titles or first lines.) After locating a poem, she recited it out loud over and over again, following the lines down the page with her finger. Using this method, she taught herself new characters one by one. In time, she could read every poem her mother knew. Then she expanded her vocabulary, as well as her repertoire of poetry. The more she read, the faster she learned.

In this adventure Guanying became her partner. They worked together figuring out new characters and difficult lines. When they were completely mystified, they asked their mother for help. Their questions seemed to draw their mother away from her devotions to the Bodhisattva Guanyin and from her sorrow. In the evening, her mother read over the day's tentative poetry drafts, written in faltering calligraphy, while Qieying sat at her feet. Once in a while, when Qieying looked up, she found her mother's eyes resting on her with great affection. For mother and daughter, poems became a bridge to a place where Juesun's death did not intrude.

The family home in Jiaxing was much quieter than the Jin mansion in Anhui, where Qieying had spent much of her early childhood. The Jin family had made a habit of inviting famous scholars and master calligraphers to come and stay with them, sometimes for extended visits. In Jiaxing, however, Qieying's father lived almost obscurely, teaching and writing. It was therefore a great event when their friend Bao Shichen came especially to Jiaxing to pay a call on the family. The pretext for the visit was condolence, but since Bao Shichen was Qieying's father's close friend, and also the entire family's preferred guest, his visit had the effect of cheering everyone up. Qieying's father and Bao Shichen resumed their passionate discussions on calligraphy, interrupted since their earlier meetings at the Jin compound in Anhui. Master Bao was deeply concerned and well informed about government affairs, and his circle of friends included many important people who relied on his advice. Yet he seemed to enjoy spending time with Qieying's family, especially with the girls. He liked to hear what they were studying, and while he stayed with them, he summoned them for that purpose without notice.

Qieying remembered clearly the very first time she read a poem aloud, at Master Bao's invitation. She felt nervous, but she was the eldest and she knew how to manage herself before guests. She kept her voice firm and let it soar as she intoned the four lines she had written. The poem was very short. It was almost an exercise: the shell of a *yongwu* verse (a "poem in praise of an object") on an object that her father had selected: the ancient sword he had inherited from his own father and passed on to his son.[4] Qieying could tell from the way Master Bao looked at her after she had finished that she had done well, and she felt an embarrassing rush of pride when she heard someone in the room mutter that Zhang Qi's eldest daughter was virtually self-taught. Retreating in confusion, Qieying tried to compose herself. She was not in the habit of being the center of anyone's attention.

Master Bao recorded his judgments on writings by all four Zhang daughters as their talent became known, and many years later, when his comments on their poetry became famous, he singled out Qieying, observing:

> Guanying's is detached and lofty (*youjun*). Lunying's is edgy and vigorous (*pai' ao*). Wanying's is harmonious and elegant (*heya*). In other words, each partakes of some element of their father's genius. As for Qieying, her writing is exceedingly sentimental (*chanmian feice*) without being trite (*bushi yu yu*). In choosing her words and in describing events (*zhuci bishi*), she always expresses her deepest beliefs. Coming as she does from a family of eminence and influence, she nevertheless produces poems that are highly original. Their form is beautiful yet they attain great heights.[5]

Qieying's self-educating project continued for three years while the family sojourned in Jiaxing and her father earned his salary and developed a medical practice, working as a teacher, a private secretary, and the occasional physician to well-off families. Then, once again, Qieying had to put her poems aside. She had a new baby brother, and with his arrival she found herself with new responsibilities. The family returned to Changzhou to live in a ramshackle rented house with only a single servant to help her mother, who had been weakened by her late-term pregnancy. Qieying's father departed almost immediately on an extended trip to the north and west, once again teaching and practicing medicine. This time he did not invite the family. Instead, he promised to send money. Qieying's mother focused all of her energy on the baby. The kitchen, the cleaning, the washing, the water, and the general management of the household fell to Qieying.

Within a few years, little Yuesun was ready to begin his own education, and Qieying's mother began teaching him characters. That was perfect timing for Qieying's little sisters Lunying and Wanying, who sat and studied with their baby brother until they were too old to mix with boys. Wanying, at only nine *sui,* was already regarded as a child prodigy. She memorized characters with a voracious appetite and turned out childish verses as soon as she could write in a legible hand. As for Lunying, she loved to recognize characters, and when she was not otherwise occupied, she liked to read the *Kangxi Dictionary.*[6] Qieying liked to quiz Lunying with whatever book she had on hand, testing her with the hardest characters. Her younger sister's memory astounded her. But she also felt a guilty twinge of jealousy, seeing how much time the little ones had for learning when she was always so busy.

When Lunying and Wanying reached the age when they too had to retreat to the women's quarters, Qieying and Guanying took over as their teachers. Wanying was so advanced by then that she was able to join rhyming games with her older sisters right away. One would set the rhyme with a poem, and the other two would match it in a response, their poems circling back and forth throughout the day. Lunying, for her part, declined to join them. She preferred to paint and practice writing with her brushes.

Qieying had so much to do that she often felt ill, but she discovered that illness could be useful. An upset stomach or a fainting spell gave her time to lie on her pallet to read. Stacks of books wobbled on her writing desk. Her tiny bedchamber was a library, and her lamp burned late at night while she turned pages, reciting softly to herself. When she felt better and resumed her duties, she could move her books into the kitchen and leave a few propped up on her dressing table. Even when she was cooking, or when someone was doing her hair, she kept a book nearby.[7]

During Qieying's years of hard work and stolen hours, with the family resettled in Changzhou and her father traveling, she spent more time with her mother. One day, soon after her father's departure, as Qieying and her mother sat sewing, her mother looked up from one of the few letters she had received from her traveling husband and said, "Your father is teaching up north in western Henan. He seems to have his own medical practice now." Since Juesun's death, medicine had become her father's passion. Qieying was old enough to understand why her father felt so driven to cure the sons of other fathers. But it struck her as ironic that while her father followed his calling and brought comfort to the sick and suffering, she and her sisters, their mother, and their new brother were left behind with almost no money.

In her husband's absence, Qieying's mother took over Yuesun's training as a scholar. A tutor was too expensive. She also began teaching all four of the girls how to do needlework. Qieying and Guanying, who had done simple stitchery for some years, were soon producing fine embroidery. As months and then years passed without word or money from Qieying's father, her mother began relying on Qieying and her sister to help support the family. Between the two of them, Qieying and Guanying could turn out several pieces of exquisite work a month. Most of it was in small pieces: sleeve and hem trimmings, pouches, and occasionally even shoes, though shoes were very personal items and most women liked to make their own. Qieying specialized in flowers and Guanying liked to do birds, so they traded off work on the same piece. They made a game of it: who could do the hardest pattern with the most colors and the prettiest effect? They let their mother be the judge.

Many years later, Qieying persuaded a friend to publish a memoir celebrating her mother's exquisite silk work, but she never mentioned its critical economic value to the family. In fact, throughout her life Qieying was forced to recall that during those hard years when her father was away, the learned Zhang ladies, senior and junior, were best known to the elite women in their neighborhood as fine provisioners of embroidered silks, catering to the exacting tastes of genteel young women in need of a dowry. Qieying cultivated an especially refined and gracious demeanor in greeting their clients, which further enhanced the steady demand for their sewing and embroidery, and thus bolstered the family's income. Yet she sighed as she folded silk pieces and thought longingly of her poems, stashed in a chest that she now rarely opened. In Changzhou, as she was well aware, the cultural currency of the *guixiu* was poetry, not embroidery. Her own mother's late development as a poet only sharpened Qieying's determination to write while she was still young.

It was Guanying who rescued Qieying's poetry and kept her hope in writing alive. Qieying compared herself and her sister to the two sides of a reversible tapestry, one gleaming rosy red, the other shining darkly green. While Qieying was consumed by her many tasks—precisely chopping the scallions into bits, firmly punching the dough into shape, calculating the amount of water needed to boil the rice, parceling out the salt for just the right seasoning—Guanying would let her mind wander, leaning against the kitchen wall humming to herself, tracing new words in the air, smiling at some secret amusement. While Guanying dreamed and sighed, turning the pages of a novel or drumming an imagined beat to an opera tune, Qieying studied the rhyming rules for regulated verse, correcting her latest drafts and recopying her polished poems. Qieying might have resented Guanying's distracted remoteness, her one-step-removed mind that freed her from the practical burdens that weighed so heavily on Qieying's own shoulders. But instead of an irritation, to Qieying her second sister was a tonic. When she felt most alone, Guanying heard her out. When the trivial concerns of the household overcame her, Guanying told her stories that lifted her spirits and freed her mind. When she produced a brilliant image in a poem, Guanying crowed with delight. And when she wept, overcome with exhaustion, Guanying hugged her close and gave her comfort.

Four years after Yuesun's birth, with her father's success in the capital and the family's move to a beautiful new garden home, Qieying began to feel calmer. Her responsibilities were no longer overwhelming. She could steal more and more time for her writing. For the first time in many years, she felt serene and confident. It was in this state that she was summoned to her mother's room one day for what she assumed was to be a reading of one of her father's rare letters. As she entered, she caught a look on her mother's face that made her uncomfortable. "Mengti," her mother began—using her courtesy name, which was unusual—"your father has found a husband for you." Qieying sat down abruptly and stared at the letter in her mother's hand. She was not prepared for this. "Let me read you what he says here," said her mother, strangely breathless herself. She skipped over her husband's customary greetings and began: "As you know," the letter said, "I have made the acquaintance here in Beijing of a fine scholar named Wu Tingzhen, who recently has taken the name Zan. He comes from a good family in Changshu. He is seven years older than our Qieying, an acceptable age for a match. His writing is excellent and his prospects for a high degree are exceptionally promising."

Qieying's mother paused. Then she rose and began to pace the room as she read: "Wu Zan's situation is complicated. Three years ago he married a woman surnamed Jiang, and she recently gave birth to a healthy baby boy.

Unfortunately, she did not survive the delivery, and he is now a widower with a young heir to raise. In my judgment, this man would make an ideal companion and husband for our talented eldest daughter. I have therefore taken the liberty of broaching a betrothal to him, and he has responded very positively. I will rely on you to convey this news to our daughter with your usual tact and persuasiveness. I am sure that when you meet Wu Zan, you will be grateful that this opportunity for a splendid match has been presented to us."

Qieying's mother stopped pacing, looked down at her daughter, and sighed. Qieying herself was too shocked to speak. She was already twenty *sui* and she was expecting that a marriage would be arranged for her at some point, perhaps even soon. But the last thing she had considered was that she might be betrothed to someone she had never heard of or met through the family, especially as a successor wife. She knew of course that the baby would grow up thinking of her as his true mother, and that in every way— in the ancestral rites and in the daily life of the Wu household—her position as a wife would be as secure as it could possibly be. Nonetheless, the thought of moving away from her family to live in a stranger's house as a new bride was enough to sweep any reasonable reactions from her mind. She immediately burst into tears and sobbed with abandon.

When her mother finally got her attention again, it was to finish the letter. Her father's concluding words were almost as astonishing as what had preceded them: "I am aware," he wrote, "that this arrangement may be a terrible shock to our daughter, who has always been so devoted to our family. Mindful of her feelings, I have spoken to Wu Zan about the possibility that our daughter might remain in our household for now, following the completion of the wedding rites, and leaving the rearing and early education of Wu Zan's son, Zonghan, to his wet-nurse and governess. Then at some future time, when it is convenient for all concerned, and after Wu Zan has completed his studies and won his *jinshi* degree, our daughter can move to join him. Wu Zan has agreed to this. Therefore please reassure Mengti that we will try to minimize the strain of this marriage on her, and give her plenty of time to adjust to her new situation, by keeping her at home with us as long as possible."[8]

This reprieve only made Qieying cry harder, and almost at once her mother joined her. The sound of their weeping soon drew the other three sisters, who on hearing the news at once lent their own voices to the fray. Wanying was the first to see the humor in the situation, with all five women sobbing into their sleeves, and as she began to giggle, the others wiped their tears.

After a while the four girls, arms entwined, went off to the kitchen to make dinner, while their mother tended their little brother. That is how it came about that Qieying would spend the first forty years of her life under her own parents' roof, despite the fact that she was a properly married daughter.

The wedding did not take place until two years later. Qieying's husband was nearing thirty years of age at the time of their wedding. He did not win his *jinshi* degree for another thirteen years, which he spent mainly in the capital preparing for the exams, making his home in the Changshu county guildhall. It occurred to Qieying many years later that the year of her marriage was the same year that Miss Fa moved into their home. At the time she was so preoccupied with the wedding plans and so hard at work on her dowry that she barely noticed.

Barely one year after Qieying's wedding came the marriage of Guanying, who promptly moved to the nearby home of her new husband and his parents. Guanying's husband and his family were well-to-do, and they were generous in their support for Guanying's natal family.[9] Whatever the virtues of Guanying's husband and his family, however, Qieying was too disheartened by her sister's departure to write to her. After her two youngest sisters, Lunying and Wanying, married, the fact that they also stayed at home was no consolation at all. Lunying was far too self-absorbed and intense. Wanying, who was blithe and quick and wonderful company, was entirely taken up with her new husband. Neither offered their bereft eldest sister the companionship she craved. In the years after her wedding, lonesome for her closest sibling and anxious about her future, Qieying tried to conceive a child during her husband's occasional visits when he came to see her from Beijing. She carried two pregnancies to term.

Qieying was in her thirtieth year before her father became a success. In quick succession, Zhang Qi won his *juren* degree, served briefly with distinction at the imperial court, and was appointed as a county magistrate. Excited by his new prospects and finding himself with a budget that could support some of his own scholarly projects, Qieying's father immediately invited her husband, Wu Zan, together with the newly married Wanying's spouse, Wang Xi, to come to Shandong and study song lyrics with him.[10] Her father's revival of his old interests and his newly defined role as a mentor and teacher to other scholars, which he described in detail in enthusiastic letters home, caught Qieying's attention. She was curious not only because of her husband's involvement; she was also rediscovering her father. Zhang Qi had traveled so much when she was young that she took his absence for granted. She did not think of herself as his pupil. Even so, Bao Shichen was heard to say in her presence: "Qieying carries on the learning of her family." Others thought of her that way too. Now, for the first time, she herself was beginning to grasp her father's scholarly persona, and with it, her place in his legacy.

Seeing her father through adult eyes made Qieying more receptive when her mother read her father's most recent missive. He was proposing that the family move to Shandong to live in the magistrate's quarters with him. She wondered: Had her father regained the *joie de vivre* that she dimly remembered from the time when Juesun was alive? Would he shed the melancholy that had begun when his brother died and intensified with the loss of his son? She also worried. What about life in the north? She had already dreaded joining her husband in the capital. But Shandong province? The Canal zone where her father began his service was considered quite livable. To be sure, it was not Jiangnan, but Qieying knew that it was against the law for a magistrate to serve in a county near his own home, so Shandong province was certainly preferable to other places more remote. Thinking positively in this vein, Qieying reviewed other reasons why moving might be a good thing. The neighbors had been talking too much—about how her father had left his wife and family on their own and about her mother's elaborate barter arrangements with everyone from the butcher to the night soil collector. Joining her father would hush the gossip.

Her father was not alone in Shandong, of course. Her husband had joined him, and with Wanying's husband, Wang Xi, they had formed a kind of song lyric club. Moving north to join him would bring Qieying a step closer to her marital family and her eventual place of residence as Wu Zan's wife. Qieying did not miss Wu Zan; in fact, she barely knew him, and the thought of a reunion with him sobered her. She decided to talk to Lunying about the move. Lunying's husband was away taking care of his own father, which made her a relatively neutral observer of the situation.

"I don't want to travel with the babies," said Lunying emphatically when Qieying approached her. Between them, they had four—three girls and a boy—and none seemed especially strong. "Besides," went on Lunying with her usual vehemence, "think of what we'll give up when we leave here. Who knows what it's like up there?" Lunying's words did not ease Qieying's mind. Her life in Changzhou was constrained by poverty and care: her babies, for example, were sickly and feverish these days, and they demanded her constant attention. Yet Changzhou itself was all she knew as home. The canals that laced the city and its suburbs were lined with beautiful houses and elegant walled gardens, shutting out the noise from the shops and restaurants that crowded the city center. Books, paintings, fine furniture, elegant fabrics, exquisite chinaware, the best Wuxi tea—Changzhou people had excellent taste for all of these things, and they knew how to spend money. Qieying herself did not participate in that part of the life in her own community. She had little in the way of spending money. But her family never wanted for books. Their own residence at Near Garden was in the neighborhood of several fine private libraries, and one of the greatest scholarly centers in the country, the Longcheng Academy, was also close by. Her father, through friends, had always found ways to see books he could not purchase, and the family constantly received books as gifts from well-wishers and relatives. She pictured Shandong as the exact opposite of Changzhou. It would be dry, dusty, poor, bleak, and completely lacking in the amenities of a cultured life.

Qieying's mother greeted Zhang Qi's invitation with still less enthusiasm. "I absolutely cannot move now," she announced to Qieying as she read Zhang Qi's letter, set it aside, and walked out of the room. Then, as if she felt required to explain herself, she returned a few minutes later. "I have many responsibilities here in Changzhou," she said, holding her daughter's gaze. "The most important are my obligations to your father's parents. Neither has been properly buried. And construction on your grandmother's memorial arch has not even begun. If I do not see to these matters now and make sure they are done properly, no one will." She turned, then paused. "It's not that I don't want to obey your father. He has not considered all that I have to think about. I will have to remind him." She then retreated to her own chambers without looking back to see how Qieying reacted.

Qieying was unsure exactly what made her mother's resistance to moving fade. She knew only that at some point her mother began methodically dispatching her ritual obligations and matter-of-factly packing the house for a move. Then, just on the eve of their departure, a messenger from Jiangyin came with the news of Guanying's death.

GUANYING

Qieying had always thought it cruel that her favorite sister was the only one of the four of them who had to leave home when she married. Guanying's husband was a gentleman, an accomplished if undistinguished scholar. His family arranged a conventional wedding for their son, naturally expecting that their son's bride would live with them and wait on them like a proper daughter-in-law. It did Guanying no good that her elder sister had set something of a precedent by remaining at home with her parents after her own marriage. Exceptions for Guanying were out of the question. Now, hearing the news of her sister's death, Qieying rehearsed in her mind the signs of trouble she might have noticed, the things she might have done to protect Guanying. She recalled that after Guanying moved to her husband's home, she almost entirely stopped writing poetry. At the time Qieying had rationalized this. After all, Guanying carried two babies to term in the years following her marriage, and new daughters-in-law and young mothers often suffered a temporary lapse in their creative lives while they adjusted to their new surroundings. Now Guanying's retreat from writing glared as an ominous warning. Qieying felt responsible somehow, as if she had neglected her sister's cry for help.

Ordinarily when a woman dies unexpectedly in her husband's home, her brother acts as her natal family's representative and goes to inspect the circumstances. The formal purpose is to ascertain the cause of death and inquire into anything suspicious.[11] Even though families like the Zhang viewed this ritual as a formality, even a courtesy, nevertheless an invitation to visit Guanying's place of death came promptly. But the Zhang had no one appropriate to send. Guanying's elder brother was dead, and her younger brother, Yuesun, was eighteen *sui*—capped, but still too young for this weighty ritual. Qieying's father was too far away—indeed, at the time he did not yet know of his daughter's death. So Qieying could learn only what her mother managed to discover by questioning servants and messengers, and by reading between the lines of communications sent by Guanying's husband's family. Her mother could only tell her that Guanying had failed to recover her health after the birth of her second child and unexpectedly passed away.

Qieying, herself bereft and shocked, could not reach out to her grieving mother while her mother immersed herself in duties and in the preparations for the journey north. It was Lunying who wrote the somber message to send ahead to their father. No one else seemed able to lift a brush. After the family had moved to Shandong the formal mourning ended, and Yuesun printed Guanying's collected poems in his father's *yamen* studio, the Wanlin Library. Qieying's father wrote this preface for his late daughter's work:

In the sixth year following the burial of my . . . daughter Guanying, her younger brother, Yuesun, assembled all the drafts of her poems he could find, proofread them carefully and made corrections, and copied them into a portfolio for printing. I have read them over and over again. I don't know where the tears come from. Guanying studied poetry from the age of twelve or thirteen *sui*. I was traveling at the time, earning a living. Each year I came home for a visit, but I was never able to spend more than a month or so. I always loved to answer her questions about her studies, but I could never instruct her on a regular basis. The most I ever did was to give her an occasional lecture on some broad interpretive question. In the fall of 1814, when I returned home from Anhui, Guanying—who was nineteen by that time—gave me some of her poems and lyrics to read and asked for my suggestions. The nuance in these poems was extraordinary, and I marveled at them. Within a month I was back on the road to Anhui, and from there I moved to the capital, where I spent more than ten years, unable to return home. The year after I left, Guanying was married to Zhhang Zhengping of Jiangyin, and six years after that she gave birth to a son. In 1823, I was appointed magistrate of a county in Shandong, and the following year [1824] the family came from the south to join me. That same year, in the seventh month, Guanying became ill and died. She was barely thirty years old.

Ah! I remember that time in the autumn of 1814 when we sat by the light of the lamp talking about everything—classics and moderns, criticism and calligraphy—with all five children gathered around me. I was so happy then! How could I have known that in just the space of a few days I would be bidding her my last farewell? Now her sisters and her brother are here before me; all are fine. But Guanying has gone and I will never see her again. What father has ever endured such misery? Even though I know she is gone forever, I will never cease to mourn her, especially because my Guanying's poetry itself is so full of sad and mournful sounds. . . . [12]

Written on the sixteenth day of the eighth month of the ninth year of the reign Daoguang [September 13, 1829], by Zhang Qi of Yanghu

Years later, reading these lines, Qieying would leaf through her sister's poems as her brother had arranged them for publication, in chronological order. The first was dated 1810, written when Guanying was about fifteen *sui,* during the period when their father was traveling; the last, a poem about plum blossoms—symbol of feminine youth and beauty—was a rare late poem composed in the year of Guanying's death, 1824. Qieying could see how her father reviewed Guanying's life through her poems and marked in his mind the times he was with her and the years when they were parted. Qieying also noted for herself Guanying's poem marking the tenth anniversary of the death of their elder brother, Juesun; the poem written in the year of Guanying's marriage lamenting her separation from her sisters; a sad little poem about recovering from illness and missing letters from home, composed in the lonely year following her marriage; and the poem dreaming of home—written the year Guanying's first son was born. [13]

A year after the printing of Guanying's poems, Wanying would write her own poem in regulated verse and send it to Qieying:[14]

READING MY LATE SISTER'S COLLECTED POEMS

Ephemeral life is like water flowing,
We have already been separated by death a full year.
Tears well up, stirred by the early autumn,
Your departed soul drops into my dream.
A crane fairy flies from the moon's great column,[15]
A flower falls, suffused with the sunset's glow.
On this day under the western window,
In a quiet moment I recite your catkin[16] verses.

Years later, after Qieying had moved away from her family and joined her husband in Beijing for the first time, she would compose this song lyric in her sister's memory, to the tune "Bodhisattva Headdress":[17]

From the magnificent dwellings of the immortals, no news;
If your soul returned, it would be hard to recover those brilliant gifts
    [of writing].
The single slim volume of your poems in my writing case
Is my only source for recovering your feelings.
Ten years of weeping[18]
Have made me thin and haggard.
Leaning toward the old moon's chill beams,
I ask: who taught you to be so perfectly round?

The night is deep, the wind is sharp, piercing my body,
Over the Clear Bright Hall flies a crisp snow.
When I roll up the bamboo screen to gaze,
Who takes pity on my pair of cold sleeves?
In the frosty glitter my wind-tossed hair is a shadow;
Events long past come unbidden to my mind.
I dare not complain that the night is long;
Knowing how you suffered so much more.

Guanying's collected poems, printed with a preface by her father and stored in a case in her eldest sister's dowry, were an enduring touchstone for the family's grief, a medium through which they remembered and communicated with her departed spirit.[19]

On their journey to Shandong after Guanying's death, the family first boarded a boat to follow the Grand Canal north. Qieying stood numbly on the deck, watching great barges loaded with imperial grain move slowly past their passenger ship, which constantly had to make way for the larger vessels. On the small houseboats that plied the Canal's edges, washing hung out to dry near inverted chamber pots. Port towns along the way were lined with docks full of vendors' stalls. More than once she recovered herself and sent a servant to buy local treats and handicrafts to amuse the babies and distract her mother, who, garbed in hemp, reclined belowdecks, mourning.

After reaching the great Canal port at Jining, they left the boat and made their way overland, traveling on the imperial courier routes northeastward through Yanzhou and Tai'an, then skirting the Tai mountains until they arrived at the grand city of Jinan. Clear streams ran down the northern slope of the mountain range, feeding into the moat surrounding the city and pooling to create the famous Daming Lake. From Jinan they planned to take the road to Zhangqiu, where her father was an acting magistrate. Qieying's brother and her brother-in-law, Wanying's husband, who had come to escort them, discussed their destination as they traveled the dry and pitted roads, blanketed time and again by clouds of dust as military convoys rode forth and imperial couriers dashed by.

Zhangqiu was a small town compared to Jinan. But it was hardly dull and quiet. On the contrary, the area exploded with energy: construction everywhere, laborers moving in gangs to transport heavy loads of brick and stone, moneylenders' shops lining the streets, and a new entertainment district catering to the rich travelers arriving in droves each day. Land developers and commercial farmers had remade Zhangqiu into an immense marketplace. The landlords of Zhangqiu were not simply rich; they were also newly wealthy, men who had made their fortunes in the booming Shandong commercial markets and in the new industries that now peppered that part of the North China plain.[20] Such men, Qieying knew, were seldom formally educated and, to hear her brother talk, their values were very far from those of scholars like the Zhang. Zhangqiu's landlords were not inclined to invest in their local communities, for example; in fact, many of them were hostile to the central government's officials and their assiduous tax recording. They were not, however, averse to using the county magistrate's court to advance their interests. Qieying was therefore not surprised to hear her father announce, shortly after their arrival, that Zhangqiu was a snake pit of litigation. His appointment there was temporary, and he couldn't wait to be reassigned.

As they lingered long over the evening meal the first day they arrived, Qieying's father told the family about his arrival there: how he had found a thousand cases waiting for a hearing, and how he had managed to pare down that caseload by working from dawn until midnight every day until his desk was finally clear. His words were bold and proud, but it was plain to Qieying that the Zhangqiu courtroom had taken its toll on her father. At sixty, his hair was almost white. He looked like an old man.[21]

No sooner were they settled in Zhangqiu than Qieying's father was ordered to move again.[22] This time he was sent to a still more challenging post in the far western corner of the province. The county of Guantao was nowhere near the Grand Canal or its hinterland. It lay just on the provincial boundary, in one of the most desolate parts of the entire North China plain. Guantao was infamous as a home for bandits and rebels, and everyone knew that a magistrate sent there could expect serious trouble. It was agreed that Zhang Qi would proceed first to his new position to make ready for the rest of the family, while his wife and daughters and their children took temporary lodging back in Jinan, where they could enjoy—at least briefly—the amenities of urban life. Qieying fancied herself boating again on Daming Lake.

As they returned to Jinan she allowed herself the luxury of feeling safe and secure. The city was a sophisticated place: fine herbal medicine shops, excellent bookstores, wonderful antique emporia, rivaling what she had known at home. She and her mother and her sisters indulged themselves, sending servants out to the finest stores in search of small luxuries that, thanks to her father's new status, they could suddenly afford.

It was the height of summer. In the crowded, densely built quarter of the city where they had rented rooms, a smallpox epidemic spread rapidly within the city walls. Shortly before they were to leave for Guantao, Qieying's two babies—a son and a daughter—were stricken and died; within a month, Lunying lost her own two young children. Far from home and sojourning in a strange place, Qieying and Lunying buried their only children.[23] In Guantao, unaware of the tragedy that had befallen the family, their father waited eagerly to see them.

To reach Guantao they had to travel entirely by land, crossing the Grand Canal at Dongchang and continuing westward on a dusty road. An armed escort, as well as several pack animals and many servants from the *yamen,* met them at the Canal crossing. As they approached the city toward the end of their journey, they could see the stark walls of Guantao rising amid vast fields that lay dry and parched, stretching far across the flat plain to the horizon. Beggars lined the road leading toward the county seat. Just below the city walls, Qieying's palanquin passed a dense crowd where vendors had set up tiny stalls dispensing hot water and snacks. On the edge of the crowd she saw a woman younger than herself holding up a sign offering her child for sale. Nearby, another group of women in shabby clothes lingered, eyeing the men milling about, most of them hauling heavy loads or looking for a load to pull. Qieying turned to the maid seated beside her, who had come out from the *yamen* to meet them in Liaocheng. "What are those women doing there?" she asked. "They are there to see the sights, madam," the maid replied.[24]

They passed through the main gate, and the crowds vanished. Qieying craned her neck to look down the length of the street. She could see the walls of the county *yamen* in the distance. As their entourage pulled up, loud shouts and gongs announced their arrival, and the doors were flung open, revealing a large compound. At the rear stood the magistrate's private quarters. The compound Qieying would call her new home was topped elegantly with curving roofs and landscaped with lush gardens, kept green and blooming with well water by an aged but devoted gardener. He hovered over a nearby flowerbed as they were escorted past him. A large staff of servants stood ready for her mother's commands. Qieying got down from her palanquin and walked as steadily as she could across the front courtyard, supporting her mother. Her father, her brother, and Wanying's husband stood at the top of the steps to receive them and draw them inside.

Many months after Qieying's arrival in Guantao, on the evening of the Mid-Autumn Festival of 1827, Zhang Qi assembled his family to celebrate their first such festival together in more than twenty years.[25] Qieying had observed the Mid-Autumn Festival every year, through good times and bad, but she had never seen preparations like this. Maids and serving boys rushed around, arranging potted plants and furniture, preparing food, hanging lanterns. Elegant brushes, inkstones, and paper were set out on fine pearwood stands for spontaneous verse-writing in case the mood should strike. Her father's chief valet made himself the foreman of the operation, keeping a sharp eye out for idlers and sloppy work. He had ordered immense ceramic pots placed along the balustrades, filled with purple, russet, gold, and deep red chrysanthemums. Behind the pots, pale autumn hibiscus blooms hung low over the railings, reminding Qieying of their old home in Near Garden. It was the first holiday she had ever known when she had no work to do.

She caught herself wondering, as she looked around, what her mother's life would have been like had her father's career unfolded differently, or had her uncle Huiyan lived. Perhaps they might have spent their lives in luxury, or at least in greater comfort. Her mother was seated off to the side under another balcony observing the scene, probably recalling her childhood and similar grand occasions. Qieying's mother had often told stories about her carefree girlhood, surrounded by cousins and her doting aunt and uncle. Now, however, her mother looked austere, somber, and alone. Instead of the holiday gowns all of her daughters had donned for the evening—they were forbidden to mourn children who died so young—Qieying's mother still wore a mourning dress of coarse white hemp. Guanying's death was more than three years behind them, so she should have long since discarded those hempen garments. But devastated by the deaths of so many grandchildren, she resolutely kept them on, defiant of convention and ritual propriety.

Gazing at her mother, Qieying felt a wave of apprehension. Her husband, Wu Zan, was not present for this grand Guantao reunion. The year before, he had reached a pinnacle in his career, winning the highest degree in the examination system. He was now officially a "presented scholar" *(jinshi)* just like her late uncle. He had been received by the emperor himself, who had offered personal congratulations on Wu Zan's distinguished examination essays and on his outstanding calligraphy. Qieying was proud and even a little excited about her husband's sudden ascent to distinction, but she was ambivalent about the examinations as a measure of talent. Her father was extremely critical of the examination system and especially of the stereotyped writing in the "eight-legged essay" form. Her late uncle, who shared those views, had managed to excel anyhow, but Qieying's father had never reached the heights now attained by her own husband. Still, Qieying liked to think that her father was partly responsible for Wu Zan's performance in the exams. Just a year before winning his degree, Wu Zan had taken a leave from his regular studies to spend a year working with her father in Shandong, in the company of her brother and friends, writing song lyrics and developing his talent. Qieying believed firmly that her father's tutelage was partly responsible for Wu Zan's excellent performance on the exams.

Of her own relationship to her husband Qieying also had doubts. She and Wu Zan had spent little time together. After their wedding in Changshu, he left the south at once for Beijing. There he lived in his native place's guildhall, preparing for the examinations. He paid occasional visits to Changzhou, the pregnancies that resulted had been difficult, and they did not write letters or constantly exchange poems the way Wanying and her husband did.

The loss of their young children would give them grief to share but little else, and in any case, Wu Zan's son remained in excellent health. There was yet another reason for Qieying's ambivalence about her husband's triumph. Now that he had established himself in the highest circles at the capital, she would finally have to leave her parents and siblings and move there to join him.

Her attention returned to the scene around her. It was a cool, clear evening, dry and calm, such as one could experience only in the north. The moon began to rise, and Qieying's family members gathered in the courtyard, which was large and grand, to toast and exchange poems: her father; her mother; her sister Lunying; her sister Wanying and Wanying's husband, Wang Xi, and their one-year-old daughter (the infant who had just been born being off with a wet nurse); and her younger brother, Yuesun. Lunying's husband was not present. Yuesun was engaged but not yet married. One by one each of them stepped forward. Qieying's father was subdued, Guanying's death still much on his mind. Clearly he remembered, as all of them did, the last time the family had gathered for the Mid-Autumn Festival, when Guanying was still very much alive. Qieying's mother, who declined to speak, stood near her husband in funereal white.

The mood, however, turned merry, and Qieying gave herself over to it. Her brother set the tone by raising his goblet to his future bride. The delightful and talented Bao Mengyi, the family's darling and a close friend of Wanying, was still living in her stepfather's home, but the mention of her pending marriage to Yuesun, planned for the following year, reminded Qieying how well Mengyi would fit into the contours of their very close family. Mengyi's stepfather, Master Bao, so like an uncle to the girls, would now become a formal kinsman. And Mengyi would make a perfect respondent in the Zhang sisters' endless exchanges of verse.

There was one other person who might have joined the gathering that evening, but she was not to be seen: Qieying's late elder brother's fiancée, Miss Fa. Miss Fa had moved in with the family in time for their Mid-Autumn Festival gathering of 1814. On that occasion, when everyone was still trying to find a proper place for her in the family, Qieying and her sisters went to great lengths to include Miss Fa in the festivities, to entice her to make herself at home and enjoy herself. But they had long since abandoned those well-meaning efforts. Miss Fa was at fault: she was too difficult. On her arrival, she had self-righteously announced that she had given up all celebrations and pleasures in the aftermath of her fiancé's death, and she was at special pains to make it known that enjoying the Mid-Autumn Festival— a time when separated lovers toasted from afar—was out of the question.

As part of what Qieying took to be a more general strategy of coping with her anomalous status, Miss Fa steadfastly declined when it came to any interaction with Qieying or her sisters beyond what was minimally required. She preferred to cast herself in the role of daughter-in-law, and she attempted to focus her attention on Qieying's mother. At the time Miss Fa first entered their home, however, Qieying's mother was preoccupied with Yuesun's education and with keeping the household solvent in her husband's absence. She had neither time nor patience—nor, as Qieying came to see, motivation—to instruct an unwanted daughter-in-law. Over the years, Qieying tried several times to integrate Miss Fa into the workings of the kitchen and the household tasks that were her own charge, but Miss Fa had no energy and seemingly no aptitude for practical duties, absent a command from her self-selected mother-in-law.

In this manner, gradually and over time, Qieying and her mother and sisters reached an accommodation with Miss Fa. Miss Fa was a living presence in their home, but she kept to herself. She dressed modestly, she ate a strict vegetarian diet that she prepared for herself and took in her room, and she devoted long hours to prayer, chanting her Buddhist rosary by the hour, reading sutras, and burning incense around the clock. As a gesture of pity or kindness, Qieying was not sure which, Qieying's mother installed a small altar to Guanyin in Miss Fa's room so she could conduct her devotions in private. Qieying often heard the sound of the wooden fish knocking as she walked past the closed door.[26] So although Miss Fa had come north to Shandong with the rest of the family, and although she was present in the *yamen* compound on the eve of the Mid-Autumn Festival in Guantao, she remained in her room, out of sight and, for the most part, out of Qieying's mind.

Following her brother's toast, it was Qieying's turn to recite a poem. Then came her youngest sister, Wanying, who put down her squirming child in order to read more dramatically. Little Caipin, at two *sui,* was already showing signs of precocity, and Wanying insisted that she be in the thick of every literary event. A servant shadowed the squealing Caipin as she toddled off toward the chrysanthemums. Wanying's husband, Wang Xi, who next to Qieying's father was probably the most learned gentleman in the family, ran to scoop up his daughter and juggle her on one arm while he chanted his own poem. Then everyone began to argue about whose poem was better and why.

As the debate rippled around the room, it skipped over Lunying. Lunying had never shown any interest in poetry, preferring to concentrate all of her energies on her calligraphy, and she always demurred in these kinds of conversations. But Qieying noticed that Lunying was standing a bit off to the side, looking distracted. Suddenly, to Qieying's utter amazement, Lun-ying stepped into the center of the company and began to chant, in a clear and resonant voice, the first verse anyone had ever heard from her lips. At the age of thirty, Qieying's calligrapher sister made her debut as a poet.[27] Here is the poem she recited:[28]

THINKING OF SOMEONE ON AN AUTUMN DAY

The jade dew gleams with autumn hues,
The *wutong* tree sheds its first leaf;
Locusts' clamor rises to the tall trees,
Fireflies glimmer through the gauzy curtain.
The nesting swallow knows it's time to return,
But my encumbered spouse can't yet come home.
From afar I worry about your thin sleeves,
Where shall I send your winter clothes?

Written in the "ancient" style using five words per line, this poem went into Lunying's writing case and was later printed in her collected works.[29] In years to come, her brother would liken her best poems to those of the great Six Dynasties poets Tao Qian (372–427) and Xie Lingyun (385–433). He wrote in a preface when he published her poems that like them, Lunying strove to create a moment in which the poet and the natural world were one.

LUNYING

Qieying was convinced that her sister's debut as a poet that Mid-Autumn Festival evening was not accidental. Lunying had just lost her only children from nearly ten years of marriage—both little girls, one still an infant. The terms of Sun Jie's marriage contract with the Zhang did not require him to provide an heir for Zhang Qi's line, even though he was a "married-in" son-in-law. Sun Jie therefore had arranged to adopt one of his younger brother's sons to carry on his own family line. Lunying was the ritual mother of this adopted boy,[30] but she had no surviving offspring of her own.

Lunying's poetry recitation at this fateful time was therefore a perfor-mance to which Qieying attached some significance, for on the eve of this particular family gathering, Lunying's husband was absent, comforting his father following the death of his mother. Qieying knew, moreover, that Sun Jie's father's financial situation was unstable, even though he was holding a magistrate's post like her father's. She was certain that when Sun Jie departed, her parents had sent him off with gifts and money. The line in the poem about winter clothes and thin sleeves, therefore, rang a bit hollow in her ears. Sun Jie and his family might be poor, but her own family was taking good care of them.

In the years to come, Qieying often recalled that scene at Mid-Autumn, when her sister stood basking in the stunned congratulations of her family. Lunying was extremely talented, but she had set herself apart from her sisters in refusing to write poetry. Instead, she won acclaim as a calligrapher, one of the very few women practicing that daunting art. Still more remarkable was Lunying's calligraphic style: she had mastered the difficult Northern Wei stele style, which their father had been teaching her from the time she was a little girl. Neither of them paid any attention to the fact that women never wrote in this heavy, manly style. Lunying disdained the fine, spidery writing on silk and paper that was considered appropriate for women, even if the model was the work of a genius like Wang Xizhi. She preferred rubbings from ancient stone tablets, and in her art she sought to capture exactly the weight and even the crudeness of carved stone characters. She used thick heavy, brushes and viscous ink on large surfaces. Her scrolls were monumental. She considered her art and her technique to be profoundly rooted in the past, and she approached it with a gravity that Qieying sometimes found unnerving. Qieying had to brace herself to watch Lunying write, every massive stroke flawlessly placed, each character perfectly balanced, the completed phrase precisely in harmony. To give herself enough leverage, she took to standing on her bed platform so she could bend over the paper.[31] Her finished work was architectonic, a grand pattern or design that fit the page exactly (see figure 3). It required utter concentration and meticulous planning, as well as powerful physical force.

As Lunying's talent blossomed, Qieying's parents began receiving visitors who had heard about the *cainü* calligrapher and wanted to buy one of her scrolls. Korean scholars and envoys visiting the capital learned of Lunying's work from Qieying's husband and from her brother, and the interest of one Korean connoisseur in particular catapulted Lunying to true fame.[32] The family quickly developed a routine for handling Lunying's following. A collector seeking Lunying's work would call at the Zhang family home, Qieying's mother would serve him tea, and then her brother would escort Lunying into the family reception hall for a consultation. Once the terms of a commissioned piece had been agreed upon, the visitor would be permitted to withdraw, leaving a red envelope discreetly behind. Lunying never

宋遜瑜妻魏氏作南征賦詞甚典美張說見之歎曰曹大家東征之流也

FIGURE 3. Zhang Lunying, "Wife of Tingyu." Nanjing Museum. Written on gold-thread-squared paper. The inscription, which honors the wife of Song Tingyu, reads as follows: "Lady Wei, wife of Song Tingyu, composed a rhapsody titled 'The Journey South,' which was deeply classical. When Zhang Yue saw it, he sighed and said, 'Truly it is in the tradition of Ban Zhao's "The Journey East."'" The original text appears in a biography in *Jiu Tang shu*—among the thirty-one biographies of women, one of the two that mention female erudition. Zhang Yue (667–730) was a well-known scholar to whom Lady Wei wrote a petition requesting his help in finding her husband an office. So impressed was Zhang Yue with her eloquence that he wrote this comment on her talent, which was preserved by Lady Wei's biographers. (See Yao 2006. From Li Lan 1999, p. 48.)

received such visitors in her studio, and the scrolls and inscriptions she created without commissions were never sold. Instead, she preferred to give them to members of her family and to friends. Qieying had several such precious pieces in her own dowry chests.

To watch Lunying at her art was a privilege reserved for family members and the occasional close friend. Lunying would stare at the blank surface, as if she were meditating, before lifting her brush. Qieying recalled her brother's image of "a slight figure who barely filled her clothes" with a giant brush and an immense piece of silk or paper. Lunying was an artist obsessed, bent over her writing desk late into the night, refusing to sleep— Qieying remembered how she used to say: "If I let a single day go by without writing, I feel lost. I cannot help myself."[33] Day after day, Lunying worked with her father in his *yamen* library, the studio later named in the title of her collected poems as the "Green Scholar Tree Studio."[34] Whenever Qieying remembered her middle sister, she thought of father and daughter assuaging their grief together.[35]

As Lunying's spouse, Sun Jie had not developed as Qieying thought he might. Perhaps his family background had something to do with this. He came from a Changzhou merchant family, not a family of scholars like the Zhang. His father had been the first in his family to win the *jinshi* degree. Qieying's father met Sun Jie's father in the course of their studies, and they agreed to a marriage contract for their children just before Sun Jie's father won his first official appointment. At Zhang Qi's insistence, the contract stipulated that Sun Jie would be a uxorilocally married son-in-law and that his primary place of residence would be with Lunying's natal family. Qieying's parents did not need Sun Jie to produce an heir for them. Therefore, Qieying had always assumed that her father insisted on these arrangements so he could keep Lunying close to him, in case the betrothal was a mistake. The Sun were so new to scholarship, and at the time of the betrothal Sun Jie's own prospects were not at all clear. Moreover, Sun Jie's parents had many sons, and it was a financial relief for them to send one son "out" in marriage. Certainly in Changzhou no stigma was attached to this kind of arrangement for either side. The terms of the contract were flexible, too, as to residency. Shortly after the wedding, Lunying and her new husband moved briefly to Huaiyuan in Anhui province to join her father-in-law at his new magistrate's office there, a stay that turned out to be mercifully brief. After their return to Changzhou, Sun Jie departed for the capital to try his hand at the examinations.

But the Sun family met a series of calamities. Within the space of a few years, every one of Sun Jie's four brothers died. By 1827, on the eve of the Mid-Autumn Festival, Sun Jie was his parents' only surviving son. When these disasters began with his eldest brother's illness at the capital in 1825, Sun Jie gave up the exams so that he could escort his brother's body home for burial. Overwhelmed by the death of his last brother barely two years later, Sun Jie declared an end to all of his examination studies. Each of his four brothers left sons and a widow behind; all were now Sun Jie's responsibility. The widows would need support; the children would need education and, eventually, suitable marriages. Lacking a means of employment himself, Sun Jie found his debts mounting rapidly.

Unfortunately, he was not the sort of person who could handle extreme difficulties. In fact, he was by nature unaccustomed to being responsible even for himself. All his life he had followed his fancies. As a youth he liked martial arts and geomancy, and he dabbled in medicine. Eventually he studied medicine with Qieying's father, and some people said he became an effective doctor. But there was a lot of debate about that. As a young man Sun Jie prided himself on his strength. He could draw the heaviest bows—ten *piculs*, he boasted, when two was the norm. Then he took up weights and, at the peak of his powers, he carried a four-hundred-pound stone three times around the courtyard of the Sun family home before collapsing with a hemorrhage. Qieying was convinced that her brother-in-law's poor health began with that unfortunate error in judgment.

Of course, when Lunying married Sun Jie, Qieying knew none of these stories. They came to light only as she grew better acquainted with Sun Jie and had to account for his peculiarities. Martial arts exploits were something of a joke in the Zhang family, mainly because Qieying and her siblings had never had much use for such things. Yet, she reminded herself, Sun Jie did have some appealing traits. He was easygoing, open, and forthright. He could be forgiving and humble. Qieying believed he was a moral person with a good sense of right and wrong. While he was living with the Zhang and studying medicine with Qieying's father, he was exceptionally kind to Yuesun, who was often at home nursing his ailments. But at the same time, Sun Jie was impulsive, and he seemed unaware of the effects of his actions on others. He would take up anything that struck his fancy and drop everything else, until he grew bored or until his new obsession became too difficult. No one could depend on him for anything. This wore on Qieying after a while, and even his devoted friends had trouble with him. Sun Jie became morose and depressed as people turned away from him, and as he entered middle age, he became harder and harder to deal with.

For Qieying, however, the worst thing about Lunying's husband had little to do with any of this. The worst thing was his attitude toward Lunying's talent. Qieying had actually overheard Sun Jie telling her father, soon after the wedding, that calligraphy was "*not* a woman's concern" (*fei furen shi*).[36] Coming from a man with so little talent of his own, his words made her stomach turn. She could only imagine her sister's reaction, for she could not believe that her sister was unaware of Sun Jie's prejudices. And her father! Her father was the one who taught Lunying her calligraphy and showed her off to Bao Shichen. Sun Jie's words were an insult to Qieying's entire family, but his gross ignorance and his narrow-mindedness were a particular affront to Lunying. That, at least, was Qieying's view of it.

Qieying knew that Sun Jie's opinions were shared by some very highly educated men; they were not just a matter of gross ignorance.[37] She was familiar, through her female friends, with an influential essay on women's learning by the noted philosopher Zhhang Xuecheng, whose work her father had greatly admired. When she had asked her father about this particular essay, however, his response was reserved. Zhhang Xuecheng's views on a number of current social issues, including the scandalous (as he thought) conduct of women who declared themselves "pupils" of a libertine poet named Yuan Mei, were outlandish from the point of view of Changzhou literati, whose wives and daughters spent much of their time interacting with and reading the poems of those very women poets. Qieying's father explained to her that Zhhang's hyperbole was typical of the conservatism of his native place, Shaoxing. Shaoxing families were renowned for their adherence to strictly literal readings of classical texts on the separation of the sexes. Qieying's father suspected that much of this conservatism was developed in a local culture where litigation and clever lawyering were rampant and where a family's only hope for respectability was to avoid being dragged into court. This meant, among other things, avoiding conflicts over property and—especially—keeping women completely out of sight.[38]

All this ran through Qieying's mind as she watched her sister read her poem. With her husband gone, Lunying's talent shone more than ever. Qieying guiltily hoped that Sun Jie would not return soon.

BEIJING (1829–1844)

Qieying could not remain indefinitely in Guantao to look out for Lunying and play with her nieces. Her husband was expecting her to join him in

Beijing. For the first time, at nearly the age of forty, Zhang Qieying tearfully left her natal family like a proper married woman.[39] As she traveled she felt a growing sense of both anxiety and anticipation: she was to join for the first time her "son," the boy born to Wu Zan by his first wife, who had died in childbirth. Zonghan had been reared by nursemaids and tutored by his father, and by now he had already passed the age of capping. Qieying had received letters from Zonghan from time to time, written in the painfully polite language of obligatory greetings. But her husband's occasional letters had assured her that the boy was studious and well behaved, eager to please and anxious to spend time with his talented stepmother.

On her arrival in Beijing Qieying was immediately swept into a new life. She became the mother of a teenaged son whom she had never met; a household manager for her husband, whom she barely knew; and the wife of a sociable official whose contacts throughout Beijing's literary circles drew her into the company of the leading female writers of the day. The whirl of Beijing society and the demands of her new household almost distracted Qieying from her extreme suffering at parting from her family. She was not prepared for the news that came within a year of her departure from Guantao.

Wanying's first letter arrived soon after Qieying reached the capital. It began with the usual chatter. A cousin from the Dong side of the family had recently visited and delivered a manuscript that offered a sequel to the collection of song lyrics published by their father and their late uncle. "Father was so pleased," Wanying went on, "that he immediately composed a preface and arranged for its publication in his own studio right here."[40] She added a few bits of news about other relatives and friends back home in Changzhou. Then her tone shifted abruptly. "Mother's health is not improving," she wrote. "I am pregnant again, and keeping up with Caipin and Caifan takes all the energy I have. Mengyi and Lunying share the housework to spare me. There are problems with Miss Fa that I cannot go into here. Lunying's husband has returned and has brought with him his own father—can you imagine!—who is himself desperately ill. Our father is supposed to cure him! So there is our Lunying, caring for Mother day and night, and now with her father-in-law to attend to while her husband frets around getting in the way, and with Father himself torn in all directions. Father has his own medical practice here in Guantao, of course, not to mention his official duties. I fear he will collapse at any moment. The two of them never have time for their writing and the Green Scholar Tree Studio is empty, gathering dust."

The next letter was brief. "My dear elder sister," Wanying wrote. "You will know already what I am about to tell you. Our mother was very ill when you left for the capital, and her condition did not improve in the weeks and months following. She died peacefully with all of us around her, but our father is disconsolate and our brother is beside himself with worry, not to mention grief. Her death came in the seventh month of this year (1831). She had almost reached her seventieth birthday."

Wanying's letters continued to come, leading Qieying through the unhappy days and months that followed their mother's death. When Yuesun left Guantao to take their mother's body back to Changzhou for burial, Sun Jie, as the senior married-in son-in-law, took his place in the Guantao quarters. Sun Jie had gotten on well with Yuesun, who had been his friend as a young man. But Sun Jie could not interact at all with Miss Fa, who was causing new problems that Wanying left vague for the time being. Meanwhile, despite their father's best medical efforts, Sun Jie's father died within the year. The strain of two deaths on Qieying's father, the doctor, combined with his weighty responsibilities as a magistrate, suddenly began to tell. Lunying and Wanying both wrote to Qieying now, and their letters were grim. Their father complained of illness but refused to see any physician but their brother, whose judgment alone he trusted. Zhang Qi died in the third month of 1833, under the care of his physician son.

On reading this last news, Qieying saw the burdens that suddenly fell on her beloved brother. Yuesun had not only failed to save his father's life. Now, with Zhang Qi's death, the Zhang siblings would also lose their home at the Guantao *yamen*. Their father had been an honest official. Therefore he had accumulated no assets during his term as a magistrate. Whatever luxury they had all enjoyed as residents of the Guantao *yamen* would remain there for the incoming new magistrate. They did not have enough money to pay for the transportation of their father's coffin back to Changzhou; in fact, two coffins required transport, since Sun Jie's father's body remained in Guantao as well. Yuesun borrowed money. He also received a substantial gift from an admirer of his father's at the capital, conveyed to him by Qieying's husband, as well as help from many other quarters. When the boat bearing Zhang Qi's coffin reached Yangzhou, where Bao Shichen was living at the time, their old friend came out to weep over it.[41]

Wanying's next letters came from Changzhou and the new home Yuesun had made for the three siblings and their families to share.[42] "Our household is transformed," she wrote. "Without Father and Mother, we are like geese who have lost their flock, scattered and strayed. But our brother is amazing all of us. He has taken on the role of family head with a strength and assurance I never expected. My own dear husband has gone off, very enterprisingly, to a teaching position in Hangzhou. Of course I miss him. Lunying is busy day and night turning out hanging scrolls for people who seem to line up outside waiting for them. I understand that you have friends up there who are interested in buying her work, especially that diplomat from Korea, Master Yi. Our brother will be bringing a very large consignment of Lunying's work up to the capital with him when he comes to visit you, which—if I may judge from his recent activities—will be very soon."[43] Wanying went on: "Besides her tremendous output of work, Lunying has taken on the instruction of all the young children in the family, which saves us a lot of money. I am trying to do more to help Mengyi with the housework."[44] The letter concluded with some very disturbing details about Miss Fa.

MISS FA

In the aftermath of Qieying's mother's death—and in her absence—the emotional life of the Zhang family took unexpected turns. Reading the letters that flew northward from Changzhou to Beijing now brought Miss Fa forcibly to Qieying's attention. The problems that Miss Fa's presence might cause in her brother's household had first come to light in Guantao, when a clerk on their father's staff took some interest in Miss Fa and went to the unthinkable lengths of attempting to approach her through a scullery maid. This maid, who was related to one of the runners at the Guantao *yamen,* was too lowly to have any access to Miss Fa directly, or even to the women's quarters. But the maid had plenty of contacts among the rest of the staff, from Qieying's father's valet to several of the serving boys with whom she was acquainted, and she induced someone to deliver a note to Miss Fa. The note, which was discovered when Miss Fa became hysterical after finding it on the floor of her chambers, was immediately destroyed. Qieying did not know if any of her sisters had even seen it. The clerk denied any knowledge of the matter, and since he was very well connected with powerful families in Guantao, Qieying's father, whose health at that point was very poor, decided against taking further steps against him. The maid was beaten and dismissed, however, and the entire *yamen* staff was turned inside out for months afterward, as recriminations flew back and forth. Miss Fa's hysteria was not easily calmed, and several visits from a local doctor took time to have their effect, Yuesun having declared himself unable to look after her out of consideration for propriety.

Problems emerged, meanwhile, from an unexpected quarter. Yuesun had married Bao Mengyi three years prior to their mother's death, and their second child, a daughter, was already in her second year when Qieying departed from Guantao for Beijing. With Qieying's departure and the death of Tang Yaoqing, Bao Mengyi, as the wife of Yuesun, was to become the head of the Zhang inner quarters. Of course Mengyi had her hands full with her young children. But as she perused her sister's letters, Qieying was greatly shocked to learn that the children were the least of Mengyi's concerns. Miss Fa, who had kept herself so quiet during Tang Yaoqing's lifetime, who had deferred to all of her sisters-in-law and retired from virtually every family function, had suddenly become the focus of the entire family's attention.

Venting her rage at last over her unfortunate life, Miss Fa found her target in the only person who was vulnerable to her anger: the hapless Mengyi. Qieying recognized at once, as she read Lunying's despairing letters, what a canny maneuver this was. In ritual terms, as well as in age, Mengyi was the junior daughter-in-law in the household; Miss Fa, as the betrothed of the eldest son and now ensconced as a *zhennü* in her late fiancé's family, held a position tantamount to senior daughter-in-law. During Tang Yaoqing's lifetime, respect for her mother-in-law demanded that Miss Fa suppress all of her feelings toward any other female member of the household. But with Tang Yaoqing no longer present to mediate and arbitrate, Miss Fa gave her ritual authority full play. At every turn she accosted Mengyi, flying into rages over her food, her room, her mood, her ailments, her clothing, her place in the family. Mengyi faced these tantrums without ever losing her own composure. She learned to placate Miss Fa by assessing each complaint and its most likely resolution, being by turns apologetic, sympathetic, soothing, or practical. Only in the privacy of her own rooms did Mengyi weep in frustration and anger.[45]

Qieying pondered the irony: Miss Fa and Mengyi were locked into their destructive relationship precisely because they were so well educated. Both understood supremely well the rituals governing relations between daughters-in-law. Both knew absolutely that as the ritual superior, in the absence of Qieying's mother, Miss Fa could exercise her power virtually unchecked. She took advantage of Mengyi's good nature and fine upbringing to assail her with every pain, every care, every complaint, and every irritation she could articulate. Moreover, Miss Fa permitted Mengyi alone to address her concerns and allowed no one else even to approach her.

Miss Fa's new visibility in the household led to other problems, brought to Qieying's attention by Yuesun in his own letters to the capital. One of these was the problem of an heir for their deceased elder brother, Juesun. Customarily a *zhennü* was expected to adopt and rear an heir who could carry on her deceased fiancé's branch of the family line. Although the senior Zhang had always insisted that they did not need an heir for Juesun, Miss Fa had other ideas. After Qieying's parents died, Miss Fa demanded that she be given Yuesun's first-born son as an adopted heir for Juesun. This demand immediately caused an uproar, described in excruciating detail in one of Yuesun's letters, with Mengyi distraught at the thought of giving up her son, and finally Lunying, desperate to calm things down, weighing in with all the wisdom of her years of diplomatic life with a brother's wife: "Of course," she soothed, "why debate? Name Yuesun's first-born son the Zhang heir, as he properly must be, and don't worry about it, because Mengyi will surely have more sons."[46] That settled the matter, at least for the time being, or so everyone thought. Qieying's brother's remaining act of grace was to petition the throne for a rescript to honor Miss Fa as a faithful maiden. The commendation arrived at last in 1848.[47]

Living in Beijing, far from her siblings and still mourning her parents, Qieying attempted to build a new life. Within two years of her arrival in Beijing she became pregnant again, but the new baby boy, her third child, died shortly after his birth. At that point, Qieying abandoned hope of rearing children of her own.[48] Zonghan became her singular focus. He was an avid reader and a remarkably affectionate young man, and she spent hours with him working on calligraphy and poetry.

Yuesun returned to the capital and settled in at Qieying's home, reviving the convivial ties he had formed earlier with her husband, Wu Zan, and his friends. He remained there for nearly six years, broken by periodic visits back to Changzhou.[49] Yuesun's aim was to earn enough money as a physician to repay the family's debts, some of which he hoped to recoup by the publication of a book on gynecology and infant care.[50] In reality, much of Yuesun's time was spent nursing his health and recovering his spirits in the company of Wu Zan and his friends, who gathered almost nightly to compose song lyrics and drink in a studio occupied by their Korean friend Yi Sang-jŏk.[51]

Yuesun brought news with every return trip: their cousin, Huiyan's only son, Chengsun, died unexpectedly;[52] Wanying had a third child, a son named Chenbi,[53] then a third daughter, Cailan. Lunying now took on the burdens of correspondence, writing to her siblings in Beijing with detailed reports about Wanying's children. Little Caipin, the eldest, had become Lunying's most apt pupil, composing poems and prose and learning calligraphy in the *li* (clerical script) style favored by her aunt. "I am so very fond of this child," Lunying wrote, "and you know, when she was born my husband commented that she must be a reincarnation of our own dear daughter who died."[54] "But I realize," she added, "that Caipin is Wanying's favorite too." Wanying, however, took her sister's longing to heart, and after Cailan's birth, she approached Lunying with a proposal. Granting that Caipin was Lunying's favorite niece, would Lunying be content to adopt Cailan as her own? It was arranged that Cailan would take the Sun surname and with it a new given name, Sihui (Heir to Excellence).[55] In one of her now-rare letters to Qieying, the busy Wanying described all of this in detail, concluding: "You should know, my dear eldest sister, that Cailan's new name is a tribute to you. May she carry on the learning of her family just as you have carried on the learning of ours!"

This news of birth and adoption came as Yuesun prepared to return to Changzhou for his wife's thirtieth birthday.[56] In the days before he left, Qieying shut herself up in her studio to compose Mengyi's birthday greeting, which she planned to send home in her brother's writing case.[57] Once he was gone, she cast about wistfully for a new writing project.

The idea came to her in the middle of one night, so forcefully that she rose from her bed, lit a lamp, made her way into her studio, and began to rummage through the stacks of bound books piled high on the table near her desk. One of these, she knew, contained the complete works of Sun Yuanxiang and his wife, Xi Peilan.[58] Qieying had not read their poems for some time. In fact, she confessed to herself, she had not opened those volumes since they were packed for the move to Shandong more than twelve years earlier. She had it in mind then to open them again, and for that reason she had carefully placed the two slim stitched books, in their matching binding, on the table in her study when she moved to Beijing and unpacked. There they sat, collecting dust and eventually covered by other books, forming the teetering stacks she now took apart to unearth the ones she sought. In those volumes were poems that Qieying needed to read again: poems by husband and wife mourning the death of their children—two sons and a daughter.[59] She found the books, placed the lamp by her chair, and began to turn the pages. She read until dawn, tears slipping unchecked down her face. As the sun began to warm her window, she started a poem. She wrote it with annotations, as if she were explaining it to herself:[60]

MOVED ON READING MASTER SUN ZIXIAO'S "THE DEATH OF APRICOTS,"
I COMPOSED THIS POEM IN THE SAME GENRE

Striking my eye, stopping my heart, a scene exactly as I knew it,
Tears course down my face, soak through my jacket.
Grievous aching of the heart, its cause the same pain,
Fraught images so vivid, the poem seems like a painting.
Twice in six years I have seen souls die,

Note: In the spring of 1827, I lost a son and a daughter; in the winter of 1832, another son.

For months at a time my whole family's had no more tears to shed.
Early in my life I was to learn the reality of "each in its own time,"

Note: The saying goes that in smallpox, it is timely for the elder to go before the younger; the reverse is untimely.

Elder sister, then younger sister, each lost precious "pearls in the palm."[61]

Note: At the time I was accompanying our late mother, lodging in Jinan; Lun-ying in that same month lost her own two daughters to smallpox.

The little souls had no symptoms, so a cure was not carefully considered,
How I regret that we used needles and herbs as if we were treating an
      ordinary illness.
The children gave no hint of dying, then suddenly they were gone,
Everyone had wished them long life, but their lives were not long at all.
As the illness worsened, we administered powerful drugs,
The doctors all insisted they had good remedies.
Hardest hit was the loving mother, her heart cut to the quick,
From sunset til dawn burning incense, praying for unseen help.
The moment when the crisis came, I now can bear to recall,
They seemed about to depart and yet unable to bear to leave.
Calling their mother in low tones, their spirits ebbing away,
Looking at their father, eyes straight ahead, tears still welling.
Their share of this life over, with no days left to live,
While for half my own life I've made empty talk about rearing children.[62]
After twelve years with a heart near breaking,
I am ready to reread "The Death of Apricots."

Qieying copied the poem onto a clean sheet of paper, folded it carefully, and placed it in her writing case. She rose from her desk and made her way through the house to the kitchen, vacant and tidy in the aftermath of the morning meal. She set a kettle of water to boil on the stove and steeped a cup of pale chrysanthemum tea. This she took out to the courtyard, where she sat in silence to sip and watch the bees mass around the flowers.

The whole family knew of Qieying's parents' wishes: after their deaths, their two younger daughters must be settled in a joint household with Yuesun and Mengyi. That charge, stated first by their mother and reiterated by their father, was very much on Yuesun's mind throughout the difficult years that followed the family's departure from Guantao. It took him six years to accumulate the money to get them a proper house in Changzhou. His two brothers-in-law, Wang Xi and Sun Jie, also put in some money, and at length the three couples began a new stage in their lives, living together under one roof with their children. Sun Jie was delegated as a tutor for the youngsters who were old enough to begin their studies. Wang Xi went out as a teacher and spent most of his time on the road.[63] Yuesun continued to practice medicine both at home and, periodically, up in the capital, where Qieying and her husband hosted him. Miss Fa inhabited a small room off to one side of the women's quarters. Qieying followed most of these changes through letters, and her brother's frequent visits north sustained her. When her brother collected her poems and song lyrics and printed them in the family's studio in Changzhou in 1840, in honor of her fiftieth birthday, she found it hard to celebrate from a distance.[64]

Her sense of distance sharpened when a letter came from Yuesun. "I decided," he announced, "that we must have a painting to celebrate our lives together here, and to honor our parents' memory." Of course, thought Qieying—that old promise Yuesun made to their parents, to look after her younger sisters. She tried to ignore the contradictory meanings of "our" in her brother's missive. "Moreover," Yuesun went on, "I found exactly the right artist—she is a cousin of our mother, a descendant of our maternal grandfather's line, and everyone knows her gifts, as she is the daughter of parents who are both painters." Qieying knew at once that her brother was talking about Tang Jiaming, whom they all addressed by her courtesy name, Bihen.[65] She imagined her siblings and her cousin conferring about the composition of the painting and the sentiments it was intended to convey. For a moment, she had to put the letter down.

The painting that Tang Bihen had now completed, her brother went on to say, was a handscroll in three parts titled "Biwu lianyin tu" (Linking verse across adjoining rooms),[66] and Lunying and Wanying had already composed poems to be inscribed at the end of the scroll. Now, concluding his letter,

Yuesun insisted that Qieying write a colophon herself for Bihen's painting. Since she could not see the painting herself, he helpfully supplied a detailed description: Three young couples, well dressed and refined in appearance. Each person holds a brush; each is absorbed in a composition. Paper lies scattered about among inkstones, water bowls, and stacks of books. Not a servant is in sight. The arrangement of the couples follows the title of the painting; that is, they are writing in separate but adjoining rooms. Each room is comfortably appointed with a desk for writing, chairs for sitting, and the elegant accoutrements of the scholar's life. There are elaborately designed inkstones together with every shape and size of brush; a scepter of fine cloisonné; many exquisitely carved red lacquer vases and boxes; fine shelves holding a few well-chosen curios and unusual jade figurines; and three large paired couplets gracing the walls, one set for each room, each in Lunying's own Northern Wei–style calligraphy. Brocade draperies and embroidered cushion covers soften the elegant lines of the pearwood furniture. Teacups sit carelessly upon side tables. In each room is also a landscape or flower painting of the type that can be inserted into a heavy carved ebony frame standing upright on the desk. This, he wrote with some pride, is a modern decoration that enables one to change a painting's seasonal theme with one's mood, or with the climate, or on a whim.[67]

Imagining the painting as she prepared to write, Qieying was struck by two things that made it remarkable. One was the mixed company. Men and women did not ordinarily sit composing poetry together, except in the courtesans' quarters. Yet this painting showed a domestic scene in a well-appointed literati home. The other unusual feature of Tang Bihen's painting was the fact that the three married couples—a brother, his two sisters, and their respective spouses—did not belong to the same patriline and therefore, properly speaking, should not occupy adjacent rooms.

Qieying read the colophons composed by her sisters, which Yuesun had copied into his letter, before she began her own. The following were her favorite lines.[68]

By Zhang Lunying:

I have lived forty-five years,
My hair is already thin and white.
How can a person enjoy long life?
Bending to and fro, I recall the old days.
When I was young I insisted on staying home with my parents,
Who grieved when I was far away from them.

Now in my middle age I lament that I can no longer care for them
And my sorrow finds no relief.

But luckily we siblings have each other,
We support one another to keep from stumbling and falling.
For ten years we have lived side by side,
With our songs and poems bringing pleasure morning til night.
My good husband is stubbornly upright,
And so our livelihood steadily slipped into distress.
A single bowl and ladle supply our modest needs,
We shut the door and immerse ourselves in books.

We are inhabitants of the age of great peace,
Subsisting on the barest of provisions.
Although each of us longs to fulfill our potential,
It's impossible to change the fate time has allotted.
The autumn winds penetrate the eastern wattle fence,
The massed chrysanthemums display beautiful color.
Let's fill our cups with unstrained wine,[69]
Let's enjoy to the fullest our shared happy sojourn.
Floating here between heaven and earth,
Our delight has no bounds.

Also by Lunying:

Long ago I returned to live with my parents,
Traveling by cart to Guantao and Zhangqiu.
Our household was happy and content;
United in pleasure, we celebrated and toasted.
Hearing us my father was filled with delight;
He said it made him forget his cares.
Before he died he commanded us to stay together,
To preserve and continue forever the happiness we shared.

Then one day he died and plunged us into grief,
Our good times were over in a fleeting instant.
The whole family moved back to our old home,
Entering the gates we wept. . . .

Qieying noted that a concluding stanza of this poem was a lament for her
own absence. Lunying wrote that the painting was a reminder of how "the
formation of the geese has been broken"—that is, her family had been separated and torn apart by death, by marriage, and by distance.

Next came stanzas by Wanying, of which Qieying singled out these lines:

We followed our father to his official post,
He commanded us to return here to share a house.
His concern for us was very great,
Generosity and love may not last forever.
Inspired and chastened, we heeded his dying wish,
Suffering hardship, we took solace in our old home.
Wishing to confirm a pledge of ten thousand generations,
We dared not lightly forget our patriline.

For the good of all the siblings,
We settled in a flowery mansion.
Raising our cups, we faced our small problems,
Within the walls, we were faithful to each other.

Putting our hearts together, we can escape the vulgar world,
Do not ask about the boats out on the Five Lakes.[70]
The distant guests have returned to the flowered rooms,
Their inner sadness borne away in the simple music of the zither.

Here Qieying made a note that in the spring of 1839, Yuesun had returned to Changzhou after visiting her in the capital, and at about the same time, Wanying's husband, Wang Xi, had come back to Changzhou from his teaching post in Zhejiang.

In a world of wind and dust that drives people apart,
How much more important are your own kin, who truly "know your
    sounds"!
Gathered together once again under one roof,
Year by year we cast aside our bitter writings.
A grieving heart still gazes north,
A thousand *li* beclouded and obscure.

Qieying read with a pang this additional reference to her own isolation in Beijing.

A splendid match, that was my brother's!
Qin and [Jin] united to carry on forever.
His writings stirred attention abroad,

That, thought Qieying, would be a reference to Yuesun's Korean friend.

His reputation entered the circles of distinguished scholars.

Between the third and fifth hours under the full moon,
We link verses in the quiet recesses of the house.
The clear dusk is like a time long past,
Old dreams recall the eastern hills.
If only our parents could be alive now,
How this scene would make them smile!
Having been painted, it is more moving still;
On my sleeves, tears blot the colors.

Taking a deep breath, Qieying sat down to compose her own poem on the painting, so that she could seal it and send it off at once to her brother. She began resolutely:

Your letter brought good news;
The peace at home remains undisturbed.[71]

That optimistic couplet was the best she could manage, however, to put a good face on her reaction to the scene in the painting. The next several lines, which practically wrote themselves, wandered first to her own advancing age and failing health, and then, in a torrent, line after line about her loneliness, her despondency, and the pain of separation from her siblings. She read the lines over, trying not to let her tears fall on the fresh ink. She made a few hasty corrections, placed the draft in a courier's satchel, and summoned a servant to post it to Changzhou the very next day.

BEIJING (SUMMER 1842)

At the capital, Qieying's circle of friends extended far beyond the people who had known her father or were acquainted with her brother or her husband. Her husband's network was extensive, to be sure. Wu Zan was especially well connected because of his leadership in the Changshu guild,[72] and through him she met the wives of scores of officials working in Beijing. Over tea, these ladies liked to gossip and discuss poetry and the arts. Qieying found some of their socializing pretentious and even annoying. Much of the conversation was at a level that she and her sisters would have dismissed as superficial, and she seldom recognized the names she heard discussed. She was also surprised to discover that her classical education, self-taught though she was, was far superior to that of many of her female peers. Few of the women whose poems she read cited the *Zuo zhuan,* for instance, which was a staple for herself and her sisters, supplying a wealth of stories and metaphorical images. Qieying often found herself criticizing the allusions in the poems that others sent for her review as hackneyed or trite. She became known as a sharp critic and an erudite writer, and female poets who found themselves residing in Beijing began to vie for her attention.

Qieying might have withdrawn entirely from the endless rounds of socializing that threatened to engulf her had she not met one woman whom she came to regard as a true "poet friend."[73] This was the young Hangzhou poet and critic Shen Shanbao.[74] Shen Shanbao was sixteen years Qieying's junior and quite unlike any of the talented women Qieying had known before, including her younger sisters. In the first place, partly out of necessity because of her father's early death, Shanbao worked on her own as a female scholar, with no male relatives to mentor or sponsor her. She had made an independent literary life for herself, and for support she often relied on her multiple ties to other, well-connected women writers. Shanbao knew of Qieying's family and its reputation. She admired Lunying's calligraphy, and she had read some of each of the Zhang sisters' work in manuscript. Qieying found it easy to befriend her, though the closer they grew, the plainer their differences became.

As Qieying came to know Shen Shanbao, she saw at once what a difference it made to lose a father early in life. Shanbao's father had committed suicide when she was only nine *sui,* and his death immediately exposed her to the cruelty of official politics. Shanbao's powerful lament for her father, written before she reached her twelfth year, made her a legend as a child prodigy. Qieying herself had long been familiar with that poem. But in coming to know Shanbao personally, Qieying came to comprehend the costs beyond grief of Shanbao's father's premature death. The economic impact, especially on Shanbao's mother, was at least as great as the emotional toll. From the time of her father's death, Shanbao's future, including her marriage, had depended on help and patronage from people outside her family, including a foster mother whom Qieying never met.

Qieying thus understood why Shanbao was so adroit in her social relationships. Shanbao knew how to make connections and how to advance herself. At the same time, she was keenly aware of the limits imposed on talented women and the difficulty of developing one's talent if one happened to be born female. She was the first woman Qieying had ever met who tried to nurture women's writing for its own sake.[75] Through Shanbao, Qieying came to know a large circle of talented female poets whose work was eventually included, along with Qieying's own and that of her sisters, in Shanbao's anthology of women's poems. Eventually Qieying came to believe that her own emerging career as a patron and tutor to women writers owed a lot to Shanbao's recommendations.

From the time she arrived in Beijing, Qieying had experimented with new themes in her poetry and with a new voice in her song lyrics. For her new voice she had in mind a model: the song lyric by Su Shi (1037–1101) titled "Thinking of the Past at the Red Cliff," which was set to a tune titled "The Charms of Niannu" ("Niannu jiao"). At the time Su Shi wrote this song lyric, it was acclaimed for its "powerful and free" *(haofang)* style.[76] This was the style that Qieying wanted for herself, and she found many women writers in Beijing who were experimenting with it. Still, using that voice was a challenge.[77] It was unconventional for a woman writer to adopt such a voice, at least according to the literary standards in Qieying's own family. In fact, it struck her that whereas men easily shifted in and out of the feminine voice in their own poetry, and although some of the most admired poems by male writers were written in a woman's voice, the reverse did not hold true at all. Women who wrote in a masculine voice were often criticized. Some were accused of plagiarizing their husband's writings, or— worse—of asking their husbands to write for them. More subtle were the general preference of literary critics for a "soft, warm" tone in women's poetry and the decided taste of anthologists for women's poems on proper womanly subjects like loneliness and motherhood.

Partly because of her disenchantment with what she regarded as hackneyed feminine styles, Qieying found it increasingly difficult to work with them. She recalled that she had once written a poem about an old family sword, now in her brother's possession. Rifling through her writing case of poems, she found it: a poem titled "Ancient Sword," composed years earlier, when her father was still alive. She read it over with fresh eyes, reviewing in her mind her father's instructions about "poems on objects." She could hear his words: "You have to try to describe the object as completely as possible, but you can't give a literal description. Your description has to be allegorical, so the reader can see the object in a new way. A good poem on an object makes the reader understand the object as much more than a material thing."

Her father did not need to tell her that allusion was the only way to meet the challenge of such a poem. The right allusion, carefully placed, could open up complex, rich images, even through an association as simple as a color or a place-name. To be sure, good poetic allusions presumed good readers. A poet friend of her father's once observed that a poem on an object is really an occasion for the poet and the reader to challenge one another about history, art, and meaning, using a simple material object as their common source of understanding. To call such a poem a "poem on a thing" (*yongwu shi*) was, in that sense, a grave misnomer. Qieying kept all of this in mind as she reviewed approvingly the allusions in this early poem, written in the 1830s:[78]

ANCIENT SWORD

Brave hearts from a hundred battles live on in you;
Why speak of the seven precious gems that adorn your surface?
Your sharp bright edge congeals a killing force,
Spirits and ghosts weep at the sight of your cold sharp point.
Your thunderous sound fills the hall with chill,
The sweep of a rainbow arching against the sky.
Must good men be forever vanquished?
In your gilded brilliance I recognize Ganjiang!

She quite liked the bravado of that poem, especially its allusion to Ganjiang. The story of Ganjiang and Moye was one of her favorites as a young girl. The skilled swordsmith Ganjiang lived a few centuries after Confucius, in the south near Qieying's old home. His swords of steel were so strong that people accustomed to bronze believed they were magical. In the version of Ganjiang's story that Qieying loved best, Ganjiang spent three years casting a great sword for the king of Chu. In fact, he made two swords, one male and the other female, because he suspected that the king planned to kill him as soon as the sword was finished. He presented the female sword to the king, but he saved the male sword for his pregnant wife, who gave birth to a son after Ganjiang met the death he had foreseen. As Ganjiang had hoped, his son received the sword from his mother and grew up to take revenge for his father's death.[79] Whenever Qieying thought of Ganjiang, she thought of swords in pairs and imagined a brave woman carrying on the mission of her husband. Her poem on a sword took her very far from the life she and her husband had built in the capital, into a world of heroism and daring.

Rereading her sword poem was like arming to meet the challenge of composing song lyrics in the new powerful style. Qieying was well schooled in song lyric composition. Her late father and his brother, her uncle Huiyan, had been the leaders of a movement to revive the art of the song lyric, long dismissed by upper-class writers as frivolous or shallow (a "lesser Way" of writing poetry). The song lyric style that Qieying's father revived, which came to be called the "Changzhou style," was not, however, powerful and free like Su Shi's. This was the heart of Qieying's discomfort. Not only were heroic song lyrics unwomanly; she had an obligation to transmit the learning of her family. How could she write in a style that her own father would not have endorsed? She reasoned out an answer as follows: Her father and her uncle had been strong advocates of using song lyrics to express political opinions, especially through allegory and metaphor. Moreover, they had never confronted the crises that she now saw threatening the country. She was confident that if they were alive, they would applaud her determination to speak out.

The tune for her song lyric, she knew, must be "The Charms of Niannu."[80] She gave her composition the title "Moved by Events" ("Gan shi"). This, too, was a bold gesture, placing her verse in a direct line of descent from the poems of a famous thirteenth-century political critic, Yuan Haowen.[81] Qieying's own "Gan shi" verse was composed in June 1842 as British troops advanced up the Yangzi River toward Nanjing in the final months of what came to be called the Opium War.[82] She wrote it to express her outrage over what had happened to the great Lin Zexu, the only official in the country brave enough to stand up to the foreigners and burn their opium. Lin alone had stood firm in support of keeping the foreigners out of the country. He was a hero of all the people Qieying had learned to admire in the capital, especially from listening to Bao Shichen, who was one of Commissioner Lin's trusted advisors.[83] Through Bao Shichen and her other contacts, Qieying knew of Lin Zexu's exile to the far west frontier in Xinjiang, despite an eloquent appeal on his behalf by the impeccably loyal official Wang Ding. When Wang Ding died shortly after Lin was exiled, Qieying believed those who said he committed suicide.[84] Wang Ding, too, was part of a circle of upright officials whom Qieying had heard her father praise before his death. Now Qieying's husband's friends and acquaintances, whose opinions she knew well from her nightly conversations with Wu Zan, were shocked by the throne's refusal to heed this high-minded minister's admonitions. Such lapses in imperial judgment could signal ominously that the dynasty was growing weak and that the ruler's hold on Heaven's Mandate was not secure.

Qieying understood that the death of a man like Wang Ding was not an isolated event. Rather, it was a symbol of defeat for a reform movement at the court that had been building for forty-some years, following the death of the Qianlong Emperor in 1799. Many Changzhou scholars were closely involved in that movement. Hong Liangji nearly lost his life as one of the first to speak out against the corruption of the late Qianlong court and the Jiaqing Emperor's failure to reverse it.[85] If Wang Ding and Lin Zexu could not survive in the current political climate, Qieying knew that honest officials like her husband and her brother had little chance of improving the situation. Her husband's friends said that the emperor had actually come to regret his recent choice of advisors, and that he had even issued a clemency for Lin Zexu. But the news from the south about the foreign invasion showed that the emperor's regrets had come too late. The Opium War was nearly over.[86] Her song lyric, set to the tune of "The Charms of Niannu," began as follows:[87]

MOVED BY EVENTS

A glowing autumn just at its peak,
When drifting clouds suddenly cover the sun!
No sooner clear than rain returns,
Transforming the face of autumn into chaos;
Song Yu's grief at autumn was so rightly bitter!
My ears roar with autumn squalls,
My breast fills with distress and indignation,
But how can my soundless words[88] make any difference?
The flowing current, how I long to turn it back!
How can I bear the pain of these passing years?
My eyes search abroad, the wilted grass laden with frost,
Amid desolate smoke, a lone tree,
Shaking, spent, utterly without direction.
The shrieking partridge cries "You can't go on [xingbude]!"
But my slip of a heart is hard to pour out.
Wu Zixu's ghost flew on the crest of the waves;
The Miluo River where Qu Yuan drowned is deep and wide;
But all I offer is the voice of an aggrieved bird-spirit [yuanqin].[89]
Deeply buried is that remonstrating memorial.[90]
What can I do? Swallow my anger forever?

Shortly after Qieying had finished her song lyric and begun circulating it among friends, Shen Shanbao came for a visit. Qieying always received visitors in her Pale Chrysanthemum Studio, the room where she kept her desk and writing implements, and her haven for escaping the intense social life of the capital. It was the twenty-fourth day of the sixth month of the year 1842 (July 31). The "Birthday of the Lotus Blossoms" *(hehua shengri)* happened to fall on that day. Lotus Day was a local festival in Changzhou, and had she been able to return, Qieying would have joined her sisters in viewing the lotus blooms along the canals near their home. The timing of Shanbao's visit was not ideal. Qieying was in bed recovering from a bout of illness when Shanbao's unexpected arrival was announced. Making her way to her studio to receive her guest, Qieying carried in her hand the notice she had received just that morning from home: the town of Zhenjiang, next to Changzhou, had fallen to an attack by British troops. Zhenjiang was a center where Manchu garrisons were quartered, and everyone had counted on the Manchu army's firm resistance to the British advance. Instead, according to the news in the note from a relative,[91] a disaster had occurred. First the Manchus turned on Chinese civilians inside the city, killing many who were suspected of treason; then entire Manchu military families committed suicide as British soldiers poured into the city. At the moment the missive was dispatched, British armies were closing in on Nanjing.[92]

As they returned to Qieying's bedroom, Qieying handed the courier's note to Shen Shanbao, who barely glanced at it. She had already heard the news. She sat down beside Qieying's bed and clasped her hands tightly. Wordlessly, Qieying pulled from her writing case her new song lyric. On an impulse, she asked Shanbao if she would do the honor of completing it. Years later, Qieying could still remember how Shanbao looked that day, sitting on a stool with her head bent over the poem. She read Qieying's lines carefully, her whole face intent on the meaning. She put her head in her hands. Then she leaped up, turned back toward Qieying's writing desk, poured a few drops of water, ground the ink, dipped a brush, and began to write furiously. More than two hours passed while she worked, now crossing out lines, now thinking, now casting aside whole sheets of paper. When she finished, she handed Qieying a draft and sat down with a gasp, her hands trembling with exhaustion. Qieying, leaning back on her pillow, read through the finished lyric. Shen Shanbao's part was heroic, brave, majestic, and angry—worthy of Su Shi himself. Her own, she quickly saw, was meek and mild by comparison. She said as much, but Shanbao would have none of her disclaimers. Shanbao took the entire lyric with her when she left.

Later, Qieying's song lyric, with Shanbao's concluding stanzas, was printed and published in Shanbao's own anthology of poetry criticism. Shanbao copied it faithfully, together with an account of their meeting. She even praised Qieying's "extremes of fineness and smoothness," which she found a pleasing contrast with her own "sharp-edged boldness."[93] Reading Shanbao's drafts for her book, Qieying felt that this judgment was tactful, perhaps even truthful, but it did nothing to change her own evaluation of the relative merits of their work. In the end, she was grateful that Shanbao saw fit to save those lyrics. Her brother's plans to print them never materialized.

Shen Shanbao's ambitious project, to compile an anthology of women's poetry and poetry criticism, encouraged Qieying to create an anthology of her own. She had long been an admirer of Wanyan Yun Zhu's collection of women's poems, *Guochao guixiu zhengshi ji* (Correct beginnings: An anthology of poems by gentlewomen of the reigning dynasty), and she also enjoyed reading the other major work in that genre, the *Xiefang ji* (A lapful of fragrant flowers). But in Qieying's opinion, Yun Zhu's approach as an anthologist was too moralistic and strait-laced. Yun Zhu had refused to include any poem with even the faintest hint of sensual or sexual innuendo, and she had excluded poems by courtesans entirely. Qieying felt her anthology was far too selective. On the other hand, the *Xiefang ji* was too frivolous and even, Qieying felt, provocative, in its conventional focus on women's romantic and erotic verse. Its editor was, in her view, indiscriminate. She decided that her own anthology would be based on criteria that were more capacious than Yun Zhu's but more rigorous than those of the *Xiefang ji*. When she set to work on the project, she asked Wanying to compile for her a short biography of each of the poets whose work she planned to include. Wanying worked so quickly that the biographies were printed in her collected prose long before Qieying had finished selecting the verses for her anthology. Time passed, and Qieying's anthology never went to press.[94]

More cognizant than ever of the difficulties of publishing and printing, Qieying admired Shen Shanbao's determination to publish her own volume of poetry criticism. Reading the drafts in progress, she was flattered to find comments on the poetry of all of her sisters, and of her mother too. She was surprised to read the linkages Shen Shanbao traced between the talents of mother and daughters. Qieying had never studied poetry under her mother's direct supervision, and she had assumed, subconsciously, that the "family learning" *(jiaxue)* she and her sisters transmitted was that of the Zhang family, her father's line, not the Tang family, which was her mother's. But Shen Shanbao did not see it that way at all. She was always looking for influence from the maternal side of any writing family. Shanbao's project made Qieying think of her mother in new ways. And this brought to mind a vivid memory.

Her mother had fine hands, and when she could take the time, she used them to create fantastic landscapes out of silk. Tang Yaoqing's embroidered and appliquéd landscapes in intricate layers belonged to a genre of miniature crafts, like the tiny peach-pit boats people liked to buy in the market from clever woodcarvers who transformed the wrinkled surface of the pit into an elaborate facsimile of a fine river boat, complete with sails and rudders. But Qieying's mother did not use peach pits. She preferred eggshells. Her fragile eggshell creations, unlike peach pits, did not survive the moments for which they were made, and in Qieying's view they were far from craft. They were truly art. On one occasion, when the wife of Qieying's son, Zonghan, created a particularly beautiful silk appliqué work of her own, Qieying wrote a poem about it. She suddenly found herself writing her memories of her mother into the poem, as she recalled her father's own poem about her mother's most beautiful creation as a young woman: an exquisite eggshell lantern.[95] On an impulse, Qieying asked Shanbao a favor: would she pay a special tribute to Qieying's mother in her poetry anthology by writing down a complete description of that silk creation? Shanbao could not refuse. Here is what she recorded, as dictated by Qieying, reconstructing it from her father's poem:

My mother was extremely clever. She was a genius with bits of colored silk, which she could fashion into flowers, birds, and landscapes that were utterly realistic. Once when she was amusing herself, she created a lantern out of an eggshell and decorated it with a pieced-silk painting titled "Streams and Mountains." The lofty mountains reached into the clouds and overhanging cliffs towered above. Atop the mountains was a Buddhist temple with seven levels, and on the left side a multi-storied pagoda. The vista was brilliantly clear, with golds and azures glowing like jewels. The mountainous rocks supplied shade against the glare of the variegated profusion of color. At the foot of a hill on the east lay the green leaves of great slant-cut trees, a comely woodcutter wandering, singing, in their midst. Along level banks and twisting torrents, hanging willows and green-blue peach trees gleamed around a small village. A tiny boat came into view, bobbing along the water as if seeking directions from the ferryman on a distant bank. Layers of mountain peaks and high cliffs surrounded the stream on three sides, as if they were a ladle out of which the stream poured into the sea. There was also a long bridge on the east which hung down over vast forests, deeply shading a mountain kiosk as if to shelter it. By the tips of the tree branches an imposing pavilion rose. The stream's clear water flowed fresh and free among duckweed and rocks. All of this was cleverly captured in just a few inches of space. There were eighteen mountains, eleven dwellings and buildings, five persons, two bridges, two fish, seven rocks in the water. The vista was surpassing, as if you were lying on your back gazing at the sky, as if you were viewing a heavenly scene, brilliant and delightful to the spirit, overwhelming to the eye, so that you could not begin to spell out all of its detail.[96]

Years later when Qieying reread those words, what she had been unable to see during the whole of her mother's life finally came to her: the richness of Tang Yaoqing's imagination, the depth of her aesthetic sensibility, and the heavy weight of silence that locked it all inside—to be released only on the face of an eggshell lantern or in the tiniest fragment of a late poem.

When Yuesun became the family head at the age of thirty-three, one of his first tasks was the mammoth printing of the family's collected writings, assembled first in the Guantao *yamen* and now due to be completed. Arranged under more than a dozen titles, which included the poems of his late sister Guanying and the complete works of his father and mother, the woodblocks required a separate storage shed as they awaited printing in Changzhou. Yuesun had been so devoted to family matters all his life that his own career had not yet begun, and, with his father's death, success in the examinations suddenly seemed a more remote goal than ever. But, resettled in Changzhou with his wife and sisters and their families, he felt his energy return. He threw himself into publishing, printing, and distributing his father's work, then hiring woodblock carvers and a master calligrapher and continuing the studio name of his father (the Wanlin Library, or Wanlin shuwu).[97] His own first publication was the complete poems and song lyrics of his eldest sister, Qieying. In a final frenzy of memorialization, he also commissioned the painting by Tang Bihen. Birthdays came, and with them still more occasions for him to display his literary talent: Wanying turned forty in 1840, and Qieying entered her fiftieth year in 1841.

Finally satisfied that he had completed his literary duties to his family, he turned once again to his own career, passing the Jiangnan provincial examinations in 1843. Then he traveled to the capital to register for the metropolitan examinations. For reasons that Qieying never understood, Yuesun did not sit for that exam. Instead, he received an immediate appointment as a magistrate-in-reserve, with a title and an office pending. Three years later, he was posted to formal duty in Wuchang, the major central city on the Yangzi River and closer to home than his wife and sisters had dared hope.[98]

As Qieying's brother's successful career began, an ominous counterpoint jarred the family's happiness. Bao Mengyi, Yuesun's wife for sixteen years, died in 1844, barely surviving to taste the triumph of his accomplishment in the examination hall.[99] Shocked and at a loss, with a new post to assume and an entire household to relocate, Yuesun asked Lunying and Wanying to pack up the family and prepare to join him. Elaborate discussions ensued, for the trauma of Mengyi's death forced other decisions on Yuesun and his family. The first was their responsibility to Miss Fa. Yuesun himself had no parental charge to see to her welfare. Moreover, Miss Fa's quarrelsome demands for recognition had made his late wife's life miserable. He had no interest in moving her to Wuchang with his family. There was in Changzhou a well-established and highly respectable home for faithful widows operated by a local consortium of public-minded gentry like himself, but such homes were not open to widows or faithful maidens whose families could support them. He made inquiries, however, and discovered that he could arrange comfortable and secure private accommodations for Miss Fa in a home near her natal kin.[100] Yuesun lost little time in making those arrangements. For her part, Miss Fa made no objection. She knew well that she could command no authority in a home managed by one of Yuesun's elder sisters. She was also aware of the unspoken antipathy toward her, on the part of Lunying especially, who had developed a special relationship with the late Mengyi. The decision to leave Miss Fa in Changzhou therefore met no opposition.

There was still the matter of Yuesun's fate as a widower. "We must find a concubine for him," Qieying wrote urgently to her sisters. "Clearly," she continued, "we don't need to make elaborate arrangements for a successor wife. Lunying is fully capable of managing the household. But Yuesun and Mengyi had only one son and a daughter—too few children for us to feel secure about the continuation of our brother's line."[101] Lunying made inquiries, and a prospect immediately presented itself in the person of the young daughter of a personal servant in the magistrate's office. Li Bin, the girl's father, had come to Changzhou as a document endorsement attendant (*qianya*) for the magistrate, bringing his family with him. The magistrate, however, had just been replaced and was about to move on, with his personal staff in tow. Li Bin and his family now faced a future on the road with no prospect of a return to their original home in Henan. His wife, concerned about their daughter's future and eager to improve her prospects, let it be known that she desired a life for her youngest child that would spare her heavy physical labor.[102] The magistrate, who knew of the Zhang family's situation, immediately intervened in Li Bin's behalf, offering his personal guarantee of the family's integrity, having employed Li Bin for many years.

On inspection, Li Bin's daughter, Luan, turned out to be appealingly attractive, both physically and in her temperament. She was escorted to the Zhang household and introduced to Wanying and Lunying, who interviewed her and her mother at some length. What they learned pleased them. Li Luan was the same age as Yuesun's daughter Xiangzhen, and she seemed likely to make an amiable addition to the circle of cousins who would live together when they moved to Wuchang.[103] By the same token, reasoned Lunying, as she wrote back to Qieying about the plan, Li Luan's age ruled out any friction over the authority to manage and run the Wuchang household. That authority would fall entirely to Lunying as the eldest female. Li Luan accordingly moved into the Zhang household and was established in a small bedchamber adjacent to the bedroom formerly occupied by Mengyi.

However, Mengyi's burial seemed to open the gates of the netherworld to other vulnerable souls. Before the family could move to Wuchang the following year, Lunying's husband, Sun Jie, was stricken with a high fever and died within a month, throwing all of the moving plans into chaos.[104]

The letter conveying this news reached Qieying at her distant home in the capital while she was still devastated by Mengyi's death. She did not know how Lunying's husband's death would affect her middle sister. Almost immediately after Sun Jie's funeral, she noticed, her brother began planning for the printing of Lunying's complete poems. By this lovely gesture he seemed to be reminding Lunying that her life depended not on marriage and children but on art. And he seemed to be telling her that her siblings valued her art above all else. Wanying wrote about this in some detail after she completed the move to Wuchang with Yuesun: "Lunying has finally moved here to join us, and our dear brother timed the printing of her poems to coincide precisely with her arrival. She seems to have a sense of new beginnings. Our house here is very grand, and she has a magnificent studio where she can return her full attention to her calligraphy."

A year later, Lunying's spirits were high enough that Yuesun declared a grand celebration of her fiftieth birthday and invited Qieying to travel south from the capital to join them. She made immediate plans to depart.

Qieying's visit to Wuchang gave her time to observe her youngest sister. In Qieying's eyes, Wanying was the sister with the charmed life. As the youngest, she always did the least housework and got the most time for her studies. As the last to marry, with a husband brought in for her, she never had to contemplate leaving home. Wanying got the best husband of the four too—Qieying and Lunying agreed on that. Wang Xi was chosen by their father after he had worked closely with him for years in the family's studios. As a near-member of the family even before the marriage, Wang Xi was a kindred spirit to Qieying and her sisters, and Yuesun always treated him like a brother. He was a man of letters. He had a modest collection of song lyrics, which Yuesun arranged to publish. Wang Xi's song lyrics were included in Yuesun's anthology from their shared time in Beijing. And because of all his personal contacts, Wang Xi was commissioned to reconstruct the history of a Shandong legend that inspired the famous opera *Injustice to Dou E*.[105] There was the additional fact that Wanying's marriage had produced four beautiful daughters and a son of her own, who, together with the babies born to Wang Xi's concubine, made her the ritual mother of nine children. Equally important, in Qieying's eyes, was Wang Xi's devotion as a husband and father. He was especially attached to his daughters, in whom all of the Zhang sisters saw a mirror image of their own youth.

Qieying considered the concubine a possible blot on Wanying's otherwise charmed marriage. But it was difficult to discern any negative consequence from the concubine's presence in Wang Xi's life. Wanying's only son, Chenbi, was her favorite child, but she had grown up in the shadow of Juesun's death, and she knew too well what the loss of an only son might mean to her husband's line. This, in Qieying's view, explained Wanying's enthusiasm when Mengyi presented Wanying with the concubine as a gift on her fortieth birthday.[106] (For all she knew, Wanying had actually proposed the gift to her sister-in-law.) Wang Xi, for his part, never allowed the concubine to intrude into his relationship with his wife. A shy and illiterate woman, quite unlike Li Luan, Wang Xi's concubine lived on the margins of the Zhang household. No one ever mentioned her, and Qieying never met her.

Like Qieying's own father, Wang Xi traveled constantly in search of work as a scholar, teaching and writing wherever he could find employment. His four daughters grew accustomed to tearful departures, reminding Qieying of her own girlhood. But (and here Qieying noted a critical difference),

Wang Xi and Wanying's children had a houseful of cousins for extra company and an uncle who was a successful official to look out for them. When he traveled, Wang Xi wrote Wanying detailed poems describing the various towns and famous places he saw on the way. She would write back in a harmonious rhyme, traveling with him through her mind's eye.[107] They had done that for years and years, and many of those poems were saved together by Wanying, so that when Yuesun went to print Wanying's collected poems, he was able to reproduce, side by side, poems by husband and wife. Qieying envied their intimacy.

Qieying's father once told her that he felt sorry for Wang Xi because he had lost his own parents and been set adrift by the powerful Wang of Taicang, the lineage from which he was descended. Qieying had never learned the full story about that family, but from what she could gather, jealousy and brotherly rivalry played a role in Wang Xi's isolation. Wang Xi was a fifth-generation descendant of the great painter Wang Yuanqi, who was in turn the great-grandson of the late Ming official and grand secretary Wang Xijue. The entire line further claimed descent from the illustrious Taiyuan Wang, one of the grand aristocratic families of the Tang period.[108] In between Wang Xijue's generation and Wang Xi's, the Wang line had produced two Grand Secretaries and nine *jinshi* degree holders.[109] On occasion Wanying remarked politely on the "towering figures and great deeds" of her husband's family, and they all knew she was not exaggerating. Her own family could offer little by way of comparable wealth or even reputation. But they gave Wang Xi a home where, Qieying knew, he was very happy.

In 1847, with the mourning for Lunying's husband a distant memory and the birthday celebrations still buoying her spirits, Qieying reluctantly prepared to return from Wuchang to Beijing. In her concern about packing for her departure, she overlooked the anxiety that grew daily in her sisters' eyes, and she was almost ready to leave when she was forced to recognize that Wanying's husband was very ill. Wang Xi had been feeling poorly ever since the move to Wuchang. Now Wanying hovered near her husband's bedroom, where he spent much of every day resting. When he moved about, it was very slowly, and his usual good humor and kind manner were muted. He did not respond to his children's teasing, and his studio sat empty, the brushes and inkstones gathering dust. As Qieying's day of departure approached, she saw with alarm that Wang Xi's condition was measurably worse. Doctors were summoned, the best Yuesun could find in Wuchang—and he was very well connected in that community by this point. As the children tiptoed through the house and Wanying grew pale and taut with foreboding, Wang Xi's fever took hold. Qieying put off her journey. She was still in Wuchang when Wang Xi died.

Now Wanying, too, had a journey to make: she must take her husband's body to the Wang ancestral home, Taicang, to be buried.[110] It was at this point that having a married-in husband revealed its costs. Wanying had never been to Taicang, and she had never met her husband's family. Qieying decided to accompany Wanying as far as possible by water before making her own way north back to Beijing. Under normal circumstances, Qieying might have tried to travel overland, since a carriage was much more comfortable than the hot and sticky quarters of a closed boat.[111] But travel overland in those days was dangerous. Bandits and rebel gangs roamed the roadways and security was minimal, especially toward the north. Their plan was to take a boat down the Yangzi all the way to Zhenjiang, where the Grand Canal crossed the great river. There Qieying would leave her sister and proceed northward along the Canal, while Wanying turned southeastward, passing through Changzhou, their old home, where she could stay briefly and be comforted among relatives before going on to her destination.

It was improper for women to travel by boat unaccompanied by male family members, and Wanying also needed companionship, so she took along her son, Chenbi, who was just past his twelfth year, along with a nephew on her husband's side. Her son could represent his father to the men in the Wang family if necessary, and her nephew would know some of the relatives they were to meet, as well as the Taicang area, which was unfamiliar to Wanying. Through Yuesun's official connections, Wanying hired a trustworthy captain, who brought his wife to wait on them, and two boat hands to manage the sails, rudder, and poles. Like any good river boat, the vessel slept six passengers. The captain himself cooked for them when they stopped along the way and supplied them with things to eat on those days when it was impossible or unnecessary to halt at a mooring. The trip would not have been a lark under any circumstance, but Qieying and her sister were traveling on the great Yangzi River in a small balance boat, with a coffin stored belowdecks.

The two sisters and their companions set out in mid-April. The river was high and the weather was awful. Below Wuchang, the Yangzi stretched wide like a giant lake. They could rarely see the opposite shore, especially in their small craft, which had to cling to the shoreline. Headwinds and rough water kept holding them up, so day after day they were stuck in moorings with nothing to see or do. Vendors and peddlers rarely ventured out in stormy weather, and sightseeing was out of the question. Qieying and her sister had embroidery silks, needles, frames, and other things to keep them busy. The young men played chess. Much of the time they all felt too seasick to concentrate. The weather was beginning to turn warm.

About two weeks into their slow journey, Qieying became chilled and developed a fever. Wanying nursed her while pondering what lay ahead, her spirits lifting slightly as they passed Taiping prefecture and Qieying began to recover. They had a full month together before they reached the point at Zhenjiang where they had to part. Wanying rented a second vessel for her own party so that Qieying, traveling alone, could continue in a boat manned by people they knew and trusted. They transferred the coffin. Sleepless and sad, the sisters talked for most of the night. As Qieying's boat pushed off, Wanying watched while tears ran down her face. Qieying had months of cramped, hot travel ahead of her, while she herself would arrive very shortly at her old home in Changzhou,[112] where relatives and friends would greet her, take her in, comfort her, and send her on her way.

Nearly one year later, Wanying sent Qieying a copy of her diary from the journey to Taicang. Qieying read it with great absorption, then carefully set it aside. She wanted to make sure that the account of Wanying's sad journey was preserved. She knew her brother was planning the publication of a special edition of Wanying's poetry and prose writings in honor of her fiftieth birthday in 1849. Wanying had recorded her trip in meticulous detail, without comment, chronicling every single stop and its duration.[113] Qieying, filling in the blank spaces between the lines, followed along as her sister described reaching Changzhou safely. In Changzhou, Wanying persuaded an old friend of her husband's who was a fine geomancer to join her on the last leg of her journey to Taicang. Little did she know how important his presence would prove to be.

When Wanying and the rest reached Taicang, Wang Xi's relatives were cool and distant. Wanying found herself lodging on the boat instead of being received in one of the Wang homes. She was further told that the family's graves had no space for Wang Xi's body, not even near the burial site of his father. So she resumed her journey, searching with her son and nephew and the geomancer for a suitable place to bury her beloved husband. It took her six months.

Re-reading Wanying's letter that came with the travel diary, Qieying sat up startled at the signature. Wanying had signed her name *laoren* (this old person). Qieying used the term always, now that she had passed her fiftieth birthday. It was quite proper to call oneself "old" at that point. But Wanying was nearly ten years younger than she, and she had at least two years left before she could really claim to be "old." What did she mean by it? Qieying puzzled. Her sister might be signaling her renunciation of sexual pleasure; that would make sense. But Qieying thought there was more to it. In the course of that journey to Taicang her youngest sister had aged. Wanying had finally met the side of life that her younger years had spared her: not only loneliness but also cruelty, jealousy, and greed, against which the greatness of the grandest old lineage offered no protection.

BEIJING (AFTER 1847)

Qieying saw the same problems at the capital. In Beijing, few were spared the same kind of rude, condescending treatment that Wanying had suffered at the hands of her in-laws. Comparing her youngest sister's life to her own, Qieying could see how far apart they had grown in the years since she had left home. Some of her friends were fond of joking about the women (and the men) at the capital who devoted all of their time to cultivating friends in the right places, giving gifts, offering bribes, plying others with unctuous flattery. Shen Shanbao herself was probably adept at such maneuvering, Qieying knew, but her own relationship to Shanbao was straightforward and direct, as far as Qieying was concerned. And she herself steered very clear of most Beijing social climbing. A genteel poet could protect herself from the crudest scholarly politics by taking shelter in the entourage of a great official, by conducting dignified correspondence with gentlewomen, and by following the example of her own father and mother: being unfailingly generous and refusing to engage in malicious gossip.

Qieying did not exactly avoid politics. In fact, she became more and more involved in politics as the safety of her loved ones, and indeed her own safety, became tangled in the fate of the country. The Treaty of Nanjing in 1842 had opened the door to foreign trade and to foreign residents, whose presence in the newly opened ports was creating a stir. Qieying was passionately opposed to allowing these foreigners to trade at their own advantage, and she discussed the foreign crisis endlessly with her friends. Their conversations were freely critical of the government and of high officials. Qieying felt no compunction about expressing her views openly, although she knew that men in the public domain had to be cautious about whom they criticized and where. No one cared particularly whether she wrote antiforeign song lyrics, and no one paid much attention to her diatribes about court politics. No one worried that she might influence an important decision. So as Zhang Qieying moved steadily away from her closed world as a *guixiu* into a poet's political world of conflict and competition, her concerns broadened, her opinions sharpened, and she began to occupy a space that even her husband could not enter.

As Qieying made her way in the poetic circles of the capital's elite women, her husband's health took a turn for the worse, and although he was still a relatively young man, he died within two years of her return from Wuchang to Beijing. Despite his twenty years in office, Wu Zan left his wife and children with neither land nor a house to call their own. Qieying's brother urged her to move down to Wuchang and live with him and her sisters as soon as she was able to attend to Wu Zan's burial. But she knew she could count on support from Wu Zan's family in Changshu, with whom she enjoyed good relations, and she wished to avoid further burdening her brother, whose vow to their parents weighed heavily on his conscience. So she demurred for the time being. History was about to take the decision out of her hands, in any case.

Between 1849 and 1850, Yuesun commenced another grand publishing project. He had his own new studio imprint in Wuchang, which he called "Dihua guan," or "Studio Where Sibling Affection Flowers." The studio's name made Qieying smile and frown at the same time. "Dihua" called to mind a favorite poem in the *Book of Odes* titled "Chang di," which celebrates unwavering sibling devotion and affection. But the poem also stresses that devotion and affection are vital in times of stressful separation and political upheaval.[114] The siblings to which the studio name referred were probably herself, her sisters, and her brother, as well as the new generation of cousins: Wanying's children, including the one adopted by Lunying, and Yuesun's own son and daughter.[115] The collected works printed in Yuesun's new project included a reprint of Guanying's short poetry collection, five *juan* (chapters) of Qieying's poems and song lyrics, two *juan* of poetry by Lunying, and four *juan* of poetry together with two *juan* of prose by Wanying, the only one of the sisters who dared to try her hand at epitaphs and biographies written in the demanding ancient prose *(guwen)* style.[116] This was followed by Yuesun's own special project: a collection of the poems of the young cousins, whose lives together were about to undergo their first big shift with the marriage of Wanying's eldest daughter, Caipin.

Hence Qieying's smile. But why the frown? Because along with its auspicious projects, the year 1850 had ominous portents. It was the year of the death of the Daoguang Emperor. It was also the year when a series of uprisings in Guangxi brought to Qieying's attention a new problem with the foreigners, far more serious than any threat posed to date. The foreigners'

Christian teachings had inspired a rebellion. The "God-Worshippers" rising up far to the south had pledged their faith in a charismatic leader named Hong Xiuquan, and Hong had declared himself the second son of the foreigners' god.[117]

As the movement of God-Worshippers spread through Guangxi in 1851 and 1852, now under a new name, "The Heavenly Kingdom of Great Peace," stories began to circulate in Beijing. The God-Worshippers aimed to bring about the kingdom of their own god on earth, in China. They intended to overthrow the emperor and replace him with a fanatic who claimed divine descent from this alien god, who was connected to the teachings of the foreigners and their religion. They taught that all people were members of one grand family, and that every man was a brother to every other man, and every woman a sister to every other. For these reasons, they housed men and women separately, and strictly forbade their members to live in conventional family units. Qieying reacted in disgust to accounts of the rebels' excesses, which extended to not only the dissolution of the family but also the forced unbinding of women's feet and their mobilization as laborers in the fields and markets outside the home. Female soldiers were part of their fighting force, and the Hakka customs prevalent among their followers dictated the broad participation of women in every rebel activity. Qieying, who herself had fancied taking up a sword to defend the country, found nothing appealing in the image of these women warriors.

At first she was not worried. Such a radical movement had no chance of success beyond the impoverished southern regions where it had taken hold. Like many distressing rebellions, such as the uprisings of White Lotus communitarians, or Miao tribespeople, which she had heard her father discuss years before, this one—known as the Taiping Rebellion—spread in remote and mountainous borderlands where the poor scratched a living from thin soil and non-Han peoples lived beyond the pale of civilization. Rebellions posed no threat to her old home in Changzhou, nor to the great Yangzi cities like Wuchang where her loved ones lived, let alone to the capital far in the north where she now resided.

Qieying began receiving letters from her brother, however, that told a different story. The Taiping rebels, far from being stopped in their tracks as everyone had expected, were breaking through government blockades and seizing market towns and county seats with a speed that left the government in a panic. Within two years, on December 13, 1852, the rebels had marched north and seized Yuezhou, a strategic town on the far northeastern edge of Dongting Lake. Yuesun sent Qieying a letter from

Wuchang describing the disaster at Yuezhou that she did not receive until the end of December that year. He wrote: "This is the gateway into Hubei province and the portal of the Yangzi River." He went on to say that the Hunan provincial commander in chief, Bolegongwu, charged with defending Yuezhou, "knows nothing about military affairs, and his soldiers are all weaklings."[118] Sarcasm fairly dripped from the rest of the letter in her hands.

The next news did not come from her brother. Qieying began reading official reports. She learned that in late December the rebels reached the outskirts of Wuchang. They occupied the city on January 12, sacked it, then abandoned it a month later when imperial troops led by Xiang Rong finally drove the rebels out.[119] Unfazed, the rebels continued eastward, taking Jiujiang and occupying Nanjing by March of 1853.[120] Changzhou at that point was in grave danger, but the rebels shifted northward on their rampage, marching toward Kaifeng and ultimately turning their attention to the capital itself. In October of 1853, Zhang Qieying fled Beijing with thirty thousand refugee families in a vast exodus that left hundreds dying in the roads as these panicked civilians tried to make their way to safety through lands they did not know. She had no idea what had befallen her niece, Caipin, now married and living not far from Kaifeng, which was on the rebels' line of march. She did not know if Yuesun was still alive, or if her sisters and their children had survived the fall of the city of Wuchang.

For the next several years, Qieying moved from sanctuary to sanctuary. She took refuge first with her late husband's relatives in Changshu. Bao Shichen was killed in 1855 while fleeing the rebels; her uncle Tang Yifen died in the battle over Nanjing; her niece Caipin's husband died in 1856. She was never able to find out the cause of his death. During the worst of the fighting, Qieying and Lunying both stayed with friends near Changsha, and Wanying traveled to Luoshan on the Yangzi River, miles upriver from Wuchang.[121] In the spring of 1857, Hubei province was secured and Wuchang was declared safe.[122] The next year, Yuesun convened everyone at the Wuchang *yamen* to celebrate Wanying's sixtieth birthday. Caipin managed to travel down from Kaifeng for the occasion; Qieying brought two of her granddaughters.

After the celebration, when she had returned north, Qieying was contacted by Yuesun's old friend, the Korean scholar Yi Sang-jŏk. He had heard from Yuesun of plans to reprint her collected poems on the occasion of her seventieth birthday, and he wanted to be the first to congratulate her. He was also seeking reassurance, for he had grieved needlessly over what he now knew to be a false report of Yuesun's death.[123] During the years that Wuchang was under siege, he'd heard nothing from Zhang Yuesun. Now he wanted to show her the letters Yuesun had written, all of which he had carefully saved. He asked if he could come in person to visit her.

Master Yi arrived with a birthday poem in hand.[124] Qieying had had occasion to greet Korean scholars before because of her sister Lunying's following among connoisseurs of fine calligraphy. But at her advanced age, and in the wake of the great danger her family had passed through, she felt a special empathy for this learned gentleman who so obviously cared for her brother. Together they sat down and pored over Yuesun's letters. "The provincial commander in chief, Bolegongwu, is a featherbrain," stormed her brother. "My every plan for defending the Yangzi basin has been completely ignored until it is too late."[125] The letter went on for page after page, detailing and decrying the disasters her brother had witnessed. For Qieying, the contents of the letter were no surprise. She had heard enough from her brother's own mouth to know the gravity of the military crisis. What still made her cringe, however, was her own sense of helplessness. After more than a decade as a widow, her sense of independence as a writer and a literary patron had grown, but she had no way to make her voice heard beyond her poems.

The historian says:

The case of Yi Sang-jŏk, Zhang Yuesun's devoted Korean friend, is a telling example of a little-studied phenomenon of the eighteenth and nineteenth centuries, when erudite Korean translators who accompanied the diplomats sent to represent the Korean court in Beijing won acclaim in Chinese scholarly circles for their consummate mastery of the classical Chinese canon and their brilliance in composition, calligraphy, painting, and poetry. Yi Sang-jŏk, who became Yuesun's closest confidant in what proved to be his final years, noted in his own memoirs his admiration for Chinese culture, where for the first time he felt free of the aristocratic pretensions of Korean society. Coming as he did from outside the aristocratic *yangban* elite, Yi was part of the growing class of "middling" commoners who were upwardly mobile, highly educated, and indispensable to the workings of the Korean Chosŏn polity. Yet it was only in China that Yi found himself judged solely on merit and talent, and not on the basis of his birth.[126] "Cosmopolitan" is not quite the word to apply to these Sino-Korean friendship networks, since the Koreans outdid the Chinese in their strict adherence to Zhu Xi's Confucian rituals. The networks did serve, however, as a capacious space where painters, poets, calligraphers, and scholars found common ground regardless of their ethnic or political background.[127]

The epistolary silence that caused so much anguish to Yi Sang-jŏk settled over the entire Zhang family after the Taiping Rebellion. Changzhou escaped attack by the Taiping in the early years of the fighting, but as the battleground shifted to the east, the walled city fell to the rebels in 1860. The city was occupied for four full years before the armies of Zeng Guofan and Li Hongzhang put a final end to the Taiping movement.[128] Zhang Yuesun's record of the rebellion, which survives only in manuscript form, is a telling indictment of the imperial government's inept early response. He recounts in detail the failure of military officials and provincial leaders to heed his warnings and advice about strategies to secure the path into the Lower Yangzi, as city after city was overrun in the rebels' relentless advance. He concludes ominously: "Alas! The masses of rebels at the end of the Yuan, and the marauding bandits at the end of the Ming—these things happened not so long ago. How can we not be apprehensive?"[129]

Zhang Qieying died sometime after 1863. The last written record of her whereabouts appears in a footnote to a poem written in 1862 by her brother. The date of Wanying's death is unknown. After the pacification, Lunying returned to Wuchang, where she continued to sell her calligraphy to support herself. She passed her seventieth year in good health[130] and was honored with the reprinting of her poetry collection, along with an additional new chapter of work, in 1868. These later poems describe her harrowing escape to Jingzhou, Hubei, in flight from the rebels, and her anguish at her separation from her brother in the years before his death.[131] Miss Fa, who remained in Changzhou, probably perished there when the city fell.[132]

We learn of Yuesun's fate from his close friend Zhuang Shouqi, whose son married Yuesun's younger daughter by his concubine, Li Luan. Zhuang offers this retrospective account of Yuesun's last years, spent entirely at war in a futile effort to change the course of history:

As the Taiping began moving north and surrounded Changsha, Yuesun requested that troops be moved south to guard Yuezhou, and northward to defend Hanyang, which he thought might at least save Hubei. But this request, like his others, went unheeded. The next year, in 1852, Taiping armies swept into Hanyang and Wuchang, which fell in rapid succession. The following year [in what became a military pattern] the Taiping withdrew. Meanwhile, the fall of Wuchang was partly blamed on Yuesun, although his protectors in Beijing were able to memorialize the throne and clear his name. In all,

Wuchang fell to the Taiping three times, and each time the collapse was predicted by Yuesun and in each case his advice was ignored by his superiors. . . .

Finally, in 1857, the city was recovered permanently, and Yuesun was promoted to the rank of prospective Circuit Intendant *(daotai)*. Encouraged, he immediately began an ambitious program to eliminate corruption from the grain tribute collection system at Wuchang, taking particular aim at the activities of the local clerks and runners. This campaign was very successful in reducing the tax payments of the people and in curbing illicit fees and gouging by government agents. . . .

In 1860, the Board of Revenue ordered Zhang Yuesun removed from office on the grounds that he had failed to fill the tribute quota to supply the army at Jingzhou,[133] and he was pressed to repay the missing funds. As Yuesun later explained in detail, the record books kept for the Board of Revenue had been incomplete since the rebellion. He therefore had to conduct a thorough audit. After three years, he was able to account for every coin. But the whole affair made him bitter, and he lost his will to engage in worldly affairs *(qiaoran wu zhi yu shi yi)*.

Then in 1863, when foreign trade issues arose in Wuchang, Yuesun became an enthusiastic advocate of taxing foreign trade to increase the revenues of the tribute system. As a result of his interest in foreign trade, he was transferred to Shanghai, but shortly thereafter he died. He was in his fifty-sixth year. It was the sixth month of 1863. His son, Jinli, died with him.[134]

Yuesun was transferred to Shanghai as part of Li Hongzhang's effort to consolidate control over the customs revenue flowing through that port in order to finance the last years of the campaign against the Taiping. This placed Yuesun, at the moment of his death, in direct communication with Zeng Guofan and other key leaders of the subsequent Restoration movement.[135]

As for Zhang Qieying, her five *juan* of poems and song lyrics, printed in 1840 at the Wanlin Studio, survived the rebellion and were carefully preserved by her granddaughter Wu Lanwan. Zhang Yuesun's plans to print a continuation of Qieying's collected poems never materialized, although an edition dated 1868 is listed in some catalogues and probably circulated in manuscript form for a time.[136] Yuesun was truly a man who never wasted a single moment, as his studio name in his later years attests, but he did not live long enough to see that project to completion. He did, however, compose the preface for a collection of the early poems of Qieying's granddaughter Wu Lanwan, a poet and painter who self-consciously carried on her grandmother's learning. These were finally published in 1866 after peace was restored. Yuesun wrote:

My father inspired his descendants with ancient poetry, and his teachings spread far and wide through his many followers. My eldest sister, Mengti [Qieying], studied poetry with him, and as her mastery developed, she created the drafts that make up her collected works, the Pale Chrysanthemum Collection. Critics said that her poems preserved a womanly style of mild and gentle yet earnest and sincere writing, while keeping alive the legacy of her father. Then when my grandniece Lanwan was a young girl and showed herself to be extremely quick and intelligent, my eldest sister instructed her in reading the classics and the histories. Lanwan could remember everything she read as soon as her eyes had passed over it. Lanwan next went on to complete her study of the poetry of the Han, Wei, and Six Dynasties masters. She always seemed to achieve an intuitive understanding of these. Every night she would chant them until long after dark. In her leisure time she also practiced stele-style calligraphy and studied the painting practice books of Nantian [the great Changzhou painter Yun Shouping]. My eldest sister took great delight in her. When I held office in Hubei as the grain intendant, my eldest sister brought her to Wuchang, where she presented me with myriad poems in the ancient and modern styles. . . . Many of these were true heirs of my sister's Pale Chrysanthemum poems.

> *Written in the first year of Tongzhi [1862], the first month, by her*
> *great uncle Zhongyuan, at the Library Where No Moment Is Wasted*
> *(Xi fenyin zhai)*[137]

Wu Lanwan married Ren Daorong, a scholar who won distinction through his leadership organizing local militias *(tuanlian)* for defense against the Taiping and *nian* rebels before going on to a successful career as a high provincial official. In 1895 Ren Daorong succeeded Wang Caipin's employer, Xu Zhenyi, as Director-General of the Grand Canal, bringing part of our story full circle.[138]

A final faint echo of the Zhang siblings' legacy sounds in an epitaph written years later for a concubine of Yuesun's son, Jinli. After Jinli's death in 1863, the concubine, whose surname was Shao, was left to carry on Yuesun's line. She arranged for an heir to be adopted from another branch of the lineage, but that young man died just at the age of capping. An heir then had to be found for *him*. This time the concubine found a promising young man among the descendants of Zhang Huiyan's son, Chengsun. The person she chose, Zhang Zhaoxian, recalled vividly in his eulogy for "Lady Shao" the pressures he faced in 1886 at the age of fourteen, moving out of his own family's home to the home of his adoptive grandmother, where he would serve as the heir for her deceased husband's line. Lady Shao made sure that Zhaoxian had no cause for regret, as he later recalled:

When I was nearing young adulthood, my grandmother treated me like a baby. She let me decide if I wanted warm clothing or something cool, what I wanted to drink, what I got to eat; she gave me everything I wanted, and her only concern was that I might not be completely satisfied. The only time she was unrelenting and strict was when it came to studies. Then she never gave me a minute to rest or relax. She would always say: "For generations the Zhang of Changzhou have been famous for 'the fragrance of books.' You are no different from any other descendant of the Zhang. You must arduously pursue your studies so you can carry on the profession of your forebears and take care never to slacken your efforts, as if you were making an offering to your ancestors."[139]

Zhang Qi's line endured, in the end, through the will of its women.

The Zhang Family and the Song Lyric

Zhang Qieying became something of a literary icon for aspiring younger women poets of her day. She was a mentor to many who became successful, especially the Zuo sisters (Zuo Xixuan and Zuo Xijia), also from Changzhou, who studied with her, and her niece Wang Caipin, whose story follows. Together with Shen Shanbao, Qieying pioneered in creating the networks of patronage and support that helped to sustain and publish the work of female writers, following in the footsteps of Wanyan Yun Zhu, also of Changzhou, whose classic anthology of women's poetry remains one of the most important sources for the history of Chinese women's literature. Qieying was best known not for her classical-style poetry but for her song lyrics (ci). In this she was also the heir to her family's learning, for her father and her uncle Huiyan were the founders of what came to be known as the "Changzhou song lyric school."

The Zhang brothers' interest in song lyrics was a bold intellectual and aesthetic move in their day. The genre, centuries old, was traced to Tang dynasty (618–906) texts set to well-known musical tunes. Although the original melodies were lost over the years, the tune patterns survived, creating patterns that were then set to words in irregular meter.[140] The combination of irregular meter and fixed popular tune patterns made the song lyric controversial among scholars for whom classical poetry in highly formalized standard meters was the most prestigious form of poetic writing.[141] In the late Tang period, the most famous song lyrics were composed by eminent literati for the female performers who entertained in the growing commercial centers of the south (Yangzhou, Suzhou, and Hangzhou), so that the song lyric was associated with the female voice, with the expression of emotion and spontaneous feeling, and with a certain air of decadence. In the Song period (960–1279), song lyrics became increasingly popular, and their aesthetic and intellectual possibilities were greatly expanded by the experiments of the eminent scholar-official Su Shi. The early Qing saw a revival of song lyrics after centuries of neglect during the Yuan and Ming dynasties.[142] Scholars studied the *ci* form and its history, and they began to write *ci* themselves, forming song lyric clubs devoted to compiling and editing *ci* anthologies, and to critiquing them.[143] The Zhang were heirs to this song lyric revival.

The Zhang brothers approached the song lyric the way they approached any scholarly topic: with thorough and meticulous research, and a certain amount of high moral purpose. This won them both praise and sardonic criticism. The Zhang brothers admired allusion and allegory—to excess, many said, comparing their taste in song lyrics to their preference for artful parallel prose *(pianwen)* rather than the ancient style of simple prose *(guwen)*. The Zhang brothers also created a distinct place for themselves in the history of song lyric criticism by insisting that the song lyric belonged to a hermeneutic tradition begun with the *Book of Odes,* according to which all lyrics could be read as political commentary. In the view of Zhang Huiyan and Zhang Qi, song lyrics were to be read "as the figuration of political concern about the state of the empire and the frustration of a loyal official at his inability to do anything about it."[144] The genre combined aesthetic and political interests and invited experimentation outside the confines of classical regulated verse, whose terse lines and complex rules of meter imposed a certain parsimony on even the most heartfelt or emotional poem.

Young poets in the Zhang family and elsewhere in Changzhou first learned to write simple short poems in the ancient style, with four lines of five or seven characters each. Since all characters were one syllable and every character was pronounced with a tone, poems were written for their auditory effect, to be chanted or read aloud, and the choice of a "word" was only one consideration in the composition. Mastery of the ancient style was simply training for composing more difficult "regulated verse" of the sort composed by the great Tang poets. Regulated verse followed strict rules: eight lines of five or seven syllables; the same rhyme ending on alternate lines; the four middle lines being two antithetical couplets; and the tone pattern fixed. These conventions set the framework for the poet's evocation of an image, an idea, or a sentiment; a truly fine poem required days and months of careful writing.[145] In contrast with regulated verse, the song lyric asked only that the poet "fill in" the words for a pre-existing tune (or, in this case, tune pattern). Song lyrics had lines of unequal length, but the tunes set limits on the number of words per line, with the result that extremely elaborate conventions grew up around the verse patterns for song lyrics, depending on the mood or tone of the tune pattern.[146] Both verse and song lyric depended on oral recitation and encouraged social interaction around the composition and shared reading of poetry. We see this in the Zhang family's domestic life, in the collegial circles of poets at the capital, among the various patronage networks frequented by the Zhang men and women, and also—in the case of the Changzhou song lyric school—in politics.

James Polachek once argued that "aesthetic fellowship . . . had by the nineteenth century become *the* dominant model through which men confirmed common values within the interstices of public life."[147] Scholars who affiliated themselves with the Changzhou song lyric school were recognized not only as admirers or associates of Zhang Huiyan and his younger brother but also as adherents to particular positions in politics as well as aesthetics.[148] Changzhou song lyric writers prided themselves on compositions whose contents were historically, politically, and morally significant. They liked to use allegory and metaphor in the manner of the *Book of Odes* and Qu Yuan's *Li sao* while adhering to the disciplined formal requirements of parallel prose, with its florid and varied syntax and its broad vocabulary. The result was writing full of obscure and complex characters intended to lend nuance and layered meanings to even simple phrases.[149] The impact of the school's new style was dramatic. As Zhang Yuesun recounts in an extant version of his preface to the collected writings of his own song lyric club, the *Tongsheng ji:* "The character of song lyrics by Changzhou writers was transformed with the publication of the anthology *Ci xuan* by my uncle [Huiyan] and my father [Qi]. As a result, song lyric writers since the Jiaqing era have followed a wholly different path from those of the previous Yongzheng and Qianlong periods."[150]

The wide acclaim for their song lyric anthology catapulted the Zhang brothers into the center of cultural politics.[151] Their poetic theory rested on two premises: first, that song lyrics could voice a range of expression that regulated verse suppressed; second, that poets were inherently critical of the bureaucracy and corruption of contemporary politics. Zhang Huiyan, for instance, was well known for his dislike of the civil service examination essay's stereotyped format and clichéd ideas. In his writing, he stressed that *ci* could express feelings and pent-up emotions that a gentleman might have in his heart but could not otherwise voice. As with a poem, the purpose of a *ci* was to give voice to one's deepest convictions *(yan zhi)*, and the larger message was always correct and true *(zheng)*.[152]

The Changzhou school's emphasis on the moralistic interpretation of poetry offended many song lyric critics and even repelled leading members of the Zhang's own circle, such as the song lyricist Zhou Ji (1781–1839).[153] Contemporary scholars of the song lyric have also faulted Zhang Huiyan for overdrawn and excessively labored allegorical readings of the song lyric.[154] The history of the Zhang family told here, on the other hand, points to broader political problems that account for Zhang Huiyan's obsession with political language and allegorical protest. In the context of his time, to claim moral integrity and use it in writing and in literary criticism was both an act of courage and an affirmation of intellectual authority in the immediate aftermath of the death of the Qianlong Emperor, who presided over an infamous literary inquisition and ended his reign under a cloud of factional scandal.[155] Zhang Qieying's political song lyrics surely bear the imprint of her father's and her uncle's *jiaxue* (family learning).

Zhang Women and the Song Lyric

In the monograph on the arts found in the draft history of the Qing dynasty, the name of each of the four Zhang sisters is given, followed by the title of her collected works.[156] All of these works are poetry, save the two slim chapters of prose written by Wanying. In a preface to that small prose collection one of Wanying's admirers comments on the rarity of women's prose writing, which he explains largely in terms of the gender division of labor. Women have so many household responsibilities that they do not have the time to read as broadly as writing prose requires. Concerning talent there seems to be little question. Poems, therefore, are the métier of the female writer. Economy of expression and a well-defined corpus of great works make poetry an aesthetic medium where talented women could excel despite their domestic burdens.[157]

With respect to the song lyrics favored by the Changzhou school, the role of the woman writer was more complicated. The canonical reading of *ci* in the Qing period, at least as interpreted by the Changzhou school, necessarily made women the object of a male poet's gaze, even in political allegory.[158] At the same time, the fact that song lyrics were usually identified with emotion made them "natural" media for female writers, in the eyes of some male critics.[159] Moreover, the "self-expressive" style of song lyric writing pioneered by Su Shi in the Song period, which favored the writing of occasional lyrics in social settings, with accompanying prefaces, was a style women freely adapted to suit their own literary and social contexts, as Grace Fong has emphasized.[160] Even though Qing female poets generally shunned the "heroic" mode of song lyric associated with Su Shi, in favor of "feminine" *(wanyue)* styles, they found ways to use Su Shi's models, either in celebration of women warriors, or in historical poems that criticized the fate of talented women in the past. The tune selected by the writer for a song lyric could send a message about her voice and her intentions. For example, the tune titled "Man jiang hong" ("Red Fills the River") was associated with the *haofang* (heroic) style, celebrating martial virtues and loyalist sentiments, usually perceived as masculine.[161] It has even been suggested that from the late Ming into the Qing period, gentry women writers could use the masculinized heroic style in *ci* as a status marker, to distinguish their poetic voices from those of courtesans, who continued to prefer the *wanyue* style.[162] Without imputing too much to the selection of a particular style, it is worth noting that the early nineteenth-century female poet Wang Yun's well-known *ci* lamenting her plight as a woman unable to use her talent by sitting for the examinations is written to the "heroic" cadence of "Man jiang hong":[163]

> That painted beauties should fade and drift
> Is a past and present regret.
> That great talents grow old
> Is cause for a myriad autumns' resentment.
> I query heaven and earth:
> Whom may I ask to hone my heart's sword and stem this sorrow?

Changzhou was a cradle of culture for women writers of the song lyric in the Qing, as the contemporary scholar Cao Hong has shown.[164] Changzhou's greatest literary families, the Zhuang and the Yun, produced countless talented women who made the prefecture and its hinterland famous in the Qing period.[165] Zhang Qi's talented female progeny constituted only one luminous example of the female talent that emerged from the confluence of cultural traits particular to Changzhou. What was distinctive about the Changzhou model of the female writer was, first, a highly developed consciousness of herself as a woman *(nüxing yishi)* and, second, direct engagement with practical worldly affairs *(yongshi guannian qiushi zhiyong)*. To illustrate, Cao Hong mentions the leading nineteenth-century anthologist

Yun Zhu, citing not only Yun Zhu's remaking of the exemplary woman *(lienü)* model in her *Langui baolu* but also descriptions of Yun Zhu as she was remembered by her biographers. The local gazetteer, for example, said of Yun Zhu that "she supported her husband with correct advice, and she instructed her sons in practical learning" *(xiang fuzi you zhengsheng, xun zi yi shixue)*. Instruction by the mother *(mujiao)*, a central tenet of the Qing discourse on exemplary women, was particularly important in Changzhou, where status-conscious, degree-aspiring families like the Zhang, who lived very much on the economic margins, sent menfolk traveling constantly in search of work to support the family and their scholarly objectives, while mothers assumed most of the responsibility for their children's education. Women at home were the mainstay of the ongoing educational enterprise.[166]

From the late Ming period, female poets enjoyed both the support of informal networks and formal patronage by established male and female writers. Changzhou was especially favored in the nineteenth century by the publication of Wanyan Yun Zhu's capacious anthology of *guixiu* poems, the *Guochao guixiu zheng shi ji.* But the role of Shen Shanbao and the prominence of Zhang Qieying as personal patrons of women writers stationed in the imperial capital suggests a new kind of consciousness about the nurturing of female talent among female writers, and a new scope for female patronage of letters. In the anthology *Qing shi hui,* which reprints extensively from *guixiu* poems of this period, we see frequent references to female poets as patrons and mentors, and to poems being exchanged among prominent female poets. Qieying was the most prominent mentor among the Zhang sisters.[167] Zhang Lunying, too, was active in poetry exchanges beyond her family. Lunying's most prominent connection was with a female writer from the north, Zhang Yin (no relation). Like Shen Shanbao and Zhang Qieying, Zhang Yin left poems that show a deep engagement with the political and even economic problems of her time. The intimacy and emotional candor of Zhang Yin's most famous poems, which resemble those of Zhang Qieying, contrast with her critical, politically aware poems on current affairs and social issues.[168] Zhang Lunying's and Qieying's links to male scholarly and official networks shaped their poetic practice as well as their political views, suggesting that the "inner Opium War" described by James Polachek was fought by female as well as male combatants.[169]

A final note should be added about the "poems in praise of an object" *(yongwu ci)* that were such an important part of the collected poetry of Zhang Qieying and her female relatives.[170] In his study of *yongwu* song lyrics, Zhang Hongsheng observes that up to the mid-Qing period such song lyrics were intended as realistic descriptions of actual objects; thereafter, however, writers began to emphasize the metaphorical and allegorical possibilities of *yongwu,* invoking poetry criticism from the *Book of Odes,* which emphasized *bi* (comparison) and *xing* (analogy) as well as "lodging meaning [in unrelated objects]" *(jituo).*[171] Zhang's observation suggests that *yongwu* song lyrics were gaining new currency and valence in the period when the Zhang women were writing, Zhang Qieying's precocious poem on a sword being one example.

In sum, native place, family ties, talent, and genre converged to create the context in which Zhang Qieying and her pupils pursued new paths in women's writing at the midpoint of the nineteenth century. Huang Yanli, who has studied the four leading female song lyricists of the Qing period, names Zhang Qieying as a crucial figure in this transformative record, one of those leading female intellectuals who "transcended the women's quarters," thus prefiguring the late Qing women writers Lü Bicheng and, of course, Qiu Jin.[172]

FOUR

Wang Caipin, Governess

(1826–1893)

CHANGZHOU (1833–1846)

On the day her family began the journey from Guantao back to Changzhou, Wang Caipin was already eight *sui,* old enough to be alarmed by the scene in the *yamen* courtyard. Her mother brushed past her, distracted, giving orders while servants packed up the donkey carts waiting outside. Her father strode from one end of the compound to the other in a vain effort to keep their departure on schedule. A passing maid touched her gently. Caipin's clothes and games, her new zither, her sewing box, all marched by and disappeared through the front gate onto the stacked luggage. It was well past noon when she and her mother and two sisters were helped into palanquins to begin the long trip home. The baby, Cailan, was in her mother's arms. Her father and brother followed behind on horseback.

In Changzhou, Uncle Yuesun and Uncle Sun, Aunt Lunying's husband, were waiting to welcome them in a spacious old rented compound. Caipin was not bothered by its run-down appearance, nor did she trouble herself with the worried conversations of her parents, who talked constantly about paying the rent on such a large place. To Caipin and her cousins, the Changzhou house was a magical place. Its corners and crannies were full of sunlight and pools of water. The gardens drew butterflies and birds. At night the courtyard sang aloud with the beating wings of giant cicadas. Games and study, study and games—the children occupied themselves all day long, while the adults worked steadily, decorating and repairing, recreating a semblance of the elegance they had known.

As soon as he was sure they were all settled, Uncle Yuesun departed for the capital. Burdened by the knowledge that he was now the sole supporter of his two sisters and their families, as well as his own wife and children, he spent most of the next ten years in Beijing. He had borrowed money from friends to finance his father's funeral, but his work as a physician paid just enough to support his studies and to send some money home for the rent. Caipin heard her mother and her aunts murmuring about the family's debts.

Caipin's father, Wang Xi, also left Changzhou, traveling south in search of employment. He sent letters from his travels: from Suzhou and from more distant cities, Hangzhou and Jiujiang. Caipin at the time was too young to see him as others did: an antiquarian, impractical, idealistic, and erudite. When he was at home, Wang Xi took Caipin on his knee and read with her. He told her special stories about his favorite people in the classics, and he liked to make funny drawings of scenes from those stories on the old pieces of paper he kept for that purpose near his desk. He bragged shamelessly to friends about his eldest daughter's brilliance, and he was never more content than when sitting in the courtyard watching his children play poetry games.

Still, Caipin was also old enough to sense the intense feelings that bound her parents. Wang Xi was her talented mother's closest companion. Caipin observed how, after her father left, her mother would watch eagerly for the postal courier, poring over her father's letters. On occasion she would begin to read a letter aloud, then stop abruptly and disappear. Caipin would later find her mother absorbed at her desk, brush in hand, composing a poem in reply to a verse that her father had sent.

With both Wang Xi and Uncle Yuesun traveling, Aunt Lunying's husband, Uncle Sun, who was unemployed, was put in charge of the family school. This saved what might have been spent on teachers. Under Uncle Sun's supervision, Caipin and her sisters took their zither lessons; painted flowers, birds, and insects; practiced calligraphy; and chanted poems from the *Book of Odes*. All the while, Uncle Yuesun remained the remote center of their universe. He wrote prodigious letters to every member of the family from his home with Aunt Qieying in Beijing, and they responded with enthusiasm. To Caipin's little missives, each containing a new poem or piece of artwork, Uncle Yuesun replied in detail, advising her on her writing, exhorting her to write more poetry, and praising her latest drafts. She came to think of him as her special mentor and enthusiastic promoter. By the time she matured, his influence on her had become so great that when she wrote, she always imagined him as her audience. Many years later, after he died, she would nearly stop writing altogether.

Aunt Lunying's calligraphy sold briskly now. The profits from her business were rarely mentioned, but Caipin occasionally heard talk of them in the privacy of the inner rooms where the women gathered. Lunying's income paid for all of the family's food and clothing. Caipin also noticed the glances exchanged among family members and friends when her own father's name was mentioned: "How regrettable that he has never come to anything, and so talented too," they would say, well out of her mother's hearing.

The Changzhou house was laid out in an orderly fashion, with a main central compound and two side wings. Caipin and her parents and siblings occupied the longest wing, which included rooms for the children and a large living space for their parents.[1] Her Aunt Lunying and her husband and their adopted son took a few rooms facing a small courtyard on the opposite side of the house. Uncle Yuesun and his wife, Caipin's Aunt Mengyi, and their two children had the main part of the house, with a large kitchen in the rear and a vast entrance hall at the front. Visitors came and went constantly, giving an air of great hospitality to the entrance hall and receiving room, while from the rear inner quarters, where the women and girls spent most of their daylight hours, streamed the sounds of chatter, laughter, and the occasional screaming child.

The configuration of that house, with its classic joint family construction, came back to Caipin's mind time and again in the years to come. For theirs was not the classic joint family. She was living with her mother's brother and sister, not her father's brothers, and she never met or even saw the home of her father's parents. Her cousins were all maternal cousins, and none of them had the surname Wang. She was oblivious to the anomaly of her situation when she was a young girl, but in time she came to see that these unusual family arrangements demanded explanation and justification, as well as celebration. In birthday greetings, in memoirs, and in the painting that was to play a crucial role in her emotional life, Caipin learned and relearned the circumstances that made her family special.

When Uncle Yuesun was away on his own travels, Caipin and her next younger sister, Caifan, studied with Aunt Lunying's husband in the family school. At first they were together with the boys, and Caipin found herself far ahead of all of them. This only served to heighten her sense—inspired by her uncle's lavish attention—that she was special and gifted: a *cainü* in the Zhang family tradition. But on reaching the age of twelve, at Uncle Sun's insistence, she had to leave the family school. Her sisters and her female cousin followed her in due course. They all "retired," as it was put to them, to spend their days in the women's quarters doing "womanly work." When Uncle Yuesun was at home visiting and resting—and sometimes recuperating, for his health was poor—he gave Caipin and her sisters and cousins daily lessons. Like proper young ladies, Caipin and her sisters always finished their embroidery first. But each day, as soon as their sewing was done, they wrote page after page of poems to each other. They staged contests to see who could create the most original and most pleasing rhymes. They challenged each other to "harmonize" or link a difficult verse or match an obscure allusion.[2]

Caipin could not reconcile her conviction that she was talented—more talented than her male cousins, certainly—with her fate as a young woman. It did not help that she knew what was proper. Life outside the formal school was dull, and studying on her own was less interesting than performing before her cousins and siblings. The poetry club was fine, but it had its limits, as she was ahead of all of the rest and they could never teach her anything. She counted on a reprieve just once or twice a month. At those moments, the timing of which she could never quite fathom, Aunt Lunying's husband would invite all the girls to what he called an "overview session," where they could discuss everything they had been reading on their own and try to see the connections between poems and classics and histories. Of course those sessions were for the girls only. They never joined the boys again.

Caipin found Aunt Lunying's husband nice enough, but as a teacher he was uninspired. He was eccentric and unpredictable, too. Privately, Caipin felt that Uncle Sun was condescending toward girls. Perhaps it was because he had no surviving children of his own, but he always seemed slightly ill at ease with his nieces. Meanwhile, at the age of barely fourteen *sui,* Caipin unconsciously began to assume a kind of scholarly authority over her siblings and cousins—even from "behind the screen," as she put it playfully, in the women's quarters.[3]

On one particular day, the girls were lounging in the back of the house feeling bored. Caipin cast about for something to liven up the afternoon. Her eyes wandered to her mother's wardrobe chest, and before she knew what she was doing, she had opened a middle drawer. Inside, neatly folded, she found skirts, vests, jackets, and underthings. She shook several out and held them up, chose an outfit, and wriggled into it. She unlatched her mother's jewelry case and stuck two large kingfisher pins in her hair, which had only recently been put up in the style of a marriageable young woman. The pins protruded at odd angles from the sides of her head. She was afraid to try the earrings, but her mother's makeup case stood open on the dressing table, and to that she turned next. Her sisters and cousin recovered from their shock and began to scramble. One grabbed the pencil, another the tweezers, a third the brush and red powder, a fourth the comb. Someone threw a cloth over Caipin's shoulders to protect the jacket, which was quite fine. After some time, satisfied, the girls stood back to admire their work.

Caipin was large enough to wear her mother's clothing. The loose jacket and flowing skirt fit her own adolescent body almost as well as they fit her slight, forty-year-old mother. A mirror was brought so that all the girls could admire the results. Slowly and with a look that perfectly captured one of her mother's haughtier poses, Caipin drew herself up to her full five-foot height and faced her audience. She was now ready to declaim a poem and lead them in their day's assignment. Positioned loftily behind Wanying's desk, she peered down at her three younger sisters, who giggled from the stools where they had arranged themselves. Their cousin Xiangzhen smiled demurely (or so she thought) from the side.

The poem Caipin recited had been composed by her uncle for her mother's birthday. Uncle Yuesun had asked the girls to respond with something appropriate, in harmony with his rhymes. This task was too much for the younger ones, but Caipin was completely engaged by it, and her dramatic reading of her uncle's poem enthralled her audience, who were by turns captivated by her uncanny resemblance to Wanying and focused on the rhyme scheme in the vain hope of writing something their uncle would approve.

While this was going on, they slowly became aware of shouting in the courtyard outside. It was boys' shouting, mostly high-pitched with an occasional croak when Caipin's brother's changing voice broke and fell into an unexpected low register. The girls turned toward the courtyard, from which several teasing queries eventually brought Caipin herself out into the sun to confront her brother and her male cousins. She told the little girls to stay inside. "Are you jealous that you can't join our club?" she asked Chenbi, who was standing in the doorway and peering into the inner quarters, though he could not see a thing past the entryway. He knew the girls were working on Uncle Yuesun's poetry assignment. "How long will it take you to produce something good?" he asked in a faintly mocking tone, winking at the boys behind him. "Our poems are already finished, we've checked them over for errors, and we are going down to the canal to watch the boats." He turned and led the boys out toward the front gate as Caipin watched and her sisters crowded out into the courtyard. "Now let's forget about them," said Caipin, "and play a game until Uncle Sun comes for our class." The girls, less exuberant now, helped Caipin to disrobe and dress for class before starting a riddle contest.

The class in question that day involved the same text that Caipin's grandmother had admired so much: Chen Hongmou's *Jiaonü yigui*. Sun Jie, who had discovered Yaoqing's well-thumbed copy and carried it from the Guantao *yamen* back to Changzhou, idolized Chen Hongmou.[4] He liked to tell stories from Chen's life to the boys, and he sometimes spoke to the girls of Chen's deep interest in women's moral development. To Caipin's mind, Chen Hongmou was unbearably old-fashioned. Chen's distaste for women's talent was evident in his single-minded focus on women's work and their correct ritual performance. His lack of interest in women's poetry or, indeed, in any sort of womanly aesthetic expression led her to question his understanding of young girls' capabilities. Besides, never having experienced any of the in-law conflicts or complex familial relations associated with life in a well-to-do gentry family herself, Caipin had difficulty understanding what all the fuss was about in some of Chen's chapters on behavior and decorum. As for dealing with servants assigned to help the young ladies, the Changzhou household was notably devoid of them. Caipin and her sisters generally took care of each other, and their mother and aunt did the same.

Uncle Sun, however, was not interested in Caipin's opinion of the subject matter. The girls read several passages in unison, then each one took a turn explaining one or two. Uncle Sun did not like to devote too much time to practical instruction of this sort, so before long they turned back to the classics. Caipin could not believe that he wanted to read the "Er nan" again.[5] Weren't there other sections in the *Book of Odes* that they could memorize? She was especially intrigued by some of the songs of Wei, which she knew were controversial because of their sexual overtones. She and her sister Caifan had read them together, struggling over the commentaries. She sighed and began another recitation of "Taoyao."[6]

The fun Caipin had in Changzhou came when her favorite uncle and her father combined forces. Late one night she finished a poem she had labored over for days. It was a seven-character four-line poem in the classical style titled "Red Plum" ("Hongmei"):[7]

> As stripes of shadow and slanted beams stretch toward the evening sun,
> Thick bamboo screens weighed low hold their subtle fragrance.
> A green beauty is naturally different from a deep red one,
> Just like colorful makeup outshines a pale face.

She ran to show it to her father, who by that time had already retired. Wang Xi got up, lit a lamp, read the poem, and reached for his brush to write a poem in response. He showed the two poems to Caipin's mother, who was still recuperating after the birth of Caizao. Caipin's mother wrote a verse of her own and gave it to a maid to deliver to Uncle Yuesun, who was at home recuperating from an illness. Uncle Yuesun propped himself up on his pillow and wrote his version, which he sent over to Aunt Lunying, who sent one back. At dawn they were still up writing poems to each other while the maid ran back and forth and the house rang with laughter.[8]

The year *gengzi,* 1840, the twentieth year of the reign of the Daoguang Emperor, arrived auspiciously. It was the year of Caipin's mother's fortieth birthday, which made for long hours in the poetry club. Every person had to be prepared with a verse for the party, even the youngest children, who were coached to produce at least a few characters in a childish hand. Uncle Yuesun, meanwhile, had finally completed the collating and editing of an enormous body of writings by Caipin's grandfather and her mother and aunts. In a frenzy of enthusiasm, he began to print them. A storage building near their home housed stacks and rows of fine pearwood blocks, each block carved with characters for printing each leaf of text. Her uncle spent nearly every spare minute in the workshop where the books were being produced, checking details and generally making himself a nuisance to the very competent printers he had hired.

On one such foray, Uncle Yuesun arranged for Caipin and Caifan to accompany him. It was one of the very few times that the girls had ever traveled formally in a sedan chair, and they paid little attention to their destination, preferring to gape and giggle at the sights on the streets through which the chair passed on its way to the shop, and then to discuss all they had seen while they followed their uncle around the premises. The Wanlin Studio series was planned as a complete compendium of the collected works by Yuesun's father, his sisters, and himself, including Yuesun's own edited anthology of song lyrics by the members of his Beijing circle and his brothers-in-law.

As her uncle's publishing project gained momentum, and his commitment to it grew, Caipin also felt in her family a sense of foreboding. Among the adults she heard disturbing conversation, hushed and earnest. Her aunt and her mother obsessively discussed reports of an invasion by foreigners from a distant country she had never heard of. She did not have the courage to ask about these things, and no one suggested that she should be interested. But browsing one day among her uncle's books, she found two short works that included in their titles the term *haiguo,* which she recognized as a reference to foreign countries across the seas. These were *Haiguo ji wen* (Record of things observed in countries overseas) and *Haiguo ji lan* (Survey of countries overseas).[9] Curious, she opened the first book and turned the pages. It contained a series of notes, which she had difficulty reading, about people described as hailing from the "Countries of Red-Headed Hollanders" *(hongmao helan zhuguo)*. After an hour of fruitless guesswork, she took the books and went to find her mother.

Wanying, looking up from her sewing, saw her teenaged daughter standing before her with three slim, hand-sewn volumes under her arm. "Where in the world did you get these?" asked Wanying. "In Uncle's library," came the reply. "I was trying to find out something about the foreigners." Wanying sighed. "These books," she said, "came to us as a gift from the author, who is Li Zhaoluo, a very distinguished scholar of Changzhou who has worked in Canton with Master Bao and some other prominent officials. Mr. Li was a great admirer of your grandfather, and his memorial biography of your grandfather was the greatest honor our family received after your grandfather's death."

Wanying paused, remembering her brother's letter written from Shandong to Li Zhaoluo and delivered in person by Bao Shichen. The letter was a death announcement for their father, and its delivery was the family's implicit request for a eulogy. Li Zhaoluo was such an eminent scholar that she and her sisters feared their request might be taken as presumptuous. Master Bao, who had pretended optimism in agreeing to deliver the letter, went hoping for a gracious and appropriately sympathetic response, and for at least a promise of a eulogy at some future time. Li Zhaoluo, he was sure, received such requests almost daily and certainly, even if he wanted to write, would wish that he had not been asked. Wanying smiled as she recalled what Master Bao later told her about the encounter. Accepting the letter, Li Zhaoluo read it quickly, looked up, and paused. Then he said, "See how old and decrepit I am! It won't be long before you'll have to return the favor." And in no time, the long eulogy was delivered.[10]

Wanying suddenly became conscious of her daughter's gaze and resumed her story. "Mr. Li was employed by an official named Ruan Yuan, the head of the Xuehai Academy in Canton and also in charge of some of the planning for the defense of the coast.[11] Canton is the port city where all the foreigners and their ships have congregated. It is the only legal port open to them. But our Mr. Li was not so much interested in coastal defense at the time he wrote this book. He simply found the foreigners fascinating. He wanted to know everything about them: their houses, their clothing, their everyday lives, and all the things they used to equip themselves so extravagantly. It's all recorded here in his book. But since he wrote the book our concerns about these foreigners have changed. They seem to be aggressive and perhaps dangerous. They have military power that may be greater than that of our own armies. We need to know who they are and what they are doing here so we can protect ourselves. This is why we keep Mr. Li's books in our house." She added: "Mr. Li is also an excellent cartographer, and his maps show the countries of the world and our own empire's place in the four seas. I can get you one of his essays on map-drawing, if you like."[12] Then she commented: "He is staying here in Changzhou now—his health is not good and the doctors do not expect him to live much longer. Otherwise, we might even try to pay him a call."

Fascinated, Caipin returned to her uncle's library and spread out Li Zhaoluo's books. Although she could not make out the meaning of some of the outlandish descriptions of foreign things and customs in Li's writings, she could read enough of his preface to see that he had based his information on a text called the *Hai lu* (Record of the seas), a transcript of observations made by an uneducated Cantonese sailor who had traveled all over the world on foreign ships, getting off at each port to poke his nose into every kind of business and entertainment, walking everywhere to see the sights and sounds, questioning people on the street, and trying to make sense of what he learned. This sailor, named Xie Qinggao, lost his eyesight some years before his death, but his memory was excellent and his skills as a raconteur made him a desirable informant. Li Zhaoluo had acquired a copy of Xie's record, which had been written down by a well-educated countryman named Wu Shihua. Li took Wu's manuscript, compared the records there to earlier accounts in old Chinese travel books, and produced what he considered to be a more reliable text, which he titled *Haiguo ji wen*.[13]

At last Caipin found a section that she could read, if slowly. It described a country she had heard of from her aunt: England (Yingjili):

> The country England is inhabited by red-haired peoples.[14] It faces the south-west coast of France. To reach it you proceed from Saint Helena north and slightly west, passing along the coast of Portugal, Spain, and France. You may reach it in about two months. It is a solitary island stretching several thousand *li*. The population is sparse but extremely wealthy, and all of the dwellings have many stories. The people work hard with the aim of earning profits, and most of their income is from seagoing trade. They will vie fiercely for access to the most lucrative markets. Their traders are spread out all over the high seas, and they have established foreign outposts in Bengal and Madras.
>
> The people are in service to the king between the ages of fifteen and sixty. They also train foreigners to act as their soldiers. Therefore although their country is small, they can command armies of one hundred thousand or more, and every country on the seas is in fear of them.
>
> Their chief port of trade is London, which can be reached by boat inland

about a hundred *li*. It is the single largest city in the country. The buildings are dense, the forests are luxuriant, the people well off and numerous. It is the capital of the country and it is governed by a high official. The water channels in the city are clean and pleasant, and there are three great bridges over the main river, called the "three decorated bridges." Each bridge has a steam pump that sends water coursing into lead pipes which are concealed below ground along the roads. When people use water in their houses they have no need to fetch it; rather, each house is connected to the roadside conduits by small copper pipes built into the walls of the house. Each household uses a small steam pump to make water flow into their cooking and cleaning vessels. The king calculates the number of people using the water and charges a water tax accordingly. The three bridges serve three districts in a regular daily rotation, so each district can draw water for an entire day at a time. People in each district are notified when it is their day to draw water. When it is a household's turn to draw water, they turn on their pump and when they have collected enough to last for three days, they turn it off. The water for an entire district is shut off when everyone in the district has had a turn to draw it. This continues until all three districts have been served, after which the process begins all over again.

Their laws are extremely strict and no one dares to steal, a situation that is rare in the maritime countries. The country has many prostitutes who, even if they have an illegitimate child, will always rear the child and never dare let it come to harm. Men and women all wear white clothes and when they put on mourning dress, it is black. Military officers wear red. Women wear dresses that sweep the ground, narrow on the top and wide at the bottom, with a tightly cinched band around the waist, wishing to appear slim and delicate. At the head of the band is attached a gold thing called a "buckle"' Over the dress on the shoulders a woman wears a silk piece decorated with flowers. For celebrations they invite guests to eat and drink, and then they will ask beautiful young women gorgeously attired to come and dance and sing songs to each other, circling lightly, which they refer to as "a dance party." The young ladies of well-to-do families all know how to do this and enjoy it regularly.

In their military, five men make up a company, and each company has a sergeant. Twenty men comprise a brigade. . . . [15]

Caipin's attention wandered. She turned the pages for some time looking for more observations about foreign women, which she failed to find before she was called off to resume her chores.[16]

A major event of the year *gengzi* was the painting Uncle Yuesun commissioned. He engaged one of the talented daughters of their famous uncle Tang the painter to come live in their home to observe the family's interactions and arrange for a leisurely posing of her subjects.[17] Her charge was to paint a scene showing Yuesun himself and his wife, Mengyi, along with his two sisters (Caipin's Aunt Lunying and her mother, Wanying) and *their* spouses, each couple composing linked verse in response to poems by the others. The painting was to be a merry one: wine and song, conviviality and friendship, conjugal harmony and sibling affection—all the symbols of the good life that Uncle Yuesun had provided for his sisters in fulfillment of his own dying parents' wishes. Moreover, the painter was asked to play with the image of "linked verse" by creating the illusion that the three couples had adjacent studios, harmoniously attached in linked fashion. Uncle Yuesun wanted a specific title: "Linking verse across adjoining rooms."

Aunt Tang worked slowly and carefully, and the painting took many months to complete. On rare occasions, Caipin and her sisters and cousins were permitted to watch her as she composed the three sections of the intricate scroll. When she finally pronounced herself finished, the family gathered to watch her slowly unroll the handscroll, one section at a time. Caipin caught her breath as she watched her parents emerge from the last section of the painting, their special rapport captured on silk by her empathic aunt.

Then came the formal ceremony, led by Uncle Yuesun, when painter and patron were toasted in turn, followed by more toasts for each of the six subjects. After the ceremony, when everyone was quite tipsy, Caipin's mother and her Aunt Lunying began composing poems on the painting, by turns weeping and laughing. These had to be revised several times before they could be copied onto the silk in the space at the end of the handscroll, a delicate task that the poets saved for another, more sober, day. Uncle Yuesun, thinking of Aunt Qieying far away, sent off at once a description of the painting and a request for a poem from her. Many years later, Caipin herself wrote a poem on that painting, which eventually came into her own hands under circumstances she could not have anticipated in the year *gengzi*.

The painting, focused as it was on their home life and its domestic idyll, diverted Caipin's attention from the ominous events that had distracted her. The signing of the Treaty of Nanjing two years after the painting was completed came to Caipin's notice only because her great-uncle Tang Yifen, who was living in the city at the time, sent word of it—along with a detailed description of the foreign emissaries—to his relatives in Changzhou. Caipin later thought that the painting might have been an act of indulgence that the gods decided to punish. Within a few years of its completion, her Aunt Mengyi died in childbirth at the age of thirty-seven *sui,* and barely one year later, Uncle Sun succumbed to a sudden illness that took his life in a matter of weeks. Mengyi's death washed out the joyful news from Beijing, where Uncle Yuesun finally won his coveted *juren* civil service degree within months of his wife's passing. Funerals and mourning blanketed the high spirits of the children. Their parents moved through the days as if paralyzed by fear and sadness. Uncle Yuesun, torn away from his ambitious new career path, resumed his publishing with a strange fervor. He put aside his literary projects and brought out a book on pregnancy and childbirth, full of remedies, prescriptions, and medical advice accumulated through his years of practice in the north and in the area around Changzhou. The book was his offering in his wife's memory, and his cry of despair that his expertise had not been sufficient to save her life. He also printed his sister Lunying's complete poems, as if to honor her creative life apart from her husband. Caipin, whose romantic sensibilities were reaching a high point, was deeply moved by her uncle's devotion, and her attachment to him grew.

On a day not long after her Aunt Mengyi's death, Caipin's mother summoned her. Wanying sat her daughter down on a stool near her own chair and began to talk. She spoke first of her brother Yuesun's loneliness as he confronted life without Mengyi. She talked about the tensions in the household that might now dissipate because Miss Fa's continuing struggle against her sister-in-law was ended. She mentioned her own long discussions with her sister Lunying about the new situation in their household. "And we have made an important decision," Wanying said. Caipin waited. "We have urged our brother to take a concubine, and in fact we have found an ideal girl. She will be joining us very soon."

Caipin did not move. What did her mother mean by "girl"? Would this be someone her own age? How would her cousins Xiangzhen and Jinli feel about replacing their mother? How would this new person make a place for herself in the intimate web of female relationships they had all been spinning for so many years? She realized suddenly that her mother was speaking again. "I want you to take charge of this new girl," her mother said. "You are older than she is, you are a good teacher, you know what a proper young lady should learn to read and write, and you will have to be the example for your sisters and cousins." Caipin knew what her mother was talking about. There would be tension, jealousy, anxiety, curiosity, and, yes, anger, too, directed at this newcomer. All this would be hers to manage. "I can't do it!" she burst out. "How can you expect me to do all of that?" And she ran out of the room.

Li Luan turned out to be just a little younger than Caipin. She was exceptionally well mannered, and she was also clever, as far as Caipin could judge, even though she had no education. Caipin vaguely recalled some discussion about Li Luan's parents, who worked for the county magistrate in Changzhou. The father was literate; the mother could neither read nor write. When the magistrate was transferred sometime after Li Luan was sent to Uncle Yuesun as a concubine, her parents had moved away. Caipin had caught Li Luan weeping several times, but always by surprise and never with an exchange of words or the slightest move toward intimacy.

Caipin's feelings about Li Luan were complicated. Li Luan represented an active sexuality that Caipin had yet to experience. On the other hand, Caipin was clearly Li Luan's superior in almost every other field of knowledge. Caipin enjoyed being a teacher, and she liked the idea of having some authority of her own over Li Luan. So she readily arranged to meet with Li Luan separately every day in the garden or, if it was raining, in her mother's studio so they could share a desk. Sometimes a younger sister or her cousin joined them, but the other girls were quickly bored because Li Luan was so far behind. In point of fact, as Caipin had to acknowledge, Li Luan was quick to learn, and within two or three years she was able to write simple poems, albeit with someone leaning over her shoulder to make suggestions or supply a sample character or phrase. Besides—and to Caipin's delight in spite of herself—Li Luan had both a sharp wit and a slippery memory, so that she punned hilariously but unintentionally when she was alone with the other girls, mixing up words and reducing everyone to stitches of glee over her malapropisms. The girls called her by her courtesy name, Ziqi, and in time the appellation sounded affectionate.

Uncle Yuesun remained in mourning for his wife as well as his late brother-in-law, yet the government did not recognize mourning for a brother-in-law or a spouse as sufficient reason to excuse oneself from official duties. He was almost immediately appointed to his first government office in Wuchang, and the family began to pack up again. Caipin was nearly twenty when she left Changzhou for the last time.

WUCHANG (1846–1850)

Wuchang was one of three walled cities clustered at the strategic midpoint of the great Yangzi River, far to the west of Changzhou. Caipin knew the area from her reading—it was part of the ancient kingdom of Northern Chu, scene of her favorite stories of famous kings and officials from the past. Her uncles loved to teach using texts from the *Zuo zhuan,* the old narrative history that chronicled the tales of the ancient states during the time of Confucius. And the great novel about the Age of Division, the *Romance of the Three Kingdoms,* set gripping tales of stratagems pitting heroes against villains beside the great Red Cliff that lay just beyond Wuchang along the Yangzi. Uncle Yuesun's announcement of their move to Wuchang, therefore, was not exactly greeted with dismay. On the contrary, Caipin was ready. Perhaps, she reasoned, living in Wuchang with her sisters and cousins might restore some sense of normalcy to the family. Aunt Lunying and Caipin's mother were also ready for the move. Recalling their days of comfort in the Shandong *yamen* with their father, they anticipated without guilt the privileges that would once again be theirs as the dependents of a local official.

Caipin felt almost giddy as the moving day approached, and she helped her sisters pack their lacquer trunks for the boat ride. Heightening her state of agitation was a letter from Aunt Qieying, who was traveling all the way from Beijing to help Yuesun arrange his new household and to give Aunt Lunying the time she needed to mourn Uncle Sun. Caipin had not seen her Aunt Qieying since she departed from Guantao years before, but she constantly heard news of Qieying's life in the capital from her mother and Aunt Lunying, who exchanged poems and letters with their sister. Caipin herself had on one occasion sent a poem of her own to her distant aunt, assuring her how much she missed her. A few months later, her aunt sent a polite comment on the poem to Caipin's mother. Reading the comment aloud, Caipin's mother explained that her busy aunt would not have time to respond directly—since leaving home, she had become one of the leading cultivated ladies of the realm, and her opinion was constantly sought by aspiring lady poets who showered her with requests for comments on their work. Caipin was eager to see her aunt, but she was also nervous. She knew Uncle Yuesun would want to show her off, and she was certain she would not measure up to her aunt's cosmopolitan standards.

The family's trip upriver to Wuchang was slow. The endless delays as the boatmen paused to avoid headwinds and turbulence gave the girls a chance to leave the boat and tour the tiny mooring spots where they stopped, under the strict eye of Caipin's mother. They arrived to a clamorous welcome by the *yamen* staff escorting Yuesun, who had arranged a huge parade with a band and flags and horseback escorts to lead the entire entourage through town to his official quarters. Caipin's mother immediately set to work arranging the family's living quarters. This task was overwhelming, since she did not know any of the servants and, worse, could not understand their speech, the local dialect being very far removed from their own and also unintelligible to a speaker of official Mandarin. Fortunately, one of her mother's personal maids had grown up in a family where the Wuchang dialect was spoken. This indispensable person became the unofficial manager of all the maids in the *yamen,* a job she relished perhaps a bit too much. They all counted the days until Aunt Qieying's arrival from Beijing and Aunt Lunying's delayed journey from Changzhou, where she was still attending to her late husband's burial arrangements.

Caipin's poetry club by now had six members: Caipin and her sisters, Caifan, Cailan, and Caizao; Uncle Yuesun's daughter Xiangzhen; and the self-effacing but increasingly at ease Li Luan. The girls self-consciously modeled their club after the one in the novel *Dream of the Red Chamber,* which all of them knew, if only secondhand from stories retold by their elders. On the day Qieying was expected, all the club members rose early to prepare. Each one had copied out a special poem to read for their imposing aunt, and they had practiced in front of each other every day for a week. Caipin, in a flurry of uncertainty, tried on three different combinations of skirt, jacket, and bodice before settling on a set of blue and turquoise garments to set off her newly embroidered shoes. From her ears, pierced long ago but usually adorned by tiny pearls, hung two gold rings. Her hair, drawn up as befit a young woman of marriageable age, was fashionably styled, parted in the middle with a slight short bang over her forehead and beaded flowers tucked into the hair pinned atop her head. She spent a long time with the mirror before proceeding carefully to the entry hall to wait.

The shout of the gatekeeper brought them all to their feet, and the rushing of servants sent the girls into a paroxysm of hugs and cries, so that when Qieying at last stepped out of her sedan chair and walked through the courtyard into her sister's and brother's arms, everyone was weeping. Qieying, who had not seen Wanying for more than ten years, was also exhausted by her journey and quite unable to maintain her composure for more than a few seconds at a time. After Caipin had calmed down long enough to step back and survey her mother and the other adults, she realized that her painstaking efforts to dress for the occasion were quite beside the point. She would not get her aunt's full attention for some time. The poems were carefully set aside in the back of the house, in Caipin's room, and the girls changed into comfortable house clothes, while Caipin withdrew to her bedroom and started embroidering a new pair of shoes. It was the only thing she could do to calm herself.

Two days passed before Qieying settled down to talk with her eldest niece. By that time Caipin's careful coiffure had disintegrated into something much less formal, the elegant blue outfit had been replaced by a plain dark purple shift over pants, and the gold earrings were back in her mother's jewelry box. The poem Caipin had originally planned to read to welcome her aunt now seemed overwrought and ornamental, so she selected a few other examples from her manuscript case and sat down beside her aunt at the big table in Uncle Yuesun's studio. Together they read, line by line. Her aunt selected one and asked her to read it again. It was titled "Lamp in the Cold":[18]

> A single volume slim and light, cast into deep shadow,
> An open lattice leaning back, shedding drops of water.
> At midnight, whose shuttle moves urgently across the loom?
> The chilly glow is a heart reaching ten thousand *li.*

Aunt Qieying's face was a mask as she read. Her brother had written a note at the bottom of the text, probably as he was selecting verses for a future printing. The note said: "The meaning lies beyond the words, which are concrete yet transcendent" *(yi zai yanwai chenzhuo shenyuan).* "This poem," she said to her niece slowly, "is very, very good. When did you write it?" Caipin felt her head spin. She had written the poem one night when she was awakened by the sound of her mother's loom, to try to capture her mother's devotion to her family, and her aching loneliness.[19] Yet what she was feeling now was not about that. She was feeling pride and the thrill of accomplishment. She was basking in her aunt's praise. Truly, she thought to herself, this is what they mean when they talk about how poetry can compromise a woman's moral convictions. Her feelings for her mother and her celebration of her mother's wifely devotion had all vanished. She was in love with her art. She had never felt so amoral.

During her sojourn in Wuchang, Qieying filled Caipin's head with news about Beijing. This was not at all the sort of news Caipin was accustomed to hearing from female members of the household, or their friends. To be sure, her aunt passed along some gossip, mostly about people Caipin had never heard of. But the news that obsessed Aunt Qieying concerned the state of the country: an invasion by foreigners from the land of Yingjili. Caipin heard the name with a start of recognition. Yingjili was the country where women wore fancy dresses and danced with men. It was the place where water came out of copper pipes in the wall. Wasn't it the country where no one ever stole anything? Then she remembered the other thing about Yingjili: so many soldiers, every man between the ages of fifteen and sixty, and foreigners as well. This was the country that would stop at nothing when a lucrative market was at stake.

Her attention snapped back to her aunt's sharp voice. Aunt Qieying was talking about officials who knew these red-haired people. The officials were friends of her husband, and they belonged to a network that stretched southward all the way to the port city of Guangzhou (Canton), where the gunboats of the English had vanquished China's own army. Her late Aunt Mengyi's father, Bao Shichen, was part of that network. Mention of Bao Shichen brought up the name of Li Zhaoluo, and at this Caipin, without thinking, blurted, "Oh! I've read his book!"

This revelation brought the conversation to a halt. Aunt Qieying had seen a few of Li Zhaoluo's maps of the empire, and she had borrowed from Bao Shichen copies of Li's two major works on the foreigners. She was unaware, however, that the *Haiguo ji wen* had found its way into her brother's library. She resolved to pay closer attention to Caipin, who blushed as she waited for her aunt to stop staring at her. Retrieving her train of thought, Aunt Qieying explained that Bao Shichen was close to the great official Lin Zexu, whom he had counseled on strategies for dealing with the foreigners. These strategies depended upon playing foreign interests off against each other,[20] to compensate for their own country's military weakness in the face of the foreigners' formidable arsenals. Bao Shichen had spent much of his time lobbying for clever diplomatic maneuvering to save bloodshed and prevent humiliation, but to no avail. Caipin, taking this in, wanted to find the *Haiguo ji wen* again. The section on the Yingjili military that she had stopped reading suddenly sounded fascinating.

Bao Shichen's name resurfaced when Aunt Lunying joined them in Wuchang. Much earlier, Master Bao had deeply influenced Lunying's studies of calligraphy. Now there developed between Caipin's two aunts an urgent dialogue about political issues that Caipin took in whenever she could by positioning herself with her embroidery near Aunt Lunying's studio. Aunt Qieying visited the studio at least once each day to talk with her sister, and they sped through their consultations about the household (meal planning, servant problems, clothing that needed to be ordered, medicine for an ailing member of the staff) so they could pursue heated discussions about the fate of the country. Aunt Lunying wanted to know everything Qieying could tell her about the foreign crisis, especially about antiforeign factions and networks: Who was in them? Where were they active? How effective were they? As Caipin listened to her aunts, she unconsciously drew pictures in her mind of the officials they discussed. Some were clearly upright, strong, honest, and courageous. Others were cowardly, corrupt, weak, and even malicious. Caipin had no doubt of her aunts' judgment of character. But she sometimes recoiled from the passion that seemed to sweep over her usually reserved Aunt Qieying, especially whenever the fate of Lin Zexu came up. At those times her genteel aunt would leap from her chair and stride angrily around the room, fairly hissing her disgust with the imperial government's policies.

It became clear to Caipin that these were matters of life and death. Caipin learned of the emperor's weighty charge to Lin Zexu, of Lin's bold rejection of the foreigners' demands to expand their trading privileges, and of Lin's courage and audacity in burning an entire shipment of foreign opium. She learned too—incredulously—of Lin's subsequent recall by the emperor and his dismissal, trial, conviction, and amnesty, which permitted him to move to exile in Xinjiang rather than face the death penalty. When Aunt Qieying discussed these things with her mother and her Aunt Lunying, Aunt Qieying cried and shouted and sat on her chair hugging her stomach and rocking back and forth. Caipin had not imagined she could ever become so upset. She had seen all of her aunts, and her mother as well, upset by grief, by something one of the children had done, by a servant's carelessness or a bill they couldn't pay. But she had never encountered a woman angry about *politics*.[21]

Caipin was then in her early twenties. Her education to that point had focused on Tang poetry, song lyrics, painting, calligraphy, and proper ladylike manners. Now, from an unlikely source, she was learning about opium smuggling, foreign trade, and the foreign merchants who profited from selling to addicts in China, first by bribing the imperial court representatives on the scene in Guangzhou and then, after the Opium War, free to sell drugs openly on the China market.

Barely a year after reaching Wuchang, Caipin found herself once again on the docks by the river. Porters gingerly lowered her sedan chair, where she crowded against her sisters Caifan and Caizao, clutching their hands. When they parted the curtains and looked out, they could see the river's edge, where their younger siblings and cousins were milling around tended by maids, and a waiting boat. They watched in silence as the boat hands lowered their father's coffin belowdecks.

Caipin looked back to see Uncle Yuesun advancing slowly toward the dock, his arm around her mother, who walked unsteadily. Aunt Qieying was following Caipin's mother and her uncle. Aunt Qieying's eyes were fixed straight in front of her, but anyone could see that they were almost swollen shut. One by one, they boarded the boat: first Aunt Qieying, then Caipin's mother, followed by Caipin's brother Chenbi and a male cousin on her father's side. Uncle Yuesun, suddenly mindful of his nieces weeping in their palanquin, walked swiftly over to reach through the curtain and hug them. The boat hands untied their moorings and pushed away from the dock. Quickly, the small craft spun out into the current and, with its passengers, disappeared from sight in the glittering waves of the vast river.

Caipin's mother did not return for almost a year, and when she came back at last, Caipin could tell that the trip had been even more difficult than expected. Her brother Chenbi too seemed different. He had grown into a young man, even though he was not yet capped. Caipin was able to learn only a little from her mother about what had transpired during those months of travel on the boat, but her brother was eager to discuss everything he had seen and heard, and Caipin proved an insatiable audience.

While Caipin absorbed the complicated story of her father's burial, Aunt Qieying, who had returned by herself to the capital, sent word that her own husband, Wu Zan, was ill and not expected to live. This news, which caused her uncle and her mother and aunt renewed distress, barely touched Caipin's consciousness. She did not know Aunt Qieying's husband well. He had visited the family in Guantao several times, but she had been a young girl then and had not paid him much attention. She kept her mind fixed on her father's spirit, faithfully attending all of the prayers and rituals that her mother observed to guide him in his lonely and dangerous passage from life through death to peaceful repose.

Wu Zan died the following year. Wearily, with the mourning for Wang Xi just over, Caipin's family tried to resume a semblance of routine. There were lessons for the children. The older cousins resumed their poetry exchanges (the girls, that is; the boys were already studying hard for the first stage of the examinations). Household duties occupied much of Caipin's time, and that of Caifan and her younger sisters as well. Her mother and her aunt seemed unable to function as they once had. Yet even in the midst of their grief, forces beyond the family claimed their attention.

The reason for this, ironically, was Caipin's mother's journey down the Yangzi to her husband's native place. Taicang, where Caipin's father's family resided and where he was finally buried, lay at the far eastern edge of the province, along the coast. At the time of Wanying's departure the previous year, no one in the family knew that the Taicang area was overrun with foreign soldiers. British troops had fanned out over the Yangzi delta area from their new base in Shanghai. They landed on the Chusan Islands, near the sacred shrines of Guanyin at Putuo. They took up residence at the port of

Ningbo, not far from Hangzhou, where Caipin's mother had visited her husband's relatives. These foreigners had no formal recognition from the imperial court because the Nanjing Treaty's provisions were not being enforced. This made their presence all the more upsetting, since no one knew how to approach them or to whom they were responsible. On several occasions during her patient search for an acceptable burial plot in Taicang, Caipin's mother had caught sight of foreign soldiers. Recalling what her sister Qieying had said about the invaders, Wanying returned to Wuchang both fascinated and frightened by her memories.

One day, some time after her return to Wuchang, she emerged from her studio deep in thought, carrying a poem in her hand, which she handed silently to her eldest daughter. Caipin was to read that poem repeatedly over the next decade, so that even in her late years she could still recite it from memory. It was, to her knowledge, the only poem about politics that her mother ever wrote:[22]

LONG RAIN FOLLOWED BY SNOW

Poet's note: At this time troops are defending Zhejiang, Fujian, and Guangdong.

Green Yang of spring is clotted in deep Yin of winter,
Heavy rains beset us through this month.
Sprouts and shoots so frozen they cannot push through the earth,
The pathway gate is closed in secluded stillness.
The window, just unlatched, lets in the sunset chill,
Stiff winds kick up a flurry of snow.
The roosting crows find no resting place,
The courtyard tree still more bitterly cold.
Snuggled in a comforter *(xiekuang)*, I remember our soldiers,[23]
For news of victory, I gaze toward the imperial court.
When will the cosmos be clear again,
The shroud of clouds swept from the empty vastness,
Until bursting with refulgent growth the myriad creatures,
Shining brightly, reach toward the beneficent sun?

Caipin loved that poem not only for its rhetoric, so unlike her mother's usual poetic voice, but also for its subtle use of the *Zuo zhuan* story about the King of Chu and the quilt. In the original version, the soldiers of the king, freezing in their thin uniforms during a winter campaign, suddenly feel warm "as if wrapped in a quilt" when the king comes out to the bitterly cold battlefield and pats them, one by one, on the shoulder. In Caipin's mother's poem, the quilt becomes her personal comfort as a privileged gentlewoman who can only think sympathetically of the freezing soldiers fighting the foreigners, but can do nothing to relieve their misery. Caipin saw instantly that her Aunt Qieying and her mother felt the same frustration: as women, the most they could do to save the country was write poems in the inner quarters expressing their outrage. Caipin's Uncle Yuesun, as a man, could hold a political office. And—though Caipin could not have known it at the time—he was soon to be tested in battle himself, in a fight to save the country from a different threat.

Inspired by her mother, Caipin determined to try her own hand at writing poems on politics. Her early efforts were quite respectable, she thought. In fact, when she read them over many years later, she was surprised at the ferocity of her language. This was one of her favorites:[24]

ON READING THE BIOGRAPHY OF QIN LIANGYU

Lamenting the times, the woman of Lu grieved for her home in Qishi;[25]
Replacing her father, [Hua] Mulan became a frontier soldier.
From ancient times, women have carried our share of unusual talent;
It is not in the boudoir alone that our fragrant virtues are seen.[26]

This female general of the Qin clan was peerless in the world,
From military arts to literary gifts, she combined the best of both.
On the furthest border, thousands of *li* away, she was made Commander
    in Chief,
A hero promoted over all the elder statesmen and notables of the time.

Her White Spike soldiers served year after year in distant campaigns,
Her Red Jacket battalion was the country's main defense force.
. . .
Triumphant with fame from a hundred victories,
Upright and austere, I imagine her as a lady from heaven.
But ceremonial dress and pearly cap she dismisses with a single laugh,
In her general's brocade gown and hanging sword, her strength endures
    forever!
. . .
Reading history, vast and distant, sets my mind to roaming,
I encounter that fortunate moment, an age of approaching peace.[27]
Who among us can leave her name in history's lasting records?
Hairpins and bracelets efface entirely the heroine's courageous aura.
A single inch of prose narrates a heart that has ever been;

The span of a single lifetime moves chaotically with the times.
The heroic energy of Heaven and Earth—can it be allowed to die away?
Set your eyes free on the rivers and mountains, deeper, ever deeper.

Her uncle here commented in the margin: "I think of the writings of Ban [*jieyu*] and Zuo [Fen].[28] Exalted minds live on eternally, transmitted from age to age. Thus Qin's heroism is revealed here without the reader's having to look for it. The line 'ceremonial dress and pearly cap she dismisses with a single laugh' is fitting indeed. Simple and plain in style, the last section—with its lofty sentiment and its far-reaching reflections—in a single moment captures myriad nuances. What intelligence this is!"

Caipin also liked this call to arms:[29]

SONG OF THE SWORD WORN BY A MING PALACE LADY

Poet's note: This sword was in the collection of my respected uncle. He composed a poem about it which he titled "Song of My Elder Cousin's Sword." The poem tells how the sword was worn by a lady-in-waiting in the Ming court. In a moment of leisure, reading my uncle's poem, I wrote this one to continue it.

The swords of Ganjiang and Moye were treasured of old,
But to repair sandals, ordinary iron is all that's needed.[30]
You, sword, seem to have a spirit within,
But before your tip was even tried, you were cast aside.
In your day you rushed to provide your services at the imperial court,
Awaiting at dawn the pealing of the Jingyang bell.[31]
Your blade shining was like autumn waters flashing against rare jade
    pendants,
Your handle sprouting lotus blossoms mirrored a jade visage.
The starry patterns on Dragon Spring's three-foot blade were hidden,[32]
Entrusted not to a general, but to a woman.
Foiling the intent of your maker, Swordsmith Ouye,[33]
Your precious energy, thrust into a sheath, disappeared into
    nothingness. . . .

At about this time, a diversion from concerns about the country and the grief of mourning presented itself in the complex machinations surrounding the honoring of the virtue of Miss Fa. The servants at the Wuchang *yamen* were completely captivated by the story of Miss Fa, whose tale had followed the Zhang all the way to Wuchang. The servants spent hours discussing the details of Miss Fa's life and her complicated relationship to the

Zhang family, of which more was known than Caipin wanted to think. Caipin herself had had almost no contact with Miss Fa as long as she lived in their home. She was also unaware that at the time of the family's departure from Changzhou for Wuchang, formal notice was served to the Yanghu county magistrate's office that Miss Fa had been living as a faithful maiden in the Zhang household for more than thirty years, and a petition was filed requesting that her fidelity to her deceased fiancé be honored by an imperial rescript or commendation, as befit a woman with her virtuous record. Because the Zhang family had lived for several years in Shandong, beyond the purview of the Changzhou prefect and the county magistrate of Yanghu, a prolonged investigation was necessary to verify the accuracy of the Zhang's claim, including a query addressed to the local authorities in Zhangqiu and Guantao. There the bureaucratic procedures ran afoul of the old story about Miss Fa and the *yamen* runner, and this too had to be painstakingly investigated and discredited before the imperial Board of Rites could approve the nomination and recognize Miss Fa as a faithful maiden. As the recipient of imperial honors, Miss Fa was acknowledged personally by the emperor himself, and also commemorated publicly in Changzhou by the engraving of her name on a memorial arch dedicated to faithful maidens and widows. All of this Caipin learned from the servants indirectly, by keeping her ears open and her mouth shut.

The cash award that accompanied Miss Fa's honor, designed to subsidize the expenses associated with the commemoration, was not necessary under the circumstances, given Zhang Yuesun's comfortable appointment in Wuchang. The award was nonetheless formally presented to Zhang Yuesun by a special emissary from the court, sent with fanfare to the gates of the Wuchang *yamen* in the company of a large crowd of curiosity seekers. Caipin's uncle arranged at once for a courier to deliver the funds to Changzhou for the carving of Miss Fa's name on a memorial arch. He then put Miss Fa entirely out of his mind.

Three years after Caipin's father's death, Uncle Yuesun decided that the family had been mourning long enough. It was the year after Caipin's mother's fiftieth birthday, and a full three years after the fiftieth birthday of her Aunt Lunying. Neither had celebrated this landmark rite of passage, and Uncle Yuesun was ready to make amends. This took some delicate maneuvering, since Caipin's mother had just completed the formal mourning period for her husband, and she was hardly in a celebratory mood. Uncle Yuesun, however, was not to be deterred, and he recorded the success of his mission in an elaborate birthday greeting to his sisters, composed for their gala combined birthday celebration. Caipin and her siblings and cousins happily stood by as the family gathered for a birthday banquet, poised for the first time in years to enjoy a party.

Caipin's uncle opened the proceedings with a reading of his birthday greeting. They all settled themselves. Clearing his throat, Yuesun began by reading the title in a loud voice: "Birthday Greetings to My Elder Sisters, from Their Younger Brother Yuesun!"[34]

Then he read a preface:

In the twenty-sixth year of the Daoguang reign [*bingwu*, 1846/7], my elder sister Wanxun [Lunying's courtesy name] turned fifty. Just a year before that, I, her younger brother, was awarded the post of magistrate in Wuchang. All my friends among the luminaries at the capital, and all the wives of luminaries who were friends of my eldest sister,[35] heard about it and sent paintings and poems to add to our joy and enhance our celebrations. Yet in that same year, in the eleventh month, Lunying's husband, Sun Jie, died at home. The following year, after we got to Wuchang, Wanying's husband, Wang Xi, also passed away. Just that suddenly, our close knit family faced one another with expressions drained of happiness and clothing devoid of joy.

When we put aside our mourning garments and another year had passed, it was 1849, the twenty-ninth year of Daoguang. Wanying had turned fifty years old, and Lunying was already fifty-three. So I resumed my plans to celebrate their birthdays. My sisters, however, vigorously objected. At that point their sons, my nephews, came to me as a delegation and made the following statement: 'Our mothers' objections are valid. Yet our uncle's wishes cannot be laid aside. For long ago, when our uncle was an infant, our mothers took his hand and guided him so he would grow strong; when our uncle was in trouble or danger, our mothers supported and protected him so he would flourish. The affection between siblings is always regarded as a deep and lasting bond. But in your case, you also had writing as a covenant and mutual understanding as an elegant embellishment, so you alternated roles as teacher and friend—your relationship goes far beyond the usual sibling attachment. What's more, our uncle is about to embark on an official career, making the proper celebration of our mothers' birthdays a matter of some urgency, and he is well aware that gifts would be unseemly. Uncle's close kin are few, and his nearest relatives are our mothers. This year, Uncle, you are already forty years old, but our mothers often recall the emotional events of your childhood together as if they had happened yesterday. If this year we do not make merry, we will be unable to give comfort to our uncle's dearest wishes or help him fulfill his role as their friend. So why don't you choose a propitious day to raise a goblet together?'

These sentiments pleased me very much. So I have chosen a proper day of the month, prepared soup and buns and duck, and offer these in greeting, together with the following words.

At this point Caipin's mother and her aunt were both wiping their eyes, and Caipin's brothers and cousin looked both proud and embarrassed. Uncle Yuesun, pleased with the reaction of his audience, now declaimed his formal greeting:

I, Yuesun, have four elder sisters. The eldest, Mengti [Qieying], is the wife of Vice-Director Wu Zan, who currently holds an appointment in the Ministry of Punishments. The next, Weiqing [Guanying], married Zhhang Zhengping of Jiangyin. The third, Wanxun [Lunying], was betrothed to Mr. Sun of our own home area. Finally, Ruoqi [Wanying], became the wife of Mr. Wang of Taicang. All of these men came from families noted for their literary and ritual accomplishments. All had a reputation for talent and good conduct. Everyone in our neighborhood praised my father for selecting such excellent sons-in-law. Wu Zan entered the Hanlin Academy as a *jinshi* and went on to a post in the central government ministries. But Zhhang Zhengping, Sun Jie, and Wang Xi all failed the civil service examinations. Zhengping's family was able to provide for him and his wife, but Sun was heir to a line of upright officials [and therefore had no money], and Wang, having lost both his parents, lived in a home of "four bare walls." They both went about "with satchel and brush" seeking a living as scholars. Lunying and Wanying, pressed by their dire circumstances, labored and suffered, helping their husbands and sons. And now that they have reached middle age, both are widows. Truly, life has left them with less than their due.

Here he paused and struggled to steady his voice before continuing.

But I know that the true gentlemen of ancient times did not find their happiness in wealth or display, nor did they sorrow over poverty and hardship. Thus Confucius said that the superior person worried about the Dao but not about being poor.[36] It is also written that "the superior person can find herself in no situation in which she is not herself."[37] Since ancient times there have been countless elegantly bejeweled and adorned women, but not one of them appears in the annals of exemplary women because of their purity and virtue, and not one has produced writings that have entered the canon of literary work. The women so honored are overwhelmingly from remote places and obscure families. Why is it that a woman who has dominated an age with her beauty or her performances is eventually forgotten?

My own sisters received their instruction from my father and my mother when they were young. They learned everything that a woman needs to be able to do, and they mastered it completely. In caring for our parents when they were ill, they would cut flesh from their own thighs to cure them. They were always like this, whether people expected it or not. They sustained the family with their industry and thrift. They were kind to the servants. They taught the youngsters reading and writing, proper conduct and moral values. There is nothing that people think a woman ought to do that they have not fully accomplished. But there is more. In writing fine poetry and prose, and in practicing calligraphy, they became very nearly like the sage who achieves everything on his own, making it impossible to apply conventional labels like "poor and lowly" or "rich and honorable" to their own heart-minds.

Lunying did not study poetry until she was in her thirtieth year. She excelled in five-character quatrains in the style of Ruan Ji and Tao Qian. More recently, she also received instruction from our father in the calligraphic styles of the Northern Dynasties masters. Her large-scale pieces, with characters several inches square and measuring many feet across, were judged the equal of our father's by those who viewed them. Wanying herself, who was writing poetry at a young age, by midlife was also composing prose-poems in the ancient style; she, too, studied calligraphy under our father's tutelage, especially seal characters.

Lunying was a superb manager, quick-witted and decisive. For over ten years she took charge of my own household for me, and even in the face of great hardship and suffering, she never complained. Wanying is by nature accommodating, and when solving problems, she strives for harmony and mutual acceptance, yet she never lapsed into indulgence or laxness.

When Lunying first was married into the Sun family, she followed her husband to an official appointment in Anhui. Later she accompanied our father to his office in Shandong, and after that she came to live with me in Changzhou. After Wanying married Wang Xi, he entered our father's household in a uxorilocal arrangement; later on, they too moved in with me. Then when my own wife died, all of my family affairs fell on my elder sisters' shoulders. My relationship with them was like this: in the best of times, we cut and polished each other's literary work; in the worst of times, we braved our difficulties and exhausted our energies. When I had doubts, they were there to resolve them; when I did well, I could count on their encouragement; when I made mistakes, I knew they would correct me. It was nothing like the usual arrangement, in which once your sisters get married, they become distant and are never close to you again. I would compare our relationship to the ties that bound Qu Yuan and his elder sister,[38] or Xin Chang and his elder sister, Xianying,[39] or Zhang Xun and his elder sister, Lady Lu;[40] each took a different path, but their feelings were exactly alike.

An ancient ode from the *Book of Odes* says: "A young woman [at marriage] leaves her parents and brothers far behind,"[41] meaning that a married woman takes as her own family her husband's family, and treats her natal family as "outsiders." Thus the ode, titled "The Spring," in depicting a young wife who longs to return home but cannot, upholds and defends the great gulf between what is "inside" and what is "outside," creating a precedent that hundreds of generations have followed. But if a woman who is "ordering the marsh plants for the ancestral sacrifices"[42] and thus performing the duties proper to a wife nonetheless returns to be faithful to her ties with her own brother,[43] if she preserves the fine distinction between what is "inside" her family and what belongs to the outer realm of the "guest" while carrying out the duties of a sibling—then her circumstances may be unorthodox but her emotions will be completely pure, just like the woman of Wei in the poem, whom the sage permitted to express her deepest longings without reining them in.[44] I feel toward my elder sisters as if we all were brothers.

Seeking meaning from ancient texts, I find my sisters described; tracing talent and conduct in the present, I find them equally exemplary. They have achieved self-fulfillment despite adversity and without shame. This is the ultimate ground on which I base my own happiness and my birthday greetings for them—why should I mourn the cycles of prosperity and adversity that lie beyond our control?

For all these reasons, is not my birthday greeting to my sisters as appropriate as it can possibly be?[45]

With this final flourish, Uncle Yuesun raised his cup with great emotion toward his sisters, who laughed while they dabbed at their eyes with their sleeves. In this balance between grief and comfort, loss and memory, Caipin's last year in Wuchang ended.

YUZHOU, HENAN (1850–1856)

While visiting her brother and her sisters in Wuchang, Caipin's Aunt Qieying became aware that in the throes of moving and mourning, no one had thought to make plans for the betrothal of her nieces, the eldest of whom—Caipin herself—was already at marriageable age. Qieying immediately set to work looking for a good match among the young men in the family networks she knew in Beijing. Her careful and diplomatic inquiries revealed that the Cheng family from Wuxi, very close to the Zhang's own native place, was seeking a bride for a bright young man named Cheng Peiyuan, who had already won the *juren* degree.[46] In short order, thanks to Qieying's efforts, a betrothal was arranged. At the time, Peiyuan's father was serving as the magistrate of Yuzhou, a county town southwest of the old northern capital, Kaifeng. Although she had lived in Wuchang for only a few years, Caipin prepared once again to move.

Her uncle was distraught. He was upset at the thought of Caipin's marriage to a distant family, far from the household he had tried so hard to keep together. He also had a practical concern: he had counted on Caipin to teach her younger sisters and his own daughter as well; if she left, he could hardly expect to find anyone as gifted and as compatible to take her place.[47] He could see how upset Caipin herself was at the prospect of separation. She had spent her whole life in the company of her mother's family, and suddenly she was bound for a place where she knew no one, where no one in her family had ever been, to live with people her own mother and uncle had never met.

Uncle Yuesun took it upon himself to cheer Caipin in the only way he knew. As part of his publishing project, he had made a selection from all of the poems the girls in the poetry club had written since arriving in Wuchang—an astonishing total of 690 verses, filling twelve chapters! He commissioned his son, Jinli, to edit the original manuscripts, and he set all the other children in the family school to work proofreading the prints from the woodblocks. Then he presented a copy of the finished book to Caipin as a parting gift.[48] The poems included her own, along with poems by her sisters Caifan, Cailan, Caizao, and her cousin Xiangzhen, and Uncle Yuesun's concubine, Li Luan. Caipin was in her twenty-fourth year when the collection was printed in 1850; Caizao, the youngest, was seventeen. Caipin had tutored all of the contributors herself.[49]

Gripping the book tightly in one hand, and biting her lip while tears rolled down her face, Caipin, leaning on a maid who was to accompany her, boarded a sedan chair and went on her way to her wedding, escorted by one of her future husband's married brothers and his wife, and a retinue of servants, porters, and even armed bodyguards. Travel overland to their destination was extremely dangerous at that time. On her way to Yuzhou, swinging in the sedan chair in the precious company of the familiar maid, Caipin recalled the words of her uncle's birthday greeting to her mother and her aunt. How ironic they seemed to her now. Why couldn't she have had a married-in husband? Why had no one thought of it? It was because of her father's death, she was sure. Had he lived, he would never have been able to part with her. Thinking of her father only made Caipin cry harder. She allowed herself to wallow deeply in sentiment before she finally opened the book in her lap.

Reading, she forgot to cry. She had not seen some of the poems in years. There were those she had written when she was only twelve, and others by her younger sisters and cousin composed when they were six or seven. The wonderful dedication by her brother Chenbi startled her. Chenbi, who had just been capped, had matured far beyond his years, and his empathy for her was now palpable. Thus absorbed, she passed the rest of the day with dry eyes, and by the time they arrived in Yuzhou, her curiosity and confidence had begun to revive.

Caipin and her entourage reached Yuzhou at almost the same time that the Taiping rebels began their march northward from the mountains of Guangxi, far to the south. The region to the east of Yuzhou was overrun by local outlaws who moved in bands called *nian,* and there were already ominous signs that the *nian* might coalesce into a massive fighting force.[50] Disastrous flooding along the lower reaches of the Yellow River, foreshadowing the great river's shift in course in 1855, drowned hundreds of thousands and destroyed the livelihood of millions more. Homeless peasants in the flood plain joined the *nian,* as they would later join the Taiping armies, for sustenance and support.

Caipin's new home in the northern province of Henan lay just beyond the area where these disasters struck home, but the disorder spreading through the countryside placed her marital family in grave danger. In June of 1853 the Taiping armies were prevented from attacking the nearby provincial capital at Kaifeng by floods that drove them back. But Kaifeng was already a political disaster, sheltering thousands of refugees who were seeking food and work.[51] By the mid-1850s, lawless bands led movements to "defy officials and kill off *yamen* underlings" *(kangguan shachai),* and a vast federation of self-styled *nian* bandits led by local strongmen stretched across the south central part of the province. Local officials tried in vain to restore order.[52]

Still not settled in Yuzhou and frightened by her surroundings, Caipin willed herself to write. She had begun two difficult pregnancies since her marriage, only to lose each baby when she was several months along.[53] Her new husband tried to pursue the normal avenues of an educated man, accepting teaching jobs when they were offered and faithfully caring for his parents when he was unemployed. But the fighting in the countryside made it difficult to pretend that life was normal. Caipin's father-in-law, who was in excellent health and a conscientious official, spent his days handling messages and delivering advice to the various local officials who arrived asking for his help or direction. Caipin remembered her aunt's impassioned verses written after the Opium War, and she decided to write her own response to the chaos unfolding around her. Her first attempt took many months of revision before she was willing to declare it finished.[54]

MOVED BY EVENTS

Valued officials, with tallies and battleaxes, guard strategic borders,[55]
"Splitting bamboo"[56] sounds an alarm that the rebels' strength is surging.
Seizing the pass, they have already signaled their move out of Guangxi and
    Guangdong,
Riding the current, they are poised to descend to the clear Xiang [Hunan].
How many in oxcarts defend the border commanderies?[57]
Whose dead bodies, wrapped in horsehide, are pledged to die for our
    country?
Who has sought the origins of the rebellion, or traced the beginnings of
    this disaster?
Since ancient times, good governance has rested upon agriculture and
    sericulture.

The published version of this poem inserts here a comment by Caipin's uncle Yuesun: "At this time of crisis she pours out her groans of righteous anger; she adopts a lofty perspective and thinks deeply; these are not merely decorative phrases."

Beacon fires at Guilin reach to the southern skies,
For one full month they besieged the city—how pitiful!
Then at midnight, startling thunder—iron storks[58] come flying;
Ten thousand families weep in the wilds, provoking the cuckoo's cry.[59]
The fish is in the pot—who will be sent to hold back the rebels who
    remain?[60]
A prairie fire is best stopped before it ever starts.
Armies have long been mustered in Sichuan and in Chu [Hubei],
Why must battle carts continue traveling in the same ruts that overturned
    others?

"Leaning on a pillar and mournfully singing,"[61] a hundred feelings stir,
Looking southward to the clouds of Chu, my thoughts turn round and
   round.
The Yangzi River is Heaven's own boundary—its defense is urgently
   needed;
Beacon fires flare in the Seven Marshes [the Hubei border area]—
   the people are easily frightened.
A decisive battle is too much to hope for from a thousand *li* away;
When times are so troubling, how can I ever calm this slip of a heart?
Were I to ask for a capstring [to fight the enemy],[62] I would fail to match
   Qin Liangyu;
If I cast aside my brush [to go off to war], it would be hard to fulfill
   wifely obligations.

In 1854, a letter arrived from Aunt Qieying, who had taken refuge in her
late husband's home in Changshu after fleeing the capital along with tens
of thousands of refugees the previous year, when the Taiping forces were
still advancing north toward Beijing. The letter made clear her aunt's panic
and also her revulsion at the news spreading north about the organization
and beliefs of the Taiping followers. Most shocking to Caipin were these
lines, which reminded her of the hiss in her aunt's voice when she was dis-
gusted or angry: "The long-haired rebels want us to call our father 'brother,'
and they would have your uncle call his daughters 'sister.' If a wife calls her
husband 'brother,' how could she possibly sleep with him? These barbaric
outlaws will put an end to the family forever!"[63] Enclosed with the letter
was a poem Aunt Qieying had composed on her journey south to Changshu. Caipin read the poem in agony, realizing that at that very moment she
had no idea whether her family members were safe or whether she would
ever see her aunt again. She immediately wrote a poem in response:[64]

RESPONDING TO MY AUNT MENGTI'S POEM "MOVED BY EVENTS, WRITTEN
ON THE BOAT RETURNING SOUTH IN FLIGHT FROM THE BANDITS"
Life-and-death partings are difficult;[65]
Throughout our family, the sound of wretched weeping.
The wagtail on the plain cries its distress,[66]
Rumors of war[67] press you on your way.
Who can send word of your progress?
My dreams jump, alarmed, from safety to danger.

Your lone boat by night in lightly falling snow,
Looking out as far as I can see, with too much feeling to bear.

Here her uncle Yuesun comments in the margin, "How restrained!"

The woman of Lu grieved and wept over the times,
Her words passed down as the Qishi lament.[68]
I carry your poetry volume in my hand;
Reading it through, my emotions well up.[69]
Frontier beacon fires burn three years,[70]
News of loved ones [stretches] the heart a thousand miles.[71]
Distant mists enfold my yearnings for my country and my family,
Bending my head, I weep upon my dress. . . .

In the year 1856, on the evening of the Double Seven festival (the seventh day of the seventh lunar month), as Caipin watched a "fishhook moon" making its way across the night sky, she undertook a new poem in honor of the Double Seven. She had attempted a poem for this particular occasion only once before, and that was when she was very young, writing about missing her father.[72] As she grew older, the theme seemed hackneyed, and it was hard to think of fresh ways to write about it.[73] What moved her hand on this particular evening was her husband's absence. He had gone to fight in one of the many local organizations mobilized by political leaders to keep the city safe. She had not seen him for more than a year. Her thirtieth birthday had passed unmarked:[74]

MOON

My hair like wild grass as the conjugal mirror breaks,[75]
Leaden tears[76] flow into the moon's gilded waves.
News makes me anxious for the green bird,[77]
My feelings one with the pale Moon-goddess.[78]
Rising from bed, my thoughts of home reach out;
Recalling my dreams, the pain of separation wells up.
All night long I rub my head,[79]
As the west wind sings its loud song.[80]

This poem was followed by another, one year later. Caipin never learned the cause of her husband's death:[81]

PREVENTED FROM ESCORTING HOME FOR BURIAL THE BODY OF MY LATE
HUSBAND, BOHOU, I COMPOSED THIS ODE TO EXPRESS MY FEELINGS

At a time of ceaseless war
A coffin on the road means loneliness and desolation.
The human soul after death[82] must lie in peace,
Thinking of this heightens my fear and anxiety.
His ancestral home is more than a thousand *li* away;
I spoke of returning to divine a gravesite,
I myself would escort the coffin[83] the entire way.
I had just begun carrying out my commitment of following
    him to the end of my days;
And now, so early, those heavy bags were emptied.
The heavenly bodies signaled a propitious day,
My black mourning dress displayed my pure widowhood,
Cart wheels were greased ready for the journey,
When suddenly the feathered call to arms shot like a star.[84]
Calamity and misfortune appeared in unexpected places,
En route to Bo bandits also rose up.[85]
And the embers from these fires were difficult to extinguish,
The long road was suddenly blocked.
So was my determination to go difficult to abandon.
After all, I was the one left behind,
Stealing breath year by month,
If I followed him in death myself,
How would I ever need fear anything again?
But at home I still have his parents to think about,
How urgent their earnest instructions!
"You must dare to taste distress and sorrow;
The inner apartments cannot be lightly abandoned.
Disaster and calamity cannot always be avoided,
How can you count on comfort in times of crisis?
Although we say of the dead that they are lamented,
The living too should be regarded with pity.
You have always understood clearly the larger principles
    of duty and responsibility;
Why are you now so disquieted?"
My son the heir is still in his tender years,
Clinging desperately to my knees.
My sister-in-law is pained by parting,
Wringing her hands and crying.

Seeing this, my own suffering deepens,
I want to leave but cannot bear the break. . . .

When in 1858 Caipin's brother stopped on his way home from the capital to take her to Wuchang for their mother's sixtieth birthday, she had not seen her natal family in eight years. The city was recovered from the Taiping occupation, and her uncle's home and authority had been restored. For four months, Uncle Yuesun presided over a reunion the likes of which, as he later wrote, they would never see again.[86] As Caipin was leaving to return to her parents-in-law in Yuzhou, her uncle parted the curtains of her sedan chair at the last minute. He pressed into her hands a brocade box. "Open this when you miss us," he said. She never saw him again.

The historian says:

Wang Caipin's life after her marriage is retrieved only in snapshots like the ones presented here: occasional poems, linked to a date or an event, that enable us to place her in space and time, and to try to locate there something of her inner state and her outer experience. Following the reunion of 1858, she became a governess, doubtless under the patronage of well-to-do householders who wanted to spare her the ignominy of residence in one of the many homes for genteel widows established following the pacification in 1864. Her sister Caifan was married to a Changzhou man named Wei Ji, who moved into the Wuchang household as a uxorilocal son-in-law soon after Caipin left home for her own wedding. Upon hearing that the rebel insurgents were bearing down on Changzhou in 1860, Wei Ji hastened home to search for his mother, and was killed in the fighting.[87] We do not know what happened to any of her sisters after that.

Upon Caipin's death in 1893, her fragmentary poems were collected, edited, and published, complete with her uncle's margin notes, by her last employer, a Shandong official named Xu Zhenyi.[88] Of her life in Xu's household, we know that she was a companion to his beloved concubine, Lady Liang, for whom Caipin composed an elegy after her death, and that she was a governess for his children.[89] The rest of her family, scattered by the rebellion, left few records by which to trace their fate.[90]

In the same year that Caipin's poetry collection appeared under Xu Zhenyi's studio imprint, China went to war with Japan over competing interests in Korea. The devastating defeat of the imperial navy and land forces one year later resulted in the treaty of 1895 that began China's rapid slide from belated reform into cataclysmic revolution. Chinese women who were born about the time of Caipin's death grew up in a republic and went on to educate themselves abroad, in Japan, Europe, and the United States. Leaders in education, politics, medicine, and science, many of these women became writers and chroniclers of their own lives in poems, short stories, and memoirs.[91] Unlike Caipin, they were known not for carrying on the learning of their families but rather for the new knowledge they mastered. In their ambition, their confidence, their creativity, and their heritage, however, they were all Caipin's heirs.

EPILOGUE
The Historian Says . . .

THE ZHANG FAMILY'S VOICES, preserved forever through the printing and publishing of their own writings, have made this history of their family possible. Those same writings also invite the historian to probe beneath the smooth surface of their elegant classical Chinese, asking questions about things the family preferred not to discuss and offering plausible answers that the sources may not readily yield. I confess to skirting some subjects: sexuality and desire for one, but also anger, jealousy, cruelty, cheating, lying, and other petty sides of the human condition that few of us want to be remembered for. The Zhang men and women were surely guilty of the latter at some time or another, and perhaps they will rest easier knowing I have not tried to invent that part of their lives for them. This epilogue begins with the silences in the record and how I have dealt with them. I then comment on other aspects of the Zhang's story that are of particular interest to me as a historian of women in late imperial China: the relationships among the imperial polity, local society, the family, and the person, and between status and gender; and finally, the temporal context in which three generations of the Zhang family lived out their lives.

SILENCES AND WOMEN'S VOICES

In the historical record of the Zhang family, we hear women's voices almost exclusively in poems. Those poems were printed because of the efforts of enterprising male relatives and patrons like Zhang Yuesun and Xu Zhenyi.[1] Children and grandchildren, pressed into service as copyeditors and proofreaders, saw their own names decorating each chapter of the poet's published work, as shown in figure 4. In that sense, making a woman's voice heard was never an individual effort. It was a corporate project, conducted with affection, pride, duty, ambition, and sentiment. Local culture also played a role: noted scholars of Changzhou were known for appending the poems and song lyrics of their wives to their own literary collections.[2] The abundant prefaces and encomia that adorn women's published poems are a boon to the historian, enabling her to trace the networks of obligation and acquaintance that framed the Zhang family's social and cultural life, and fleshing out the human contours of their lives beyond letters. Those same editors, colophon writers, calligraphers, proofreaders, and preface authors, on the other hand, as the corporate sponsors of a woman's poetry collection, remind us that "voice" is hardly pure or spontaneous—never mind the poems written "on the spur of the moment" *(ou cheng)*. I like to think of those sponsors benignly, as genteel censors dedicated to their own standards of good taste and literary excellence.[3]

Still, the presence of all the production assistants calls to mind the self-censorship that must have intruded on women as writers. To be preserved and published, a woman's writing always (even if unconsciously) had to pass muster with a raft of relatives, editors, sponsors, and critics. This self-censorship surely affected the printing of references to footbinding, resulting in one of the most cavernous silences in the historical record on elite Chinese women. What can this silence tell us? For the historian setting scenes in her mind, the silence itself cracks open some insight. Zhang Qieying may well have written a poem on footbinding, but I doubt that she would have saved it in a writing case where her brother might look to collect poems for publication. Were she to save such a poem, on the other hand, she would be secure in the knowledge that her brother would never print it. The leading scholars invited to compose prefaces and colophons for the poetry of a respected woman like Qieying always relied on their own sources of critical authority. They also tried hard to draw the most flattering comparisons possible between the author and the poets they most admired. So we see in the published poems of the Zhang women interlinear comments and prefaces dropping the names of the towering poets of the Six Dynasties era, Tao Qian and Meng Haoran. And we see the Zhang women themselves picking up images and phrases from poets of the Tang, Song, and Yuan periods: Du Fu, Meng Jiao, Su Shi, Yuan Haowen. All of these poets were men. Often women writers use those images and phrases with deep sensitivity and originality to express a meaning that is intensely personal, even original. But a poem on footbinding would not find a place in a collection intended to celebrate a female poet's mastery of regulated verse or song lyrics whose standards were set by male connoisseurs.[4] In that sense, the silence surrounding footbinding in the Zhang women's poetry sends us powerful signals about the con-

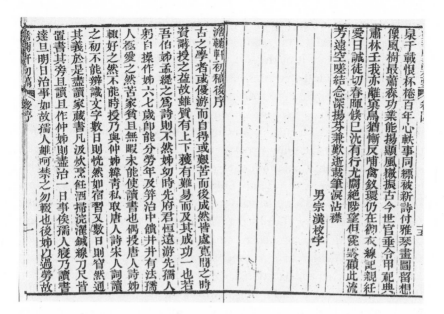

FIGURE 4. Leaf from the collected poems and song lyrics of Zhang Qieying, showing (on the right) the name of her son, Zonghan, as copyeditor, and (on the left) part of an afterword composed by her youngest sister, Wanying. The publisher is her brother Yuesun. (Source: Zhang Qieying, *Danju xuan chugao*, 1840.)

straints, as well as the enticements, of poetic criticism. Unspoken norms of poetic criticism circumscribed not only language but also subject matter, leaving bound feet in the margins of the female poet's lexicon, accessible at best as a frivolous, playful, or intimate poetic gesture,[5] or consigned to the writings of courtesans, whose reputation for vulgarity in the nineteenth century was directly associated with references to their bound feet.[6]

If intimate womanly matters were not suited to the poetics of elite publishing, neither, it appears, was there an effort to trace a literary lineage of women poets. Although the Zhang women's writings single out many female role models and heroines, from Ban Zhao to Qin Liangyu, neither the Zhang women poets themselves nor their supporters and patrons celebrate the poems of the female poet Li Qingzhao (1084–c. 1151). Li Qingzhao is commonly referred to as "China's greatest woman poet,"[7] and her work has become a centerpiece for the history of literary women in China. Li Qingzhao was not invoked as a model, however, by the women writers of the Zhang family, and their male admirers and critics did not try to place them in a lineage of "women poets." Li Qingzhao's intensely personal and autobiographical writings[8] may have been an inspiration for the talented women of the Zhang family, but they never acknowledge this in writing. The praise they won is of the sort we read in an encomium one admirer wrote on the cover leaf of Wang Caipin's collected poems, which extols their bravado and beauty and "no trace of the boudoir" *(wu guige qi)*.[9]

In an encomium written for Zhang Qieying's collected poems, Xue Ziheng, a friend of the family, comments on how few notable women poets there had been in the Qing dynasty up to his time (perhaps thirty-four, among whom twenty had produced work that was worth preserving, in his view), and he notes that recently only two had compared with Qieying: Wang Caiwei (wife of Sun Xingyan) and Qian Mengdian (daughter of Qian Weicheng). Xue Ziheng also observes that Qieying shared with both of them certain outstanding traits, such as being tutored by a gifted scholarly father, and marrying a man of great accomplishments and exchanging poems with him. But only Qieying, he stressed, could claim an additional mark of distinction: the fact that she, her younger brother, her sisters, and even her mother were also poets.[10] So the rarity of excellent women's writing was worthy of note, but not women's poetry as a genre unto itself.

This returns us to the relationship between a woman's written work and the publication of that work by her male relatives. Who made the selections, and with what aim? For Zhang Yuesun, we know, the aim was to carry on the honor of the family's distinguished literary reputation, to secure the welfare of his sisters, and to carry out his parents' wishes. Yuesun is the person who invited scholars to write prefaces for those collected works, and just whom he would invite must have been in the back of his mind as he selected the poems. In addition, Yuesun wrote his own interlinear comments on some poems, calling attention to phrases he particularly admired or nuances that an outsider might miss. So in the end, it is Yuesun's selections and Yuesun's aims that we encounter when we read most of the poems of the talented women of the Zhang family. What they themselves might have said or thought that would contravene his judgments can never be known. On the other hand, as their poems show, the heavy hand of patronage hardly stifled the creative energies of the Zhang women. We see them clearly, through their published writings, as emotional individuals with great intellectual and aesthetic gifts. When, as with Wang Caipin, a woman's poems are the only surviving evidence of her mature life and death, the slimmest volume becomes a precious record. The historian must settle for that, and be grateful.

Many poems, moreover, were lost or destroyed, or never preserved in the first place (like Tang Yaoqing's recited verses that were never copied down).

When women's scant writings are finally published, the imprimaturs of their male sponsors (colophons, prefaces, dedications, afterwords, and other literary gestures) all glorify their accomplishments and make them seem larger than life. Women writers are further spoken for by the men who celebrate their memory in inscriptions on massive memorial arches *(pailou)* and modest gravestones, as well as in hagiographic eulogies and memoirs dripping with sentiment. Again and again from those voices we hear of women's overwhelming strength, endurance, generosity, forbearance, and competence. They replaced husbands and fathers as authority figures, educators, financial wizards, and breadwinners while simultaneously doing proper "women's work" and handling all the matters pertaining to "rice and salt," "drawing water and pounding rice"—i.e., cooking, cleaning, sewing, laundry. In upper-class households, these matters involved not only material production but also the delicate management of human producers: directing servants, attending to the emotional and physical well-being of males and females of all ages who remained at home and were in constant interaction with one another, and—perhaps above all—making sure that the women of the household got along together. To such massive responsibilities, we are told, wives and mothers rose without fail, unflinchingly and even with flair, tickling an elderly in-law's listless taste buds with delicious tiny treats while serving up multicourse banquets for the carousing young friends of a son home to celebrate a break from examination studies. Such were their formidable capabilities. Truly they were, as we are constantly reminded, *zui nenggan*—they could do everything, and do it well. When women are quoted (word for word) in biographies and epitaphs, they say exactly what their virtues require of them.

Amidst this barrage of rhetoric and between the slender lines of refined poetry, hearing a woman's true voice seems nearly impossible. Still, from the silence enfolding each woman's psyche, we sometimes detect a plaintive cry, and often it comes from an unexpected quarter. Such a cry escapes from Zhang Huiyan's childhood memories of his mother's attempted suicide, which we have already heard secondhand from his sister-in-law, Tang Yaoqing:

> I recall that when I was five, my mother wept constantly for nearly a month. Then suddenly one day she lay down and was very still. I was playing at the foot of her bed and I remember thinking that she must have cried herself to sleep. In a little while my grandmother came and only then did I realize that she had tried to strangle herself with her sash. Fortunately, they were able to revive her.[11]

In this text we see Huiyan's mother as she felt after her husband's death: not strong, not omnicompetent, and with no apprehension of imperial rewards. She is also heedless of her two sons (one an infant) and her daughter (nine *sui*), whose own reaction to all of this will never be known.

Huiyan's memoir, by breaking the silence surrounding his mother, emboldens us to probe other silences in the record of the Zhang family's women. These silences blanket the dead: the boy Juesun, as well as the youthful Guanying, whose short collection of poems printed after her premature death are framed by the anguished cries of her father and continually celebrated in the sentimental verses and memoirs of her sisters and brother. Guanying's place as a tragic figure and as the emotional fulcrum of the family's remembered past is enshrined by her father in his preface to her printed poetry collection, quoted nostalgically by Qieying elsewhere in this book. Zhang Qi's words in that preface are deeply sad:

> Ah! I remember that time in the autumn of 1814 when we sat by the light of the lamp talking about everything—classics and moderns, criticism and calligraphy—with all five children gathered around me. I was so happy then! How could I have known that in just the space of a few days I would be bidding her my last farewell? Now her sisters and her brother are here before me; all are fine. But Guanying has gone and I will never see her again. What father has ever endured such misery?[12]

His words, notably, focus on himself and his travels and his long periods of absence from home, not on Guanying. They tell us nothing of her life, her personality, her talent, or even her appearance. Instead, Zhang Qi's preface turns a mirror on the father and his own deepest emotions—a self-critique of his obsession with success, a bitter reflection on his misgauged priorities, a protest against the pressures besetting all men of his class. Here we see a silence of a different kind, broken when, for a fleeting instant, a male writer finds a venue where he can rebel against the social conditions of his work and its emotional privations. Zhang Qi's preface may also bear witness to the relentless sense of failure that haunted him from the moment of his brother's death. Where could such a man find comfort? Perhaps only in mourning a much-loved daughter.

Probably no silence in the Zhang history is more compelling than the massive silence that envelops the elusive character of Miss Fa, whose ghostly presence in the shadows of the Zhang records virtually consigns her to the living dead. As evidence of her existence we have five cryptic references. The first is the brief observation dropped by Zhang Qi into the middle of his epitaph for his late wife, Tang Yaoqing, where he says of Miss Fa: "My wife took pity on her and welcomed her into our household so that she could fulfill her vow as a faithful maiden."[13] The second is a notice in the Changzhou local history of 1879: "In 1848, the twenty-eighth year of Dao-guang, an imperial commendation was conferred on the faithful maiden Fa, from Yanghu." The appended note adds: "She was betrothed to Zhang Juesun."[14] This notice contains a telling omission. According to the Zhang genealogy (our third source), Yuesun's son, Jinli, was named "simultaneous heir" *(jian si)* to Juesun, so he could carry on the deceased Juesun's line.[15] Adopting an heir is one of the virtuous acts of a true faithful maiden. Thus the formal announcement of Miss Fa's faithful maiden status in the local history, quoted above, should have paid her this tribute. Why the silence? Perhaps the silence is telling us that Miss Fa's agency played no role in Jinli's adoption, that the adoption was a decision of Yuesun's and she had no say in it. In fact, as it turned out, the adoption came to nothing in the end. Jinli himself was without an heir, and an heir had to be adopted for *him* as well. But that heir carried on Yuesun's line, and Juesun's was simply allowed to die out. That the issue of Juesun's heir was fraught is only revealed in passing in a birthday greeting, where we hear praise for Lunying's practical advice on the problem of getting an heir for Miss Fa and Juesun's line.[16] Here the point is made to stress Lunying's cool good judgment and common sense, but the need for cool judgment tells us that the heir question made at least some Zhang family members hot-headed. Whatever the fate of Jinli and his adopted heir, it seems clear that Miss Fa did not rear Jinli, nor was she involved in the care of Jinli's adopted son. She did not secure another successor to continue her deceased fiancé's line. The Zhang line-age genealogy also says of Miss Fa that she died in Changzhou in 1860.[17] This notice of her time and place of death serves as the fragment support-ing my narrative of her separation from the Zhang family in 1846 with the move to Wuchang.

A precious final source of information on Miss Fa comes from another unlikely place: a eulogy for Bao Mengyi, her sister-in-law. The eulogy, writ-ten by a family friend named Fang Junmo, was commissioned immediately following Mengyi's death in 1844. In his zeal to celebrate Mengyi's virtue, Fang seized upon her relationship with Miss Fa as the quintessential exam-ple of Mengyi's understanding of proper family relationships and respon-sibilities, and the ultimate testimony to her moral character. By dissecting that relationship, Fang's epitaph inadvertently lays bare the raw emotional tensions surrounding Miss Fa's presence in the Zhang household. Fang Junmo declares outright that Miss Fa was mentally ill *(xinji)*, flying into uncontrollable rages. Mengyi, he recalls, was unfailingly deferential toward Miss Fa. Mengyi met her every demand, and when Miss Fa was unappeased, Mengyi would quietly weep but accept responsibility for whatever had displeased her sister-in-law, resolving the conflict. Miss Fa herself, reports Fang, said: "My younger sister-in-law respects me." Mengyi's skill here involved more than psychological strength or insight. In fact, Miss Fa, as the "wife" of the eldest son in the family, was Mengyi's ritual superior, the person to whom she was required to defer in every household decision. As Fang remarks admiringly, most daughters-in-law of his day no longer understood the ritual hierarchies that distinguished the wife of a first-born son *(zhongfu)* from the wife or wives of the younger son(s) *(jiefu)*.[18] Thus Bao Mengyi's deference to Miss Fa, despite Miss Fa's mental illness, showed her to be exceptionally exemplary in this regard. Fang Junmo's comment at the end of his epitaph is worth quoting, as it explains why he fastened on that particular relationship to illustrate Bao Mengyi's character:

Lady Bao's wise actions and constant rectitude are confirmed by the testimony of her family members, all of whom, without exception, describe her this way. Truly she was a splendid person, but the hallmark of her wisdom was the knowledge of the foundation of the rites that she displayed in her submissive service to Miss Fa. . . . Miss Fa's illness was severe and beyond her control. Only by faithfully adhering to the standards governing the conduct of a junior wife was Lady Bao able to correct her heart. If we imagine how she bore her tribulations in silence and resolved her difficulties by herself, we can expand upon the meaning of that to understand other things: as she honored her sister-in-law so she filially served her parents; as she treated her sister-in-law with intimate concern, so she supported her husband—and lived in harmony with other members of the household, and treated the servants and concubines with motherly kindness. It cannot be otherwise. If we deeply examine the meaning of the ritual systems established by the ancients *(zhi li zhi yi)*, we see that only this kind of conduct truly fulfills the meaning of the "wifely way" *(fu dao)*—yet there was no hint of self-aggrandizement to be found in her anywhere. For this reason, whether she was interacting with those above her or those below her, she made them all happy; and when she was carrying out a duty, she was always mindful of the essential principles *(li yao)* behind it. The orderly state of governance of all under heaven is based entirely on just such conduct. Alas! We must tell this to all the wives of future generations! Therefore I say: truly this woman knew the foundation of the rites *(neng zhi li zhi ben)*.[19]

It may of course be true that, by some definition, Miss Fa was "mentally ill." As Weijing Lu has shown, emotional and sexual tensions tore at the veneer of moral resolve surrounding faithful maidens.[20] Eccentricity, neurosis, depression, and suicide are common themes in the stories told about these young women. Miss Fa's own situation was also unique, filled with stress peculiar to the circumstances of the Zhang family. We know that Miss Fa was betrothed to Juesun as a young girl, possibly as early as her birth. This betrothal made sense at the time because of the stature of the Fa family in the Changzhou area, a stature based on generations of distinction in the local community. And since the Fa were the leading physicians in Changzhou at the time of Juesun's death, it is likely that Zhang Qi's son died while in the care of members of the Fa family, including Ruhe, Miss Fa's own father. According to one account, as we have seen, Zhang Qi himself began to study medicine after his son's death, out of disgust with the "mediocre doctors" whom he held responsible.

In the shadow of the effusive outpourings of emotion from other females in the Zhang family, Miss Fa at first appears to be a pathetic figure, doomed to a sorrowful life because of her fiancé's death, and then overshadowed by the dazzling company in which she found herself once she had entered the Zhang household. And in fact, in the midst of all of the writings by those lively, articulate, hyper-responsible Zhang women—a whole houseful of them—Miss Fa is completely eclipsed. Not all *zhennü* were silent, as Weijing Lu has shown; the words of many of them have been carefully preserved in local gazetteers, literati memoirs, and literary anthologies, mostly as poetry, occasionally as biography.[21] But in the context of Changzhou's brilliant *cainü* culture, to be a drab *zhennü* was to invite historical oblivion.

Yet, as we see, the silent Miss Fa was far from silent. She screamed her rage and frustration at female members of the Zhang family. To Zhang Qi, whom she probably rarely saw, her very person was a living and present reminder of Juesun's death and, worse, I have suggested, its immediate cause: her own father's school of medicine and her natal family's medical practice. To Yuesun's wife, Bao Mengyi, whom she tormented, Miss Fa represented living misery. To my own surprise, in the end Miss Fa entered my history of the Zhang as a dramatic and even domineering presence, her powerful emotions piercing the screen of silence that surrounds her in the documents. Published sources on intimate family matters, in other words, occasionally tip the writer's hand, revealing for a fleeting moment the fault lines beneath the smooth façade of virtue they are supposed to display.

Silence in the historical record is also a problem with respect to money. Ellen Widmer has called attention to the expanding market for women's writing in the first half of the nineteenth century, when women as readers were becoming economically important to commercial publishers and authors, and when the line between private family publishing and commercial publishing began to blur.[22] This reminds us that the writings of the Zhang women were a potential source of not only fame but also income. The Zhang exchanged poems widely, and their poems were anthologized in commercially published works, which—though they did not pay royalties—conveyed other kinds of premiums in the form of connections, referrals, and gifts. The Zhang never mention money in reference to their writings, nor does anyone else who writes about them. But we know that Lunying sold her calligraphy[23] and that Yaoqing sold her embroidery (and that of her daughters) when the family's needs required it. The family's private publications may have been mainly distributed as gifts, but the literary works and medical books published by Zhang Yuesun and his father and uncle before him, as well as Yuesun's attempt at fiction—his sequel to *Dream of the Red Chamber*—were surely money-making enterprises.[24] At the same time, the complete absence of reference to financial arrangements of any kind in the sources reminds us how powerful the taboos surrounding literati commercial activity remained during the lifetime of the Zhang family.

Silences about money return us to the question of Tang Yaoqing and her mysteriously deep pockets. Here a cue from Fang Junmo's strategy in writing Bao Mengyi's eulogy can be helpful. Fang Junmo was well aware that Miss Fa's mental illness was not a seemly topic for literary composition. But he also knew that in order to celebrate Bao Mengyi's exceptional virtue, Miss Fa's mental health would have to be explained. Once he had decided on that approach, his responsibility to protect the family's reputation was upheld even while he divulged to his readers the juicy details of Bao Mengyi's domestic situation. In just the same way, we find the authors of our sources on the Zhang women using well-accepted conventions about virtue—perhaps we might think of them as circumlocutions—to talk about women's use of money and profit.

In the case of *guixiu* like the talented women of the Zhang family, there are several ways to point at the coarse subject of money while talking about refinements like virtue. One way is to praise womanly work: the shuttle that flies all night under the glowing lamp, the embroidery that fills the family pot with thin rice gruel—both show us money changing hands. Our sources also gloss money management and profit by celebrating a woman's use of her dowry. Since the dowry is a bride's personal fund from her natal family, the wife who uses her dowry for her husband's needs, or those of his parents, is always performing a virtuous deed. Purchasing books for a spouse who is studying for the exams is one of the most common virtuous uses of dowry wealth, but dowries can pay for anything, from food to weddings and funerals. In the Zhang records, we are not always told that dowry is the source of income that makes possible the delicacies served to an aged mother-in-law or the banquets ordered up for visiting guests or the fine piece of stone purchased for a memorial arch. But clearly a woman who could make her dowry (or her income from her work) go farther by investing it, or by pawning it—as was the case with Tang Yaoqing—could exponentially enhance the record of her virtue. Thus, we can surmise, women who were most loudly celebrated for their hard work and generosity were also those who were shrewdest and most financially successful in managing their money.[25]

IMPERIAL GOVERNMENT, LOCAL SOCIETY, THE FAMILY, AND THE PERSON

Turning from the Zhang family's literary, emotional, and material lives and the silences that surround them, let us now consider their public life: the cultural, social, and political context that made it possible for them to flourish. The public lives of educated persons like the Zhang were shaped by the Qing imperial state, the unique local culture of Changzhou, and the family system as it was normatively constructed there.

The Zhang family lived in the cultural and economic heartland of the Qing empire, the Lower Yangzi region. This fact lends their lives a dual character. On the one hand, they worked and wrote in a local society where scholarly life flourished in famous libraries and academies, often without the explicit patronage of the court. Teaching jobs, the elusive mainstay of the Zhang men and in-laws, were hardly sufficient to keep the family afloat; the men's additional learning as *ruyi,* or literati physicians, supplied a cash flow that was perhaps more secure. Regardless of how hard they tried to sustain an independent scholarly life, the looming presence of Beijing shadowed the family at all times: whether in the unending struggle for success in the exams, which shaped the life course of Zhang Qi and his brother, and Zhang Yuesun as well; or in the strategizing to marry off daughters into the families of successful officials, which placed Qieying in the capital and sent Caipin off to Yuzhou.

Marriage strategies were not only framed by the larger context of mobility in the imperial examination system. Among Changzhou's elite, marriage strategies included a marked preference for uxorilocal marriage and for the use of affinal ties (through married women's kin networks) to shore up and ramify the patrilineal descent lines of fragile families like the Zhang. Just how friable lineage ties could be within the scholar elite is dramatized in the tenuous relationship between Zhang Wanying's husband, Wang Xi, and his wealthy kinsmen in Taicang. The infamous *wangzu* (leading families) who have gotten so much attention in recent scholarship in China left many members out even as their leaders dominated local politics and the economy.[26] The reputation of a *wangzu,* at the same time, served as a kind of life raft to which downwardly mobile members clung, insisting on their scholarly pedigree in the face of diminishing returns. This makes it more striking that, in the Zhang story, *wangzu* who ignored their own agnatic kin often acted effectively and even vigorously in support of in-laws. Tang Yaoqing's father seems to have had little support from his own lineage, relying instead on the help of a married sister and her husband. By the same token, Tang affines often came to the aid of the Zhang. In fact, the Tang, the Dong, and the Qian—all related to Zhang Qi by marriage—surface constantly in records of Zhang finances, helping out with money, gifts, patronage, and connections, as well as with housing, when the situation required it. Zhang Qi and his son, in turn, were the main sources of support for two of the married Zhang daughters and their spouses and families, and they saw to it that the younger descendants of in-laws got help when they needed it. In other words, in the Zhang family, financial support often traveled more readily through women's networks (marital, maternal, sororal) than through men's.

Another noteworthy aspect of marital relations in the Zhang family is the sororate marriage of Wanying's fourth daughter, Caizao. Caizao's older sister, the third daughter, Cailan—it will be recalled—was adopted by Wanying's sister, Lunying. Wang Cailan (renamed Sun Sihui) was betrothed to Lü Maorong but died soon after the marriage, whereupon Maorong immediately married Caizao. Although little attention has been paid to sororate marriage in Chinese families, at least one study has suggested that it was common and that laws enforcing the incest taboo were lenient with respect to sororate marriage, which was legitimized by the marriage rites of the Zhou period.[27]

How did women figure in the relationships among Changzhou's leading families? Clearly, help that came through in-laws was negotiated not by men but by women, whose appeals to brothers and fathers as well as sisters may have rung less like a rival's claim on resources and more like an emotional claim on shared childhood bonds that could not be denied. Cross-cousin marriage in the Zhang family history foregrounds the importance of women's family connections, as do the close marital ties linking the Dong, Qian, and Zhang families, all of Changzhou.[28] In the Zhang family, the centerpiece of the cross-cousin marriage strategy was the wedding of Wang Chenbi to Zhang Xiangzhen. (Wang Xi famously teased his niece, Zhang Xiangzhen, for having the good fortune to study with her future husband, his son Chenbi, while she was a child.)[29] As for the marked preference for uxorilocal marriage in Changzhou, the Zhang history sheds new light on this as well. Scholars who study uxorilocal marriage have stressed that it was favorable to women, as it enabled them to remain in the natal home without the stress of becoming reproductively active while in service to a demanding mother-in-law who was also a stranger.[30] But there were other consequences of uxorilocal marriage and the accompanying close ties between affinal kin. Women who grew up in families that preferred such marriage patterns were reared from the start to use their family connections pragmatically and skillfully, not only in their own interests but in the interests of their husbands and offspring. This points to patterns of child socialization in which women are brought up to assert and pursue their interests by articulating them in persuasive and morally compelling language, by nurturing their emotional bonds with brothers and all siblings, by giving generously to kinfolk on all sides, and by maintaining written contact with a wide network of collateral kin, mainly through the exchange of poems and letters.[31]

Equally important to the Zhang was the complex local culture that nurtured talent and gave both men and women the means to support themselves. As rich as their literary lives were, we need to ask about the relationship between the self-avowed "poverty" of the Zhang and its virtues. In many such families, where a widowed mother presides, the harsh realities of life force family members into destitution and suffering.[32] Yet the Zhang found ways to support married-in sons-in-law even in the face of extreme economic hardship—if we are to believe their stories. Why were they able to stay together so amiably for so long? The Zhang family's own chronicles point to the filial son carrying out his parents' charge: Zhang Yuesun. After his parents' death, Yuesun became the fulcrum of the family, the powerful center who saw to the continued closeness of all its members. He was also the family's chronicler, obsessed with collecting, printing, and preserving the records of their lives. But in this role Yuesun had powerful backers. He is a paradigmatic example of what G. W. Skinner has called the blessings of "sister influence"—the humanizing, emotionally satisfying, morally inspiring, and ambition-driving attention of elder female siblings, an attention deepened and focused by the loss of their elder brother.[33] Furthermore, the elder sisters were themselves products of their local culture; talented, articulate, dedicated, and smart, they supplied a rich family environment such as few young men could have imagined or enjoyed at the time.

Let us now look more closely at the configuration of siblings in the middle generation of the Zhang family's history, a generation dominated by four sisters. In the Chinese kinship system, birth order was of critical importance, and generic terms identified the birth order of close relatives in everyday speech. These terms connoted ritual seniority, and they were commonly used in letters and other family writings to specify which sister (or daughter, or granddaughter) the writer meant. For offspring sets of four (of the same sex), these terms are *bo, zhong, shu,* and *ji,* meaning eldest, next eldest, third eldest, youngest; thus, for Yuesun, his sister Qieying was *bo,* Guanying *zhong,* Lunying *shu,* and Wanying *ji.*

As a four-daughter cohort, the Zhang girls were considered very special (especially by their father's elder sister, who had no daughters of her own),[34] and as the eldest, Qieying was often singled out. In writings about the four Zhang sisters, they are sometimes compared to other famous sets of sisters, particularly the three Ye sisters, daughters of Shen Yixiu and Ye Shaoyuan.[35] Like the Ye sisters and sisters in other families of their station, the Zhang daughters were given special, gendered "generation" names that shared a common character, *ying,* which conveys the double meaning of talent and beauty. (The gendered generation name for the girls' brothers, Juesun and Yuesun, was a more prosaic choice, *sun,* meaning "descendant.") This common character *ying* was used as the second character in a compound name, with the first character specially chosen for each child. For additional aesthetic appeal, the girls' unique characters shared a common radical, a "silk" tag. Two of the names Zhang Qi and Tang Yaoqing selected for their daughters were exotic: Qieying's *qie* is so rare that it cannot be printed using standard software for Chinese classical writings, and Guanying's *guan,* which can refer to a kind of seaweed or an ancient style of cap, has an obscure pronunciation (it can be confused with *shan,* an overused term in women's names) found only in specialized dictionaries.[36] Qieying's name may refer to rich color, especially in fabric;[37] the name of the youngest daughter, Wanying, conveys the meaning "pure white," while Lunying's *lun* refers to fine thread.

The Zhang story, with its dense networks of siblings and cousins, calls attention to a central feature of upper-class Chinese family life in the nineteenth century: the unique experience of elite children in "grand families," where cousins treat one another as siblings, and where sibling influence appears far greater than the influence of parents or grandparents on the developing psyches of the young. Yuesun's bonds with his sisters, abundantly clear in his comments on their poetry, are richly remembered in his sisters' writings as well. Wanying, in a poem celebrating her brother's fortieth birthday in 1845, recalled that "from your birth to the present day, we have never lived apart. That is why our friendship is so deep, and our understanding of each other is so keen."[38] Such a children's world is the centerpiece of the great eighteenth-century novel *Dream of the Red Chamber.*[39] The novel's exploration of the complex ties joining young people of both sexes explains its popularity with both male and female readers in China. Nor is it surprising that Zhang Yuesun, who presided over just such a coterie of talented youth, joined the raft of writers who composed sequels to the novel during the nineteenth century.[40] For himself and his sisters, siblings were more important than parents; and he doubtless hoped, as the provider for his niece Wang Caipin and her siblings and cousins, that they could inhabit a youthful world like the idyll in the garden of the magnificent Jia estate in the novel. Yuesun was surely also taken with the parallels between the marriage of the novel's cousins Jia Baoyu and Xue Baochai and that of his own daughter, Xiangzhen, to her cousin Wang Chenbi.

Studies of the Chinese family system seldom address the profound impact of siblings on child socialization, preferring to stress the importance of parental or even grandparental dominance over the young.[41] The youthful Zhang of Yuesun's generation and their children—like Jia Baoyu and his cousins in *Red Chamber*—created a world apart from that of their hardworking elders. Their elite youth culture—in contrast to the youth culture of the contemporary United States—was nonetheless grounded in the home. Its heart lay in the inner quarters, where respectable young women were necessarily confined. Baoyu, the hero of *Red Chamber,* led a life resembling that of Zhang Yuesun, who came from the same part of China as Cao Xueqin, the author of *Dream of the Red Chamber.* In the context of Changzhou's local culture and its family practices, the Zhang story evokes the experience of grand families throughout the Lower Yangzi area.

In Yuesun's youthful education his sisters played a dominant role. Recalled Wanying, "When my brother was born he did not cry. At the age of several months he would laugh when he heard books being read. When he couldn't sleep at night, all of his sisters would hold him and read him poems and song lyrics. So when he was able to talk, he could recite whole verses of what he had heard."[42] Her brother's delicate health prevented his teachers and others from pressing him too hard, and it was not until Yuesun was well past the age of thirty that he began to show signs of promise as a scholar-official. The complex psychology of Yuesun's early childhood, including everyone's awareness of his mother's vow to rear him as a physician, makes his later success as an official all the more remarkable. Clearly, his sense of duty and obligation, instilled by his female relatives, made the difference.[43]

Turning from youth culture to the person, we should pause to consider Zhang Yuesun's unusual responsibilities as the youngest child and the only surviving son. By accident—his elder brother's death, his own position as youngest child and sole surviving son, and the uxorilocal marriages of two of his four sisters—Yuesun emerged as the patriarch in a family where two of his elder sisters and their children were his primary charge. We know from anthropological fieldwork that a brother can play a crucial role in a sister's welfare after her marriage, dramatized in the special responsibility of a brother to inspect personally the circumstances surrounding a married sister's death.[44] The Zhang story, however, reveals another dimension of this special relationship between a married woman and her brother. In a family where a sister's husband "married in," as did the spouses of both Lunying and Wanying, her brother acted as the family head after the death of their father. Thus Yuesun assumes a paternalistic role in the lives of his sisters' children, especially their daughters. The mother's brother's role in the lives of Chinese children has not been much studied, but we might suspect from watching Yuesun in action that in places like Changzhou, the mother's brother was intimately involved in the education, marriage, and support of his sister's children.[45] This affinal bond, which transgresses the boundaries of the male descent line, comes to life in other aspects of the Zhang family experience when we see affinal kin on the mother's side offering her and her spouse and children housing, financial aid, and emotional sustenance. A further irony is what happens to the father of Sun Jie, who came to stay with and died in the care of his son's wife's family; or what happens to the ill-fated Wang Xi, whose own patriline cared little about what became of his dead body.

Finally, we note the tensions that uxorilocal marriage brought to the delicate relationships among adult women living in the same household. Seniority, as measured by generation, gave power to Tang Yaoqing in the Guantao household, but upon her death a serious crisis of authority was evident. The next-senior woman in the household, ritually speaking, was the wife of the eldest son: hence the difficulties with Miss Fa. But we also detect hints that Bao Mengyi and Zhang Lunying had to tread very carefully to negotiate their joint responsibilities in a household where an elder married sister remained in the household of a younger married brother. The relationship between a married woman and her husband's unmarried sisters was notoriously fraught, but at least it had a termination point in the case of conventional patrilocal marriage, since the sisters would eventually marry and leave the household. A uxorilocally married sister, on the other hand, was there to stay. The Zhang history does not contradict the rules of patrilineal descent; rather, it underscores both the flexibility of the Chinese family system, where descent rules bent far to accommodate local practice, financial need, taste, and affect, and the tensions inherent within it.[46] The lives of the Zhang and their talented progeny, in other words, reveal kin relations that complicate our understanding of the family system in late imperial China.

Women's Literary Culture

Thanks to the local culture, and to the reputation of the Zhang sisters and other local women writers, a distinctive model of cosmopolitan womanhood can be identified in Changzhou in the early nineteenth century. The Changzhou female literary patron Wanyan Yun Zhu married into the Manchu aristocracy and displayed in her anthologizing a keen interest in the civilizing project of the Qing court, celebrating the spread of Confucian values and culture among non-Han peoples.[47] The Zhang, as we have seen, extended their family networks into the circles of Korean literati. Like other women of the Lower Yangzi region during this period, Changzhou's women writers read widely in history and philosophy, carrying on the learning of their families, scornful of stereotypes that denigrated women's education.[48] As a home for talented women, Changzhou may be compared with the native place of another family of talented female writers, the Brontë sisters. Haworth and the environment where Charlotte, Emily, and Anne grew up could hardly contrast more sharply with the social and cultural milieu enjoyed by literati women (the *guixiu,* or gentlewomen) of early nineteenth-century Changzhou. The most striking of these contrasts is the density of human networks and relationships that nurtured and fed the talents of the Zhang daughters and their own talented offspring.[49] These were partially family networks, such that even in death and privation (which surely confronted the Zhang as often and as bitterly as they weighed on the Brontës), relatives by the score offered support and comfort. As we have seen, the women in this book spent much of their lives in the homes of extended kinfolk, and the Zhang family members seldom had a place to call a home of their own. Although this pattern of moving in and out of relatives' houses, rented spaces, and official residences may have taken its own toll, it spared the Zhang from the brooding, lonely silences that surround the writings of Charlotte Brontë, and it gave comfort in times of bereavement that the Brontës could never have hoped to find. The exception to this pattern in the history of the Zhang family is the plight of the widowed Wang Caipin after the Taiping Rebellion. In this respect, as in so many others, the rebellion tore a lasting rupture in the culture of the literati elite, both men's and women's.

A second dimension of the rich local culture that nurtured female talent in Changzhou, including the Zhang women, was the networks of intellectual and personal friendship that joined them with other writers, both male and female, who took an interest in their work and saw to its circulation and critical acclaim. These networks, thanks to the examination successes of Changzhou's local elite, reached all the way to the capital. China's late imperial culture as a whole may indeed have marginalized women's talent, if so grand a generalization can have any meaning at all. But Changzhou's local culture was probably one of the friendliest environments of its time for talented women, making it the ultimate colorful contrast with the dour environs of Haworth. In other words, in certain times and places, China's late imperial culture gave elite women choices and opportunities never imagined by their Western counterparts.

What became of Changzhou's history of female talent? Unlike the illustrious record of men's leadership in Changzhou culture, the history of Changzhou's elite women is barely known to contemporary observers, and apart from drawing the attention of a handful of scholars, it has been ignored.[50] The Changzhou women celebrated in recent historical memory have all been "new women," or modern revolutionaries, the most notable among them Chen Hengzhe (1890–1976)[51] and Shi Liang, mentioned in chapter 2. Both of them products of Westernized education and both deeply immersed in twentieth-century Chinese language and society, neither Chen nor Shi appears descended directly from the talented women who preceded them in Changzhou's nineteenth-century literary culture. Yet Chen had an aunt (*guma*) who taught her classical poetry and calligraphy in the Changzhou tradition (this was the elder sister of her husband's father, Chen Tao),[52] and Shi got her start at a school for girls in Changzhou. Thus even the ruptures that seem to divide Changzhou's modern women from their classically trained forebears point to continuities in their roles and status in China's most advanced cultural and economic regions, as they made the painful leap from the nineteenth century into the twentieth.[53]

Status and Gender

For the men of Changzhou, networks of patronage and clientage, like those on which Zhang Qi and his brother relied in their early careers, made it possible to meet leading scholars from all over the realm long before entering the empire-wide networks focused on the capital. One of the most striking features of those networks is their social range, which encompassed members of the lower and upper gentry and extended to foreigners as well. Bao Shichen, perhaps the best example of this networking in the Zhang family's experience, never held a formal office and did not even win a civil service degree. Yet his brilliance in both the arts and the study of statecraft made him a sought-after consultant to countless important officials and placed him at the center of lively intellectual circles. Through Bao Shichen, the name and reputation of the Zhang spread through circles of statecraft reformers in the mid-nineteenth century, with the result that Zeng Guofan, Feng Guifen (1809–1874), Hu Linyi, and other leaders of China's self-strengthening movement knew the names of the Zhang daughters and were among those invited to compose prefaces for their work. Li Zhaoluo and—through him and Bao Shichen—Ruan Yuan are among the other scholars of note whose fame attached itself to the Zhang family's own records.

These broad social contacts came at the cost of long years of living on the road and sojourning far from home. The high mortality rates among men and the prominence of widows in the Zhang family history are not unrelated, I think, to the peripatetic lives of scholars of this period. As I have reconstructed their stories, old age and childbirth were the main causes of death for adult women in the Zhang family.[54] The deaths in childbirth of his sister and his wife, I suggest, drove Zhang Yuesun to focus on gynecology in his own medical practice and publishing. Zhang menfolk, on the other hand, died prematurely with no reported cause. We do know that Zhang Qi's eldest son, Juesun, who perished at fourteen, was ill with a fever when he died. But regarding the cause of death of other Zhang males and kin (Sun Jie, Wang Xi, Zhang Yuesun, Zhang Jinli, Cheng Peiyuan—not to mention the Zhang grandfathers, and the husbands of the widows Bai and Jiang), we know nothing except that war was not responsible. (We also know that Bao Shichen died fleeing the Taiping, and Tang Yifen was killed in the siege of Nanjing.) The Zhang family's otherwise obsessively detailed memoirs supply no detail concerning the cause of death of many precious kinsmen. This is all the more puzzling because of the family's deep interest in medicine. It is possible that the cause of death was simply too delicate a matter to insert into a lasting memorial, out of consideration for the reputation of the physicians in charge. Readers will recall that no names were attached to the complaints about "mediocre physicians" responsible for the death of the young Zhang Juesun.

Left to her own devices, the historian can posit the causes of male mortality in the Zhang record using studies of the history of disease. Historians of medicine have identified a range of diseases endemic to the Jiangnan region in the nineteenth century, any one of which could explain the mortality rates we observe in the Zhang family history. Cholera, smallpox, chicken pox, measles, typhoid, dysentery, diphtheria, scarlet fever, and malaria were all common in the region where the Zhang spent most of their lives. Because of the climate and the pervasive waterways of Jiangnan, and because of the local practices of water use and consumption, which placed human waste and human use of water in close proximity, typhoid, cholera, and dysentery were especially widespread and were the most serious infectious diseases in that region.[55] Yu Xinzhong has identified outbreaks of cholera *(huoluan)* in Shanghai in the early 1860s, leading me to conjecture that this may have caused the death of both Zhang Yuesun and his son.[56] Diphtheria was commonly a fall and winter disease, while scarlet fever outbreaks were concentrated in the spring and summer, so the season also gives us some parameters for guessing the cause of death.[57] And malaria was so widespread in the Changzhou area that the prescribed treatment took advantage of the close ties among affinal kin in the local culture. For instance, in Changshu, when a child under the age of 4 or 5 *sui* contracted malaria, a relative from the child's mother's natal family was expected to come and offer a sacrifice before the stove god in the child's home.[58]

Zhang male relatives who died before their time probably died of these infectious diseases. And that calls attention to one of the unsung advantages of being a *guixiu*. Living a cloistered life at home with the children, surrounded by pathogens that were familiar and consuming food and drink prepared in their own kitchens, the Changzhou *guixiu* could expect to live a long life. By contrast, Changzhou's menfolk, who spent a great part of their time out on the road, exposed to all manner of crowded inns, new germs, unfamiliar water, and food prepared by strangers, were constantly vulnerable to the endemic diseases that eventually took most of their lives. Zhang Yuesun, the hardiest among them, complained constantly of illness, and accounts of his childhood describe him as sickly. Perhaps he suffered from malaria; he is frequently described in the family's records as "lying abed ill" or "returned home sick."

In sum, the Zhang family's record, with its relatively high male mortality rates, hints at a broader pattern of elite family practice in the late empire: a pattern of sojourning males and sequestered females that protected the health of cloistered upper-class women while constantly exposing their traveling menfolk to the threat of premature death from disease.

With their scholarly authority and their critical stance when it came to politics, the Zhang brothers were linked to two related yet discrete reformist discourses in the official world. The first was an agrarian reformist group associated with Bao Shichen, whose special interest in grain transport and agricultural output led to his successful career as a professional policy advisor to officials who had to deal with practical administrative problems at posts along the Grand Canal and in Nanjing.[59] The second was a cluster of officials who were drawn to Western learning, especially science and mathematics. This group included Li Zhaoluo and his pupil Feng Guifen. Agrarian reformers and experts in foreign affairs were drawn together inexorably during the mid-nineteenth century, if only to deal with the practical problems of transporting the imperial grain tribute by sea, for during the collapse of the Grand Canal transport system in the 1820s due to silting, transporting the grain required intelligence, maps, and other information about seafaring in the coastal waters where Western warships and commercial vessels were active.[60] During the Opium War, the influence of the Changzhou song lyric school inspired writers to compose patriotic song lyrics in response to the new problems they faced.[61]

Did these prestigious scholarly connections place the Zhang among the "governing class"? We have seen how difficult it is to characterize the "class" of the Zhang family. To be sure, they belonged to the elite. Yet their lives were insecure and peripatetic, except when they attached themselves to wealthier families who could employ teachers or support guests in residence. Only late in life, and then under great strain, did the heads of families like the Zhang win the prize of their labor: a government office. How, then, did they continue to define and even reinvent themselves as members of the elite? The Zhang history gives us several answers to this question. Men had to be versatile and ingenious in using their talent in order to maintain their reputation for learning. Thus we see the Zhang men shifting nimbly from study, scholarship, and writing to teaching or to technical or managerial work or to medical practice. Men also had to know how to cultivate patrons—to be a collegial member of a scholarly circle or a sociable and cultivated "guest in residence" in an official mansion. Women committed to the same standards had other roles to play. They had to be scrupulous about sexual purity and social propriety. They had to be resigned to the constraints of gender segregation. They had to be quick learners, both in the arts and in crafts (sewing or weaving and embroidery). They had to be as dedicated as their male partners to maintaining elite status, and their dedication was crucial at every turn. A final key element in the reproduction of status for the Zhang was their denial of commercial interests. Lunying's well-known popularity as a calligrapher is never directly tied to profit making.[62]

The versatile careers of the various Zhang men and their affines and in-laws give us new insight into the vagaries of literati status in the nineteenth century. Much has been written about changing employment opportunities in that period: the expansion of commercial networks, the foreclosure of official appointments and examination options, the lure of new jobs in the treaty port sector, and also surges in emigration from coastal areas in the southeast. But what we see in the sources describing the careers of Zhang Qi and Zhang Yuesun, and Xu Zhenyi as well, is something else. We see the costs of the steady deterioration of social order and economic security in the countryside, costs that were borne largely by officials posted to remote or difficult areas. In Zhang Qi's case, public office required him to deploy a new range of skills and technical expertise, confronting the overwhelming tasks of famine relief, tax collection, and jurisprudence as a hapless county magistrate in a region where the social fabric was unraveling. Ironically for Zhang Qi, the medical training and expertise he acquired as a sideline to his scholarly education turned out to be one of the most practical and useful parts of his long years of study. Medical training demanded health-care delivery, which prompted Zhang Qi to open a medical clinic in his first permanent public office. That clinic, we know, was a key to the strong support he enjoyed among the local population when he tackled his other problems.

For Zhang Yuesun, the sudden call to military duty just after he took office in Wuchang required instant mastery of strategies of defense and siege warfare, and the development of all kinds of new communications skills, from appeals to the higher administration for military aid to calls to town and village leaders in the surrounding countryside for local mobilization of militia defense forces. And according to the epitaph written by his close friend Zhuang Shouqi, at the end of his life Zhang Yuesun was being asked to enter yet another new field, foreign trade management, for which he was at best marginally prepared.

The defining characteristic of elite status in the nineteenth century for men remained the capacity to pursue scholarship in any form while staying attuned to the practical writings of officials engaged in problem solving in the field. To women fell the other parts of the support system: instructing the young (thus women too had to have an excellent education), exhorting the lazy and inept, and managing scant resources so that education was a priority. Furthermore, the women themselves labored, in housework but also in manual production of embroidery and other kinds of textile work to support themselves and their children when their menfolk were away or unemployed, or to pay for the other things respectable elite families had to spend money on, particularly rituals and the entertainment of the friends, mentors, patrons, and relatives who could further the careers of their menfolk. In sum, women who married into scholarly families like the Zhang had to resign themselves to privations associated with that lifestyle even while committing themselves wholeheartedly to its values. As a compensation for these stressful conditions, the luxuries of *yamen* life that every official's family expected offered a kind of hardship pay for the burdens the menfolk took on. For the Zhang, servants and spacious quarters, gardeners and porters and sedan chair carriers and cooks, the secluded elegance of inner courtyards, the pomp of rank and power—all these brought a reprieve of ease and comfort to lives that, especially for the women, demanded constant self-denial.

Being on the road was a way of life not only for Zhang Qi but also for his son and his sons-in-law. Their travels, occasionally chronicled in poems that sound, on first reading, like delightful travel diaries, show the range of their quest for work. Travel was expensive, dangerous, and—as the disease and death rate among the Zhang makes clear—a risk to one's health.[63] Measured in these terms, we can see what a struggle it was to maintain status and perform class identity in nineteenth-century Jiangnan literati culture. In the tenor of the Zhang family women's commitment to this lifestyle in the face of overwhelming odds—especially as widows—we see their very realistic grasp of what the struggle entailed and how much it would cost them.

Also evident in the Zhang family record is the way in which, because of the hypergynous workings of the family system, women could "move up" through servitude, concubinage, and marriage, sometimes crossing status boundaries as they went. The life of Yuesun's concubine, Li Luan, illuminates this process. Her background as the daughter of a personal servant in the county *yamen* placed her firmly in the class of manual laborers, from whom the Zhang kept a determined distance. Li Luan's entry into the Zhang household as a concubine, on the other hand, immediately freed her from the stigma of manual labor—her mother's explicit aim in making the match—even while her status set her apart from the other Zhang women and their daughters. Other factors complicated her position. The first was her age: she entered the Zhang household in the same generation as her master's daughter, which made it possible for the family to treat her as something like a cousin to the children of Yuesun and his sisters. That is how she appears in the *Dihua guan* poetry collection and in the affectionate poems addressed to her by Caipin and the other female cousins. So among the younger generation to which she belonged, Li Luan was embraced and welcomed.

Not so among her elders, the sisters of Zhang Yuesun. We have observed the complex negotiations required of the Zhang sisters and their sisters-in-law because of uxorilocal marriage and the presence of a faithful maiden in the household. Tensions erupted in Bao Mengyi's relationship to Miss Fa, as we have seen. But they did not end there. Lunying, too, had to be careful about her relationship to her brother's wife. Wanying comments specifically in a memoir for Mengyi that her sister Lunying, who was almost ten years older than Mengyi, took care to be absolutely and consistently deferential to her younger sister-in-law, in order to ensure that the household was harmonious.[64] Once Mengyi was dead and Miss Fa had departed, on the other hand, the domestic power of Yuesun's sisters, especially that of the elder, Lunying, was completely unchecked. Thus it was Lunying who made the arrangements to purchase Li Luan from her willing parents. The power of Yuesun's sisters over his concubine is displayed coolly in an encomium on the *Dihua guan* collection, where Wanying remarks with unembarrassed condescension that Li Luan's poetry skills were coming along well, considering she'd had only three years of training at the hands of her betters. Such criticism is never seen in a preface to published poetry. (Wanying wrote: "Ziqi [Li Luan's courtesy name] is meek and demure although lacking in spirit. She is well aware of her shortcomings and strives to be rid of them in order to realize her utmost potential. Although her learning is limited, she always succeeds in what she sets out to do. All the other girls encourage her.")[65] Finally, of course, Yuesun's own emotions and desires figure in Li Luan's fate. Like his nieces and daughter, Yuesun seems to have grown very attached to Li Luan. Moreover, he was completely free to develop this attachment in the wake of Mengyi's death. Yuesun also secured his concubine's future in the best way he could by betrothing the daughter she bore him to a son of his closest friend, Zhuang Shouqi. This arrangement paid off later with a handsome reward, when Li Luan's son-in-law, Zhuang Yuntai, rose to a position of the fourth rank in the imperial bureaucracy and his wife's mother received the prestigious title of *gongren* (Respectful Lady).[66]

Li Luan's privileged position as Yuesun's concubine contrasts poignantly with the fate of Wang Xi's concubine, who is barely mentioned in the family's writings. Wanying herself refers to the concubine by her given name in a short poem written to her husband while he was off teaching in Dongchang during their sojourn in Shandong. Wanying gives the poem to the concubine (whom she refers to as a *bi*, or "maid") to take to her husband, dispatching her to keep him company on his travels and observing pointedly in a note to the poem that the maid was a gift to her from her sister-in-law Mengyi.[67] I suspect that the gift arrived on the occasion of Wanying's fortieth birthday, perhaps because at the age of forty a *guixiu* might gracefully withdraw from sexual intercourse and the risk of further pregnancies, and the gift of a concubine would be an apt token of that rite of passage. In the years before Wang Xi died, the concubine bore him three sons and a daughter, but—in a further telling comment on this concubine's lack of influence—the marital status of these children is not preserved in family records. By contrast, Wanying's only birth son, Chenbi, was married to Yuesun's elder daughter, and Wanying's four daughters each made a proper match.

In other words, within the Zhang family, the status of a concubine was very much a function of the power of the women in the household.[68] As the presiding female, Bao Mengyi could claim the prerogative of presenting a concubine to her husband's elder sister as a sign of respect. By the same token, had she lived, Mengyi doubtless would have curbed or checked her husband's attachment to the concubine Li Luan—or, indeed, prevented him from taking a concubine altogether.[69] After Bao Mengyi's death, when Lunying moved into the senior position and purchased a concubine for her brother, Li Luan's age as well as her inferior status (she was only seventeen *sui* when she entered the Zhang household) ensured that she would pose no threat to Lunying's power. This still left Li Luan free to cultivate an affectionate and close relationship with her husband as well as with his daughter and his nieces. Wanying, by contrast, outlived her husband, marginalizing his concubine while Wang Xi lived and (perhaps) benignly neglecting the fate of the concubine's children after Wang Xi died. We know nothing, for instance, of marriage arrangements for the concubine's offspring.

If females entered the Zhang household through concubinage and marriage, males entered through uxorilocal marriage or adoption, or through a temporary arrangement such as Tang Yaoqing's fostering of Qian Zizhen. Formal adoption of males across patrilines within a lineage in order to "get an heir" was very common among the Zhang. In fact, two adoptions in a row were necessary to continue Zhang Yuesun's line after his death, since his only son died with him. The Tang, on Zhang Qi's wife's side, also practiced adoption across patrilines on a regular basis. In all cases, they adhered strictly to the legal and ritual injunction that an adopted heir must come from the same lineage.[70] Such adoptions did not involve class or status mobility. They were quite different in kind from the social mobility of the concubine Li Luan, who left her status group behind. The fluidity of female status illustrated by Li Luan is probably part of what made uxorilocal marriage such an appealing arrangement for Changzhou families like the Zhang. Even though Lunying's marriage was far from ideal, having her rather feckless husband, who never could have supported her, move into the Zhang household ensured that one of the Zhang daughters would not slip down the status hierarchy. The careful placement of elite women in marriage emerges here as another key piece in the fragile yet resilient scaffolding that kept the Zhang where they were.

A final piece of the puzzle concerning women and the maintenance of elite status is the inordinate concern we see regarding the economic and social security of women without husbands. Miss Fa is the most extreme example of the lengths to which elite families went to stabilize the status of their women. But the widow halls, and the genteel employment of governesses like Wang Caipin, which became increasingly common in the aftermath of the Taiping Rebellion, remind us that maintaining and performing class identity was a corporate project to which all members of the elite—male and female—subscribed.

CRISIS AND CHANGE IN THE NINETEENTH CENTURY

In concluding, the historian must return to the temporal context of the nineteenth century. The century begins with Tang Yaoqing in her prime, her classical education and her values the key to her marital family's success and her own honor. The century ends with the death of Wang Caipin, on the brink of a crisis that called into question every premise of Caipin's classical education and her womanly values.

Mid-Qing Rebellions and Rural Unrest

Zhang Qi's short-lived official career pulled him out of his Lower Yangzi homeland in his final years and consigned him to life in one of the country's poorest regions—Shandong, home to decades of rebel movements and agrarian destitution. In reading his reflections on those years, we see how well prepared he was to cope with the challenges he faced. He knew the techniques and the language for dealing with ordinary people and their problems; he knew the bureaucratic procedures for handling flood and drought control; he was clever in his manipulation of popular beliefs to serve official ends; and he was a no-nonsense judge in the courtroom, never taken in by smooth-talking litigators. Even allowing for his wish to present himself as competent, and taking into account the terrible stress (his hair turned white in the space of a year), we have to be impressed that he managed the task at all, given the privileges he had enjoyed as a highly educated person throughout his life. How did he learn all of that? In the family's records, Zhang Qi is lauded exclusively for his literary talent, his medical skills, and his devotion to calligraphy. Nowhere are we told that he read magistrate's casebooks or studied statecraft policies or was fascinated by administrative problems. His most likely source of advice and counsel was his friend Bao Shichen, whose reputation for administrative problem solving was legendary and whose writings ranged over every possible topic in current affairs.[71] The other source of Zhang Qi's commitment to public service and concern for local governance must have been his own brother. Zhang Huiyan's studies of ritual took a pragmatic view of court and family ritual as the mechanism by which the government encouraged and nurtured the innate moral proclivities of its subjects. In particular, Zhang Huiyan's specialized writings on the local security system of mutual surveillance called *baojia* advocated leadership by members of the local gentry instead of rotating responsibility among commoner households.[72]

The problems Zhang Qi faced in office, daunting as they were, appeared routine to him. He had no sense of impending doom, no inkling of massive official incompetence, no need to concern himself with anything beyond the welfare of his county and the future of his family. Still, he was part of a network of scholars who were critical of governmental corruption, skeptical of the value and meaning of the civil service examinations, and deeply interested in medicine and the healing arts as an antidote to the social and economic problems of the time. He was also well connected with scholars like Li Zhaoluo, whose ties to the southeast coast and its problems had led them to study problems and peoples beyond China's borders.[73] But concern about the foreigners or foreign invasion is hard to find in the writings of Zhang Qi. Indeed, right through the period of the Opium War, after an outcry over Lin Zexu's plight and a short-lived panic during the British invasion of Lower Yangzi cities, the Zhang family did not pay much attention to the foreigners who arrived in the newly opened treaty ports after 1842. Yuesun's close friendship with Yi Sang-jŏk and Li Zhaoluo's undying curiosity about the "countries across the sea" point to a positive interest in foreigners and a remarkable lack of condescension toward or alienation from persons who were not imperial subjects. Changzhou lay beyond the line of the British movement up the Yangzi in the first phase of the war, so Changzhou residents escaped the fighting that took such a toll in Zhenjiang. Whether the bloodbath at Zhenjiang affected the Zhang family's feelings about the Manchu Banners as a defense force and Manchu leadership in general, we do not know. It was the Taiping rebels who posed a threat that they could comprehend.

The Impact of the Taiping Rebellion

Readers will recall Wang Caipin's reaction to her aunt's distress when Taiping armies pushed all the way to the gates of Tianjin. To the best of our knowledge, however, Caipin never lived close to the actual fighting. By contrast, because Wuchang fell early in the Taiping advance, Zhang Yuesun saw the rebellion at its most violent extreme. His horror of the barbarism of the Taiping only fueled his bitter disillusionment with the leadership that failed to put them down. Those feelings, which were politically dangerous, might never have seen print had he not been able to confide in his Korean friend Yi Sang-jŏk.[74] After Wuchang's capture, the Taiping assault on Jiujiang was followed in 1852 and 1853 by the rapid fall of Nanjing, Zhenjiang, and Yangzhou. This put the Zhang's native place of Changzhou in great danger. In fact, Changzhou was passed over in the early years of the advance as the rebels strategized to seize key cities. Only much later, after Manchu battalions drove Taiping armies back out of Hangzhou, in the second month of 1860, did those armies finally attack Changzhou. Governor-General He Guiqing, charged with defending the city, sized up the situation and decided to flee. Guards escorting him shot their way out of town, killing many people in their path. For six days Changzhou's beleaguered townsfolk held off the Taiping assault. Twenty thousand people died in the fighting, and just as many committed suicide when the Taiping forces finally poured through the gates and over the walls.[75]

The collapse of Suzhou that same year galvanized others in the Zhang's literary and political circles. The collapse also brought new leadership to the fore, including the eloquent statecraft scholar Feng Guifen, whose flight to Shanghai made him the first to plead with Zeng Guofan to come to the defense of the Lower Yangzi region. That plea brought Li Hongzhang to Jiangsu just before Zhang Yuesun, his name now clear of the false embezzlement charges brought against him, was himself transferred to Shanghai in 1863. A year after Yuesun died, shortly after arriving at his new post, Li

Hongzhang's troops drove the Taiping out of Shanghai's hinterland for good, freeing Changzhou and marking the beginning of the end of the civil war.[76] In the aftermath of the fighting, a commemorative stele placed before the shrine honoring the martyrs at Changzhou estimated the loss of lives at more than one hundred thousand.[77]

Dislocation and the Destruction of Writings and Literary Networks   The tragedies of the Taiping Rebellion are well recognized in histories of nineteenth-century China. The impact of the disaster on the Zhang family was personal, taking the lives of loved ones and turning the entire family into refugees. At the same time, it reveals effects of the rebellion and its spread that demographic and military statistics cannot convey. Most stunning among the costs is the complete obliteration of the rich written record of their intimate lives. Zhang Yuesun's books burned in the fall of Wuchang, and his entire collection was lost save a few precious volumes. Some of the family's works were later reprinted from surviving woodblocks, or recopied and reissued. But those reprintings from the 1860s and 1890s leave us only with records of the period before the rebellion. The turmoil of the rebellion and the subsequent recovery period was so great, and the shock so deep, that few had the emotional wherewithal to return to writing as they had once done it. Readers who locate sources printed from that period are more likely to find captivity narratives than poetry collections.

Wang Caipin, whose collected poems are among the few surviving Zhang family mementos of the post-Taiping era, could barely bring herself to write after her uncle's death in 1863. The end of Zhang Yuesun's life seems to have been synonymous, in her mind, with the end of an era. In post-Taiping China, much more so than in post–9-11 America, people felt they were living in a different world. For many, the practical needs of survival dominated all else after the rebellion. Wang Caipin's employer, Xu Zhenyi, remarks that Caipin had to spend the last three decades of her life struggling to support herself. With her parents-in-law deceased and her natal family scattered, and lacking a spouse or an heir, Caipin was completely on her own. One suspects that many literati families like Xu's felt obliged to assist the widows of officials and scholars who had failed to survive the Taiping Rebellion years. At the same time, one may detect in Wang Caipin's life a growing trend for educated women to seek income through respectable employment. Zhang Lunying's calligraphy was one such source. Wang Caipin's talents as a governess served her equally well, and they put a roof over her head in years when she lacked a family home.[78]

These costs of the rebellion are just beginning to attract scholarly attention. Benjamin Elman has commented that the "relatively secular learned community that encouraged and rewarded with livelihoods original and rigorous critical scholarship" had, by Zhang Yuesun's time, developed "an almost autonomous subsystem of Ch'ing society with its own marks of status . . . in the Yangtze delta." This academic community, whose intellectual legacy long outlived it, "perished during the Taiping Rebellion."[79] However, contemporaries were well aware of these costs of the rebellion. The anthologist and bibliophile Jin Wuxiang remarked after the rebellion on how many scholars from the Lower Yangzi turned to military careers during the Xianfeng and Tongzhi reigns because of the Taiping and *nian* rebellions.[80] Zhang Yuesun is a fine example of what Jin was talking about.

Crisis of Confidence in Manchu Leadership   In Zhang Yuesun's candid letters to his Korean friend Yi Sang-jŏk, we see vividly the costs of the Taiping Rebellion through an official's eyes. Yuesun certainly was not prepared to lead a military campaign when he accepted his post in Wuchang. He was a paragon of literati virtue: gifted in poetry, skilled in calligraphy, an amateur painter, an accomplished physician, and an enterprising literary critic and publisher. Yet once the city in his charge was threatened, he seems to have been remarkably successful in obtaining military intelligence and seeking sound military advice. This was due, no doubt, to his solid connections to the statecraft networks that were coalescing around strategies for local defense, in response to the bungling by the central government's armies. Although anti-Manchu sentiment cannot exactly be inferred from Yuesun's scathing indictments of official ineptitude, which he hurled liberally against Han and Manchu alike, he was unquestionably appalled at the central government's inability to rout the rebels, and at the manifest cowardice of commanders specially delegated by the court to lead the defense of local communities.

Local records of the rebellion show that anti-Manchu sentiment did in fact emerge in the area around Changzhou, especially in the wake of the fall of Zhenjiang and the massacre of the Banner troops stationed there, who were thought to be the sure protection of the entire Lower Yangzi area. Thousands were trapped inside walled cities that had been sealed off by the officials in charge, dooming the population inside to almost certain death under siege. As reports of massacres circulated in advance of the Taiping armies, fear and panic spread. It is possible, as Mark Elliott has argued, that latent anti-Manchu sentiment dating from the first deployment of Manchu banners to Jiangnan revived and stayed alive after the Manchu garrison lost Zhenjiang to advancing British troops during the Opium War.[81] The writings of the Zhang family, especially those by Qieying and Yuesun, allude to failed leadership during the Opium War and the Taiping Rebellion, and the officials they criticize are overwhelmingly Manchu. Still, it is hard to read anti-Manchu consciousness into their words.

Mary Rankin's study of shifting political consciousness in Zhejiang, to the southeast, locates the rise of anti-Manchu sentiment there relatively late, in the period of the Boxer Uprising of 1900.[82] Consciousness about Manchu ethnic identity and its political meanings may have come late to Zhejiang because the Taiping devastation there was relatively short-lived, concentrated mainly in the last years of the rebellion, between 1861 and 1864. As we saw earlier, the Taiping forces turned their final fury on Changzhou and Lower Yangzi cities in Jiangsu precisely because of the vigorous resistance at Hangzhou and elsewhere in Zhejiang. The Lower Yangzi basin, in contrast, fell victim early to the Taiping assault. The fall of Yuezhou in 1853 sent Taiping armies pouring directly into downriver cities along the Yangzi, and although some cities that fell early were retaken once or even twice by imperial troops, the specter of government weakness played out time and again before panicked Lower Yangzi residents. Even so, anti-Manchu sentiment seems to have been less salient than a general frustration with the inefficacy of the court's military leadership, at least in the records of the Zhang family.

Talented Women in Times of Trouble

One of the most striking fallouts from the politics of the mid-nineteenth century is the reemergence of women's political poetry, a phenomenon seen in the fall of previous dynasties but never so articulate and pronounced as in the period beginning with the Opium War and continuing through the fall of the Qing dynasty.[83] In the case of the Zhang women, it is clear that serendipity, in the form of connections through male relatives, played a crucial role in their rising awareness of the empire's political crises. Qieying, as a patron of female poets in Beijing, was also associated with one of the most politically astute women residing there: Shen Shanbao. Caipin, isolated by her widowhood and by the post-Taiping devastation, seems to have written largely to an imagined audience consisting of her aunt and uncle. Even so, her impassioned political poems reveal the deep influence of political discussions in her family and of information gleaned from the letters and poems sent by her aunt and uncle during the most critical years of the Taiping Rebellion.

Both Zhang Qieying and Wang Caipin were honored for their poetry by "new women" of the next century. Zhang Qieying and her sisters are listed, for example, in an early twentieth-century catalog of "female literary heroines" of the past.[84] Some of Wang Caipin's poems were published, along with her Uncle Yuesun's critical comments, in the "Writers' Garden" feature of the early issues of the *Women's Journal (Funü zazhi)*, printed between 1915 and 1920, a period when the talented women of Caipin's time were still celebrated.[85] As they tell their stories across three generations, the Zhang women whose lives fill this book also show us how changes in nineteenth-century China—changes wrought by war, colonialism, economic crisis, and political strife—affected women's consciousness, their life chances, and what they chose to write about. The stories of Tang Yaoqing and her granddaughter Wang Caipin show us how dramatic these changes were. Tang Yaoqing is firmly grounded in the literati culture of the High Qing era; Wang Caipin, in her life, her writings, and her politics, is on the cusp of the next century.

Why Women Were Not a Problem in the Nineteenth Century

The talented women of the Zhang family flourished at a critical point in the history of Chinese women. The culture and society of the nineteenth century valorized women's roles in domestic economies and labor, both productive and reproductive. Patrilocal marriage was accompanied by a dowry system and a system of women's managerial household production that secured each woman's place in the domestic economy by supplying a fund of wealth to serve the interests of a vast woman-centered network.[86] The debates about learned women that flared up at the end of the eighteenth century had subsided, and the "woman problem" *(funü wenti)* that dominated elite discourses of the early twentieth century had yet to surface. In the nineteenth century, "women" as figures of controversy or as subjects of historical change were almost invisible.

As a result, one can read histories of nineteenth-century China by the tome—whether written in English or in Chinese—without finding women mentioned at all before the 1890s. Christian missionaries had Chinese women much on their minds from their first entry into China, and during the last half of the nineteenth century they wrote earnestly and urgently about the need to educate young girls, unbind their feet, and release them from the confines of the home and the oppressive structures of the Chinese family system. But these foreigners' concerns went largely unheeded by China's educated elite—male or female.[87]

The turning point came four years after Wang Caipin's death, when Liang Qichao (1873–1929) published his "General Discussion on Reform" ("Bianfa tongyi"), in which he devoted a special section to "women's learning" *(nüxue)*. Liang's sweeping blueprint for saving the empire located "the very source of China's cumulative weakness" in the lack of women's education.[88] It was this salvo that opened the discourse on the "woman problem" that occupied China's twentieth-century reformers and revolutionaries. Liang Qichao's tract did not specify which women he was talking about, but it is clear that he had in mind *guixiu* writers—the very *cainü* who are the subject of this book—and he singled out for ridicule their finest achievement, classical poetry, which he dismissed as "ditties on the wind and moon."[89] Others quickly joined Liang's criticism of classically educated women of talent. Among them was Kang Youwei's (1858–1927) influential daughter Kang Tongwei (1879–1974), who accused *guixiu* writers of chasing fame and adulation at the expense of their virtue. Immodest posturing of that sort, she wrote, had no place in an age of crisis; in fact, it invited men to restrict women's activities even further.[90] Of course, the reader of the present book can see that such attacks on women's learning were rhetorical sleights of hand. They erased elite women's poetry on politics, maritime affairs, and the defense of the country, as well as the historical changes in women's consciousness that produced those poems. Liang's and Kang's attacks also erased the countless differences of status and region that made the category "women" problematic.[91] Yet the words of Liang Qichao and his followers found a ready audience. "Women" were made a fulcrum of China's nation-building project because their roles in the old empire, in Liang's view, rendered them useless for the challenges facing the new nation. Educating women as the good wives and wise mothers of future citizens and putting them to productive work in the factories of an industrializing country became twin goals of the late Qing reform effort.[92]

To grasp the radical nature of this shift, we must recall how central elite women's education was to family, society, and the polity in the Qing period. Without question, in nineteenth-century China women's learning was intimately tied to the state of the country. If the shape of the polity was to change, so, inevitably, must women's learning. Let us consider again how "learning" secured elite women's integral place in family, society, and the polity of the Qing empire.

Throughout most of the nineteenth century, an elite woman's learning was essential to the maintenance of her family's status in the scholarly world, and this learning included all the techniques of family financial management.[93] Women in elite families were responsible for marshalling the resources that would keep their menfolk free to travel about in search of respectable employment, patronage, and connections, and, of course, to study and sit for the examinations. In other words, a *guixiu* was expected to maintain her household in the absence of a male wage earner. As we have seen, the absent men often failed to send money. This was partly because their income was low, often paid in kind in the form of room and board, so to speak; partly because reliable methods for remitting funds were limited; and partly because elite men expected their women to make do without them—that is, they were ready to rely on the labor, dowry, and invested income of their wives and mothers. Elite women, in other words, were an essential part of the masking process that shielded every scholarly family's commercial activities from view. It was elite women, and not men, who took primary responsibility for the many contracts and exchanges that brought cash into the home, and for the proto-industrial and artistic commodities (embroidery, calligraphy, decorative arts, and fashion design) that the household sent to market. Women kept the accounts, performed the manual labor, executed the works of art, and marketed the products of their labor. Their menfolk saw to it that praise for their virtue found its way into the historical record. If a deal was struck, if money changed hands, if interest was earned, if profits were made, no one had to be told. Hence Zhang Qi's continued assurances to us, his readers, that his wife was skillful in concealing the family's poverty and that all were deceived by her genteel dissembling and her boundless generosity. Learned women of elite families like the Zhang understood full well the conflation of moral rectitude and practical skill represented in the womanly Confucian virtues. They knew that the family's status and security depended on those virtues.

The urgent investment of every mother in the education and dowering of a daughter was a tactic designed to secure the daughter's future in the context of her marital family and its heirs. Aunts and grandmothers took a similar interest in their nieces and granddaughters. These investments in education gave young women practical and social skills in both manual and mental labor. They learned how to invest money, earn interest, produce goods and services and artwork, and collect commercial profits. The social skills of well-mannered and intellectually conversant women enabled them to cultivate relationships and build elaborate far-flung networks of kinfolk, friends, and patrons. These networks in turn facilitated the circulation of gifts, credit, services, and clientage on which women's income and profit making depended. In this manner, the circles of women's connections remained unbroken and kept expanding. Writings by and about learned women largely skirt these topics. In the case of the Zhang, they hint, they tease, and they deny, comfortably screening commercial interests and the marketing of products of manual labor and artistic creativity with the rhetoric of Confucian virtue and womanly conduct.

In sum, if the governing class of scholar-officials was the bedrock of the Qing imperial system, then womanly virtue and womanly managerial skills were central to it. Inevitably, then, those womanly virtues and skills would be devalued in the wrenching transition after 1895, when the education and functions of scholar-officials like Zhang Qi and Zhang Yuesun lost their meaning. Classical scholarship, song lyric writing, literati medicine, calligraphy—such pursuits had no utility in the twentieth-century drive for modern industry; military strength; new enterprises such as banking, railways, shipping; and new professions such as journalism, science, law.[94] Like the men, women needed a new learning for the new age.

The vast literature describing this transition has focused attention on the "new woman" invented to accommodate the changing times, with barely a backward glance at the *guixiu* who are the subject of this book. As a result, like Liang Qichao, historians have tended to dismiss the significance of learned women and their place in the polity of nineteenth-century China.

The distinctive voice of the woman writer *(nü zuojia)* that emerges so clearly in the early twentieth century is not easily heard during the nineteenth century, even among the talented women of the Zhang family. Anthologizing and the protocols of publication deferred heavily to the classical canon, dominated by male writers. Still, womanly voices sound distinctly in the late writings of the Zhang family women during the times of trouble that followed the Opium War. The dynastic crisis gave them a legitimate venue for adopting the voice of the woman warrior from classical precedent and historical example[95] while safely winning the praise of their male critics. The strong twentieth-century woman writer's voice is doubtless a consequence of women's coming into consciousness of themselves as citizens of a new nation, which also called them to an awareness of their place in a gendered constituency separate from men, with a literary voice and political and economic roles all their own. Many of these writers, Qiu Jin among them, read and were inspired by the writings of the late Qing *guixiu*.

How dramatically the transition from empire to nation affected every aspect of the history of Chinese women has barely begun to be understood. Late imperial thought and culture valorized and celebrated women's domestic labor as well as women's talent on a scale that the modern nation-state has never matched. As for historical change, the talented women of the Zhang family show us that nineteenth-century *guixiu* were becoming "new women" all along.

ZHANG FAMILY CHRONOLOGY

Note: Age in Chinese reckoning was calculated by taking the lunar year of one's birth as year one and adding a year at each lunar New Year's Day. On average, therefore, a Chinese child is about a year older in *sui* than she would be if her birthdays were counted by the Western pattern, and in cases where birth occurs late in a lunar year, the difference may be nearly two years.

1733   Zhang Jindi, paternal grandfather of Zhang Qi, dies at the age of 35.

1736   Mother of Zhang Qi (née Jiang) is born.

1759   Paternal grandmother of Zhang Qi (née Bai) dies (March 28) at the age of 64.

1761   Zhang Huiyan is born (July 11).

1763   Tang Yaoqing is born (third month).

1764   Zhang Chanbin (Zhang Qi's father) dies.

1765   Zhang Qi is born (5 January).

1769   Li Zhaoluo is born.

1771   Tang Dashen, Tang Yaoqing's grandfather, dies at the age of 74; Tang Yaoqing's father moves the family to live with the Qian and enters a three-year period of mourning.

1774   Huiyan begins teaching (at 14 *sui*).

1775   Bao Shichen is born in the Jing district of Anhui. Sometime in the period between 1775 and 1785, the elder sister of Huiyan and Qi marries Dong Dingyuan. The sister's mother-in-law, a Qian, is particularly fond of Lady Jiang (her daughter-in-law's mother), and she makes a house available for her and her sons, so they can move back into the city.

1785   Deng Shiru (seal carver and calligrapher) meets Zhang Huiyan and Zhang Qi at the home of Jin Bang (1735–1801) in Huizhou, Anhui. Wu Zan is born. A famine strikes Changzhou, where Jin Yunhuai is serving as magistrate. In the autumn, the Zhang brothers move to Huizhou, probably through a Jin connection.

1786   Zhang Huiyan attains the *juren* degree. Tang Yaoqing's great-uncle and uncle are killed in the Lin Shuangwen rebellion in Taiwan.

1787   Zhang Huiyan tutors in the school for Manchu bannermen in the Forbidden City, where he meets Yun Jing, who becomes his lifelong friend. Zhang Qi first begins to study poetry, according to his self-preface to his collected poetry.

1788   Zhang Qi becomes a licentiate of the first class *(xiucai)*. A famine spreads throughout Jiangnan.

1789   Zhang Qi (age 24) and Tang Yaoqing (age 27) are married; Huiyan's son (Chengsun) is born.

1790/91 Zhang Juesun is born.

1792   Qieying is born.

1794   Mme. Jiang (Zhang Qi's mother) dies (November 10) at the age of 59, her life span corresponding almost exactly to the reign of the Qianlong Emperor. Huiyan returns home for the funeral.

1795   Guanying is born.

1796   Zhang Huiyan works in the office of Yun Jing while the latter serves as magistrate of Jiangshan, Zhejiang. Together, the two become known as the founders of the *guwen* (ancient-style prose) writers school known as the Yanghu *pai.* Lu Wenchao dies in the middle of compiling a new gazetteer for Changzhou, dooming Tang Yaoqing's father's project.

1797   Zhang Qi goes to She *xian,* Anhui, having buried his mother in this same year, to join his brother teaching. There he befriends Bao Shichen, who is working for Zhu Gui while Zhu is governor of Anhui, at his office in Anqing. Bao Shichen's adopted daughter later marries Zhang Yuesun. While in She *xian,* Zhang Qi and Zhang Huiyan complete their famous anthology of song lyrics *(ci),* titled *Ci xuan.* Sun Jie is born (December 11).

1798   Lunying is born. Lady Jiang receives an imperial commendation as a faithful widow.

1799   The Qianlong Emperor dies; his favorite courtier, Heshen, falls from power, opening the way for reform. Huiyan attains *jinshi* with Zhu Gui and Ruan Yuan supervising the examinations, enters the Hanlin Academy, and moves his wife and son to the capital; Qi's family remains in Huizhou. Tang Yaoqing's father, Tang Xiuye, dies in the first month, his death coinciding with the death of the Qianlong Emperor.

1800   Wanying is born.

1801   Jin Bang dies; Zhang Qi returns from Huizhou to Changzhou.

1802	Huiyan dies in Beijing. Meanwhile, Bao Shichen has settled in Yangzhou and Shanghai (1801/2); Zhang Qi visits him en route back to his old home. Bao lives for a time in the home of Li Zhaoluo in Changzhou.
1803	Juesun dies (at 14 *sui*) in the spring. At about this time, when she is past 40, his mother begins writing poetry. The family moves to Jiaxing.
1804–7	Leaving his family in Jiaxing, Zhang Qi travels extensively.
1807	The family returns to Changzhou, where Yuesun is born. Wanying is 9 *sui;* her mother forbids her to pick the baby up, fearing she is not strong enough. Tang Yaoqing herself is 44 years old and relies heavily on her elder daughters for assistance with the baby and the household. Zhang Qi travels in Zhejiang, Anhui, Henan, Shandong, and the capital, returning home sometimes once a year, sometimes once in three or five years. He departs in winter, in the eleventh month of 1807, shortly after celebrating the Mid-Autumn Festival (Zhongqiu) with his family (see entry for 1827).
1808	Bao Mengyi, Yuesun's future wife, is born to the Wang family of Bao Shichen's sister. Guanying first begins to study poetry.
1809	Zhang Huiyan's collected prose is printed.
1811	Zhang Qi finally returns home, after a trip to the capital. The family relocates to the Near Garden.
1812	Yaoqing turns 50, but Zhang Qi is back in the capital studying and no notice is paid.
1813	In his fiftieth year, Zhang Qi passes the *juren* exams after eleven failures. About this time, the family receives word of Miss Fa's intention to enter their household as a *zhennü.* Qieying is married to Wu Zan as his successor wife; Wu Zan's first wife has died and left three children, the eldest a son called Sihan in some sources, Zonghan in others. Qieying becomes their mother.
1814	Zhang Qi returns home in autumn to celebrate his success before departing shortly thereafter (in the tenth month) for Henan and thence again to Beijing. En route home he loses three hundred poems in manuscript that he leaves behind at an inn.
1815	In Beijing, Zhang Qi publishes his study of late Zhou geography, titled *Zhanguo ce shidi;* he also edits and writes a preface to an anthology of poems from the Han through the Sui dynasties (c. 200 BCE to 600 CE), titled *Wanlin shuwu gushi lu.* Guanying is married to Zhhang Zhengping at the age of 20 (21 *sui*).
1817–19	Zhang Qi and Bao Shichen are together at the capital and in Jinan.
1820	Zhang Qi is appointed a copyist in the bureau compiling the Veritable Records *(shilu)* for the late Jiaqing Emperor. Li Zhaoluo accompanies

newly appointed Guangdong governor Kang Shaoyong (1770–1834) to Canton, where he spends more than one year and meets Ruan Yuan. There Li becomes interested in the Europeans and publishes two books on Western countries: *Haiguo ji wen* and *Haiguo ji lan.*

1821　Guanying gives birth to a son at the age of 26. At about this time, first Lunying and then Wanying are married. Yuesun reaches 15 *sui,* the age of capping.

1822　The Veritable Records completed, Zhang Qi is appointed at the rank of magistrate in Shandong.

1823　Zhang Qi sets out for Shandong, reaching the province in the fourth month; in the twelfth month, he is appointed acting magistrate of Zouping.

1824　Zhang Qi returns home before taking up an appointment as acting magistrate of Zouping. (This marks the end of the ten-year absence recorded in all the family chronicles.) In the fifth month he is released from office; in the seventh month he moves to Zhangqiu as acting magistrate. Guanying dies in the seventh month (this year Zhang Qi is 60 years old). Tang Yaoqing at first declines to join her husband in the north, citing the need to see to her parents' burial and to the construction of a chaste widow arch for her mother-in-law. When Tang Yaoqing does follow Zhang Qi to Shandong in the eighth month, one month after Guanying's death, her three surviving daughters accompany her. She arrives in the ninth month.

1824–25　Zhang Qi remains in Zhangqiu (Shandong) as acting magistrate for thirteen months; he leaves in the seventh month of 1825. His sons-in-law Wang Xi and Wu Zan study *ci* with him.

1826　Qieying's husband, Wu Zan, attains the *jinshi* degree; Wang Caipin is born. Zhang Qi is made acting magistrate in Guantao, Shandong, the incumbent having deserted his post during a famine. Bao Shichen works in Guangzhou on coastal affairs.

1827　Wang Caifan is born. Qieying's two children, a son and a daughter, die of smallpox in the spring, while sojourning in Jinan. In the same month, Lunying's two daughters also die of smallpox. Yaoqing continues to wear mourning for Guanying. Zhang Qi is promoted permanently to the post of magistrate of Guantao. His family arrives there in the sixth month. Lunying studies calligraphy with her father in the Green Scholar Tree Studio. On the Mid-Autumn Festival (October 5), Zhang Qi invites his family to join him in composing poems to celebrate their first such festival together in twenty years. This is also Lunying's thirtieth year, when she begins writing poetry.

1828   Yuesun marries Bao Mengyi in Guantao; his mother is still in mourning for Guanying.

1829   Qieying departs to join her husband in the capital at the age of 39, not to return to her natal family until 1846, when she travels to Yuesun's post in Wuchang. She is en route to the capital on the day of the Mid-Autumn Festival (September 12). Her father remarks that she is leaving her natal family for the first time in her life. On the eve of the Festival, Tang Yaoqing catches a cold, which begins the deterioration of her health, ending in her death a few years later. Zhang Qi's annotations on the great classic of Han medicine, *Su wen shi yi,* are printed for the first time. Zhang Qi composes the afterword to his late father-in-law's collected works and the preface to his deceased daughter Guanying's collected poems, also printed in his studio.

1830   Yuesun's daughter Xiangzhen is born. Yuesun's future concubine, Li Luan, is born. Zhang Qi's grandnephew Dong Sicheng visits Guantao with a manuscript to continue the original *Ci xuan.* Zhang Qi writes a preface and prints it in his studio. Lunying begins her practice of calligraphy with her father.

1831   Zhang Qi is in his sixty-eighth year. Tang Yaoqing dies in the seventh month at the age of 69; Yuesun escorts her body home and sees to her burial. Sun Jie brings his father to the Guantao *yamen,* where his father dies. Wang Xi's *Donghai ji* is printed for the first time. In this same year, the Daoguang Emperor issues a decree calling for an investigation of opium smuggling in Guangdong.[1]

1832   Li Zhaoluo completes his atlas of the Qing dynasty, the "Huangchao yi-tong yutu," which is printed as a wall map in eight scrolls in 1842 and can be seen in the Library of Congress. This atlas becomes the basis for the geographical atlas produced under the sponsorship of Hu Linyi and completed in 1863. Wang Cailan (Sun Sihui) is born. Qieying's only surviving son dies of smallpox in the winter. On August 9 (seventh month, fourteenth day), Zhang Qi lays aside mourning garments after grieving for a full ritual year in memory of his wife. This is the year when fighting first breaks out in the Hu-Guang area because of tensions between Han members of the Heaven and Earth Society and Yao minority people living in the hills along the borders.[2] In this year, too, British vessels call at ports in Fujian, Jiangsu, and Zhejiang and are rebuffed; they also anchor off the coast of Shandong. Their requests for the opening of ports beyond Canton (Guangzhou) are rebuffed. The king of Korea rejects a request to open trade with the British.[3]

1833   Zhang Qi dies (third month, twelfth day—April 12) at the age of 70, while still holding office in Guantao. Early in the eleventh month, the boat bearing his coffin reaches Yangzhou, and Bao Shichen comes out to weep over it. Lunying moves into Yuesun's household in Changzhou. Yuesun purchases a home where he can live with his two sisters and their husbands, following his father's dying wish. Li Zhaoluo engages a coppersmith to assist him in constructing some astronomical instruments. These were probably used to produce the map of the heavens he printed the following year. That map served as the prototype for a similar map made a decade later by Li's student Feng Guifen, who owned the printing blocks. Feng Guifen, an admirer of Wang Caipin's poetry, shared Li's interest in foreign learning, especially science and mathematics.

1834	Zhang Yuesun comes to the capital to see his elder sister and stays for a long visit.
1835	Wang Chenbi is born.
1837	In the summer, Yuesun and his Korean friend Yi Sang-jŏk visit Qieying's husband, Wu Zan, at the capital and stay in the Naliang guan. Yuesun's book on childbirth and infant care, *Chanyun ji*, is completed, and a preface is composed in the tenth month by an admirer. The governors of Zhili, Shandong, Jiangsu, Zhejiang, Fujian, and Guangdong are put on notice by the court to stop the flow of silver out of their ports.[4]
1838	Huiyan's son, Zhang Chengsun, dies. Lin Zexu, as governor-general of Hu-Guang, announces a ban on and confiscation of opium in Hunan and Hubei. A furor about opium ensues.[5]
1839	Wanying turns 40. In the same year, she begins to write prose. Yuesun returns home from the capital, and Wanying's husband, Wang Xi, returns from Hangzhou, where he had been temporarily employed; Qieying remains in the capital. Qieying sends a birthday greeting to Bao Mengyi, who is in her thirtieth year, and she composes a poem of mourning in memory of her lost children. Wang Caizao is born.
1840	Zhang Qi's collected works are printed. (The printing blocks are later destroyed in the Taiping Rebellion; a descendant of Sun Jie and Zhang Lunying reprints the collection in 1891, working from a copy saved in a family library.) Qieying writes a poem to celebrate her youngest sister's fortieth birthday (also dedicated to Lunying and to Yuesun). The poems of Zhang Qieying, Lunying, and Wanying are collected for printing under the Wanlin Studio name. Zhang Yuesun commissions Tang Bihen to paint *Linking Verse across Adjoining Rooms*. Lin Zexu is dismissed from office and ordered into exile in Yili.
1841	Qieying turns 50. Li Zhaoluo dies. Sun Jie travels to Anhui, Wang Xi to Jiangxi.
1843	Yuesun wins the *juren* degree.

1844   Yuesun's wife, Bao Mengyi, dies at the age of 37, and in the same year her husband is named an expectant appointee at the rank of magistrate. They were married sixteen years. Zhang Yuesun compiles and publishes the song lyric collection of his literary group in Beijing under the title *Tongsheng ji.* Wang Xi's collected song lyrics, *Lumen ci,* are printed.

1845   Yuesun is awarded a magistrate's rank in the city of Wuchang, Hubei. Before he departs for his new office, he acquires a concubine, Li Luan, age 17 *sui.* Wanying prepares to move to join him in Wuchang. In the eleventh month (December 14), Sun Jie dies at 49 *sui.* Lunying's collected poems are printed by Yuesun in three *juan.* Yuesun's medical book on childbirth and infant care, *Chanyun ji,* is published for the first time. (The text is destroyed in the Taiping Rebellion; new plates are prepared by publishers in Fujian for a new publication in 1871.)

1846   Yuesun arrives in Wuchang. Lunying's fiftieth birthday passes unmarked, while she is in mourning for her late husband. Lunying and Wanying travel from Changzhou to Wuchang, and Qieying joins them there for a reunion.

1847   Yuesun turns 40; in Wuchang, Wanying's husband, Wang Xi, dies; accompanied part of the way by Qieying, who is returning to the capital to rejoin her husband, Wanying escorts her husband's body to Taicang, his family's native place, for burial. Lunying's poems are reprinted under the Wuchang Dihua Studio imprimatur in honor of her fiftieth birthday.

1848   Wanying returns to Wuchang and moves permanently into her brother's household; she remembers to celebrate her brother's birthday. Miss Fa is honored with an imperial commendation as a *zhennü.*

1849   Wanying celebrates her fiftieth birthday; Qieying and Yuesun send her greetings; Lunying turns 53. Wu Zan dies. Wang Chenbi is capped.

1850   Zhang Yuesun completes the preface to the collected poems of six of the family's young women: his four nieces, Wang Caipin, Caifan, Cailan, and Caizao; his daughter Zhang Xiangzhen; and his concubine, Li Luan. The collection is copyedited by Yuesun's son, Jinli. A copy is presented to Caipin as a farewell present when she leaves Wuchang for Kaifeng to marry the *juren* degree holder Cheng Peiyuan, in her twenty-fifth year. This year, Wanying's two *juan* of collected prose are also printed under the Wuchang Dihuaguan imprimatur, and the collected works of Qieying are reprinted. By the time the preface to the *Dihua guan* anthology is being written, Chenbi has already married Yuesun's daughter Xiangzhen.

1851   Lin Zexu dies.

1852   Taiping rebels move down the Yangzi River from Changsha through Wuchang, reaching Jiujiang by winter of that year.

1853	The Taiping take Nanjing, Zhenjiang, and Yangzhou and for the first time threaten Changzhou. Qieying, now a widow, flees the capital in the panic of October, when thirty thousand families leave Beijing for safety. Caipin, in Kaifeng, is also threatened.
1855	Bao Shichen dies trying to take refuge from the Taiping rebels.
1856	Caipin's husband dies of an unknown cause; his body is shipped back to Kaifeng by boat.
1858	Caipin travels to Wuchang for a visit, escorted by her younger brother, who is en route home from the capital. Wanying celebrates her sixtieth birthday.
1859	Caipin returns home to Kaifeng in the summer.
1860	Taiping rebels attack Changzhou; the commanding officer, He Guiqing, flees the city, which local gentry and commoners continue to defend for six days before it falls. The rebels enter through the east and south gates, killing about twenty thousand people. One chronicler suggests that an equal number committed suicide. Miss Fa dies in the fighting. Manchu negligence and cowardice are widely cited as reasons for the rebel victories. The fall of Suzhou on June 1 galvanized many leaders there, who fled to Shanghai, among them Feng Guifen, and went on to spearhead the post-Taiping Restoration.
1861	The family is scattered.
1862	The Korean envoy Yi Sang-jŏk writes an encomium for the reprinting of Zhang Qieying's collected works on the occasion of her seventieth birthday.
1863	Yuesun and his son, Jinli, both die in Shanghai.
1864	Changzhou is recovered from the Taiping by Li Hongzhang's armies.
1868	Lunying's collected poems are reprinted, including a new chapter and an afterword by Wanying and others, to celebrate her seventieth birthday.
1871	Yuesun's *Chanyun ji* is reprinted by a Fujian publishing house.
1891	Zhang Qi's collected works are reprinted by one of Sun Jie's descendants, to fulfill a long-standing family obligation.
1893	Wang Caipin dies.
1894	Wang Caipin's collected poems are published posthumously, under the imprimatur of the Office of the Director-General of the Grand Canal in Shandong by her employer, Xu Zhenyi.

GLOSSARY OF NAMES

An Lushan 安祿山
Bai *shi* 白氏
Ban *jieyu* 班婕妤
Ban Zhao 班昭
Bao Mengyi 包孟儀
Bao Shichen 包世臣
Bi Yuan 畢沅
Bolegongwu 博勒恭武
Chen Hengzhe 陳衡哲
Chen Hongmou 陳宏謀
Chen Kangqi 陳康祺
Chen Lunjiong 陳倫炯
Chen Tao 陈韜
Cheng Menghua 程孟華
Cheng Peiyuan 程培元
   (Bohou 伯厚)
Cixi 慈禧
Deng Chuanmi 鄧傳密
Deng Shiru 鄧石如
Ding *shi* 丁氏
Dong Dingyuan 董定園
Dong Shixi 董士錫
Dong Sicheng 董思誠
Dong Sipei 董思培
Dong Wanzhen 董畹貞

Du Fu 杜甫
Du Yu 杜宇
Duan Yucai 段玉裁
Fa Ding 法鼎
Fa Qianyi 法謙益 (牧亭 公)
Fa *shi* 法氏
Fa Zhenglin 法徵麟
Fan Pang 范滂
Fang Bao 方苞
Feng Guifen 馮桂芬
Feng Shusen 冯树森
Feng Xuan 馮諼
Gu Yanwu 顧炎武
Gu Zuyu 顧祖禹
Guan Hanqing 關漢卿
Gui Youguang 歸有光
Hailing 海陵 (齡)
He Guiqing 何桂清
He Shaoji 何紹基
Heshen 和珅
Hong Liangji 洪亮吉
Hong Xiuquan 洪秀全
Hu Linyi 胡林翼
Huang Jingren 黃景仁
Huang Yuanyu 黃元御

Jiang *shi* 姜氏 (Zhang Qi's mother)

Jiang *shi* 江氏 (Wu Zan's wife)

Jin Bang 金榜

Jin Changpu 金長溥

Jin *shi* 金氏

Jin Yunhuai 金雲槐

Kang Shaoyong 康紹鏞

Kang Tongwei 康同薇

Kang Youwei 康有為

Lan Dingyuan 藍鼎元

Li Bin 李斌

Li Ciming 李慈銘

Li Hongzhang 李鴻章

Li Luan 李鑾 (Ziqi 紫畦)

Li Qingzhao 李清照

Li Zhaoluo 李兆洛

Liang *shi* 梁氏

Lin Shoutu 林壽圖

Lin Zexu 林則徐

Ling Tingkan 凌廷堪

Liu Changchuan 劉長川

Liu Dakui 劉大櫆

Liu Fenglu 劉逢祿

Lu Fu 盧復

Lu *gu* 陸姑 (Lady Lu)

Lu Wenchao 盧文弨

Lü Bicheng 呂碧城

Lü Junsun 呂儁孫

Lü Kun 呂坤

Lü Maorong 呂懋榮

Mei Zengliang 梅曾亮

Meng Jiao 孟郊

Mujangga 穆彰阿 (M.)

Muting *gong* 牧亭公

Naxunlanbao 那遜蘭保

Pan Shi'en 潘世恩

Pan Zengwei 潘曾瑋

Peng Shaosheng 彭紹升

Qian Daxin 錢大昕

Qian Hansi 錢漢思

Qian Lusi 錢魯思

Qian Lüzhao 錢履昭

Qian Mengdian 錢孟鈿

Qian Ranxi 錢然晰

Qian Weicheng 錢維城

Qian Yong 錢泳

Qian Zizhen 錢子貞

Qin Xiangye 秦緗業

Qishan 琦善

Qiu Jin 秋瑾

Qu Qiubai 瞿秋白

Qu Yuan 屈原

Ren Daorong 任道鎔

Ruan Ji 阮籍

Ruan Yuan 阮元

Shen Shanbao 沈善寶

Shen Yunying 沈雲英

Sheng Xuanhuai 盛宣懷

Shi Liang 史良

Sima Qian 司馬遷

Song Tingyu 宋庭瑜

Su Shi 蘇軾

Sun Jie 孫劼

Sun Shangxian 孫尚賢

Sun Sihui 孫嗣徽 (aka Wang Cailan)

Sun Xingyan 孫星衍

Sun Yuanxiang 孫原湘 (Zixiao 子潇)

Sun Zenggu 孫曾穀

Tang Dakui 湯大奎

Tang Dashen 湯大紳

Tang Jiaming 湯嘉名 (碧痕, 碧春)

Tang Xiongye 湯雄業

Tang Xiuye 湯修業

Tang Xunye 湯荀業

Tang Yaoqing 湯瑤卿

Tang Yidian 湯貽典

Tang Yifen 湯貽汾

Tang Yimo 湯貽謨 (also written 模)

Tang Yiyan 湯貽燕

Tang Yunqing 湯韻清 (aka Tang Yidian)

Tao Qian 陶潛 (Yuanming 淵明)

Tao Zhu 陶澍

Wan shi 萬氏

Wang Ang 汪昂

Wang Boxin 王柏心

Wang Caifan 王采蘩

Wang Cailan 王采藍 (aka Sun Sihui)

Wang Cailu 王采綠

Wang Caipin 王采蘋

Wang Caiwei 王采薇

Wang Caizao 王采藻

Wang Chenbi 王臣弼

Wang Chenjin 王臣藎

Wang Chenkai 王臣愷

Wang Chenliang 王臣諒

Wang Ding 王鼎

Wang Guowei 王國維

Wang Hui 王翬

Wang Qi 汪淇

Wang Shimin 王時敏

Wang Shizhen 王士禎

Wang Xi 王曦

Wang Xijue 王錫爵

Wang Yuanqi 王原祁

Wang Yun 王筠

Wanyan Yun Zhu 完顏惲珠

Wei Ji 魏驥

Wei shi 魏氏 (Lady Wei)

Weng Fanggang 翁方綱

Wu Han 吳晗

Wu Jin 吳謹

Wu Lanwan 吳蘭畹

Wu Lanze 吳蘭澤

Wu Shihua 吳石華

Wu Siqian 吳似潛

Wu Tingzhen 吳廷珍

Wu Xu 吳煦

Wu Zan 吳贊

Wu Zhiying 吳芝瑛

Wu Zonghan 吳宗漢 (sometimes written Sihan 似漢)

Xi Peilan 席佩蘭

Xiang Rong 向榮

Xie Daoyun 謝道韞

Xie Lingyun 謝靈運

Xie Qinggao 謝清高

Xin Chang 辛敞

Xin Xianying 辛憲英

Xing Shu 邢澍

Xu Dachun 徐大椿

Xu Jiyu 徐繼畬

Xu Zhenyi 許振禕

Xue Fucheng 薛福成

Xue Ziheng 薛子衡

Yan 炎 (Emperor)

Yan Yuan 顏元

Yan Zhitui 顏之推

Yang Fang 楊芳

Yang Ximin 楊希閔

Yang Zhaolu 楊兆魯

Yao Nai 姚鼐

Ye Gui 葉桂

Yi Kezhong 儀克中

Yi Sang-jŏk 李尚迪 (K.)

Yidian 貽典

Yin Hao 殷浩

Yuan Cai 袁采

Yuan Haowen 元好問

Yuan Mei 袁枚

Yun Jing 惲敬

Yun Shouping 惲壽平 (Nantian 南田)

Yun Zhu (see Wanyan Yun Zhu)

Zeng Guofan 曾國藩

Zeng Jifen 曾紀芬

Zhang Chanbin 張蟾賓

Zhang Chengsun 張成孫

Zhang Dejian 張德堅

Zhang Duan 張端

Zhang Guanying 張䌹英
 (Weiqing 緯青)

Zhang Huaizhen 張懷珍

Zhang Huiyan 張惠言

Zhang Jindi 張金第

Zhang Jinli 張晉禮

Zhang Juesun 張玨孫

Zhang Lunying 張綸英
 (Wanxun 宛紃)

Zhang Menglong 張孟龍

Zhang Mu 張穆

Zhang Qi 張琦

Zhang Qieying 張緗英
 (Mengti 孟緹)

Zhang Ruidou 張瑞斗

Zhang Shaozeng 張紹曾

Zhang Tailei 張太雷

Zhang Wanying 張紈英
 (Ruoqi 若綺)

Zhang Xiangzhen 張祥珍

Zhang Xuan 張萱

Zhang Xun 張巡

Zhang Yin 張引

Zhang Yue 張說

Zhang Yuesun 張曜孫 (仲遠)

Zhang Yuniang 張玉娘

Zhao Huaiyu 趙懷玉

Zhao Yi 趙翼

Zhhang* Pei 章沛

Zhhang* Xuecheng 章學誠

Zhhang* Yuezhen 章岳鎮

Zhhang* Zhengping 章正 (政) 平

Zhong Jun 終軍

Zhou Ji 周濟

Zhu Gui 朱珪

Zhu Guizhen 朱桂楨

Zhu Jian 朱珔

Zhu Yizun 朱彝尊

Zhu Yuanzhang 朱元璋

Zhuang Cunyu 莊存與

Zhuang Shouqi 莊受祺

Zhuang Shuzu 莊述祖

Zhuang Yunyi 莊允懿

Zuo Fen 左芬

Zuo Xixuan 左錫璇

*Note special romanization to distinguish this Zhhang from its surname homophone.

GLOSSARY OF TERMS

"Ai ming" 哀命
anchashi 按察使
ba 跋
baimiao 白描
"Baojian pian" 寶劍篇
bi 婢
Bi 邲
bi xing 比興
bingwu 丙午
"Biwu lianyin tu" 比屋聯吟圖
bo, zhong, shu, ji 伯仲叔季
Bo 亳
"Bo xi" 伯兮
bushi yu yu 不失於愚
"Cai fan" 采蘩
"Cai pin" 采蘋
cainü 才女
"Chang di" 常棣
Changsha 長沙
Changzhou 常州
Changzhou *cipai* 常州詞派
chanmian feice 纏綿悱惻
chi qu 馳驅
Chu 楚
chun hui 春暉

"Chun wang" 春望
Chuzhou 滁州
ci 詞
congjiu 從舅
Da Nanmen De'an li 大南門德安里
Daming hu 大明湖
daotai 道臺
de yan rong gong 德言容工
De'an 德安
di 弟 (younger brother)
dihua 棣華
Dihua guan 棣華館
Dongchang 東昌
"Donghai ji" 東海記
"Donghai xiaofu mu bei ji" 東海孝
　婦墓碑記
"Du Qin Liangyu zhuan" 讀秦良
　玉傳
"Du Ruan Yuan tai xiansheng xiyang
　mi dao jishi you gan" 讀阮元臺
　先生西洋米到紀事有感
Du shi fangyu ji yao 讀史方輿紀要
"Dui yue huai jia daren" 對月懷
　家大人
duilian 對聯
dujuan 杜鵑

duliang dao 督糧道

duoduo 咄咄

duoduo guaishi 咄咄怪事

"Er nan" 二南

fan 番

fei furen shi 非婦人事

feng he 風鶴

fenli 分隸

fu dao 婦道

"fu lu" 附錄

fuhu 扶護

gan miao 趕廟

"Gan shi" 感事

Ganjiang 干將

"Gengshen bikou dao Chu cheng zhu zunzhang" 庚申避寇到楚呈諸尊長

gengzi 庚子

gongren 恭人

goujushu 鉤距術

"Gu jian" 古劍

Guantao 館陶

guantian 官田

gui 歸

Guifan 閨範

guixiu 閨秀

guju 古居

guma 姑媽

Guochao guixiu zheng shi ji 國朝閨秀正始集

guwen 古文

Hai lu 海錄

Haiguo ji lan 海國集覽

Haiguo ji wen 海國紀聞

Haiguo wenjian lu 海國聞見錄

"Han deng" 寒燈

han hui 寒輝

hanjian 汗簡

Hanlin 翰林

Hanyang 漢陽

hao ge 浩歌

haofang 豪放

he 和 [falling tone]

hehua shengri 荷花生日

heya 和雅

Honglou meng 紅樓夢

hongmao helan zhuguo 紅毛荷蘭諸國

hongmei 紅梅

"hou xu" 後序

Huaibei 淮北

Huaiyuan 懷遠

Huang Di nei jing [*su wen*] 黃帝內經 [素問]

Huang Yun 黃運

"Huangchao yitong diyu quantu" 皇朝一統地輿全圖

"Huangchao yitong yutu" 皇朝一統輿圖

"Huangchao Zhong wai yitong yutu" 皇朝中外一統輿圖

Huanyu fangbei lu 寰宇訪碑錄

"Hubei houbudao Zhang jun muzhiming" 湖北候補道張君墓誌銘

huimin ju 惠民局

Huizhou 徽州

hunpo 魂魄

huoluan 霍亂 (亂)

"Ji" (Record) 記

"Ji Yanghu Zhang Wanxun nüshi" 寄陽湖張婉紃女史

jian si 兼嗣

Jiangyin 江陰

Jianli 監利

Jianwo yigao 繭窩遺稿

Jiaonü yigui 教女遺規

Jiaxing 嘉興

jiaxue 家學

jiazhang 甲長

jiefu 介婦

jiemei 姐妹

jiling 鶺鴒

Jin 晉

jin sihu yuan 近似乎園

Jin yuan 近園

Jinan 濟南

Jingzhou 荊州

jinshi 進士

jiqu 繼娶

jituo 寄托

jiu mo ze gu lao, zhongfu suo jisi binke, mei shi bi qingyu gu, jiefu qingyu zhongfu 舅沒則姑老，冢婦所祭祀賓客，每事必請於姑，介婦請於冢婦

"Jiu yu hou xue" 久雨後雪

Jiyin gangmu 濟陰綱目

juexue 絕學

junzi 君子

"Junzi you dao buyou pin" 君子憂道不憂貧

juren 舉人

Kaifeng 開封

kaishu 楷書

kan renao 看熱鬧

kangguan shachai 抗官殺差

Kangxi zidian 康熙字典

Langui baolu 蘭閨寶錄

laoren 老人

Lengyan jing 楞嚴經

"Li Fengtai zhuan" 李鳳臺傳

"Li sao" 離騷

li yao 禮要

liangzhang 糧長

lianyin 聯吟

lienü 列(烈)女

lijin 釐金

lishu 隸書

liu xu 柳絮

lizhang 里長

Lu 魯

Lumen ci 鹿門詞

Luoshan 螺山

mai ji shi yu 買姬侍余

"Man jiang hong" 滿江紅

"Ming gongren peijian ge" 明宮人佩劍歌

ming jiao zhi qibian 名教之奇變

Moye 莫耶

mufu 幕府

mujiao 母教

muyu 木魚

Naliang [zhi] guan 納凉之館

"Nan gui ji cheng" 南歸紀程

"Nei ze" 內則

neng zhi li zhi ben 能知禮之本

ni tian bei li buzhi zhangyou zunbei zhi xu 逆天背理不知長幼尊卑之序

nian 捻

"Niannu jiao" 念奴嬌

nüxing yishi 女性意识

nüxu 女婿

nüxu zhi chanyuan xi shenshen qi li yu 女婿之嬋媛兮申申其詈余

Nüxue 女學

nüzi wu cai bian shi de; neiyan buchu kunwai 女子無才便是德，內言不出閫外

nüzi you xing yuan fumu xiongdi 女子有行遠父母兄弟

ou cheng 偶成

pai' ao 排奡

pailou 牌樓

"*Pengmen xian mu*" 蓬門賢母

pianwen 駢文

Piling 毗陵

po zhu 破竹

Qi 齊

qi 氣

"*Qi jian*" 七諫

qianya 簽押

qiaoran wu zhi yu shi yi 悄然無志於世矣

qie 篋

Qishi 漆室

"*Quan shui*" 泉水

renzhi xinfu weixi pengren yi he jing ye 稔知新婦未習烹飪抑何精也

rusheng 入聲

ruyi 儒醫

san buguan 三不管

sangluan 喪亂

sanjun zhi shi jie ru xiekuang 三軍之士皆如挾纊

Shangqiu 商丘

sheng ping 升平

shengsi bie 生死別

Shennong benjing 神農本經

"*Shi gao zi xu*" 詩稿自序

shi gen zhong qian 始艮終乾

shi ru po zhu 勢如破竹

shijian 尸諫

shilu 實錄

shixue 實學

shou ci 壽辭

"*shu hou*" 書後

Shuchang guan 庶常館

shujishi 庶吉士

Shuowen jie zi zhu 說文解字注

"*Si sheng xinyuan hou xu*" 四聖心源後序

Si yan gui jian 四言闺鉴

side 四德

sifang qian 私房錢

Sisheng xinyuan 四聖心源

Su wen shi yi 素問釋義

Suiyang 睢陽

sun 孫

"*Sun Shuxian aici*" 孫叔獻哀詞

Su'nan 蘇南

tai 胎

Tancheng 郯城

"*Tao Yuefei xi*" 掐粵匪析

"*Taoyao*" 桃夭

Taying lou ci 塔影樓詞

tianxia zhi min bu si yu bing er si yu yi 天下之民不死於病而死於醫

tiba 題跋

"*tici xuke*" 題辭續刻

Tongcheng 桐城

"*Wang shi Tang ruren xing lüe*" 亡室湯孺人行略

wangzu 望族

Wanlin 宛鄰

Wanlin shuwu gushi lu 宛鄰書屋古詩錄

Wanxi 宛溪

wanyue 婉約

Wei bei ti 魏碑體

wei ci wei zui le zhi jing kong ci sheng buke fu de yi 惟此為最樂之境恐此生不可復得矣

Wei nü 衛女

Wen xuan 文選

wenbing 瘟病

wenzhi hou shen 文摯後身

Wu 吳

wu bumou yu zi, ji buhuo yu yi! 吾不謀於姊幾不獲於義

wu Chang wenxian 吾常文獻

wu guige qi 無閨閣氣

wu xing 五行

Wuchang 武昌

Wujin 武進

Xi fenyin zhai 惜分陰齋

xiali xingwen dong, huanbian yueying can 匣裏星文動，環邊月影殘

"Xian fujun xing shu" 先府君行述

"Xian zubi shi lüe" 先祖妣事略

xiang fuzi you zhengsheng, xun zi yi shixue 相夫子有政声，训子以实学

Xiefang ji 擷芳集

xiekuang 挾纊

xin shihuan jieji 新仕宦階級

xing shang 杏殤

xingbude 行不得

xingshang, hua ru, shuangjian er luo. yin bei xi ying, gu zuo ci shi 杏殤，花乳，霜剪而落. 因悲昔嬰，故作此詩

xingwen 星文

xinji 心疾

xiongdi 兄弟

Xiyuan wen jian lu 西園聞見錄

"Xu" (Preface) 序

Xuannan *ci she* 宣南詞社

Xuannan *shi she* 宣南詩社

xuba 序跋

Xuehai tang 學海堂

yan zhi 言志

yangban 兩班 (K.)

Yanghu 陽湖

yangwu pai 洋務派

Yangxian 陽羨

yangxue 洋學

Yanjing shi xu ji 揅經室續集

"Yi shu tu tici" 疑書圖題辭

yi zai yanwai chenzhuo shenyuan 意在言外沉著深遠

yin 蔭 (hereditary privilege)

ying 英

Yingjili 英吉利

Yixing 宜興

Yiyang 益陽

yong yi 庸醫

yongshi guannian; qiushi zhiyong 用世观念；求实致用

yongwu ci 詠物詞

"You zi yin" 游子吟

youjun 幽雋

yuanqin 冤禽

Yueman tang riji 越縵堂日記

Yuezhou 岳州
Yuzhou 禹州
"Zei qing huibian" 賊情匯編
zhang zhu 掌珠
Zhangqiu 章丘
Zhanguo ce 戰國策
Zhanguo ce shidi 戰國策釋地
zheng 正
Zhenjiang 鎮江
zhennü 貞女
Zhexi 浙西
zhi li zhi yi 制禮之意
zhongfu 冢婦

Zhongqiu 中秋
"Zhuan" 傳
zhuang shi ben wu qu, lao mou he suo cheng 壯事本無取，老謀何所成
zhuangyuan 狀元
zhuanshu 篆書
zhuci bishi 屬詞比事
zide 自得
Zouping 鄒平
zui nenggan 最能幹
Zuo zhuan 左傳, "Xuan gong" 宣公

APPENDIX
Selected Poems and Song Lyrics

"讀先姊緯青遺稿"
張紈英

浮生若流水
死別忽經年
淚眼警秋早
離魂有夢牽
鶴飛華表月
花落夕陽天
次日西窗下
空余咏絮篇

"秋日有懷"
張綸英

玉露潤秋色
梧桐一葉飛
蟬聲出高樹
螢影入羅帷
梁燕知時返
羈人未得歸
遙憐雙袖薄
何處寄寒衣

"古劍"
張緝英

百戰雄心在
千秋寶氣揚
風霜凝慘色
神鬼泣寒芒
雷掣青鋒冷
虹橫碧落長
良才未淪沒
光彩識干將

"感事"
張緝英

秋光正好
甚浮雲翳日
纔晴還雨
做弄秋容狼藉甚
宋玉悲秋正苦
聒耳商
填膺憂憤
咄咄終何補
流波欲挽
何堪更惜遲暮
極目衰草緊霜
荒煙獨樹
搖落渾無主
啼煞鵙行不得
一片精誠難訴
伍相潮飛

汨羅江闊
只共冤禽語
沈埋諫草
誰教飲恨千古

"紅梅"
王采蘋

疏影橫斜倚夕陽
重簾深押護幽香
清姿自與嫣紅異
便作濃妝勝淡妝

"久雨後雪"
張紈英

青陽鬱沈陰
甚雨苦經月
萌芽凍不抽
徑戶閴幽寂
窗虛掩暮寒
風勁忽飛雪
棲烏無定止
庭樹益凜冽
挾纊懷我軍
捷音盼金闕
何時天宇清
雲翳掃空闊
欣欣萬物榮
晶瑩仰瑞日

"讀秦良玉傳"
王采蘋

魯女憂時悲漆室
木蘭代父為戍卒
古來女子負奇才
不獨闈幃著芳烈
秦氏將軍世無匹
武略文詞兼峻節
萬里窮邊拜總戎
一時勳望推人傑
白桿頻年事遠征
紅妝一隊作干城
…
百戰功名成馬上
端嚴想見天人相
象服珠冠一笑空
錦袍劍佩千秋壯
…
讀史蒼茫發遐思
遭逢幸際昇平世
姓字誰能汗簡留
筓環銷盡英雄氣
一寸陳編萬古心
百年身世漫浮沉
乾坤閒氣寧消歇
放眼江山深復深

"明宮人佩劍歌"
　王采蘋

干將莫耶古所貴
補履不如凡鐵利
此劍相看若有神
及鋒未試中捐棄
當日趨承清禁中
侍朝曉聽景陽鐘
光函秋水侵瑤佩
鍔吐蓮花映玉容
龍泉三尺星文隱
不付將軍付紅粉
孤負當年歐冶心
匣中寶氣消磨盡...

"感事"
　王采蘋

重臣節鉞鎮巖疆
破竹驚聞賊勢強
奪險已教過越嶺
乘流便欲下清湘
牛車幾輩防邊郡
馬革何人誓戰場
誰究盜源推禍始
古來善政在農桑
桂林烽火接南天
匝月圍城亦可憐
半夜驚雷飛鐵鶻

萬家野哭促啼鵑

釜魚誰使留餘逆

原燎終宜救未然

川楚軍興是前事

那堪覆轍又相連

...

倚柱悲歌百感生

楚雲南望思回縈

大江天塹防應亟

七澤烽煙衆易驚

決勝空勞千里外

憂時那得寸心平

請纓我愧秦良玉

投筆難為盡室行

"和孟緹從母避寇南歸舟中感事詩"

王采蘋

生死難為別

全家痛哭聲

原鴒歌急難

風鶴促歸程

消息誰能達

安危夢履驚

孤舟殘雪夜

極目不勝情

魯女憂時淚

曾傳漆室吟

攜來詩一卷

讀罷感難禁

烽火三年戍
音塵千里心
蒼茫國家恨
回首欲沾襟

. . .

"月"

王采蘋

飛蓬臨破鏡
鉛淚瀉金波
消息懷青鳥
心情共素娥
下床鄉思遠
窺夢別情多
永夜頻搔首
西風發浩歌

NOTES

PROLOGUE

1. Erie Vitiello, personal communication, February 2003.
2. *The Emperor and the Assassin,* directed by Chen Kaige, is a case in point.

1. JINING, SHANDONG

1. It is not clear when or how Xu was introduced to Wang Caipin. I have surmised that they met while he was serving as provincial judge *(anchashi)* in Henan in 1885, when—to the best of my knowledge—Wang Caipin was still living in that province, in the home of her in-laws. They might have been introduced earlier through their respective connections to Zeng Guofan, a longtime friend of the Zhang family through his acquaintance with Zhang Yuesun and a patron and former employer of Xu Zhenyi. See Cai Guanluo 1984, vol. 1, p. 511. In his notes on her collected poems, Xu reveals nothing about the extent of their acquaintance, and only in a very late poem (1891 or 1892) does Caipin herself allude to instructing Xu's children. We know only that Caipin's parents-in-law died in succession sometime after her uncle Zhang Yuesun's death in 1863, and that she spent the years afterward moving about, writing little and living in seclusion. See Xu's interlinear comments in Wang Caipin, *Duxuan lou shi gao* 1894: 9/6a.
2. Xu Zhenyi, "Xu" (Preface), in Wang Caipin, *Duxuan lou shi gao* 1894: s.p. 1a-b.
3. Lunar months in the Chinese calendar were divided into thirds, reckoning time in ten-day units rather than in seven-day weeks, as is customary in the modern Western calendar.
4. Xu's first political appointment came informally in the employ of Zeng Guofan during the campaign against the Taiping rebels, when he served in Zeng's *mufu* (private secretarial staff) before winning a high civil service examination degree. Under Zeng's leadership, Xu became involved in mustering local defense militias when the Taiping rebels were capturing city after city in Jiangxi. Because of his distinction in these campaigns, he was selected to serve as a county magistrate even

before he obtained the *jinshi* degree. See his own recollections in the self-preface to his collected works, *Cai diao ji* 1894; also his biographies in Cai Guanluo 1984, vol. 1, pp. 510–514; and *Qing shi gao jiao zhu* 1986, vol. 13, pp. 10550–10551.

5. Wright 1957 remains the classic study of the Tongzhi Restoration, which lasted from 1862 to 1874.

6. Official titles were ranked according to nine grades, with nine being the lowest, and each grade was divided into two ranks (a and b, in translation). See Mayers 1966, pp. 125–126.

7. See Pomeranz 1993, esp. pp. 128 ff. The plains surrounding the Yellow River were flooded almost continuously from 1851 until 1855, when the dikes failed, allowing the river to move disastrously from a path that brought it out to sea south of the Shandong Peninsula to its present northern route (Kuhn 1978, p. 313).

8. Mayers 1966, p. 43.

9. *Cainü,* "talented woman," was the conventional phrase for a gifted wife or daughter among the families of the literati class.

10. Xu Zhenyi may also have been thinking of another aspect of this story. Fan Pang was falsely charged with corruption and sentenced to death. As he was being led off to prison, he saw his mother standing by the road, and he called out to her, lamenting that he was dying before his time and would fail to carry out his duty as a filial son. His mother, unmoved, said: "Your fame is equal to the greatest of our statesmen; why should you complain about death? Having established such a good name, do you also need to live a long life?" Fan Pang's mother was speaking of the difficulty of achieving both integrity and longevity. But Wang Caipin had managed both.

11. *Jiaxue,* "family learning," commonly referred to the teachings passed down from parent to child across generations. Interestingly, family learning was not transmitted strictly or primarily by patrilines; women carried the learning of their natal families into their marital homes, particularly in places like Changzhou, the native place of the Zhang family.

12. Quoted in Cai Guanluo 1984, vol. 1, p. 513.

13. As I began to write the story of the Zhang family, I was inspired by Annping Chin's book about four talented daughters of a later generation, also surnamed Zhang, who called themselves "the last of the *guixiu*." *Guixiu* (lit., a lady "cultivated in the women's apartments") refers to a woman who is highly educated as well as refined and proper. *Guixiu* studied Confucian texts on history, philosophy, and morality. They knew how to write good classical poetry, and usually they mastered other classical arts such as music (playing the zither), calligraphy, and painting. To be the "last" of the *guixiu* was to belong to the last generation associated with this Confucian tradition of women's learning before it was abandoned in the twentieth-century embrace of Western-style education and professional training for the new, modern Chinese woman. See Zhang Yunhe 1999 and Chin 2002.

14. The shock and pain of these coercive policies provoked such bitter resis-

tance that they were abandoned in the vicinity of the Taiping capital at Nanjing, despite their seeming promise of emancipation, in order to ensure sufficient order to maintain the economy, and the policies were rescinded in most occupied areas after 1855. See Jen 1973, pp. 120–121. As Jen points out, however, many Taiping policies inspired by the Taiping belief in equality among the faithful promised to improve the status of women (pp. 150–151).

15. Shi Yihui 1995, pp. 42–46, quoting Zhang Dejian, "Zei qing hui bian," and Zeng Guofan, "Tao Yuefei xi," on pp. 45–46.

2. TANG YAOQING

1. In his afterword to her collected poems, Yaoqing's son Yuesun recalls her early education in the *Four Books* under her father's tutelage. See Tang Yaoqing, *Peng shi ou yin* 1840: "Ji," 1a. I have placed her in her grandfather's studio in this opening scene for my own reasons. Later, as we shall see, her father assumes primary responsibility for her education. For the reference to the *Analects,* consult Legge 1991, vol. 1, p. 137.

2. *Tang shi jiasheng* 1874: 5 n.p. See also *Guangxu Wujin Yanghu xian zhi* 1879: 23/37b-38a; *Wujin Yanghu xian hezhi* 1842: 17/35a, 26/40a-b.

3. *Fa shi jiasheng* 1900: "Shi" (Poetry), 5a. The poem was originally inscribed on a painting titled "Lord Muting Making Merry," evidently portraying Fa Qianyi taking his ease. Fa Qianyi was a descendant in the sixth generation of the founding ancestor of the Changzhou Fa lineage (*Fa shi jiasheng* 1900: 1/1b).

4. Yiyan was the eldest son of Yaoqing's father's elder brother. See *Tang shi jiasheng* 1874: 1/7a-9a for lines of descent.

5. The tensions between the successful father and his failed son are never made explicit in my sources. Yaoqing's grandfather is directly quoted in several biographies delivering admonitions to his son, Yaoqing's father, and I attribute Yaoqing's father's obsession with propriety to her grandfather's lectures. For the admonitions, see *Guangxu Wujin Yanghu xian zhi* 1879: 23/38a, and *Wujin Yanghu xian hezhi* 1842: 26/40a-b.

6. This often-told story about Yaoqing's father appears in the local gazetteer. *Wujin Yanghu xian hezhi* 1842: 26/40b; *Guangxu Wujin Yanghu xian zhi* 1879: 23/37b-38a. The suggestion that people thought him extreme is mine, though it seems implicit in these accounts.

7. Zhang Qi, in his biographical sketch of his wife's life, says that her father "knew everything about history since the Ming" and was "our Changzhou reference library" *(wu Chang wenxian).* My nickname attempts to convey the nuance in English.

8. Bai 2005.

9. These two chapters, which begin the classic, illustrate the virtues of the refined young lady.

10. Hou 1986, pp. 177–179.

11. On the differences, see Handlin 1975. The biographies of talented women never mention study of such contemporary instruction books, preferring to dwell on the classics. I have therefore surmised this part of Yaoqing's curriculum.

12. Carlitz 1991.

13. The story of the "woman from Qishi in Lu" (*Lienü zhuan* 3, biography 13) figures in several parts of this book. The story emphasizes that a woman working dutifully in the home has an elevated political consciousness precisely because state policy so closely affects herself, her work, and her ability to support herself and her family. See Raphals 1998, p. 233. On the "Discriminating Woman of Chu" (*Lienü zhuan* 6, biography 5), see Raphals 1998, p. 47.

14. Such advice books were extraordinarily popular in the Qing period. See Hui-chen Wang Liu 1959, pp. 70–71. On Lan's work, published in 1712, see Chen Dong-yuan 1994, pp. 275–78. Chen Hongmou's advice book for women was printed in 1742, as part of a much larger compendium of moral instructions for various audiences. See Rowe 1992; also Rowe 2001, p. 542n85. Rowe favorably compares Chen Hongmou's work and that of Lü Kun to Lan Dingyuan's book, which was too severe, in his judgment. Rowe also mentions (2001, p. 7) that Zeng Guofan read Chen Hongmou daily.

15. These included "family instructions" or rules for living, such as those of Yan Zhitui or Yuan Cai. See Ebrey 1984 for a translation and comments on the genre.

16. *Tang shi jiasheng* 1874: 1/7a-9a. Yimo was the grandson of one of Yaoqing's grandfather's younger brothers.

17. No poems by Yaoqing survive from these early years, so I have invented this poetic image for her.

18. This scene is my invention, although its plausibility is supported in a scene featuring Lin Daiyu, the heroine of the novel *Dream of the Red Chamber* (Cao Xue-qin [1791] 1988: vol. 3, 97/1368–1369; Hawkes and Minford 1973–1986, vol. 4 [1982], p. 353). Burning one's poems was a gesture implying humility (they are unworthy), shame (they should never have been written), or despair (my talent will never be recognized). See Chang 1997, esp. p. 240; also Mann 1997, pp. 115, 217. To say that one had burned one's poems might also be a rhetorical gesture, as Maureen Robertson has shown (Robertson 1997, pp. 183–186). As for Yaoqing's father's hostility toward her poetry writing, which was not characteristic of elite men's attitudes in Changzhou and was virtually unknown in the rest of the Tang family, my portrayal of his character here is intended to dramatize his very rigid devotion to ritual propriety, which caused much comment among his peers and even prompted mildly critical remarks from his biographer in the local gazetteer. At the same time, as Kang-i Sun Chang (1997) has emphasized, Yaoqing's father's attitudes were widely shared among certain segments of the literary public. The trauma of a beloved father's disapproval is my way of explaining why Tang Yaoqing stopped writing poetry until a later crisis in her life—recounted later in the chapter—restored her will to express herself.

19. Yaoqing's embroidery, as recalled by her daughter Qieying, is described in loving detail in Shen Shanbao, *Mingyuan shi hua* 1863: 8/5a-b. See also Zhang Qi's elegiac biography, "Wangshi Tang ruren xinglüe," in his *Ming fa lu* 1840: "Xinglüe," 3a; and Qieying's own story in chapter 3.

20. Zhang Qi's earliest aspiration as a scholar was to complete a new and corrected edition of Gu Zuyu's (1631–1692) *Du shi fangyu ji yao* (Essentials of geography for reading history). Because of his admiration for Gu, he chose as one of his own studio names Wanlin, after Gu Zuyu's courtesy name, Wanxi, i.e., "close to Wan[xi]."

21. Biographies of Zhang Huiyan, in addition to the English-language summary in *EC* (pp. 42–43), are collected in Miao Quansun 1896: 15/1a-2b.

22. *Guangxu Wujin Yanghu xian zhi* 1879: 24/29a-30a. The much-touted martyrdom of the Tang in the Lin Shuangwen rebellion on Taiwan was later followed by Tang Yifen's own martyrdom during the Taiping Rebellion. See *Tang shi jiasheng* 1874: 7a-b.

23. Mann 1997, p. 132.

24. Furth 1999, p. 210.

25. Furth 1999, pp. 210–213.

26. Zhang Huiyan, "Xian zubi shi lüe," *Mingke wen er bian* 1869: "xia" 22b.

27. Zhang Huiyan, *Mingke wen er bian* 1869: "xia" 24a.

28. Zhang Huiyan, *Mingke wen er bian* 1869: "xia" 25a-b. In the biographical sketch of Zhang Huiyan's mother's life by Chen Kangqi (1840–1890) ("The worthy mother of a poor scholar's family" ["Pengmen xian mu"]), Chen remarks that when he read Huiyan's memoir of his mother "it was as if the sound of his weeping arose from the paper" (Chen 1997, p. 68).

29. *Renzhi xinfu weixi pengren yi he jing ye.* Zhang Qi, "Wangshi Tang ruren xinglüe," *Ming fa lu* 1840: "Xinglüe," 3b.

30. *Tang shi jiasheng* 1874: 12/1a-b. Lu Wenchao died in 1796. See also *Guangxu Wujin Yanghu xian zhi* 1879: 27/62b.

31. Huiyan and Qi's elder sister was married to Dong Dingyuan, whose mother was a Qian. Lady Qian was particularly fond of her daughter-in-law's mother, Lady Jiang, so while Huiyan and Qi were still young, Lady Qian made a house available for them and their mother so they could move back into the city of Changzhou, where education was more readily available. See Zhang Huiyan, *Mingke wen er bian* 1869: "xia" 24b.

32. The move coincided with a famine in Changzhou, where a member of the Jin family, Jin Yunhuai, was serving as magistrate at the time. When the Zhang brothers moved to Huizhou in the autumn, when food shortages were most dire, it was probably thanks to a Jin connection. See Wu Hongyi 1970, p. 127.

33. On Jin Bang as a patron of letters, see *EC*, p. 715. The Jin brothers were both *jinshi* degree holders and themselves sons of a *jinshi*, Jin Changpu. See *She xian zhi* 1937: 7/6a-b, 16a-b, 67a-b.

34. See Nakata 1982, p. 209.

35. Deng Shiru particularly admired the tablets engraved during the Northern Wei period (386–534), when north China was ruled by Turkish invaders. (The Wei rulers, despite their foreign origin, were devoted to aristocratic Chinese culture, and they left stone-carved records that still survived in different localities throughout the country.) See Nakata 1982, p. 209. Deng met Zhang Huiyan at the home of Jin Bang in 1785, and it was through Zhang's influence that he later gained the attention of prominent officials in the capital (*EC*, p. 715). Deng befriended Bao Shichen during his later travels. Both Bao and Deng were natives of Anhui who preferred to move in Lower Yangzi circles. Deng's work was scorned by Weng Fang-gang and other members of the rival calligraphy school at the capital, partly for reasons of class difference, it seems. Much later, in 1834, Bao Shichen wrote a biography of Deng, praising him as "the greatest master of the *zhuan* [*zhuanshu* (seal script)] and *li* [*lishu* (character or official script)] scripts among his contemporaries." See Chang and Miller 1990, p. 102.

36. T'ien 1988.

37. On Zhu Gui's relationship to the Jiaqing Emperor, see *EC*, pp. 185–186. It was well known in Zhang Huiyan's circle that patronage of the sort commonly practiced in the capital embarrassed and irritated him. He insisted that his advancements be based entirely on his own merit, not on the favoritism of his superiors. See in particular comments quoted in Miao 1896, which include Yun Jing's eulogy for Zhang Huiyan (15/1b). The eulogy is printed in *Bei zhuan ji* 1973: vol. 922, 51/11b-13a. See also biographical accounts in *Guochao qixian lei zheng chu bian* 1966: 132/34a-40b, where a biography by Ruan Yuan is also reprinted.

38. Bao Shichen later compared the two Zhang brothers this way: "Huiyan was bold and imposing; Qi was retiring and introspective." See his eulogy in *Guochao qixian lei zheng chu bian* 1966: 247/50b. In Zhang Qi's own preface to his collected prose, written in 1815, he confesses his lack of assurance as a young man. His sad description of the loss of most of his early work echoes this self-effacing tone. Zhang Qi, "Shi gao zi xu," in *Wanlin wen* 1891: 1/21a-22a.

39. See Bao Shichen's biography in *EC*, pp. 610–611; also the account of his ultimately disappointing career in *Xu bei zhuan ji* 1973: vol. 990, 79/1a-b. On Bao's genius as a statecraft thinker and policy planner, see Liu Guangjing 1981.

40. Zhang Qi's eulogy "Wangshi Tang ruren xinglüe," in *Ming fa lu* 1840: "Xinglüe," s.p. 7a.

41. His biographer specifies "plague" as the cause of death in *EC*, p. 42. See the discussion of gender, mortality, and disease, in the epilogue.

42. Zhang Qi, "Wangshi Tang ruren xinglüe," in *Ming fa lu* 1840: "Xinglüe," s.p. 5b. Physicians of this period believed that "breast milk from the child's natural mother was his best choice" (Hsiung 2005, p. 83). Hsiung notes (p. 98) that mothers were advised to breastfeed until the child was at least two years old or had begun to walk. The birth intervals in Yaoqing's record of fertility suggest that she

breastfed each child for at least two years, with the shortest birth interval, separating her son Juesun from Qieying, being the first.

43. A list of medical works by members of the Fa family appears in *Guangxu Wujin Yanghu xian zhi* 1879: 28/25b.

44. *Fa shi jiasheng* 1900, "Shi" (Poetry), 5a. On Fa Qianyi (1689–1753), also known as Master Muting (Muting *gong*), see p. 1/1b.

45. According to the Zhang genealogy, Miss Fa was the fourth daughter of Fa Ding, identified as a "student in the imperial academy," a widely purchased degree. She was born in the same year as Juesun (Qianlong 54, 1789; 1790 in Western reckoning because Juesun was born in the twelfth month of the year) and she perished in the fall of Changzhou in the fourth month of 1860. The genealogy also records that she adopted as a "simultaneous heir" Juesun's nephew Jinli, who was later born to Juesun's younger brother. See *Zhang shi zong pu* 1947: 33/2: 44a-b. For Fa Ding's place in his own line, see *Guangxu Wujin Yanghu xian zhi* 1879: 26/17b.

46. Details of Zhang Qi's emotional life are poignantly recorded in a biographical sketch by his son Yuesun in Zhang Yuesun, "Xian fujun xing shu," *Ming fa lu* 1840: "Xing shu," s.p.

47. Footbinding in the Changzhou area was less severe than in the northern part of the country, according to evidence analyzed by Dorothy Ko. Among elite families like the Zhang, small feet were a mark of gentility and propriety, necessary for wearing the elegant "ladder-rung" shoes favored by elite women (Ko 2001, pp. 122–123). But to what extent "small" feet were also extremely tightly bound remains unknown. Ko cites an observation by the Jiangnan scholar Qian Yong (1759–1844) that in the Lower Yangzi area, mothers had too much sympathy for their daughters' pain and so delayed binding until the age of seven or eight, when the process was actually much more painful. Ko suggests that this may have been tied to the economic value of women's labor in the area. Qian Yong, however, was a classical scholar deeply skeptical of the practice of footbinding, which, as he pointed out, had no precedent in the classics and, on the contrary, was actually associated with courtesan culture (Ko 2005, pp. 139–141). It is not unreasonable, I think, that highly educated women like Tang Yaoqing were reluctant to take extreme measures in binding a daughter's feet.

48. Her newly intense devotions are described by Bao Shichen in his epitaph for her, printed in *Ming fa lu* 1840, "Muzhiming," s.p. 2a.

49. This year is noted in poems written ten years after Juesun's death by Yaoqing's second daughter, Guanying. See poems dated 1812, third month, and 1813, in Zhang Guanying, *Weiqing yigao* 1829: 3a, 5a. In his afterword for his mother's collected poems, which were printed by Zhang Qi after Yaoqing's death, their later-born son, Yuesun, also comments that she did not begin to write poetry until after her fortieth year. See Tang Yaoqing, *Peng shi ou yin* 1840: "Ji," 1a. My own telling of Yaoqing's story has attempted to explain her long silence, after her promising

beginnings as an educated young woman. Wu Hongyi (1970, p. 136) also dates Yao-qing's earliest poems to these years in Jiaxing, before Yuesun's birth.

50. See her poem complaining of his absence on the New Year for the second year in a row, in *Peng shi ou yin* 1840: 2b-3a.

51. In this particular sojourn, between 1807 and 1811, Zhang Qi traveled through Zhejiang, Anhui, Henan, Shandong, and the capital, returning home at most once a year, usually less often. See the preface to his untitled poem reprinted in Zhao Zhen 1922: 4/22a.

52. Much of what follows is my attempt to explain how Tang Yaoqing fared during the long years of her husband's absence. There is nothing in the family's records to justify or account for it, beyond the inference that he was in search of teaching positions or employment by an official or scholarly patron. I take the silence in the records as an invitation to explore the resources available to elite women whose husbands were continually traveling. See my discussion of dowry and women's support networks in the epilogue.

53. According to Wu Hongyi (1970, p. 137), it was only at this time that Guanying began the serious study of poetry. I have suggested, based on the memoirs of the various Zhang sisters, that informal training in poetry began much earlier.

54. In his memoir of his late wife, Zhang Qi says that "the four girls did embroidery to exchange for rice" (*Ming fa lu* 1840: "Xinglüe," 3b). Because of the girls' ages at this point in my narrative, I have altered his observation slightly, assuming that the younger girls would not have been capable of embroidery before the age of twelve or so. They might, of course, have had a hand in sorting thread.

55. This harbinger of Lunying's later fame as a calligrapher is my invention; the family's records emphasize her studies with her father later in Shandong. I cite her early interest in calligraphy by way of explaining why she did not write poems at this age.

56. Somehow during this interlude, arrangements were made to publish Zhang Huiyan's collected prose: the first imprint appeared in 1809. See Wu Hongyi 1970, p. 137.

57. A stele recording the garden's history, by a member of the notable Yun family and dated 1674, is listed as "lost" in *Guangxu Wujin Yanghu xian zhi* 1879: 28/60a.

58. The "Near Garden" or "Almost a Garden" (Jin yuan) was modestly named by the original owner, Yang Zhaolu, a retired Changzhou official ("it's almost a garden"—*jin sihu yuan*—he wrote). Yang began work on the project in 1664, shortly after the worst of the fighting in the south had ended. The garden became famous during Yang's lifetime as a gathering place for prominent literati, including the painters Yun Shouping and Wang Hui. Wang Hui painted the garden for his host. The garden changed hands several times before the end of the nineteenth century, then fell into disrepair, to be rediscovered in 1978 by a professor who remembered its past and led the drive to restore it. Tourists and travelers may now enjoy it as guests at the Changzhou Hotel (Changzhou binguan). See Tong Jun 1997, pp. 35,

173 (photograph); Luo, Shi, et al. 1984, p. 123; also *Zhongguo yuanlin jianshang cidian* 2000, pp. 76–77; and *Zhongguo renmin gongheguo diming cidian: Jiangsu sheng* 1987, p. 504.

59. In Zhang Qi's afterword for his late father-in-law's published work, he describes Yunqing's role and identifies him by his lineage generation name, Yidian. This would make him the grandson of Yaoqing's grandfather's younger brother. Yidian was an adopted heir who was removed from his father's branch and given to his father's elder brother at a young age, leaving him highly vulnerable as the only son in a dwindling line. See *Tang shi jiasheng* 1874: 1/7a-9a for a chart of the Tang genealogy. Zhang Qi, "Shu Tang Yinling Feng gong shi," *Wanlin wen* 1891: 2/3b-4b. In a prose tribute for Yidian's seventieth birthday in 1843, Wanying calls him "maternal uncle" *(congjiu)*. See Zhang Wanying, *Canfeng guan wenji chubian* 1850: 1/4a-5b.

60. See his eulogy for his wife, s.p. 5a.

61. This story also comes from Zhang Qi's eulogy, s.p. 5b.

62. See Hawkes' history of the novel in Hawkes and Minford 1973–1986, vol. 1 (1973), pp. 15–16.

63. For the consultation with the physiognomist, see notes on a poem by Qieying in *Danju xuan chugao* 3:7a. According to the note, the physiognomist pronounced Yuesun a *wenzhi hou shen*.

64. The Fa family's reputation in medicine in Changzhou is detailed in *Guangxu Wujin Yanghu xian zhi* 1879: 26/17a-b.

65. Lu forthcoming.

66. Zhang Qi, "Wangshi Tang ruren xinglüe," in *Ming fa lu* 1840: "Xinglüe," 6a.

67. In his eulogy for his wife (*Ming fa lu* 1840: "Xinglüe," s.p. 3b), Zhang Qi describes his travels during those years.

68. Bao Shichen's epitaph for Qi says that after years of travel he went to the capital, where friends persuaded him to sit for the next year's Shuntian *juren* examinations. See *Guochao qixian lei zheng chu bian* 1966: vol. 14, 247/50b. See also Zhang Qi, *Ming fa lu* 1840: "Shu," p. 3a; Zhang Weixiang 1944, p. 4; and Wu Hongyi 1970, p. 139.

69. Wu Hongyi 1970, p. 140.

70. In his eulogy, Zhang Qi says that two of her sons-in-law also gave the family loans through pawnbrokers. See Zhang Qi, *Ming fa lu* 1840: "Xinglüe," s.p. 4a.

71. During his time at the capital, Zhang Qi wrote and printed his study of late Zhou geography, *Zhanguo ce shidi;* he also completed and wrote a preface to an anthology of early poems from the Han through the Sui dynasties, titled *Wanlin shuwu gushi lu*. On these years, see Wu Hongyi 1970, esp. p. 141, describing Zhang Qi's and Bao Shichen's travels and collaborations in Beijing and Jinan between 1817 and 1819.

72. On Zhang Qi's experiences as a magistrate in Shandong, the most detailed records are supplied by Bao Shichen in his eulogy for Zhang. The words of Zhang

Qi here are based on Bao's account, and Bao must have learned everything he knew from Zhang Qi directly, in either letters or personal conversation. See *Guochao qi-xian lei zheng chu bian* 1966: vol. 14, 247/31a-34a.

73. In an afterword to Guanying's collected poems, her brother Yuesun remarks that virtually all of them were written before her marriage. See Yuesun's colophon *(ba)* for the collected poems of Zhang Guanying, *Weiqing yigao* 1907.

74. *Guangxu Wujin Yanghu xian zhi* 1879: 7/20b.

75. Zhang Qi, *Ming fa lu* 1840: "Xinglüe," s.p. 6b, notes the identity of the stone buyer. Yaoqing's travails are detailed on pp. 4a-6a.

76. Yaoqing's concerns about her father's death and burial began when she was unable to prepare his body for interment because she was living in Huizhou when he died. According to Zhang Qi, she regretted this for the rest of her life. See Zhang Qi's memoir of his wife, "Wangshi Tang ruren xinglüe," in *Ming fa lu* 1840: "Xinglüe," 7a.

77. Zhang Qi, "Wangshi Tang ruren xinglüe," in *Ming fa lu* 1840: "Xinglüe," 5a, stresses that his wife never let anyone outside the immediate family know of their difficulties, leading me to believe that some must have guessed.

78. This is based on Zhang Qi, "Wangshi Tang ruren xinglüe," in *Ming fa lu* 1840: "Xinglüe," 4a-b.

79. On the pettifoggers, or "litigation masters," of this era, see Cole 1986, pp. 118–129 (he points out that Changzhou was one of the leading centers training these people), and Macauley 1998. The term "managerial landlords" was coined by Jing Su and Luo Lun to describe the new class emerging in Shandong during the eighteenth century as the economy commercialized and the population grew. By the time Zhang Qi arrived there, the effects were apparent. See Jing Su and Luo Lun 1978, especially the discussion on pp. 138–149.

80. There is little evidence of piety in Yaoqing's records, apart from her prayers to Guanyin after the death of her first son, which are well documented in many accounts. I have taken the liberty here of expanding her spiritual life by referring to the testimony of the female Changzhou poet Wanyan Yun Zhu, who turned to this Buddhist scripture for relief from domestic pressures (Mann 1997, pp. 71, 182, 187–189), and to comments by Zhang Huiyan in his memoir of his grandmother, where he remarks that she had a rich spiritual life as a Buddhist, reading scriptures and keeping a vegetarian diet, even though she never visited temples "because of her sense of propriety" (*Mingke wen er bian* 1869: 22b).

81. Zhang Qi, "Wangshi Tang ruren xinglüe," in *Ming fa lu* 1840: "Xinglüe," 6b.

82. Zhang Yuesun, "Xian fujun xing shu," in *Ming fa lu* 1840: "Xing shu," s.p. 2b: "At the age of sixty, his black hair had turned half white."

83. While in Zhangqiu, Zhang Qi spent time with his son and his son-in-law Wu Zan, who was visiting from the capital, composing song lyrics, as recalled by Zhang Yuesun in his second preface to the *Tongsheng ji.*

84. See the poem by Zhang Qieying in *Danju xuan chugao* 1850: 3/7b-8a, and also the events described in chapter 3.

85. This story bears a disconcerting resemblance to an anecdote in the voluminous "private history project" by the late Ming official Zhang Xuan (1558–1641), cited in Sutton 2004, p. 224. Sutton makes the point that late imperial officials avoided a skeptical stance toward the gods, preferring to use popular belief in deities for their own purposes. On Zhang Xuan and his *Xiyuan wen jian lu,* see *DMB* vol. 1, pp. 78–79.

86. *Guantao xian zhi* 1936: 8/64a-b records these stories in a section on biographies of local officials.

87. Polachek (1992, pp. 321–322n31) notes that in 1826 Bao received information on conditions in Singapore from the cartographer Yi Kezhong (1796–1838), who at the time was working in Canton with scholars involved in coastal defense planning.

88. *Yamen* is the term for the building and grounds of an official government headquarters.

89. Lunying's studies of calligraphy with her father in the Green Scholar Tree Studio (Lühuai shuwu) in Guantao were celebrated in a painting for which Zhang Yuesun's Korean friend Yi Sang-jŏk wrote a colophon. See Yi Sang-jŏk, *Unsong dang chip* 1847: vol. 1, 8/2b.

90. Described by Lunying's brother Yuesun in explaining the history of her studio name, "The Green Scholar's Tree Studio," in his inscription on a painting of the scene, reprinted in Zhang Lunying, *Lühuai shuwu shi gao* 1845, "Fu lu," 4/1a-b.

91. In his inscription on the painting of his father and his sister engrossed in their calligraphy, Yuesun observes that his sister did not begin to study calligraphy until her thirty-first year. See Zhang Yuesun, "Yi shu tu tici," reprinted in Zhang Lunying, *Lühuai shuwu shi gao* 1845, "Fu lu," 4/3a.

92. Praising his father's conduct in the courtroom, Yuesun—in his memoir of his father's life—remarks that "he did not make use of crafty strategies in the courtroom, such as 'hooking from a distance' *(goujushu)*." Zhang Yuesun, "Xian fujun xing shu," in Zhang Qi, *Ming fa lu* 1840: "Xing shu," 3a. For help with this colloquial term for judicial entrapment I am indebted to Matthew Sommer.

93. Zhang Yuesun recalled: "My father, who was not good at managing his assets, died without even the means to transport his body home." "Xian fujun xing shu," in Zhang Qi, *Ming fa lu* 1840: "Xing shu," s.p. 7b.

94. These and other details of Yaoqing's virtue are affectionately chronicled by Bao Shichen in his eulogy for her, reprinted in *Bei zhuan ji bu* 1931: vol. 1000, 59/17a-18b.

95. Zhang Qi's eulogy in *Ming fa lu* 1840: s.p. 6b.

96. We can be certain that Yaoqing's concern about Ruidou's line stemmed from her intimate knowledge of the life and dedication of Lady Bai, the mother of Ruidou and of Zhang Qi's father as well. Lady Bai's decision not to kill herself when her husband died and her vow to her father-in-law that she would continue the Zhang

family line or die with her children were moral lessons deeply ingrained in Yao-qing's consciousness. Zhang Huiyan's memoir of his Grandmother Bai is the most detailed and dramatic account of her life. See "Xian zubi shi lüe," in *Mingke wen er bian*, "xia," 21a-b.

97. Zhang Qi's eulogy in *Ming fa lu* 1840: s.p. 5b.

98. In later poems recalling this time, Zhang Yuesun notes that his concubine, Li Luan, was born in the same year as his daughter. See *Jinyan shenhao zhi ju shiji* 1904: 10/4a-b, 5a-6b.

99. Tang Yaoqing, *Peng shi ou yin* 1840: 5a. Qieying's poem written en route, on the day of the Mid-Autumn Festival (September 12), appears in Zhang Qie-ying, *Danju xuan chugao* 1840: 1/9a-b.

100. Zhang Qi records her death in a poem titled "Writing My Feelings as I Set Aside Mourning Garments for My Wife, on This the Fourteenth Day of the Seventh Month of the Year *renzhen* (August 9, 1832)." See *Wanlin shi* 1891: 2/13a. Bao Shichen's epitaph for Tang Yaoqing places her death on the fourteenth day of the seventh month of Daoguang 11 (August 21, 1831), noting that she was sixty-nine *sui* at the time. He also says that her son Yuesun accompanied the body home for burial in Jiangyin, which took place on December 27 that same year. Burial in Jiangyin may be an error, or perhaps Guanying's marital family, the Zhhang, took a hand in the arrangements, since they had land in Jiangyin and had offered assistance to Yaoqing on other occasions. See *Bei zhuan ji bu* 1931: vol. 1000, 59/17b, 18b. Contradictory details are common in Zhang family documents.

101. Yuesun's memoir of his father marks the date as April 12, 1833, and his father's age as seventy. See Zhang Yuesun, "Xian fujun xing shu," in Zhang Qi, *Ming fa lu* 1840: s.p. 7a.

102. At the time of our story, Changzhou was actually a prefectural capital housing the county governments of two subordinate jurisdictions: Yanghu county and Wujin county. The Zhang are identified in county histories, and in biographies, memoirs, and just about everyplace else, as persons from Yanghu or Wujin. Changzhou was not a meaningful local identity for individual persons, although it was a legitimate choronym, or "place-name component," for literary schools. (On choronyms see Johnson 1977, p. 165n46.) In some sources, Changzhou is referred to by its ancient classical name, Piling. For the sake of the reader's sanity and my own convenience, I use the place-name Changzhou throughout this book.

103. On Changzhou's rank among Lower Yangzi walled cities, see Skinner 1977b, p. 238; on the importance of prefectural capitals that housed the seats of two or more counties, see Skinner 1977a, pp. 343–344. Skinner argues that in such centers where merchant and gentry power were concentrated, a divided county admin-istration served to fragment and thereby weaken the parapolitical power of local interest groups.

104. On Shi Liang, see "Shih Liang," in Klein and Clark 1971, vol. 2, pp. 764–766; and "Shi Liang," in Lee 2003, pp. 450–455.

105. Hong is famous as the native son who had the temerity to write an out-spoken letter criticizing the decline of imperial authority in the final years of the Qianlong reign. See Jones 1972; Elman 1990, pp. 284–290 *et passim;* Waley-Cohen 1991, p. 82.

106. Sheng's biography appears in English in Boorman 1967, vol. 3, pp. 117–120. The classic study is Feuerwerker 1958.

107. This list of luminaries comes from the preface (1939) to a wartime catalog of writings by scholars from Changzhou. See *Qingdai Piling shu mu* 1944. For in-dividual biographies, see *EC.*

108. See Vittinghoff 2004, p. 104 *et passim.*

109. See Shi Mei 2001; statistical comparisons of all counties in Jiangsu appear in a table on p. 81. Shi's research substantially updates and expands the figures re-ported in Hu Wenkai's standard work on the subject, which are summarized in Mann 1997. I am grateful to Shi Mei for making her research and this journal avail-able to me, and for referring me to the work of Jiang Qingbo (1999), who also offers a detailed analysis of the structures supporting women writers in the Lower Yangzi region.

110. See *Wu Yang zhi yu* 1887: 12/28b; *Wujin Yanghu xian hezhi* 1842: 31/10a gives the details of Lady Jin's meeting with the Empress Dowager, repeated in *Guangxu Wujin Yanghu xian zhi* 1879: 27/21a. Qian Weicheng was in fact a *zhuangyuan* (he had placed first in the palace examinations), so the Empress Dowager was obvi-ously well briefed by her own ladies-in-waiting. Qian Weicheng's daughter Meng-dian was a noted poet in her own right, far outshining her husband, whose poems were appended to *hers* when they were published (Jiang 1999, p. 159). Interestingly, unlike her daughter, Lady Jin herself was not recognized as a *cainü* by the editors of the local gazetteer; she is listed alongside faithful widows like Lady Bai, Zhang Qi's grandmother. See *Wujin Yanghu xian hezhi* 1842: 31/10a, 56a-b, 67b.

111. Chang 2007.

112. Huiyan and Qi's branch of the lineage, which was identified with Chang-zhou's De'an Neighborhood by the Great South Gate, took as its apical ancestor Zhang Duan (1440–1497), who was the first to establish residence in that part of Changzhou. The De'an Zhang began their own ancestral rites in the Hongzhi period (about the turn of the sixteenth century), positioning themselves to pursue the mul-tiple mobility strategies that were wide open at that moment. Zhang Yuesun sup-plies a history of his family in his biography of his late father, "Xian fujun xing-shu," reprinted in Zhang Qi, *Wanlin shi* 1891: s.p. 1a; see also Zhang Huiyan's biography of his father, "Xian fujun xingshi," *Mingke wen er bian* 1869: "xia" 19b. Wu Ren'an (2001, pp. 61–62) discusses the families who rose during the flourish-ing age when the new empire had been established, families who moved into the area between the Chenghua (1465–1487) and Hongzhi (1488–1505) reigns. The au-thoritative biography of Zhang Huiyan (*Guochao qixian lei zheng chubian* 1966: 132/36a-37b) by Yun Jing says that Huiyan's Zhang ancestors moved to Wujin at

the beginning of the Song dynasty, relocating from Chuzhou, Anhui (to the north-west of Nanjing, on the other side of the Yangzi and over the Anhui border). Zhuang Shouqi's eulogy for Zhang Yuesun, by contrast, says the Zhang lineage's earliest home was Sichuan. He chronicles the movement of Zhang lines within the Changzhou area following the move but offers no dates (see Zhuang Shouqi, "Hubei houbudao Zhang jun muzhiming," *Fengnan shan'guan yiji* 1875: 1/3a-b). The Zhang genealogy (*Zhang shi zong pu* 1947) supplies details for the Da Nanmen De'an *li* branch of the lineage in *juan* 33. See 33 "xia" 1a for Zhang Duan.

113. Cao Hong 1996, pp. 36–56.

114. Lu 1998 identifies these practices throughout the Lower Yangzi region.

115. Guo Songyi 2000, pp. 333–34.

116. I use an alternate spelling here and elsewhere to signal a surname different from that of the subjects of this book, even though the surnames are homonyms.

117. Mann 1992b.

118. Wu Ren'an 2001, p. 59.

119. Wu Ren'an 2001, pp. 63–68. On the pages following, Wu presents detailed examples of various mobility strategies, including an analysis of the success of Wang Xi's own Taicang lineage on pp. 71–72.

120. Wu Hongyi 1970, p. 127. On *mufu,* see Folsom 1968.

121. Polachek 1992, pp. 36–43 ff.

122. See Elman 2000, pp. 158, 162. This appointment means that Zhang Huiyan also successfully passed a special examination at the court, above and beyond the metropolitan and palace exams that made up the regular *jinshi* test (Elman 2000, p. 536).

123. See Wu Hongyi 1970, p. 132, where this sequence of events is detailed and documented. On Hong Liangji's exile, see Waley-Cohen 1991, pp. 82 *et passim.*

124. This is the description by Suzhou University professor Hua Rende, in Hua 1999, p. 105.

125. Hua 1999, p. 112.

126. Admirers of this style also studied the steles containing engraved epitaphs that were produced as part of the imperial campaign to spread Chinese burial customs among non-Han peoples living in the area around the new capital of Luoyang (Hua 1999, pp. 118–123).

127. Hua 1999, p. 125.

128. Hua 1999, pp. 127–128. Bao Shichen (who wrote a treatise on calligraphy in this style) and his school were greatly admired by Kang Youwei, who took their teachings as his own model (Hua 1999, pp. 128–129), noting that Bao had "collected and passed on the method of Deng Shiru" (translated quotation on p. 128). Bao and his followers scorned the use of model books and instead devoted their energy to collecting, mounting, and preserving steles that could serve as an inspiration to student calligraphers.

129. Guy 1987.

130. See Nakata 1982, pp. 154–55, quotation on p. 154.

131. See Bai 2003, p. 259. The latter was printed in 1802 by Sun Xingyan and a coauthor, Xing Shu (*jinshi* 1790). See also Shen 1994 on traveling to visit famous steles.

132. Nakata 1982, p. 209.

133. Readers will recall that Deng Shiru met Zhang Huiyan and Zhang Qi in 1785 at the home of Jin Bang (1735–1801) in Huizhou, Anhui, and it was through Zhang's influence that he gained the attention of prominent officials in the capital. See *EC*, p. 715. Only later did Deng befriend Bao Shichen during his travels. Deng's work was scorned by Weng Fanggang and other "copybook" partisans at the capital, perhaps because of his less-than-august class background.

134. Nakata 1982, p. 156. In 1834, Bao wrote a biography of Deng, praising him as the greatest master of the *zhuan* (*zhuanshu*, "seal script") and *li* (*lishu*, "character" or "official" script) scripts among his contemporaries. See Chang and Miller 1990, p. 102.

135. Bai (2003) writes: "With paleographic correctness now a prime consideration, . . . [character forms] in works by calligraphers of the middle and late Qing are far less bizarre and surprising [than those we find in the work of earlier calligraphers like Fu Shan]" (pp. 258–62, quotation on p. 259).

136. Bai 2003, p. 260.

137. Unschuld (2003, p. ix) compares the place of the *Su wen* in the history of Chinese medicine to Hippocratic writings in the history of medicine in Europe, except that—as he stresses—the *Su wen* continues to be consulted as a source of both theoretical and practical knowledge in modern Chinese clinical settings. As Unschuld observes, the *Su wen* and other texts from that era "mark the beginning of medicine in China" by attempting "to explain disease and health . . . solely on the basis of natural laws" (pp. 319–320). See also the approving discussion of Zhang Qi's scholarship (pp. 71–72).

138. The *Chanyun ji* was complete in manuscript form in 1837, but it was published for the first time only in 1845. Although the text was later destroyed in the Taiping Rebellion, new plates were prepared by publishers in Fujian, who reprinted the book in 1871. See postscripts to the text reprinted in Zhang Yuesun, *Chanyun ji* 1936, p. 60.

139. Widmer 1996, pp. 96–99.

140. Translated in Widmer 1996, pp. 101–102. Widmer (1996, p. 99n83) notes elsewhere that a modern edition of this text (Shanghai: Keji weicheng chubanshe, 1958) stresses the value of these annotations because they are based on practical experience.

141. Drug therapies developed by Song physicians depended upon elaborate classification systems in which drug properties were linked to these broad correspondences. See Unschuld 1985, pp. 154–188, esp. pp. 187–188. Unschuld notes that these elaborate theories never achieved a satisfactory level of practical use.

142. See Handlin 1983, pp. 140–141.

143. Leung 1987.

144. See Unschuld 1986, pp. 196–97.

145. Unschuld 1986, pp. 183–197.

146. Unschuld 1985, esp. pp. 194–212.

147. *EC,* p. 323.

148. Zhang Qi's interest in medicine, and particularly in the writings of Huang Yuanyu, following his first son's death is described in his biography by Li Zhaoluo. See *Guochao qixian lei zheng chu bian* 1966: vol. 14, 247/51b.

149. Hanson 1998 provides a concise and clear description of this traditionalist school and its critics, who were part of an emerging *wenbing* ("warm factor") school stressing the distinctive climate and diseases of the Jiangnan area. The "warm factor" physicians ultimately rejected Zhang Qi's classical canon and founded a separate southern medical tradition that distinguished "robust northerners" from "delicate southerners." Zhang Qi died before this distinction would have been clear.

150. *EC,* pp. 902–903.

151. Pomeranz 1993, pp. 128 ff.

152. See Naquin 1981; Perry 1980, esp. map, p. 114; and Esherick 1987, pp. 7–37.

153. See McDermott 1990; also the discussion of dowry in Watson 1991, pp. 352–358, and literature cited therein; also Ocko 1991, pp. 317–318. Bernhardt's analysis of women's property rights focuses on inheritance and widows' control over property and does not deal with dowry even as a form of premortem inheritance (Bernhardt 1999). Dowry and its uses are discussed further in the epilogue.

154. Ocko (1991, pp. 314–315) remarks that Qing law "gives scant attention to dowry and impinges not at all on dowry as a relationship between a daughter and her natal family."

155. Ocko 1991, p. 318; Watson 1991, pp. 356–357. See in particular discussions of *sifang qian* in Cohen 1976, pp. 178–184; Cohen's fieldwork identifies many uses of dowry that correspond to what we observe in the Zhang family records. On keeping the dowry in a locked alcove, see Bray 1997, pp. 139–140. See also Wolf 1972, pp. 131–132, on the dowry and the uterine family. The epilogue returns to the subject of dowry.

3. ZHANG QIEYING

1. "People in the world don't die from illness, they die from doctors" *(tianxia zhi min bu si yu bing er si yu yi).* Zhang Qi, *Wanlin wen* 1891: 2/21a. Note that Zhang Qi makes no reference here or elsewhere to the Fa—the interpretation of his comment offered here is strictly my own.

2. Zhang Qi's reference to the "quacks" *(yong yi)* responsible for his son's death does not name the Fa. I have guessed that the Fa physicians cared for his son because of their leading role in the literati medicine of Changzhou, which is well documented. Reference to quack doctors *(yong yi)* appears in Li Zhaoluo's biog-

raphy of Zhang Qi, reprinted in *Ming fa lu* 1840, s.p. 1a. Bao Shichen refers to a "medical error" as the cause of Juesun's death and attributes Qi's devotion to medicine to that misfortune (*Ming fa lu* 1840, "Muzhiming," s.p. 6a). For Unschuld's discussion of *yong yi*, for whom he prefers the term "common physicians," see Unschuld 1979, pp. 69–71. On Zhang Qi's frustration with medical practitioners of his time, see his complaints in "Sisheng xinyuan houxu," in *Wanlin wen* 1891: 1/20b-21a.

3. In her afterword to Qieying's collected poems, Wanying, her youngest sister, wrote: "When my sister was young, our father was always traveling far away, and our mother was heavily burdened. So from the age of six or seven *sui*, my eldest sister took on some of our mother's work, and by the time she pinned up her hair, she was in charge of the entire management of the kitchen. Our mother loved her deeply but suffered because our family was so poor that Qieying had no leisure time to read." Zhang Wanying, "Hou xu," in *Danju xuan chugao* 1840, s.p. 1a-b.

4. On "poems in praise of objects" and their place in riddles and word games of the sort relished by the Zhang family, see Saussy 1997, pp. 290–291.

5. In her assessment of Zhang Qieying as a poet, Shi Shuyi foregrounds this passage, quoting from Bao's collected works, *Yizhou shuang yi* (Shi 1987, pp. 512–513 [orig. ed. 9/2b-3a]). In the original text, Bao uses the Zhang daughters' adult names rather than their given names; for clarity, I have used given names in my translation. I have invented this encounter between Bao Shichen and Qieying, which could have happened at any time during her youth.

6. Recalled by Zhang Yuesun in an encomium on a painting of Lunying practicing calligraphy. See Zhang Lunying, *Lühuai shuwu shi gao* 1845: "Fulu," 4/1a. The *Kangxi zidian*, published in 1716, is the largest of the character dictionaries for classical Chinese, containing 47,035 characters, of which 40 percent are graphic variants, and including many exceedingly rare characters, some of which were used "rarely or only once." See Wilkinson 1998, p. 67.

7. This image of the young Qieying lying in bed ill, surrounded by books, is repeated in many accounts of her life. The original source is Wanying's afterword to Qieying's collected works. See *Danju xuan chugao* 1840: "Hou xu," s.p. 1a-b. See also Zhang Weixiang 1972: 11/8–9.

8. Wu Zan went by a number of names during his lifetime; the two given here are the most commonly used in my sources. I have fabricated Zhang Qi's letter, but not the facts it contains. I was unable to determine the precise timing of Qieying's betrothal and wedding, which must have been around 1813. Evidence for Qieying's status as a successor wife comes from the eulogy for Wu Zan by Zong Jichen. According to Zong, Wu Zan's first wife, née Jiang, gave birth to a son. Zong gives the child's name as Sihan. Zong also says that Qieying gave birth to a son who died before his name could be recorded in the genealogy. This would be the child who died of smallpox. A concubine of Wu Zan's bore a third son, whom Zong names as Siqian, and also a daughter. See Zong Jichen 1856: 10/50a-51a, kinship data on

p. 50b. I have concluded that Sihan and Zonghan are the same person. A son named Zonghan (not Sihan) appears as the copyeditor of Qieying's complete poems, and to Zonghan are also dedicated a couple of poems in her collected works: one sending Zonghan off to the south to marry (*Danju xuan chugao* 1840: 2/2a), the other mourning the death of Zonghan's wife, née Ding (*Danju xuan chugao* 1840: 2/4b-5a). These poems were written before 1837, assuming that they are in chronological order, because they precede a poem honoring Bao Mengyi's thirtieth birthday in that year. Since the poem to Zonghan refers to six years of being inseparable, Qieying must have had six years with him following her move to the capital for the first time, in 1829, and he would have been married in 1835, placing his birth date right about the time of Qieying's marriage to Wu Zan. Hence my story, which makes Qieying a successor wife married to Wu Zan following the death of his first wife in childbirth.

9. Guanying and her spouse for a time supported both of her newly married younger sisters, whose husbands were less successful. The Jiangyin Zhhang (no relation; the character is different, hence the variant romanization of the name) also helped to purchase the stone for Yaoqing's mother-in-law's chaste widow arch (see chapter 2).

10. Wu Zan's song lyrics were published under the title *Taying lou ci* in Zhang Yuesun's anthology of *ci* by his own circle of friends, titled *Tongsheng ji*. In his preface to this work, Yuesun describes his brothers-in-law studying song lyrics in Guantao with his father.

11. One must assume that such queries were for personal satisfaction only, since it was almost impossible to convict a husband or the parents-in-law of causing injury or death to a spouse or daughter-in-law. See Ch'ü 1961, pp. 107, 115–117. The accused could always plead that the victim was insubordinate and deserved to be punished, and that death or injury was an accidental result. A spouse could be convicted of homicide if his wife died of a beating he claimed she deserved, but that, too, was avoidable if he could show that he killed her accidentally.

12. In Zhang Guanying, *Weiqing yigao* 1829: "Xu" (Preface). Zhang Qi's emotional tribute to his dead daughter has centuries of precedent in the writings of distinguished literati lamenting the loss of beloved daughters and nieces, beginning with the great Tang scholar and prose stylist Han Yu. See Wu Pei-yi 1995, pp. 138–144. Han Yu too had four daughters; he lost the youngest when she was only twelve (p. 138). Hsiung (2005) argues that the sentimental and emotionally involved father became a more familiar figure in elite Chinese families from the seventeenth century onward (p. 115).

13. Zhang Guanying, *Weiqing yigao* 1829: 1b, 9b-10b, 5a, 6a, 6a-b, 7b-8a (in order of mention).

14. Translated in Mann 1997, p. 101. Reprinted in Xu Shichang 1929: 187/31b. Original in Zhang Wanying, *Linyun youyue zhi ju shi chugao* 1849: 1/2b. For the Chinese, see appendix.

15. A human who left home to learn magical arts and returned as a crane fairy. The crane fairy figures in a poem by Tao Qian (365–427), whose writing was greatly admired by the Zhang sisters.

16. A "catkin" verse alludes to the brilliance of poetic imagery in the writings of the late fourth-century female poet Xie Daoyun, who won a poetry contest by likening falling snowflakes to the flossy seeds of a willow tree (a "willow catkin," *liu xu*) floating through the air. The *locus classicus* is translated in Mather 1976, p. 64.

17. Printed in Zhang Qieying, *Danju xuan chugao* 1840: "Ci," 8a-b.

18. The reference to a decade of mourning dates this poem to the year 1834, when we know that Yuesun paid a visit to his sister in the capital. The visit could well have triggered the impulse to reread Guanying's work.

19. Biographies of Guanying frequently mention her famous absorption in poetry: "When I read a poem," she once said, "it is as if I had entered the poem myself; when I write a poem, it's as if my heart has wandered outside myself. My heart can travel to places I have never visited; my heart can embrace emotions that I have never uttered." Quoted in Zhang Weixiang 1972: 11/9.

20. Jing Su and Luo Lun 1978. A map showing the route the Zhang family traveled appears on p. 104.

21. See Yuesun's biographical sketch of his father, printed in Zhang Qi, *Wan-lin shi wen* 1840: s.p. 2b.

22. This was the seventh month of 1825.

23. Smallpox was the "preeminent" threat among the many diseases threatening children in late imperial times (Hsiung 2005, p. 135). Mourning rites for infants were minimal; most of Qieying's and Lunying's grief would have to be carried in their own hearts. See Waltner 1986, p. 679. See later in this chapter for Qieying's poem "The Death of Apricots," composed twelve years afterwards.

24. This euphemism *(kan renao)* is my invention, extrapolated from a custom at the Anguo Medicine King Temple Fair in Hebei, where women who worked as prostitutes spoke of "going to the temple fair on time" *(gan miao)*. See Zheng Hecheng 1932, p. 121.

25. Zhang Qi, *Wanlin shi,* in *Wanlin shi wen* 1840: 2/12b.

26. The wooden fish *(muyu)* is a hollow block of wood carved with the shapes of fish or fish scales. In devotions, a mallet is knocked rhythmically on the wood to focus the mind and steady the pace of chanted prayers.

27. Zhang Lunying, *Lühuai shuwu shi gao* 1845: "Xuba," 2/1a.

28. Zhang Lunying, *Lühuai shuwu shi gao* 1845: 1/3a. For the Chinese, see appendix.

29. A writing case or chest *(qie)* made of bamboo was used to store drafts of poems and other writings.

30. Zhang Yuesun's lament for Lunying's late husband, Sun Jie, reprinted in Zhang Lunying, *Lühuai shuwu shi gao, fu lu* 1868: 5/4b.

31. On women and Northern Wei stele–style calligraphy, see Zhang Zhong-

xing 1995, especially p. 25, quoting Deng Zhicheng, *Gudong suo ji*. Zhang claims that even Qiu Jin's close friend Wu Zhiying, the other famous female practitioner of Northern Wei stele–style calligraphy, did not achieve the mastery displayed in work by Zhang Lunying. I am grateful to Clara Ho for calling my attention to Zhang's article. On Qiu Jin and Wu Zhiying, see Hu 2004.

32. Some sources mention both Korean and Japanese envoys when describing foreigners who were interested in Lunying's calligraphy. See Zhang Weixiang 1972: 11/9. I have yet to locate evidence for the Japanese, but they are mentioned in a local gazetteer. See *Wu Yang zhi yu* 1887: 11 (part 5)/3b-4a.

33. This quotation is repeated in biographical accounts of Lunying's life and art.

34. This was the subject of a painting for which Yuesun and many others composed inscriptions. See Zhang Lunying, *Lühuai shuwu shi gao* 1845: "Fu lu," 3. Yuesun elsewhere recalls that both Lunying and Wanying took their studio names from their adjacent rooms in the Guantao *yamen*. See Zhang Yuesun, *Jinyan shenhao zhi ju shiji* 1904: 6/7a-8a.

35. Actually, this observation is Yuesun's, not Qieying's, in reflections on her life offered in his birthday greeting for Lunying, composed in January 1845. See Zhang Lunying, *Lühuai shuwu shi gao* 1845: "Fu lu," 4/3a.

36. In his eulogy for his late brother-in-law, Zhang Yuesun comments: "My father personally instructed [my sister] in the calligraphy of the Northern Dynasties. Sun Jie at first was displeased by this, believing that it was unseemly for a woman. But when she had completed her studies, he reluctantly pronounced that my sister was worthy of continuing her father's teachings. He would often take out her poems and calligraphy to show his friends, always with great delight" (Zhang Lunying, *Lühuai shuwu shi gao* 1845: "Fu lu," 5/5b-6a). The account of Sun Jie's life here is largely based on this eulogy, titled "Sun Shuxian aici," reprinted in a supplement to Zhang Lunying's collected poems. See Zhang Lunying, *Lühuai shuwu shi gao* 1845: "Fu lu," 5/3b-6a, quotation on p. 5b. See also Zhang Yuesun's encomium *(xuba)* for this collection.

37. Kam Louie and Louise Edwards have pointed out that calligraphy was considered a particularly "masculine" art demanding strength that lay beyond the capacities of a woman. See Louie and Edwards 1994, pp. 144–145.

38. Qieying refers to the arguments about women *(querelle des femmes)* that were especially vehement in her grandfather's time. See Mann 1992a, 1992b. On legal disputes and women's involvement, see Theiss 2004.

39. See the poem her mother wrote bidding her farewell, in Tang Yaoqing, *Peng shi ou yin* 1840: 5a. Also compare with her father's much longer poem on the same occasion, in Zhang Qi, *Wanlin shi wen* 1840: 2/12a-13b (in the edition of 1891, see 2/13b-14a). Cf. Xu Shichang, *Qing shi hui* 1996: 187/24a, 28a-b.

40. The young cousin in question was Dong Sicheng; the sequel, a continuation of the *Ci xuan*. See Wu Hongyi 1970, p. 144. Dong Sicheng later won the *juren* degree, in 1840. He was a grandson of Zhang Qi's elder sister's husband. See Zhang Weixiang 1972: 7/16-17.

41. Wu Hongyi 1970, p. 145.

42. Zhang Wanying, *Canfeng guan wenji chubian* 1850: 1/6a. See also Zhang Yuesun, *Dihua guan shi ke* 1850, "Xu," 1a, on their unusual living arrangement and his responsibility to fulfill his parents' wishes.

43. Yi Sang-jŏk (1804–1865) came to China as a professional translator, accompanying the diplomats of the elite *yangban* class who served as the Korean king's envoys to the Qing court. In the course of his career, he made twelve trips to China. As a member of the "professional class" *(chungin)* of highly educated Korean scholars who were "specialists in foreign languages, law, medicine, and accounting," Yi and his colleagues performed invaluable services for the aristocratic *yangban.* See Hwang 2004, pp. 2, 107–160. In Yi's time, the *chungin* had begun a literary movement promoting connoisseurship of classical Chinese arts and letters, in part to distance themselves from other commoners. Yi's delight in the company of Qieying's husband, Wu Zan, whom he first befriended, was soon extended to Zhang Yuesun and other Chinese scholars in his circle. Their companionship was founded on classical learning, Yi's excellence in poetry and scholarship being one of the traits that his Chinese friends most prized and admired. This in turn deeply impressed Yi, because clearly Chinese scholars paid no attention to the fine class distinctions that were so important in Chosŏn society. He obviously felt more at home intellectually in China than he did in his own country. Mr. Yi eventually became an avid purchaser of Lunying's calligraphy, buying up her finest scrolls from Yuesun when Yuesun brought them to Beijing. Pastreich (1997, p. 188) observes of Yi that despite his commoner status, Yi's learning and his embrace of Chinese gentry values, including the compilation of his own lineage's genealogy, made him a lively participant in Chinese literati circles. Korean male intellectuals at the time also evinced a growing interest in Chinese vernacular fiction (pp. 157 ff), including translations of *Honglou meng* (p. 185). Pastreich notes further that interpreters and translators like Yi were the main purveyors of the trade in Chinese books marketed in Korea (p. 85). See also Hŏ 1997, pp. 248–252; Ch'a 2003, pp. 273–308; and Chŏng 1990. Yi's role as a publicist for Lunying's calligraphy is one I have invented for him.

44. The contents of this and Wanying's other letters are my inventions. Such details of moneymaking or art for profit are not acknowledged in the Zhang's published writings except by implication, as when we learn that Lunying's admirers included Korean and Japanese connoisseurs.

45. These details from Fang Junmo 1931. See also the discussion in the epilogue.

46. Lunying's wisdom here and on other occasions, and her extreme tact in deferring to Mengyi at every turn, despite the fact that she was nearly a decade Mengyi's senior, are all detailed in Wanying's long birthday greeting composed in honor of Lunying's fortieth year (dated June–July 1845). See Zhang Wanying, *Canfeng guan wenji chubian* 1850: 1/6a-7a.

47. The notice of the award, which was later printed in the Changzhou county gazetteer, made no reference to an adopted heir. Officially, and in the Zhang line-

age genealogy, Yuesun's son, Jinli, was named the "simultaneous heir" of the two lines; unofficially, Juesun's line was simply allowed to die out. Miss Fa died in the siege of Changzhou during the Taiping Rebellion, in 1860. See *Zhang shi zong pu* 1947: 33/2/44a-b. Jinli died in 1863, while accompanying his father on the move to Shanghai. The cousin who was adopted to take Jinli's place is shown in the genealogical chart as continuing Yuesun's line, not Juesun's (33/12a-13a).

48. In her afterword to Qieying's collected poems, Wanying comments that her sister bore three children, none of whom survived. See Zhang Qieying, *Danju xuan chugao* 1840: "Hou xu," s.p. 2a.

49. See Zhang Qieying, *Danju xuan chugao* 1840: 3/1a, where she complains that she hasn't seen her brother for five years.

50. Yuesun's *Chanyun ji* was probably completed in 1837, the date when the first preface was composed. It must have circulated in manuscript for years; the first publication date is 1845.

51. This was the Naliang guan. See Yi Sang-jŏk 1847: vol. 1, 7/1b, 10/2a *et passim*. Yi's collected works are full of sentimental reminiscences recalling those days; he commissioned paintings of himself surrounded by his Chinese friends in Beijing. See Yi Sang-jŏk 1847: vol. 1, 7/1b-2a, for a poem on the first painting in this series; the second painting included seventeen literati. On Yi's Chinese friends and his book-collecting enterprise, see Chŏng 1990, esp. pp. 65–84, 126–225.

52. See Yi Sang-jŏk 1847: vol. 1, 7/1a; also *Zhang shi zong pu* 1947: 33/2/43b-44a.

53. A poem written for Chenbi's capping ceremony, dated 1849, is printed in Zhang Yuesun, *Jinyan shenhao zhi ju shiji* 1904: 10/4b-5a.

54. Recalled by Zhang Yuesun in a poem presented to Caipin when she left home after her marriage. See *Jinyan shenhao zhi ju shiji* 1904: 11/9b.

55. On adoption and surnames, see Hsiung 2005, p. 167. Bao Mengyi, also adopted, was born a Wang but took the surname of her adoptive uncle, her mother's brother.

56. Details in Zhang Wanying, *Linyun youyue zhi ju shi chugao* 1849: 2/8a.

57. Zhang Qieying, *Danju xuan chugao* 1840: 3/3b-4b.

58. On Sun Zixiao, whose proper name was Sun Yuanxiang (1760–1829), and his poet wife, Xi Peilan, a noted member of Yuan Mei's poetry circles, see *EC,* pp. 685–686.

59. On laments for children, especially girls, in poetry and prose, see Hsiung 2005, pp. 196–198.

60. Zhang Qieying, *Danju xuan chugao* 1840: 3/7b-8a. This poem was probably composed in 1839, since Qieying alludes to the "twelve years" since the death of her daughters. The *locus classicus* for the motif "the death of apricots" *(xing shang)* is a verse by the Tang poet Meng Jiao (751–814). In a preface to his poem by this title, Meng Jiao wrote: "'The death of apricots' refers to a young tender blossom that falls in the frost before it opens. I wrote this to mourn the death of my baby so long ago" (*Hanyu da cidian* 4: 776); or, in Stephen Owen's translation: "Apri-

cots die young: their flowers are nipples which the frost cuts and they fall. They lead me to grieve over my late child and to write these poems." On Meng Jiao, see Owen 1975, and Owen's notes in *ICTCL,* vol. 1, pp. 622–23. Owen reads this poem metaphorically as a commentary on the dark forces that govern politics as well as nature, but clearly Qieying takes the poem literally, as apparently did Sun Yuanxiang. For Owen's translation of these poems, see Minford and Lau 2002, pp. 850–851. Another translation appears in Hinton 1996, pp. 41–51. In her poem, Qieying remarks on how so many deaths came within six years, between 1827 (when four babies died of smallpox, her two and Lunying's two girls) and 1832 (when Qieying lost another son, also to smallpox). So she and Lunying were bereaved together in 1827. See also Chang and Saussy 1999, pp. 484–485, for translations of two of Xi Peilan's sixteen quatrains mourning her six-year-old son, whose death was followed only a day later by that of his three-year-old brother. Xi Peilan and her husband had an unusually close relationship, and it is of interest that Qieying read their poetry yet here she mentions only Sun's and not Xi Peilan's. Doubtless this is because she wanted to use the apricot motif in her own poem.

61. The phrase *zhang zhu* (lit., pearl in the palm of the hand) is a metaphor for a beloved child, most often referring to a daughter.

62. This heartbreaking line reminds us that Qieying reared her husband's children but never her own.

63. In reality, both of Yuesun's brothers-in-law traveled a lot of the time, presumably in search of teaching positions or other patronage, to Anhui and to Jiujiang, Jiangxi. See poems in Zhang Yuesun, *Jinyan shenhao zhi ju shiji* 1904: 6.

64. On the birthday, see various tributes printed with Qieying's collected poems, especially *Danju xuan chugao* 1840: "Tiba," 2a, 4b, 8b. The *tiba* by Zhhang Pei (4b) remarks that Qieying was so homesick that Yuesun used to travel to the capital and spend a year or two at a time there to be near her, alternating residences between Changzhou and Beijing.

65. Tang Bihen was one of the seven offspring of Tang Yifen and his wife, Dong Wanzhen. Other sources record her courtesy name as Bichun; her given name was Jiaming. Tang Jiaming was a painter who was noted for her *baimiao* (fine ink-outline) portraits. See Zhang Weixiang 1972: 11/10.

66. The phrase *lianyin* in the title, literally "linked humming," might also be translated "versifying together," but the linking means that each poet must use the last character or phrase from the preceding poem as the beginning of his or her new poem. The linking is a kind of poetic game that also requires humming or chanting lines to each other. The image is one of thin walls and sympathetic minds. Accounts of this painting appear in Jin Wuxiang's chapbook *Suxiang wu bi* 1894: 2/6a-7b. See also Lei Jin 1922: 2/15a-16b. Zhang Yuesun's Korean friend Yi Sangjŏk was invited to write a colophon as well, which he recorded in his collected works under the date 1842. See *Ŭnsong dang chip* 1847: vol. 1, 7/1a-b.

67. This description is my own invention, based on the colophons that follow.

68. These colophons have been reprinted many times. The texts translated here are found in Jin Wuxiang, *Suxiang wu bi* 1894: 2/6b-7b.

69. An allusion to the sixth of Tao Qian's twenty poems on drinking wine.

70. The "five lakes" are the various lakes in the area near Changzhou; her meaning here is "let us ignore the outside world and its gossip."

71. Qieying at the time was closely following events along the southern coast outside Canton, since her husband moved in the circles of officials who supported Lin Zexu. Two years later, she wrote an impassioned song lyric lamenting the foreign invasion and decrying the cashiering and exile of Lin Zexu. So "peace" here probably refers not simply to family harmony but also to the state of the country, especially in the south.

72. The gazetteer of Changshu county, Wu Zan's native place, notes: "When people from our native place took the exams in the capital, no one who came to him in need ever went away dissatisfied. The Fellowship Hall of his native place guild was in an inferior location, so he consulted with geomantic specialists and collected funds to relocate and rebuild it. Within ten years the guild claimed four top-ranked graduates in the Hanlin palace examinations." *Chongxiu Chang Shao hezhi* 1904: 27/42b.

73. See Ko 1994, pp. 226–242.

74. On Shen Shanbao's life and work, see Fong 2000; also Fong 1998.

75. Qieying never had a chance to meet Wanyan Yun Zhu, who was actually from her same home area, Changzhou. By the time Qieying might have gone looking for her, Yun Zhu had left home to live with her son, and their paths did not directly cross.

76. See Ku Sui 1980, pp. 163–166.

77. The leading women poets who wrote song lyrics in the heroic style, including Shen Shanbao, are discussed in Li Xiaorong 2005.

78. Zhang Qieying, *Danju xuan chugao* 1840: 1/5b. Reprinted in Xu Shichang, *Qing shi hui* 1996: 87/24b. For the original poem, see appendix.

79. In the other version of the legend, Moye casts herself into the cauldron as a sacrifice to ensure that the sword's steel will set properly, with the result that two swords (one female, one male) emerge from the forge and are named after husband and wife as a yin and yang pair. The suicide image is the one not favored by Qieying. Lu Xun retells the former version of the legend in a story titled "Forging the Swords," translated by Yang and Yang 1972, pp. 74–95.

80. For other *ci* written to this tune by female poets, see Li Qingzhao's (translated in Chang and Saussy 1999, p. 93); and Zhang Yuniang's (translated in Chang and Saussy 1999, p. 145).

81. According to Morohashi (v.4, 10953.65), the first poet to use the phrase *gan shi* ("to be moved by events," "to express concern about events") in a title was the most distinguished poet of the Jin period, Yuan Haowen (1190–1257), in a verse containing the following lines: "If I sought nothing during the years when I was

young and robust, / How can my schemes as an old man ever come to anything?" *(zhuang shi ben wu qu, lao mou he suo cheng)*. Perhaps this poem was composed on the eve of the Mongol conquest of Kaifeng, where Yuan was serving as a prominent official in the waning years of Jin rule. J. Timothy Wixted, in his biography of Yuan, says that Yuan "is . . . famous for his poems lamenting the demise of the [Jin]" (p. 953), the tone of which led critics to compare him to Du Fu. Yuan was associated with the *haofang,* or "heroic," style of *ci* poetry (*ICTCL,* vol. 1, p. 847). See also West 1974, pp. 142–169. Both Weng Fanggang and his disciple Ling Tingkan wrote chronological biographies of Yuan Haowen, a measure of the revival in his poetry during Qieying's lifetime (*EC,* pp. 515, 857–858). A modern example of a *gan shi* poem is Qiu Jin's verse of that title, reprinted in Ji 1978, p. 234; for translations of poems in this mode by Qiu Jin, see Chang and Saussy 1999, pp. 651–655.

82. For a dramatic account of the British advance and the fall of Zhenjiang in July, see Elliott 1990.

83. Bao Shichen's concerns about the fate of the country well predated the Opium War troubles. He attributed his broad learning to his efforts to come to terms with the country's problems and to deal with them effectively throughout his life. In a letter to a friend, he once wrote: "I was born in the Qianlong reign, and by the time I was a young student, everything was falling apart. Bribery was pervasive and open, the administration was contaminated and vile, and the people's energy was taut like a spring, as if there might be a rebellion. I thought then of how to prevent violence and ward off chaos, so I studied the arts of war. When I saw how the people's livelihood had grown so precarious that with a single drought, they were reduced to starving on the roadsides, I wondered how to restore the foundations of our economy and enrich their lives, and I turned to the study of agriculture. Then I saw that while most people trod innocently through life, villains preyed on them as if they were ducks and came away with immense profits. Wondering how to punish wrongdoing and eliminate crime, I studied the legalists" (quoted in Chen Weizhao 2001, p. 199). Bao's sense of practical engagement with the problems of his day must have been imparted to the Zhang both through his adopted daughter, Mengyi, and through his close relationship with Lunying and the rest of the family. To him, directly or indirectly, we probably owe much of Qieying's political awareness.

84. Wang Ding was part of a cohort of reformist officials who emerged as leaders in the post-Heshen era, when the Jiaqing Emperor made a futile attempt to eradicate the corruption that laced the bureaucracy. Qieying's fervent identification with Wang Ding is another sign of her male relatives' close affiliation with that post-Heshen reform effort.

85. Elman 1990, pp. 284–290 *et passim;* Waley-Cohen 1991, p. 82.

86. As a result of Lin Zexu's blockade of British supply lines in Canton, British ships had moved northward to occupy Dinghai, Zhejiang, on July 5, 1840. Lin's dismissal, which followed Qishan's conciliatory settlement with the British at Tian-

jin, came on September 28 of that same year. Ordered exiled to Yili, Lin got a reprieve in the autumn of 1841 because of floods on the Yellow River, when he was ordered to Kaifeng to assist in Wang Ding's flood control efforts. After this work was successfully completed, and despite Wang's positive report on Lin's participation, however, Lin was forced to proceed to Yili, in 1842. Wang Ding subsequently died in Peking, reportedly (according to some sources) committing suicide as a protest against Qing policies toward the British and, especially, the exile of Lin Zexu. Lin was exonerated in 1845 and lived long enough to accept an appointment as acting governor of Guangxi during the early years of the Taiping Rebellion. He died in 1850, en route to his post. See *EC*, p. 513, for details; also Zhang Zhenhuai's notes on this poem (Zhang Zhenhuai 1997, pp. 146–147).

87. Reprinted in Zhang Zhenhuai 1997, pp. 145–147. Original in Shen Shanbao, *Mingyuan shi hua* 1863: 8/6a. See appendix.

88. "Soundless words" *(duoduo)* is an allusion to a story about Yin Hao (fl. 350), who, after being dismissed from office, lived in Xin'an in western Zhejiang and spent all day, every day, writing characters in the air. When closely observed, he was seen to be writing only four characters over and over again: *duoduo guaishi* ("what a strange thing it is!"). See Mather 1976, p. 451.

89. "Aggrieved bird spirit" is a reference to the spirit of the daughter of Emperor Yan, who drowned in the Eastern Sea and turned into a pheasantlike seabird.

90. Here she alludes to Wing Ding's so-called corpse admonition *(shijian)*, a memorial showing that he was ready to die for his cause, which he allegedly prepared to submit to the throne before it was suppressed by the opposition party led by Mujangga.

91. Zhenjiang fell on July 20, closing the Grand Canal to north-south transport and opening the way to Nanjing. See Wakeman 1978, p. 206. The optimal speed of courier service from Nanjing to Beijing at that time was ten days. See Fairbank and Teng 1960, p. 30. A more recent study of the fall of Zhenjiang focuses on the rise of ethnic consciousness emerging out of policies to single out "traitors" among the civilian population by the Manchu garrison commander, Hailing. See Elliott 1990. Eyewitness accounts of the fall of Zhenjiang are translated in Waley 1958, pp. 197–221.

92. The story of the British advance is well told in Wakeman 1978, pp. 206–210.

93. Shen Shanbao, *Mingyuan shi hua* 1863: 8/5b-6a. Shi Shuyi, who quotes these comments, offers her own observation: "Qieying's sensitivity to the conditions of her time, as evidenced here, is rarely seen in the women's quarters of that period." See Shi Shuyi 1987, pp. 512–13; also Zhang Zhenhuai 1997, pp. 147–149. Su Zhecong singles out this coauthored lyric as the earliest example of women's "patriotic" writings in the period following the Opium Wars. See Su Zhecong 1988, pp. 5, 227–228. The song lyrics by Zhang Qieying and Shen Shanbao, translated in Mann 2003, self-consciously quote the Su Shi lyric.

94. Shen Shanbao, describing Qieying's anthology in her *Mingyuan shi hua* (1863: 8/3a), observed that it had yet to go to a printer. Wanying's biographies, on the other hand, appear in her collected prose, *Canfeng guan wenji chubian*. On poetry anthologies of this sort, which coupled poems with biographies of their authors to narrate the history of an age, see Meyer-Fong 2004, esp. pp. 19–20.

95. Zhang Qieying, *Danju xuan chugao* 1840: 3/2a-b.

96. Shen Shanbao, *Mingyuan shi hua* 1863: 8/5a-b.

97. On the origins of this studio name, which honors the historical geographer Gu Zuyu, see chapter 2.

98. Details summarized in Zhang Weixiang 1972: 7/19. According to Yuesun's old friend Zhuang Shouqi, he was appointed to the rank of magistrate in the city of Wuchang in 1846. He immediately won praise for his skillful handling of the flood crisis that he encountered shortly after taking office, particularly for his flood victim relief program. Within a year he had been promoted to the post of department magistrate, one rank higher; in this capacity he reported directly to the provincial governor. In 1850, as the Taiping Rebellion was just beginning, he was transferred to a magistracy in the adjacent city of Hanyang. See Zhuang Shouqi, *Fengnan shan'guan yiji* 1875: 1/4a.

99. See Zhang Wanying, *Canfeng guan wenji chubian* 1850: 1/32a.

100. The well-established home for chaste widows mentioned here would be the venerable institution founded in 1774 by the lay monk Peng Shaosheng (1740–1796), a Changzhou scholar whose philanthropic vision inspired others in Jiangnan to create similar shelters for the protection of the widows and orphans of impoverished scholars and degree-holding families. See Leung 1993, pp. 11–12. The placement of Miss Fa in a private accommodation is, like other parts of her fragmented story, a fiction I created to explain disparate and unrelated facts of her life. Private accommodations were common in the nineteenth century, particularly in areas where widow homes were full (Tao 1991, pp. 116–118).

101. It is not clear who among the sisters initiated these conversations about a concubine for their brother, but Yuesun left a poem thanking Lunying for "buying a concubine to keep me company" *(mai ji shi yu)*. See *Jinyan shenhao zhi ju shiji* 1904: 7/1b-2a.

102. Zhang Weixiang 1972: 11/10.

103. Zhang Yuesun, *Jinyan shenhao zhi ju shiji* 1904: 10/4a-b, 5a-6b.

104. See Zhang Wanying, *Canfeng guan wenji chubian* 1850: 1/31a. Wanying marks this journey as a decade after her return from Shandong to Changzhou in 1834. Meanwhile, of course, the Opium War had been fought and lost. The family's records take little note of this.

105. The opera, by the great playwright Guan Hanqing (c. 1120–c. 1307), was based on a series of local legends about a filial woman in Tancheng county, Shandong. The occasion for Wang Xi's work, which was commissioned as a history of the legend and its sources, was the rebuilding of a shrine in the woman's memory

by the incoming magistrate, who was a native of Changzhou and knew Zhang Qi through local connections. This would be a fine example of the sorts of employment that kept young literati like Wang Xi afloat. See his preface to the "Record of the Eastern Seas" ("Donghai ji"). Wang Xi was also following in distinguished footsteps, as stele inscriptions for the shrine had been composed earlier, in 1797 and again in 1808, by the distinguished Changzhou scholar Sun Xingyan ("Donghai ji," "fu lu").

106. The concubine's children, three boys and a girl, were born between 1828 (the year of Mengyi's marriage) and 1844 (the year of Mengyi's death). If Mengyi gave Wanying her "present" on an important birthday, we might surmise it was in the year 1839, Wanying's fortieth year, following the birth of all of Wanying's own children: Caipin was born in 1826, Caifan in 1827, Cailan in 1832, and Caizao in 1839; Chenbi's birthdate was 1835. See the poem for Wanying on her fortieth birthday written by Qieying, in Xu Shichang, *Qing shi hui* 1996: vol. 3, 187/25b.

107. See Ko 1994, pp. 224–226, on this kind of vicarious travel; also Mann 2005.

108. Johnson 1977.

109. On the more famous Wang of Taicang, including the painters Wang Shimin and Wang Yuanqi and the statesman Wang Xijue, see *Rengui zhi gao* 1880: 2/38a–41a, 46b–47a, 62a-b, 66b–67a; 5/14a-b *et passim; Taicang zhou Zhenyang xian zhi* 1919: 19/1a-2b, 7b-10a, 30a-b; 20/13b-14a *et passim*. Wanying refers specifically to her husband's ancestor "Lord Wensu," Wang Xijue (19/10a, 25/19a). The first gazetteer contains no mention of Wang Xi, but *Taicang zhou Zhenyang xian zhi* 1919 found space to list him (25/75a) as a poet; the same gazetteer also records the work of his talented daughter, Wang Caipin (25/70b). See also the biography of Wang Xijue in *DMB,* pp. 1376–1379.

110. After death the body was placed in a coffin made of the finest wood the family could afford. Coffins were sealed and made airtight by treating them with lime and varnish, which were applied in several layers, often in combination with crushed crockery, to produce a very hard surface. Such coffins, properly treated, permitted families to delay burial for months or even years if necessary. See Doolittle 1867: vol. 1, pp. 213 ff. Such delays were common because of the importance of selecting and purchasing an auspicious gravesite and because, as in the case of Wang Xi and Zhang Qi, death often occurred far from the ancestral home, where the body must be buried. Escorting the coffin home was a duty reserved for the wife, if she outlived her spouse. The journey is described in detail in Zhang Wanying, *Canfeng guan wenji chubian* 1850: 1/29a-31a. See also Mann 2005.

111. See Ko 1994, p. 221, for a graphic description.

112. The Grand Canal stretched 650 miles from Hangzhou northward as an inland passage to the capital; the distance from Qieying's departure point near Zhenjiang to her destination was about 400 miles. Her boat would travel against the current, which was about three miles per hour, all the way to the Yellow River crossing, perhaps covering 20 miles in a week, then moving more quickly as the current

changed direction and flowed north. In the year of Qieying's journey, 1847, the official grain tribute had to be transshipped in Shandong because of low water, making delays unavoidable. In fact, so problematic had transport on the Canal become by this time that a year later the court shipped as much tribute grain as possible by sea. See Williams 1900, vol. 1, pp. 32–37; Hinton 1956, p. 18. On problems in Canal shipping earlier in this period, see Leonard 1996.

113. Zhang Wanying, "Nan gui ji cheng," *Canfeng guan wenji chubian* 1850: 1/29a-31a. See also Mann 2005.

114. See *Book of Odes (Shi jing)*, "Xiao ya," book 1, ode 4, "Chang di," or, "The mountain cherry" (Legge 1991, vol. 4, pp. 250–252). *Di*, flowering plum (homonym for *di* ["brothers"]), embodies the metaphorical language of the poem, which celebrates brotherly affection and brotherly bonds, which are superior to the bonds joining spouses: the wagtail as it bobs is an emblem of the unity of brothers and cousins of the same surname (when one end rises, the other falls). In the poem, the wagtail, a water bird, finds itself displaced by war to the dry plains, just as brothers may be cast apart in times of disorder. But at the same time, it is brothers who will most diligently seek one another out and save one another; in this, as in other times, brothers are always better than friends. (See also notes in *HYDCD*, vol. 1: 434–435.)

115. In a letter dated 1850, Zhang Yuesun says his household in that year numbered twelve, including his own children, his sisters' children, and two concubines (Yi Sang-jŏk, "Haerin ch'ŏktok" n.d., 5a).

116. Wanying did not begin writing prose until the year of her fortieth birthday. See *Canfeng guan wenji chubian* 1850: "Xu," 1a. Her first prose success was her afterword for Qieying's poetry collection, *Danju xuan chugao*, reprinted in her own collected prose, *Canfeng guan wenji chubian* 1850: 1/1a-2b.

117. Spence 1996. Rudolph Wagner has shown that Hong's vision of himself as a son of God was first recorded in 1848, though the original testimonial did not survive. See Wagner 1982, pp. 18 ff.

118. See Jen 1973, p. 100, quoting from Zhang Yuesun, "Chu kou jilue," n.d.

119. Yuesun's biographer explains that subsequent investigations cleared his name, though he was initially blamed for the fall of the city. See Zhuang Shouqi, "Hubei houbudao Zhang jun muzhiming," in *Fengnan shan'guan yiji* 1875: 1/4a-b.

120. For details, see *Wu Yang zhi yu* 1887: 5/4/1a-b.

121. Zhang Yuesun, *Jinyan shenhao zhi ju shiji* 1904: 16/3b, note to a poem dated 1861. Luoshan is in Jingzhou prefecture, Hubei; Yiyang is part of Changsha prefecture in Hunan. It is not clear why the sisters were separated. Possibly Wanying stayed in the home of Yuesun's old friend Wang Boxin, who was a native of Jianli, Hubei, the closest town to Luoshan; Zeng Guofan's ties to the family would have found them a safe haven in the area around Changsha. In a letter to his Korean friend Yi Sang-jŏk, dated winter 1859, Yuesun explained that all of his sisters had been able to continue instructing the children in their charge throughout the rebellion. See Yi Sang-jŏk, "Haerin ch'ŏktok" n.d., 17a.

122. Jen 1973, p. 322.

123. Yi Sang-jŏk 1847–1862: vol. 3, 2/5b, 4/8a, 5/3b; vol. 4, 78/10b.

124. The poem is printed in Yi Sang-jŏk 1847–1862: vol. 4, 9/3b-4a.

125. Zhang Yuesun, "Chu kou ji lüe," n.p. I am grateful to Wang Yan for copying this rare manuscript from the Nanjing Library. This is the source of Jen Yu-wen's (1973, p. 100) quotation in his discussion of the ineptitude of the Manchu military leadership. The entire account by Yuesun narrates his military strategies (all excellent and foresightful) and the leadership's astounding capacity to ignore or contravene his advice. The source of Yuesun's own military expertise is unclear, but his close ties to members of what Polachek (1992) has identified as the "war party" may have supplied him with advisors who were sophisticated military strategists.

126. On the "middling," or professional, class, see Hwang 2004; on Yi's appreciation for China's open mobility system, and for the friendship of Chinese literati who esteemed his talent, see Hŏ 1997, p. 251.

127. These networks were also political. He Shaoji, a protégé of Ruan Yuan and a founding member of the Gu Yanwu Shrine Association, one of the "vigorously nonconformist" circles in the capital during the Daoguang period, wrote a preface for Yi's collected poems. On the political circles of the time, see Polachek 1992, pp. 227–230 *et passim*.

128. *Guangxu Wujin Yanghu xian zhi* 1879: 6/11b. The gazetteer editors mince few words in describing the cowardice of Governor-General He Guiqing, who abandoned the city and fled for his life, leaving the city's residents and defenders trapped inside. They managed to hold out for six days. See also the impassioned record of the city's fall reprinted in *Wu Yang zhi yu* 1887: 5/4/1a-3b, estimating that 20,000 were killed and an equal number committed suicide.

129. Zhang Yuesun, "Chu kou ji lüe," n.p.

130. Deng Zhicheng, *Gudong suo ji* 1933: 7/10b-11a. Deng, citing Li Ciming's famous diary, *Yueman tang riji,* says that according to Li, Lunying lived past seventy, and that "during the Tongzhi reign, she lived at her brother's official residence in Wuchang, supporting herself by selling her calligraphy and her paintings." This suggests that Lunying found a way to remain in Wuchang for years following her brother's transfer and death. Li Ciming's diary covers the years 1863–1888.

131. Jingzhou is the present-day city of Shashi. Zhang Yuesun himself had planned to republish her work, but he did not live to see his project carried out. He mentions his plans in a letter to Yi Sang-jŏk dated early 1862, explaining that the woodblocks for the original edition were destroyed in the fighting at Wuchang ("Haerin ch'ŏktok" n.d., 10b). The reprinting was undertaken by Lü Junsun, a scholar-official from a Changzhou family who was related by marriage to Lunying, probably through her adopted daughter, Sihui, who married a Lü. See Zhang Lunying, *Lühuai shuwu shi gao* 1868, "tici xuke." Comments on Lunying's excellent health appear in the afterword ("shu hou").

132. According to the *Zhang shi zong pu* 1947 (33/2/44b), the date of her death was May 26, 1860.

133. Jingzhou is located upriver from Wuchang just below Yichang.

134. This account is paraphrased from Zhuang Shouqi, *Fengnan shan'guan yiji* 1875: 1/4b-6b.

135. In 1862, Yuesun, charged with carrying out a "thorough investigation of corruption in the Shanghai customs administration," wrote to Zeng Guofan to complain about the conduct of the chief official at Shanghai, the *daotai* Wu Xu. He also criticized Li Hongzhang himself, along with Zeng Guofan, for a failure of leadership. See Spector 1964, p. 56; also Jen 1973, pp. 492–494 (both refer to Yuesun by his courtesy name, Zhongyuan).

136. Sun Dianqi 1980, p. 294. See also Liu 1970.

137. Wu Lanwan 1866, "Xu" (Prefaces), 4a-8a. Biographies of Wu Lanwan appear in Li Junzhi 1990, "*gui xia*," 38b; and Shi Shuyi 1987, pp. 598–599 [10/16b]. Wu Lanwan's poem about her visit to Wuchang is printed in her collected works (1866: 10a). Wu Lanwan's younger sister, Lanze, may have accompanied her grandmother and her elder sister to Wuchang. A poem from her own collected works, which were circulated in manuscript form with a preface by Zhuang Shouqi dated 1863, describes escaping from unrest in Hubei in the year 1860. In this case, the escape may have been from *nian* activity in the north, and the implication is that Qieying spent more than a year staying with her brother. See Wu Lanze, "Gengshen bikou dao Chu cheng zhu zunzhang" (1863: n.p.). Like their grandmother, Wu Lanwan and Wu Lanze wrote poems of "death and destruction" *(sangluan)* in an attempt to capture and commemorate the suffering of their time. See Mann 2003.

138. See chapter 1 on Xu Zhenyi; for the biography of Ren Daorong (1823–1906), see *Qing shi gao jiao zhu* 1986, vol. 13, pp. 10549–10550.

139. Reprinted in *Zhang shi zong pu* 1947: 33/12a-13a.

140. The term *ci* is translated here as "song lyric" following the usage in Yu 1994.

141. Egan 1994.

142. Pauline Yu (1994, p. 93) attributes the widespread fascination with the *ci* form during the early Qing period to the leadership of critics like Wang Shizhen (1634–1711) and Zhu Yizun (1629–1709), who were in turn influenced by the antiquarian scholasticism of their day, as well as by regional scholarly loyalties.

143. The best known of these was the Xuannan song lyric club (Xuannan *ci she*), identified by Polachek as the Xuannan poetry club (Xuannan *shi she*) (Polachek 1992, esp. pp. 47–50). It is unclear whether or not the two groups were overlapping or identical. In tracing links between the Zhang brothers and the Xuannan circle listed by Polachek (1992, p. 299n49), there are few clues. One of the founding members, Zhu Jian (*EC*, pp. 177–178), was sometimes compared to Yao Nai and Li Zhaoluo in his classical scholarship (*EC*, p. 177). Another, Tao Zhu (*EC*,

pp. 710–711), had ties to Bao Shichen (e.g., in 1826 he delivered the grain tax quota by sea, at Bao's suggestion, while serving as governor of Jiangsu). Likewise, at the suggestion of Bao and Wei Yuan, he adopted the salt ticket system in 1832 while serving concurrently as governor-general at Nanjing and as Liang-Huai salt commissioner. And one of Tao Zhu's seven daughters married a son of Hu Linyi. But these are at best tenuous connections.

144. Yu 1994, pp. 95–96, quotation on p. 96. The rival scholarly circle was the Tongcheng *xuepai,* which traced its origins to Gui Youguang and included Fang Bao, Liu Dakui, and Yao Nai. Ultimately it was the Tongcheng school, not the Changzhou school, that proved most influential in the subsequent history of literature, despite the fact that the Changzhou writers were much more influential among their contemporaries. Zeng Guofan, among others, was an admirer of the Tongcheng school. See Chow 1994; also *ICTCL,* vol. 1, p. 498 *et passim.*

145. See Liu 1962, pp. 20–29.

146. Liu 1962, pp. 30–32.

147. Polachek attributes this partly to Qianlong politics, in particular the reforms in the examination curriculum that restored verse writing to the examinations in the decade 1751–1760 (Polachek 1992, pp. 27–28, quotation on p. 28). Among the other causes of the shift toward "aesthetic fellowship" Polachek names the importance of cultivating sources of insider information on the basis of relatively fleeting and superficial contacts, the need to cast one's circle of "mentors and friends" as widely as possible, and the popularity and relative ease of publishing stylistic pieces that would attract the attention and interest of aspiring literati. See pp. 25 ff.

148. They were opposed to two other approaches to contemporary song lyrics: the so-called Western Zhejiang (Zhexi) group, which sought elegance and refinement over content or significance; and the Yangxian group, named for the founder's home county in present-day Yixing, Jiangsu, which advocated unrestrained expression, according to the standards used by critics at the time.

149. See the discussion in *ICTCL,* vol. 1, pp. 225–226; also pp. 230–231, 238–239, 846–49.

150. The work Yuesun refers to here is the *Wanlin ci xuan,* a song lyric anthology that not only transformed the writing of lyric poetry in China but also attracted attention abroad in Japan. First published in 1797, the book touted 116 selected lyrics by forty-four Tang, Five Dynasties, and Song poets. See Wu Hongyi 1970. The quotation, which appears on p.3, is taken from a copy of the preface that appears in Miao Quansun's *Guochao Changzhou ci lu.*

151. One of the best statements of the philosophy of *ci* composition as it was practiced by the Zhang is found in a preface to seven song lyrics by Pan Zengwei in Zhang Yuesun's *Tongsheng ji.* Pan himself was the son of Pan Shi'en, a prominent supporter of Lin Zexu (*EC,* pp. 607–608). The preface contains a lengthy critical discussion of Mao Odes 84 and 85 and the problems of interpreting meaning in poetry. On the relationship between anthologies and canon formation, see Yu 1994.

152. These are ideas about poetry that can be traced to Su Shi. Yet Zhang Huiyan had reservations about the *haofang*, or heroic, style, associated with Su Shi's most outspoken and candid song lyrics. For a discussion of Zhang's poetic theory, see the essays in Changzhou shi wenhua ju 1997.

153. See Lo and Schultz 1986, pp. 24–25. The most important critic of the Zhang was Wang Guowei (1877–1927), who called Zhang Huiyan's treatment of *ci* "absurd," and accused him of assigning "abstruse and involved interpretations" to great song lyrics that were in fact simply "evocative expressions of sentiment with no hidden meaning implied." Translated in Rickett 1977, p. 78.

154. Ye Jiaying, for example, goes so far as to suggest that the Zhang brothers' interest in song lyrics was purely instrumental, the result of their need to produce appropriate teaching materials for the young men they were tutoring in Jin Bang's household in Huizhou. See Chia-ying Yeh Chao (1978) for her sometimes caustic assessment of Zhang Huiyan's literary theories, citing equally critical contemporary scholarship by Chinese literary historians, especially p. 161, on the Jin family as consumers of *ci*. Pauline Yu's view of the Changzhou school's legacy is more benign (Yu 1994, p. 96).

155. On the oppressive effects of censorship, cumulative in the Qianlong literary inquisition and continuing through the compilation of the Four Treasuries compendia, see Wu Hongyi 1970, pp. 10–14; also Guy 1987, pp. 157–200. On the aftermath of the scandals surrounding the Manchu courtier Heshen (1750–1799), see Polachek 1992; also Jones and Kuhn 1978, pp. 116–119.

156. *Qing shi gao jiao zhu* 1986: 55, "zhi" 130, "yiwen" 4:4198.

157. See Wu Jin's preface to Zhang Wanying, *Canfeng guan wenji chubian* 1850: s.p. 1a-b.

158. Yu 1994, p. 96.

159. Fong 1994, p. 121.

160. Fong 1994, p. 135.

161. Fong 1994, pp. 140–143. Fong points out that the late Qing revolutionary martyr Qiu Jin specifically embraced the heroic martial mode and used it to express her own political voice, in a self-conscious echo of the Song loyalist general Yue Fei, who made the tune famous in his own song lyric.

162. Chang 1994, pp. 185–186. She stresses that, in the end, no rigid line can be drawn between these two classes of writers and their works. But her proposition should be kept in mind when reviewing the tunes chosen by women writers, if in fact tunes send a signal about one's poetic voice.

163. Translated by Kathryn Lowry in Chang and Saussy 1999, p. 533.

164. Cao Hong 1996, pp. 36–56. See also the discussion of women in the leading families of the Su'nan region in Jiang 1999, pp. 150–173.

165. Like Cao Hong, Zhang Hongsheng has stressed the importance of female *ci* writers in the Qing period, pointing not only to the concentration of these writers in the Jiangsu-Zhejiang area but also to the importance of family in nurturing

female talent. He associates successful women writers with flourishing literati families like the Zhang (Zhang Hongsheng 1998, pp. 180–182).

166. Cao Hong 1996, pp. 38–42 ff. Quotation, citing the *Wujin Yanghu he zhi,* is on p. 40.

167. Qieying was a mentor to, among others, Zhang Menglong of Xiangyin, near Changsha, Hunan. Menglong's father was a *jinshi* of 1811, making him a rough contemporary of Zhang Qi (Xu Shichang 1996, vol. 3, p. 3174 [*juan* 188: 44a]). Zuo Xixuan of her own native place, whom Qieying had instructed as a young girl, sent her a poem titled "To my 'mother' Mengti who has now been in Hunan for half a year, written to express my feelings" (Xu Shichang 1996, vol. 3, pp. 3206–3208 [*juan* 190: 1a-5b]). And the Mongol woman poet Naxunlanbao (d. 1873) sent a poem to Qieying thanking her for deigning to write an inscription on a small portrait of herself (Xu Shichang 1996, vol. 3, p. 3207 [*juan* 190: 2a-b]).

168. See, for example, her poems "Ballad of a Soldier's Life" and "Because of the Long Rains I Was Concerned about the Peasants, and So I Wrote This Poem as a Prayer on Their Behalf," translated in Idema and Grant 2004, pp. 663–666.

169. Polachek 1992. Reading the list of authors who contributed prefaces and encomia to the Zhang sisters' work, we find the names of noted scholars and officials, including Feng Guifen, Zhang Mu, Mei Zengliang, Qin Xiangye, two sons of Pan Shi'en, and the father of Xue Fucheng. (See their various greetings to Zhang Lunying on the occasion of her fiftieth birthday, when her collected poems were printed by her brother, in Zhang Lunying, *Lühuai shuwu shi gao* 1845: "Fu lu," 1/1a-7a; "Xu ba," 1/1a-2a.)

170. See the forty poems in praise of things by Yuesun's nieces, concubine, and daughter, in Zhang Yuesun, *Dihua guan shi ke* 1850: 12/5b-11a. Subjects include a sword, a fan, a potted plant, a bookcase, a banana tree, a brush holder, and a mirror stand.

171. Zhang Hongsheng 1998, p. 56.

172. Huang Yanli 2002, p. 5. On Lü Bicheng, see Fong 2004. Qiu Jin's writings have been extensively studied, most recently by Joan Judge (2005). See also Idema and Grant 2004, pp. 767–808; Chang and Saussy 1999, pp. 632–657.

4. WANG CAIPIN

1. Caipin's third sister, Caizao, was born six years after their return to Changzhou, during her father's prolonged visit home to honor her mother's fortieth birthday. Shortly thereafter, her father took a concubine. The concubine gave birth to three more boys and a girl, so that by the time Caipin was twenty, she had four brothers and four sisters. In upper-class families where concubines were present, all offspring of the concubine were considered the children of their father and his wife, not the concubine. Thus Caipin would make no distinction between siblings born to different mothers. Her mother, however, definitely drew

distinctions, of which the children doubtless grew more conscious as they grew older.

2. The phrase is *he,* pronounced with a falling tone, meaning to respond in kind by matching the form and content of a poem. The "linked verse" of the painting commissioned by Zhang Yuesun invokes this term, with the meaning "chanting back and forth in matched rhymes."

3. Caipin's little joke is a learned one: it is a classical allusion to the story of Lady Song, who sat behind a screen to instruct scholars at the court in the lost texts of the classic *Rites of Zhou,* which she had committed to memory. See Mann 1997, p. 81. The Empress Dowager Cixi also ruled "from behind the screen" in the late nineteenth and early twentieth centuries, evoking this classical ideal of the learned lady who removes herself from the public politics of the court.

4. See Rowe's biography of Chen (Rowe 2001), which sympathetically traces the origins and development of Chen's deep moralism and his devotion to improving the lot of women through productive work and proper education.

5. A reference to the first two chapters in the *Book of Odes.* See next note.

6. The poem "Taoyao," or "The elegant peach," celebrates the virtue of a young woman about to marry (Legge 1991, vol. 4, pp. 12–13). It appears in the first of two chapters in the *Book of Odes (Shi jing)* containing poems from the south; hence the term "Er nan," or the "two south" chapters. These poems, representing the essence of the cultural teachings of King Wen, were considered particularly desirable for young women to study to prepare themselves to be good wives. It appears that Uncle Sun did eventually recognize the precocity of his charge, for he went on to introduce the youthful Caipin to the difficult and wide-ranging treasury of medieval poems and prose in the sixth-century *Anthology of Literature (Wen xuan).* See Zhang Yuesun, *Jinyan shenhao zhi ju shiji* 1904: 11/9b.

7. See appendix for original poem.

8. This story is recounted by Wang Chenbi in his colophon on the *Dihua guan shi ke,* p. 1b. The original poem is reprinted with Wanying's and Wang Xi's responses in Wanying's own collected works, *Linyun youyue zhi ju shi chugao* 1849: 2/10a-b. Caipin's age at the time was thirteen *sui* (p. 10b), which may have conveyed to an adult reader a slightly erotic nuance. The choice of the red plum *(hongmei)* as a subject is itself daring, because of the association of the red blossoms with rouged beauty (as opposed to the pale white of the true plum, idealized for its connotations of snowy purity and solitude). See Bickford 1996, esp. pp. 12, 47–48, and 69–72; also Frankel 1976.

9. *EC,* pp. 448–449.

10. Bao Shichen, "Li Fengtai zhuan," in Li Zhaoluo, *Yangyi zhai quan ji* 1878–1882: "Zhuan," 1a-4b, dated the eighth lunar month of 1845.

11. On Ruan Yuan and the Xuehai Academy, see Miles 2006.

12. Li Zhaoluo was one of the early nineteenth-century cartographers who worked with a hybrid form of mapmaking that incorporated latitude-longitude lines

derived from Jesuit maps with the rectangular grid system of map drawing favored by Chinese mapmakers beginning in the Han dynasty. See Needham 1959, vol. 3, p. 586 (describing Li Zhaoluo's 1832 map, the "Huangchao yitong diyu quantu"), and pp. 537 ff. (on the origins of the grid system). One of Li's early maps, dated 1842, in eight scrolls, is held in the Library of Congress.

13. Li Zhaoluo's original text has been lost. Only his preface survives, in his collected works. An account of the probable origins of the original text on which Li's text and similar works were based is found in An Jing's detailed recent edition of Xie's work (2002). See preface, pp. 1–5. For other discussions of Xie Qinggao, see Mirsky 1964, pp. 265–266, and Fairbank and Teng 1960, p. 185. For Li's preface, see Li Zhaoluo 1878–1882: 2/23b-24a; also Jiang Tong 1913: 2/13a-14a.

14. The text uses the word *fan,* which designated a vassal or subject population that was less than fully civilized in Qing foreign affairs. See Millward 1998, p. 158, for a discussion suggesting that the term was not synonymous with "foreigner."

15. An Jing 2002, pp. 250–251. For a slightly different translation from a different version of the original *Hailu,* see Mirsky 1964, pp. 269–270. Mirsky's is based on an original translation by Kenneth Ch'en in *Monumenta Serica* 7 (1942).

16. Li Zhaoluo incorporated technical skills from the Jesuit science of mapmaking introduced into China in the sixteenth century by Matteo Ricci and others. See the longer discussion of this process, a reciprocal exchange of geographic knowledge, in Needham 1959, vol. 3, pp. 583–586; see also Needham's description of one of Li's own references, the *Haiguo wenjian lu* (Record of things seen and heard about the maritime countries) by Chen Lunjiong, which was printed in 1744 (p. 517). See also Teng 2004, p. 55, where she notes that Chen's focus was on the colonization of Taiwan, not on the foreigners from Europe. Drake (1975) does not mention Li Zhaoluo's work, although it seems highly likely that Xu Jiyu made use of it in 1848.

17. Tang Jiaming, known in family sources by her courtesy name, Tang Bichang (also written Bihen), was the daughter of painter and polymath Tang Yifen (1778–1853), Yaoqing's distant paternal cousin (he was the son of her father's cousin Xiongye). Tang Yifen and his talented wife, Dong Wanzhen, had seven children, all of whom—remarkably—were painters, and the family was famous for producing an album together. Tang Yifen died when Nanjing fell to the Taiping rebels. See Liu Wanlang 1990, p. 153. Tang Yifen and his wife enjoyed a famously companionate marriage; a love letter she once wrote to him is reprinted in Hu and Wang 1941: 5/140. On Tang Jiaming, see Zhang Weixiang 1972: 11/10.

18. Wang Caipin, *Duxuan lou shi gao* 1894: 1/1a.

19. The poem alludes to a poem by the late Tang poet Meng Jiao, whose work was also admired by Zhang Qieying, as we saw earlier in Qieying's poem based on Meng Jiao's "The Death of Apricots." The poem by Meng Jiao quoted by Caipin, titled "You zi yin," uses "spring glow" *(chun hui)* to invoke the labor of a devoted mother who makes clothing for her traveling son (compare with Caipin's "chilly glow" *[han hui]*).

20. See Waley 1958, pp. 137–138. When in February 1841 the distinguished general Yang Fang was under orders to travel from his commanding position in Changsha to Canton to fight the British, he stopped in Nanchang and consulted Bao Shichen. Bao's advice was [in Waley's rendering]: "We [Chinese] cannot compete with the English either in ships or guns. But the other foreign countries are equipped as the English are, and though no one country is capable of standing up to the English, if they united they could certainly inflict a crushing defeat. Our policy should be to fan the grievances of the nations whose trade has been stopped owing to the behaviour of the English, and get them to join in an attack. These other nations should then be rewarded, according to the amount of help they have given in achieving this victory, by Customs concessions, and so on."

21. Later poems show Wang Caipin closely attuned to her aunt's political sensibilities, but Caipin's childhood impressions of Zhang Qieying, conveyed through this invented conversation, are the product of my own imagination.

22. In Zhang Wanying, *Linyun youyue zhi ju shi chugao* 1849: 2/11a-b. For the original poem, see appendix. The poet's choice of a *rusheng* mode (a tonal pattern dominated by falling sounds) casts the poem in a mournful tone. I have followed Stephen West's suggestions for a language of translation that draws out what he calls "the interplay of blocked Yang and overabundant Yin" as "a metaphor of the imperium and the rebels" (West, personal communication, February 12, 2003).

23. *Xiekuang* is a reference to padded cotton clothes; the original phrase is *sanjun zhi shi jie ru xiekuang* ("the soldiers, though cold, were as if clad in padded garments" [because of the sympathy they felt when the king came out in person to pat them on the shoulder and urge them on]). The *locus classicus* of the story is *Zuo zhuan*, "Xuan gong," 12, which describes the prelude to the great Battle of Bi between Chu and Jin, in 597 BCE. See Watson 1989, pp. 84–102. This story, which celebrates the empathic leadership of the Chu king, is adapted from Legge's translation as follows: "Wuchen, Duke of Shen, said to the king, 'Many of your soldiers are suffering from cold.' At this, the king went around to all three armies, comforting the soldiers and encouraging them, which made them feel as if they were wearing quilted clothing" (Legge 1991, vol. 5, p. 321). In this allusion to the *Zuo zhuan*, Zhang Wanying displays the familiarity with that text that came from growing up in Changzhou's rich intellectual culture. On Changzhou studies of the *Zuo zhuan*, see Elman 1990.

24. Wang Caipin, *Duxuan lou shi gao* 1894: 3/8b-9a (composed 1848). The original poem appears in the appendix. As a girl, the Ming loyalist woman warrior Qin Liangyu (d. 1648) was trained in military arts together with her brothers. After her marriage to a native chieftain in southwestern Sichuan province, she was widowed and inherited his title. In 1620, the Ming Emperor ordered her to lead an army in the northeast against the invading Manchu armies, and she fought for the Ming loyalist cause on several occasions thereafter. She and another late Ming woman warrior, Shen Yunying (1624–1661), became the subjects of a popular eighteenth-

century opera. Both appear frequently in women's poems of the late nineteenth and early twentieth centuries. For Qin Liangyu's biography, see Peterson 2000, pp. 306–312; also *EC*, pp. 168–169.

25. The woman of Lu from the town of Qishi explained to her neighbors why women should be concerned about the state of the kingdom, pointing out that the present ruler was perverse and negligent, citing ways in which she suffered under his rule (including having her gardens trampled and her food supply destroyed by occupying armies), and concluding that the heir to the throne was still young and evidently foolish. How could such a situation *not* have anything to do with women? she demands. See Liu Xiang 1936: 3/13 (pp. 87–88); also O'Hara 1945, pp. 95–97.

26. Stephen West (personal communication) notes the elegant juxtaposition here of phrases associated with womanly and manly virtue, playing on the nuances in both.

27. Her use of the phrase *sheng ping* (approaching peace) suggests that Caipin was influenced by the thinking of Changzhou scholars who studied the Gongyang commentary on the early classic that was said to be Confucius's record of the history of his time. That commentary identified three ages: disorder, approaching peace, and great peace. Its utopian vision inspired late Qing reformers Kang Youwei and others. See Elman 1990, esp. pp. 231 *et passim.*

28. Ban *jieyu* was a Han palace lady whose eloquent "Rhapsody of Self-Commiseration" gave lyrical expression to her reflections on her youthful days as a favorite in the imperial palace and her isolation in her declining years. Unlike Lady Ban, who was an aristocrat, Zuo Fen was a talented woman from an "undistinguished" family who became a lady-in-waiting for the Western Jin Emperor and wrote poems at his command. Her most famous work used the voice of an imperial concubine to express the loneliness of palace ladies and their isolation from their families. See David R. Knechteges, "Ban *jieyu*" and "Zuo Fen," in Chang and Saussy 1999, pp. 17–21, 30–35.

29. *Duxuan lou shi gao* 1894: 3/9a-b. See appendix for the original poem.

30. In other words, for a mundane task you do not need the finest talent.

31. The bell in the Jingyang Tower was rung by Emperor Wu of the Southern Qi; it rang nightly from the third to the fifth watch, alerting the palace women to rise and adorn themselves, according to a standard dictionary. For a different explanation, see Chang and Saussy 1999, p. 270n.

32. The allusion here to the sword's starry pattern *(xingwen)* may be to lines from "Precious Sword" ("Baojian pian") by the Tang writer Liu Changchuan: *xiali xingwen dong, huanbian yueying can.* See *HYDCD* 1994, vol. 5, p. 671.

33. The swordsmith Ouye, who once made five swords for the king of Yue, then worked with Ganjiang and made another three swords for the king of Chu.

34. This birthday greeting ("Shou ci") is reprinted as an appendix *(fu lu)* to Wanying's collected poetry, *Linyun youyue zhi ju shi chugao* (1849).

35. Mengti (Qieying) was living in Beijing with her husband at the time.

36. *Analects* 15.31: "Junzi you dao buyou pin" (Legge 1991, vol. 1, p. 303).

37. He quotes here from *The Doctrine of the Mean* 14.2. The chapter is discussing the conduct of the "superior person" *(junzi)* in various kinds of circumstances: "In a position of wealth and honor, he does what is proper to a position of wealth and honor. In a poor and low position, he does what is proper to a poor and low position" (adapted from Legge 1991, vol. 1, p. 395). The crucial phrase here, *zide,* is one that Yuesun returns to later in his greeting. It means, literally, "self-possessing" or "self-fulfilled," or, in Legge's rendering of the commentators, "happy in conforming himself to his position." I have translated the quotation using the feminine pronoun because obviously in Yuesun's mind it was applied here to woman as "person" and, in this case, a "superior person."

38. Yuesun here uses the phrase *nü xu,* which appears in Qu Yuan's poem "Encountering Sorrow" ("Li sao") in the following stanza: *nüxu zhi chanyuan xi shenshen qi li yu.* According to the *Shuo wen,* the character *xu* was used in the state of Chu to refer to an elder sister, but a different commentary on the poem asserts that *nüxu* was the name of Qu Yuan's sister. David Hawkes adopts the latter interpretation in his translation of Qu Yuan's "Seven Remonstrances" ("Qi jian"), when he literally translates the phrase as Nü Xu. However, in a long explanatory note he argues that the term as it was used in the "Li sao" itself means "maidens," a collective reference to the women surrounding the poet, who is representing himself as a woman in the elegy. See Hawkes 1959, pp. 131, 26, 214. In both poems, the poet describes a woman's "sorrowful entreaties" (p. 131) and her "sobs and sighs" (p. 26). Yuesun seems to have in mind the "Ai ming" section of the "Seven Remonstrances." *Ai ming* means literally "mourning my lot" and describes a person of spotless purity who is living in a time of disorder and has therefore met with disgrace. As the poet wanders far from his homeland, which is sinking into destruction, he recalls the entreaties of his sister before he commits suicide in the Miluo River (Hawkes 1959, pp. 130–131).

39. Xin Chang was an aide to a powerful general in service to the Wei dynasty (third century) who had offended the reigning emperor and as a result was condemned to die. Saving his commander meant risking Xin Chang's own life, not to mention defying the ruler. To decide what to do, Xin Chang consulted his talented and intelligent elder sister, Xianying. Said he of her advice: "If I did not consult my elder sister, I would risk losing my integrity!" *(wu bumou yu jie, ji buhuo yu yi!) Jin shu* 1974: 96/2508.

40. Zhang Xun (709–757) was a noted high official and loyalist general during the rebellion of An Lushan in the Tang dynasty. He and his descendants were honored for their extraordinary heroism at a temple dedicated to his memory located in the city of Suiyang, which he recovered and helped to hold from rebel forces. His elder sister married into the Lu family (hence her name, Lu *gu,* or Lady Lu) and became personally involved in the military negotiations defending the court. In the siege of Suiyang by An Lushan's forces, both she and Zhang Xun perished

in a sordid end detailed in his biography in the *Xin Tang shu* 1975: 192/5540. Another story about Lady Lu identifies her as an expert in military arts. See Feng Shusen, *Si yan gui jian,* cited in Zhang Fuqing 1996, p. 302.

41. The poem from the *Shi jing (Book of Odes)* cited here is Mao no. 39, "Quan shui" (The spring) (Legge 1991, vol. 4, pp. 63–64). The passage in question reads: "When a young lady goes to be married / She leaves her parents and brothers" *(nüzi you xing yuan fumu xiongdi).* The poem describes the longing of a young married princess for her home, made more agonizing by the fact that her parents have died and she no longer has a legitimate reason to return there.

42. The allusion here is to two poems in the "Shao nan" section of the *Book of Odes:* "Cai fan" (Gathering artemisia) [Mao no. 13] and "Cai pin" (Gathering duckweed) [Mao no. 15]. Both poems describe the diligence and reverence of a young wife of a prince or official as she assists in the ancestral sacrifices. See Legge 1991, vol. 4, pp. 22, 25.

43. This allusion too is to a poem from the *Book of Odes,* in this case one of the "Lesser Elegantiae," titled "Chang di" (The mountain cherry) [Mao no. 164]. The first line in the third stanza of the poem compares brothers who come to one another's assistance to the wagtail *(jiling)* on the plain, the idea being that wagtails, which flock together, bob their heads and tails in concert, just as brothers respond to one another (unlike friends, who, though "they may be good, will only heave long sighs"). See Legge 1991, vol. 4, p. 251. The wagtail nests in large communal groups, sometimes numbering in the thousands, but in the poem a solitary bird has become isolated when the flock scatters, just as siblings may be cast apart in times of disorder.

44. The phrase *Wei nü* here refers to the subject of the poem "The Spring," who is a daughter of the house of Wei. The phrase *chi qu* occurs in one of the "Greater Elegantiae," titled "Pan" (Return), where it is glossed as a reference to "following one's passions." The literal meaning of the phrase refers to horse charioteering, as in "driving furiously about." See Legge 1991, vol. 4, p. 504.

45. To this greeting Yuesun appended the following biographical note: "Lunying's son is named Zenggu; her daughter's name is Sihui. Wanying's son's name is Chenbi, and she also has three sons by a concubine, named Chenliang, Chenjin, and Chenkai. She has three daughters of her own: Caipin, Caifan, and Caizao; and a daughter by a concubine named Cailü. All read with utter clarity and diligence, and all of the girls compose classical verse and lyric poems, as well as doing calligraphy and painting, well enough to amuse themselves, though we cannot anticipate their future luminous achievements." Note that Yuesun has carefully regrouped his nieces to show the formal adoption of Wang Cailan by her aunt.

46. Li Junzhi's biographical note on Caipin refers to Cheng Peiyuan as "a *juren* from Wuxi" (1990, p. 519), but I've been unable to confirm this elsewhere.

47. Wang Chenbi, encomium for the *Dihua* collection of 1850.

48. Zhhang Yuezhen, "Preface," *Dihua guan shi ke* 1850: s.p. 1b. See also the

preface by Deng Chuanmi, s.p. 2a. Yuesun himself says (in his own preface, p. 1b) he created the collection to send to his eldest sister, Qieying, in the capital to assuage her loneliness.

49. The instruction of younger girls by older girls is a theme in many of the prefaces to the *Dihua guan* collection. Yuesun's own remarks singling out Caipin appear in his preface, p. 2a.

50. The term *nian* originated as a numeric marker, referring to groups of outlaws known by various names ("Red-beards," "Swordwielders"). See Kuhn 1978, pp. 311 *et passim.* Kuhn traces "the first manifestation of unity" among these bands to the early 1850s (p. 313). On the *nian* heartland, see Perry 1980.

51. See Jen 1973, pp. 172–174.

52. See Liu 1978, pp. 456–477, esp. pp. 462–464; map on p. 458.

53. Caipin's poems refer to an heir, but there is no evidence that she reared a child who survived her. Had she done so, he would surely have seen to the publication (or at the least, the copyediting) of her collected poems.

54. Wang Caipin, *Duxuan lou shi gao* 1894: 6/1b-2a. For the original poem, see appendix.

55. The poet may refer here to Zeng Guofan, but Zeng's Hunan Army was not fully mobilized until 1853.

56. Wang Caipin's use of the phrase *po zhu* underscores the irony of her tone. "Split bamboo" was usually used in the context of imperial victories, when the tide of battle was about to turn decisively in favor of the government's armies (the phrase was *shi ru po zhu,* "at this moment we smash them like splitting bamboo"). Here the poet instead hands the momentum to the enemy.

57. This is a sarcastic comment on antiquated weaponry and blind reliance on traditional defenses. She refers to a battle of the Tang emperor Suzong, who, in fighting the An Lushan rebels in 1756, ordered his generals to imitate the ancient military arts. Two thousand oxcarts were assembled for battle, backed with soldiers on horseback and on foot. The rebels used noise to panic and stampede the oxen, then lit fires that burned downwind and destroyed the resistance. Forty thousand imperial soldiers died.

58. Stephen West (personal communication) notes: "Because storks cannot cry out, they can only clack their bills," hence the sound of horses' hooves.

59. The cuckoo *(dujuan)* is associated with the spirit of King Du Yu of the ancient kingdom of Shu. Its cry was heard by exiles from Shu as a call to return home, hence its invocation in this context. Some sources also say that the cuckoo cries up blood.

60. Here she may be referring to the fact that the siege of Guilin was lifted.

61. The poet here invokes the story of Feng Xuan of Qi from the *Zhanguo ce.* Having gained admission to the retinue of the Lord of Mengchang, Feng Xuan is given only coarse greens as food by the other retainers, who despise him for his poverty and his self-professed lack of talent. At length he leans on a pillar, taps the

hilt of his sword, and sings: "Long sword, let us return home; we have no fish to eat here." Word of his song reaches the Lord of Mengchang, who commands that Feng Xuan be fed as befits a guest. Feng Xuan keeps this up until he gets everything he wants: a horse, a chariot, and, finally, provisions for his mother too. Here the poet alludes to a particular nuance in the tale; that is, Feng Xuan in his quest for office was forced to leave his mother and could no longer care for her as a proper son. The poet's final line returns us to this conflict between political aspirations and family responsibilities. For another reading of Feng Xuan's story, see Paula Versano's note in Chang and Saussy 1999, p. 393.

62. The request for a capstring, a convention for departing to take up arms, invokes the story of Zhong Jun of the Han, who asked for a capstring for his helmet before going to battle for control of the kingdom of Nan Yue (present Vietnam); he used it to tie up the king and bring him to court to submit to Emperor Wu of the Han.

63. These comments by Qieying are my invention, based on information she would have received through networks associated with Zeng Guofan, who described the Taiping beliefs on family relationships in graphic detail. See chapter 1.

64. Wang Caipin, *Duxuan lou shi gao* 1894: 6/4a-b. For the original poem, see appendix.

65. *Shengsi bie* refers to a farewell that may be the last, said of seeing a loved one off on any long journey whose outcome is not certain.

66. The wagtail signals Caipin's allusion to the *Book of Odes* poem "Chang di," with its description of separated families and its celebration of sibling bonds. See note 43.

67. Her poem here alludes to a fourth-century story about terrified soldiers awaiting attack by overwhelming forces, who confuse even the "sound of wind or cranes" *(feng he)* with the approach of the enemy. *Jin shu* 1974: 79/2082.

68. The story of the woman of Lu from Qishi is told in note 25.

69. I have not been able to locate the poem by Qieying to which this responds.

70. Invoking Du Fu's famous poem "Chun wang."

71. Quoting here the phrase for news of home that she could not hear, used by Cai Yan in her "Eighteen Songs on a Nomad Flute." See Idema and Grant 2004, pp. 121–127.

72. "Dui yue huai jia daren," Wang Caipin, *Duxuan lou shi gao* 1894: 1/2b. Written sometime between 1840 and 1846 (Wang Xi died in 1847); probably composed when Caipin was about fifteen or sixteen *sui*.

73. The Double Seven Festival marks that singular time of year when the stars of the Herdboy and the Weaving Maid cross the Magpie Bridge over the Milky Way to spend one precious night together. For lovers who watch the starry skies on that night, the story of Herdboy and Weaving Maid is also the story of all great lovers, like Emperor Ming Huang and his beloved "Precious Consort," Yang Guifei.

74. For the original poem, see appendix. Wang Caipin, *Duxuan lou shi gao* 1894: 7/2a.

75. "Flying grasses" tells us the poet has in mind a poem from the *Book of Odes* ("Odes of Wei," Mao no. 62, "Bo xi"), in which a wife mourns the long absence of her husband, who is a leading charioteer in the king's armies. In the poem, her hair resembles the wild floss of the *peng* (a kind of artemisia), left unwashed and unattended because she has no one for whom to adorn herself (Legge 1991, vol. 4, p. 105). The broken mirror is an emblem of conjugal separation: husband and wife each keep half, in token of mutual love and trust.

76. "Leaden tears" is an allusion to the moon and to longing for an absent lover or mate. In a Yuan song lyric, the allusion is invoked for the Double Seven Festival.

77. The term *xiaoxi* refers to word of triumph or failure arriving from afar—an allusion from a poem by Du Fu that plays on an earlier meaning, that "triumph is always followed by defeat, flourishing by decline." The "green bird" augurs the coming of the Queen Mother of the West, in an old tale associated with the court of Emperor Wu of Han; the green bird in this story attended the Queen Mother as she arrived on the Double Seven. Since the advent of the Queen Mother signals a tryst, the green bird would promise the same to anyone who received its message.

78. Caipin uses *su'e* as a name for the Goddess of the Moon. *Su* (pale, colorless) invokes the moon's paleness and purity while at the same time playing against the parallel "green" in the line preceding. The poet jars her reader by juxtaposing "green" and "pale" in these parallel lines. "Green" is often coupled with "red" or "rosy" in descriptions of sensual pleasure, but here the "rosy" *(hong)* face of a seductively made-up woman is replaced by an abstemious, unsexed visage. In her reference to Chang'e, Goddess of the Moon, Caipin again recalls the Queen Mother of the West, who gave the herb of immortality to the Goddess's husband, the archer Hou Yi. While Hou Yi was away, Chang'e tasted the herb and ascended into the sky as an immortal, where she became the moon, while Hou Yi, vainly pursuing her, was transformed into the sun. Thus Chang'e, like the Weaving Maid, is a woman separated forever from her mate.

79. The phrase comes from the *Book of Odes* poem on the "Retiring girl" (Mao no. 42), which celebrates the virtues of the ideal young lady (Legge 1991, vol. 4, p. 68). The poet is anxiously searching with his eyes for his beloved but cannot see her. Caipin has reversed the image to place herself as the "retiring" beloved, seeking the man who has married her.

80. The "loud song" *(hao ge)* invokes a phrase from a poem by Du Fu decrying the state of the country as he contemplates his life as a refugee, "singing of injustice" (as translated by Rewi Alley) or (in another translation by David Hinton) mourning the people in a "song brimming with lament." See Alley 2001, p. 51; Hinton 1989, p. 19. Kang-i Sun Chang (2005, pp. 519–522) has shown how Du Fu's "concern for the destiny of the world," as she puts it, inspired women poets of the late Qing who bore witness to the fall of their country.

81. Wang Caipin, *Duxuan lou shi gao* 1894: 7/3a–4b.

82. She uses the term *hunpo* to refer to the soul's two parts: the ethereal part

that disperses into *qi* after death, and the sentient part that remains lodged in and decays with the body.

83. These two parallel phrases may play ironically on her transformed status as the wife of a dead man: *gui,* or "returning," by convention refers to marriage; *fuhu* (supporting and protecting) now makes it her charge as a good wife to escort her husband's coffin home (a different return).

84. A feather was attached to messages about military action to indicate urgency.

85. Bo is an ancient capital of the Shang emperor Tang, in present-day Shangqiu on the eastern edge of Henan province, the first stop in that province for anyone traveling from the provincial capital, Kaifeng, to Caipin's husband's native place.

86. In a note on Caipin's poems from that visit, Yuesun wrote: "Since we parted in Wuchang we had not seen her for eight years. This was the happiest moment, such as I fear I shall never have again in this life *(wei ci wei zui le zhi jing kong ci sheng buke fu de yi)."* Wang Caipin, *Duxuan lou shi gao* 1894: 8/3a.

87. According to the local gazetteer's account, Wei Ji was speared to death protecting his mother, who, thanks to him, escaped. See *Wu Yang zhi yu* 1887: 11/5/4a.

88. Some sources say that Wang Caipin was employed as a governess in the household of Li Hongzhang, but I have been unable to verify this. See, for example, Li Junzhi 1930: 39a-b.

89. Xu's concubine (Liang *shi*) is described in a sketch of her life by Xu Zhenyi that was printed in his collected works *(Yiwei ji* 1897: 1/1a-3a). Caipin's poem celebrating Liang's life is printed in Wang Caipin, *Duxuan lou shi gao* 1894: 10/1a-2b.

90. Lunying's collected poems were reprinted once, in 1868, on the occasion of her seventieth birthday. She probably outlived all of her siblings. Shortly before Caipin's work was published, Sun Shangxian, a grand-nephew of Zhang Qi, reprinted Zhang Qi's own complete poems and prose *(Wanlin shi wen* 1891). These reprintings do not comment on the family's fate after the pacification of the Taiping Rebellion. Zhang Wanying lived to see her sixtieth birthday, celebrated in a poem by her brother. See Zhang Yuesun, *Jinyan shenhao zhi ju shiji* 1904: 14/7b-8b.

91. For examples, including Chen Hengzhe and Shi Liang, both of Changzhou, see Lee 2003.

EPILOGUE

1. Ho 1999, pp. 314–322, discusses the importance of men as preservers, collectors, editors, publishers, distributors, and introducers (through prefaces, biographical sketches, memoirs, and so forth) of women's writings in Qing times.

2. Jin Wuxiang, *Suxiang wu bi* 1894: 6/33a.

3. As Clara Ho points out, positive appraisals were *de rigueur* for male writers invited to comment on women's literary collections: "critical review almost did not exist among these courtesy writings" (1999, p. 318). Self-censorship, in other words, probably worked both ways. At the same time, as Ho notes, these same male

writers often made sure that their prefaces and other contributions to women's literary collections were republished in their *own* collected works.

4. A poem on footbinding would find a place in other genres, such as a collection of folksongs sung by commoners, or the intimate poems composed in the so-called women's script from southern Hunan province. On folksong collections, see Ko 2005, pp. 183–186; on the women's script, see Wang Ping 2000, pp. 145–173; also Silber 1994.

5. See the sensitive discussion in Ko 1994, pp. 167–171.

6. Ko 1997.

7. *ICTCL*, vol. 1, p. 534. She is also described as "a major link in the poetic tradition—the successor to Su Shi" (Chang and Saussy 1999, p. 89).

8. This is especially clear in the discussion and translation of her work in Idema and Grant 2004, pp. 204–221.

9. Copy in the Rare Book Room, Beijing University Library.

10. Xue Ziheng, "Tiba," in Zhang Qieying, *Danju xuan chugao* 1840: s.p. 1a-b.

11. Zhang Huiyan, *Mingke wen er bian* 1869: "xia" 25a-b.

12. Zhang Qi, "Xu" (Preface), in Zhang Guanying, *Weiqing yigao* 1829: s.p.

13. Zhang Qi, "Wangshi Tang ruren xinglüe," in *Ming fa lu* 1840: "Xinglüe," 6a.

14. See *Guangxu Wujin Yanghu xian zhi* 1879: 9/6a. The timing of the award of the imperial commendation *(jingbiao)* is somewhat anomalous, since (according to the Zhang genealogy), Miss Fa did not die until 1860, twelve years later, and *jingbiao* were generally conferred posthumously. Juesun died in 1803, and Miss Fa declared herself a faithful maiden *(zhennü)* a decorous ten years later. A plausible explanation for the timing of the *jingbiao*, then, is that applications were made after Miss Fa had served her late fiancé's family for more than thirty years (in other words, after 1843). Perhaps the award was timed to serve as compensation for Miss Fa's severance from the family, since Mengyi died in 1844, and shortly thereafter Yuesun moved his sisters and their families to Wuchang, leaving Miss Fa, duly honored, in Changzhou, where I have taken the liberty of placing her in a charitable home for widows.

15. *Zhang shi zong pu* 1947: 33/2/44a-b.

16. Zhang Wanying, *Canfeng guan wenji chubian* 1850: 1/6a-7a.

17. See *Zhang shi zong pu* 1947: 33/2/44a-b. The genealogy is also the only source of Miss Fa's birth and death dates, and it is the only indication we have that she remained alive until the fall of Changzhou during the Taiping Rebellion. The genealogy, of course, was much more concerned with establishing formal lines of descent than with the actual practice of kinship observed in the Zhang family's other writings, and those of their friends.

18. The text on which the case rests is a passage in the *Li ji*, "Nei ze": *jiu mo ze gu lao, zhongfu suo jisi binke, mei shi bi qingyu gu, jiefu qingyu zhongfu* (when the father-in-law dies and the mother-in-law is old, the wife of the eldest son makes sacrificial offerings and waits upon guests; concerning every particular, she must

consult with her mother-in-law, and the wife or wives of the younger sons shall consult with her).

19. Fang Junmo 1931, quotation on pp. 12a-b.

20. Lu, *True to Their Word* (forthcoming).

21. Lu, *True to Their Word* (forthcoming).

22. Chow 2004, esp. pp. 90–148; Widmer 2003, pp. 294–302; also Widmer 2006.

23. Many references to Lunying speak of the collectors who sought her work, without mentioning prices. There is also a tantalizing letter from Yuesun to Yi Sang-jŏk, dated January 1850, in which—after carrying on about how poor he is and how many relatives he must support—Yuesun provides with some embarrassment an inventory of items, some of which the members of his household produced. I suspect that Yi Sang-jŏk regularly purchased such items from him, either for resale or to present as gifts himself to his networks of collector friends both in Beijing and at home in Korea. Yuesun's list includes, among other things, thirty-two paintings, a pair of *duilian* (couplet scrolls of calligraphy), four bronze seals, seventeen small seals ("specially carved to be suitable as gifts"), four curios for decorating a scholar's studio, four volumes of his sisters' poetry, and eight inkstones and four brushes in cases ("Haerin ch'ŏktok" n.d., 5a).

24. See Pastreich 1997, who documents the growing interest in Chinese vernacular fiction among Korean male intellectuals during the nineteenth century (pp. 157 ff.), an interest that included fascination with translations of *Honglou meng* (p. 185). He also notes considerable evidence that interpreters and translators like Yi Sang-jŏk, who accompanied Korean delegations to China, were the primary purveyors of the trade in Chinese books sold to Korea (p. 85). Perhaps the Korean book market was an added incentive for Yuesun to write his sequel to *Dream of the Red Chamber.*

25. See the discussion of dowry and household financial management in chapter 2.

26. See Wu Ren'an 2001 for one of the best examples.

27. Granet 1920, pp. 3–5.

28. Marriage to mother's brother's daughter (for Dong Shixi and Wang Chenbi), and marriage to father's sister's son (for Zhang Xiangzhen).

29. Wang Chenbi, "Ba" (encomium), in Zhang Yuesun, *Dihua guan shi ke* 1850: s.p. 1b.

30. Lu 1998.

31. See Bossler 2000, especially pp. 87–91, on elite women's ability to "act to channel political advantages to their natal or affinal kin" (quotation on p. 90) in late imperial times.

32. See Grace Fong's account of the troubled fate of Lü Bicheng, whose widowed mother, along with her daughters, suffered terribly among both affinal and agnatic relatives (Fong 2004).

33. Skinner 1992, pp. 959–962, especially on older sisters as "little mothers."

34. Dong Sicheng, recalling his grandmother's affection for his aunt, in an encomium for Qieying's collected poems (*Danju xuan chugao* 1840: "Tiba," 6a).

35. See the "tiba" for *Danju xuan chugao* by Xue Ziheng, s.p. 1a-b. On the Ye sisters, see Wu Xiuhua and Lin Yan 2001; also Ko 1994, pp. 202–209 *et passim*.

36. *Kangxi zidian*, "*wei* ji zhong, si bu" (*wei* collection, middle section, silk radical), p. 22c.

37. The *locus classicus* is Qu Yuan's *Chu ci*, and the character has two pronunciations, *xi* and *qie*. I have used the latter, following the judgment of the authors of Zhang Qi's biography in *EC*.

38. Zhang Wanying, *Canfeng guan wenji chubian* 1850: 1/8a.

39. For an analysis of family relations and adolescent worlds in *Dream of the Red Chamber* that takes a very different approach from the one developed here, see Miller 1995. For the novel itself, see Cao and Gao 1988; Hawkes and Minford 1973–1986.

40. See Widmer 2006, chapter 7, especially pp. 241–242, on Zhang Yuesun.

41. Again, the exception is Skinner 1992.

42. Zhang Wanying, *Canfeng guan wenji chubian* 1850: 1/8b.

43. See Hsiung 1994.

44. Wolf 1972, pp. 34–35.

45. For discussions of the importance of sister-brother relations after marriage, see Wolf 1972, pp. 34–35; Fei 1939, pp. 66, 87. Janet Theiss's study of eighteenth-century court cases shows brothers actively and sometimes aggressively involved in the defense of a married sister's honor (Theiss 2004, pp. 92–94 *et passim*).

46. As Bossler remarks (2000, p. 98), "Affinal relationships could be used to subvert the patrilineal kinship system, but those same affinal relationships also provided that system with a flexibility that helped it to survive."

47. Cao Hong 1996, pp. 38–39. On Wanyan Yun Zhu and the civilizing project, see Mann 1997, pp. 94–98.

48. Jiang 1999, pp. 157–172, discusses the unique structures of familial and social support that fostered this unusual women's culture.

49. See the discussion of dense emotional support in Hsiung 2005, pp. 156–179.

50. Cao Hong 1996.

51. Chen Hengzhe is also known in Western-language sources as Sophia H. Chen Zen. For biographies of Chen Hengzhe, see Lee 2003, pp. 58–61; "Ch'en Heng-che," Boorman 1967, vol. 1, pp. 183–187; also Wang Wenqiang 2000, pp. 158–162. A short story written by Chen Hengzhe is translated under the title "One Day" in Dooling and Torgeson 1998, pp. 87–99. Chen Hengzhe is identified there as a member of a "scholarly Hunanese family" (p. 87), but her birthplace was Changzhou and her local history is traced to that place. See also the memoirs of Chen Hengzhe's daughter, the distinguished U.S. scholar E-tu Zen Sun, in Ren 1993. I am grateful to Lin Man-houng for supplying me with a copy of this book.

52. E-tu Zen Sun, personal communication, 21 March 2003.

53. See Wang Lingzhen's account of Qiu Jin's transition from her youth as a talented *guixiu* to her young adulthood as a revolutionary leader (Wang 2004, pp. 27–60). She stresses the development of Qiu Jin's writing voice that resulted from her classical education.

54. I blame both Guanying's death and the death of Bao Mengyi on childbirth because of the ages at which they died, twenty-nine *sui* and thirty-seven *sui,* respectively, well within the norm for the reproductive years of a married woman in this period.

55. Yu Xinzhong 2003, p. 92. Cholera made its first documented appearance in China about 1820, spreading to the Lower Yangzi from Ningbo and Shanghai inland (pp. 92–93).

56. In the year of Yuesun's death, 1863, Shanghai and environs were the scene of a massive epidemic (whether smallpox or not is unclear), preceded a year prior by an outbreak of cholera, which took the lives of several hundred people in Shanghai in the summer of 1862. See data in Yu Xinzhong 2003, p. 367. Yu cautions, however, that records of outbreaks of cholera and other diseases are not a completely reliable guide. Many of these diseases were so common that few local gazetteers record them exhaustively, making it difficult to use the few records we have to track the spread of pathogens (Yu Xinzhong 2003, pp. 82–88).

57. Yu Xinzhong 2003, pp. 105–110.

58. Yu Xinzhong 2003, pp. 111–112.

59. Liu Guangjing 1981.

60. Leonard 1996, Dodgen 2001, Polachek 1992.

61. See Zhang Hongsheng 1998, esp. pp. 14–31.

62. On markets for the work of female calligraphers and painters, see Hsiung 2005, pp. 214–215. On the other hand, as we have seen, since it was a mark of women's virtue to make do in men's absence, there are frequent references to women's ability to marshal resources through their own labor, especially embroidery and, in the case of Lunying, calligraphy. In the rhetoric of our texts, these activities support the family; they do not make money as profit, and they most certainly are not business or commercial operations.

63. On the hazards of travel, see Lufrano 1997.

64. Zhang Wanying, *Canfeng guan wenji chubian* 1850: 1/6a-b.

65. Zhang Wanying, *Canfeng guan wenji chubian* 1850: 1/12b.

66. *Zhang shi zong pu* 1947: 33/2/45a.

67. Zhang Wanying, *Linyun youyue zhi ju shi chugao* 1849: 1/9a.

68. See Rubie S. Watson 1991. Watson stresses that the market transaction that brought a concubine into a household also effectively cut her ties to her natal family, and with them a vital source of power and support. According to Guo Songyi, Li Luan's experience as a concubine was increasingly the norm in her day. See Guo 2000, pp. 378–385, on the changing status of concubines in the Qing and on the

status of the children to whom they gave birth. He identifies two changes in the status of concubines during the Qing. One is the increasing historical evidence that upper-class men were moving a concubine into the status of proper wife following a wife's death—instead of taking a second wife *(jiqu)*. The other change is that sons of concubines who became successful officeholders were increasingly able to provide honorary titles for their concubine mothers, as well as for their "official" mothers. Guo also observes in marriage records that no distinction was made in the quality of the match for children born of concubines as opposed to children born of proper wives.

69. Hence my reading of this concubine as a gift Wanying could not refuse, but one whose impact she was in a position to minimize.

70. Waltner 1990, pp. 48–71.

71. Liu Guangjing 1981, esp. pp. 996–997. Bao wrote a series of essays that K. C. Liu calls "a template for early nineteenth-century reform" (p. 996), in which Bao discussed matters such as the role of clerks and runners in local government, the government's system of mutual surveillance and security called the *baojia* system, and the rationale for bureaucratic administration of county-level units. Liu notes that all of Bao's essays were inspired by his own broad experience after 1797 working as a professional advisor to officials in posts from Anhui to Hubei and Sichuan, and on his interactions with local people as well as with civil and military officials. Recalling that Zhang Qi and Bao Shichen began their friendship at the Jin *yamen* in Anhui, we can surmise that Zhang's "education" for his Shandong posts began long before he actually took office.

72. Luo Jianqiu 2006, pp. 201–203. Luo discusses the influence of both Bao Shichen and Zhang Huiyan in developing this practical concern with governance as one aspect of Han learning. I am grateful to Li Guotong for calling this new work to my attention.

73. On Bao Shichen's ties to Lin Zexu, see Waley 1958, pp. 16–17, 137–138, 153; on Li Zhaoluo, see *EC*, pp. 448–450.

74. For chronology, see Jen 1973, pp. 100–107.

75. See *Wu Yang zhi yu* 1887: 5/4/1a-3b; also the briefer account in *Guangxu Wujin Yanghu xian zhi* 1879: 6/11b. On He Guiqing (1816–1862), see *EC*, p. 621. Du Lianzhe, the author of his biography, notes that, for his cowardice, He Guiqing was tried and executed in 1862, despite the efforts of many people to save him.

76. See *EC*, p. 242.

77. *Guangxu Wujin Yanghu xian zhi* 1879: 28/64a-b.

78. According to some accounts, Caipin once served as a governess in the household of Li Hongzhang, whose many indirect ties to the Zhang family are recorded in his own life history. Unfortunately, I have been unable to document Wang Caipin's relationship to the Li family anywhere beyond occasional comments in bibliographic sources.

79. Elman 2002, quotation on p. 420.

80. This remark is found in Jin Wuxiang's chapbook *Suxiang er bi* 1883: 6/12a-b.

81. Elliott 1990.

82. Rankin 1986, p. 194.

83. Li Wai-yee 2006.

84. See Xu Dingyi 1909, p. 45a. I am indebted to Joan Judge for this reference.

85. Hu Siao-chen [Hu Xiaozhen] 2004: 174–178.

86. Margery Wolf's model of a uterine family, strictly defined as a woman's own mother and her mother's children (Wolf 1972, p. 33 *et passim*), shows how to conceive of meaningful bonds constructed by women within the framework of the patrilineal kinship system. The "uterine family" is the core of a unit whose elasticity permits it to expand and contract with a woman's own life cycle and in response to her affective bonds with female relatives. The womanly networks described here work the same way. Wolf's observations about a mother's use of her dowry for her daughter's benefit appear on pp. 131–132.

87. Hunter 1984, pp. 1–26, reviews the background of the twentieth-century missionary enterprise, observing that "for years, missionaries . . . advanced a consistent program for Chinese women with little to show for it. Only when Chinese nationalist reformers made the cause of female education their own did Chinese attitudes begin to change" (p. 21). See also Kwok 1996 and Ross 1996.

88. Liang Qichao 1978, p. 38. See also Hu 2000, p. 163.

89. Hu 2002; Judge 2002.

90. Judge 2002, pp. 166–167.

91. On the problematic construction of the subject "women" in this discourse, see Barlow 2004.

92. Judge 2001. Liang's legacy lives on: the status of women in contemporary China is still considered a key measure of the success or failure of the modern Chinese nation-state, as Gail Hershatter (2006) has emphasized.

93. See Joseph McDermott's seminal discussion of women's managerial roles in elite family finances, based on his analysis of a set of "family instructions" written by Zeng Guofan's daughter Zeng Jifen (1852–1942) and intended for an audience of the elite women who managed their family's consumption and savings. The instructions give advice on drawing up and keeping a budget, and so forth. Moreover, Zeng Guofan's daughter's own diary describes her cleverness in loaning, pawning, and investing her dowry. As McDermott observes tartly, such evidence "should be the last nail (if it is still needed) in the coffin of the belief that the pursuit of profit and the Confucian Way were necessarily considered irreconcilable opposites in late traditional China" (McDermott 1990, p. 272). Notice that men's celebration of women's virtue was a rhetorical device designed to distance their profit making from the Confucian Way, even though the rhetoric was transparent to all. For the autobiography of Zeng Jifen, see Kennedy 1993.

94. On the new configurations of elite status, new occupations, new fields of

learning, and new social actors, see Vittinghoff 2004 and Bastid-Bruguiere 1980, pp. 536–571. Both show that these new configurations began with the Taiping Rebellion.

95. Kang-i Sun Chang 2005; Li Wai-yee 2006.

CHRONOLOGY

1. Qi Sihe 1958, p. 787. (Notes are provided only for references not otherwise cited in the body of the book or accessible by consulting *EC.*)

2. Wu Hongyi 1970, p. 145.

3. Qi Sihe 1958, pp. 787–788.

4. Qi Sihe 1958, p. 791.

5. Qi Sihe 1958, p. 792.

Alley, Rewi, trans. *Du Fu: Selected Poems.* Beijing: Foreign Languages Press, 2001.

An Jing 安京, ed. *Hailu jiao shi: Xie Qinggao kou shu, Yang Bingnan bi lu; An Jing jiao shi* 海录校释：谢清高口述，杨炳南笔录，安京校释 (An annotated edition of *Record of the Seas:* Based on the dictation of Xie Qinggao, as written down by Yang Bingnan, and edited by An Jing). Beijing: Shangwu yinshuguan, 2002.

Bai, Limin. *Shaping the Ideal Child: Children and Their Primers in Late Imperial China.* Hong Kong: Chinese University of Hong Kong Press, 2005.

Bai, Qianshen. *Fu Shan's World: The Transformation of Chinese Calligraphy in the Seventeenth Century.* Cambridge: Harvard University Press, 2003.

Bao Shichen 包世臣. "Li Fengtai zhuan" 李鳳臺傳 (Biography of Li Zhaoluo), in Li Zhaoluo 李兆洛, *Yangyi zhai quanji* 養一齋全集. Edition of 1878–1882.

———. *Yizhou shuang ji* 藝舟雙楫 (Collected works of Bao Shichen). In *Anwu si zhong* 安吳四種. Edition of 1851.

Barlow, Tani E. *The Question of Women in Chinese Feminism.* Durham: Duke University Press, 2004.

Bastid-Bruguière, Marianne. "Currents of Social Change." In John K. Fairbank and Kwang-Ching Liu, eds. *The Cambridge History of China,* vol. 2, *Late Ch'ing, 1800–1911,* part 2. Cambridge: Cambridge University Press, 1980, pp. 535–602.

Bei zhuan ji 碑傳集 (Collected eulogies from stele inscriptions). Comp. Qian Yiji 錢儀吉. First printed 1893. Repr. Taipei: Wenhai chubanshe, 1973.

Bei zhuan ji bu 碑傳集補 (Collected eulogies from stele inscriptions, supplement). Comp. Min Erchang 閔爾昌. Edition of 1931. Repr. Taipei: Wenhai chubanshe, 1973.

Bernhardt, Kathryn. *Women and Property in China, 960–1949.* Stanford: Stanford University Press, 1999.

Bickford, Maggie. *Ink Plum: The Making of a Chinese Scholar-Painting Genre.* New York: Cambridge University Press, 1996.

Boorman, Howard L., ed. *Biographical Dictionary of Republican China.* 3 vols. New York: Columbia University Press, 1967.

Bossler, Beverly. "'A Daughter Is a Daughter All Her Life': Affinal Relations and

Women's Networks in Song and Late Imperial China." *Late Imperial China* 21.1 (June 2000): 77–106.

Bray, Francesca. *Technology and Gender: Fabrics of Power in Late Imperial China*. Berkeley: University of California Press, 1997.

Cai Guanluo 蔡冠洛. *Qingdai qibai mingren zhuan* 清代七百名人傳 (Biographies of seven hundred famous persons of the Qing dynasty). 2 vols. Beijing: Zhongguo shudian, 1984.

Cao Hong 曹虹. *Yanghu wenpai yanjiu* 阳湖文派研究 (The Yanghu school of literary writing). Beijing: Wenhua shuju, 1996.

Cao Xueqin 曹雪芹 and Gao E 高鶚. *Hong lou meng* 红楼梦 (Dream of the red chamber). 3 vols. Beijing: Renmin wenxue chubanshe, 1988.

Carlitz, Katherine. "The Social Uses of Female Virtue in Late Ming Editions of *Lienü Zhuan*." *Late Imperial China* 12.2 (1991): 117–148.

Ch'a Yong-ju 車溶柱. *Hanguk wihang munhak chakka yŏn'gu* 韓國委巷文學作家研究 (Literary writers of the Korean "middling classes"). Seoul: Kyŏngin Publishing Company, 2003.

Chang, Kang-i Sun. "Liu Shih and Hsü Ts'an: Feminine or Feminist?" In Pauline Yu, ed., *Voices of the Song Lyric in China*. Berkeley: University of California Press, 1994, pp. 169–187.

———. "Ming-Qing Women Poets and the Notions of 'Talent' and 'Morality.'" In Theodore Huters, R. Bin Wong, and Pauline Yu, eds., *Culture and State in Chinese History: Conventions, Accommodations, and Critiques*. Stanford: Stanford University Press, 1997, pp. 236–258.

———. "Women's Poetic Witnessing: Late Ming and Late Qing Examples." In David Der-wei Wang and Shang Wei, eds., *Dynastic Crisis and Cultural Innovation: From the Late Ming to the Late Qing and Beyond*. Cambridge: Harvard University Press, 2005, pp. 504–522.

Chang, Kang-i Sun, and Haun Saussy, eds. *Women Writers of Traditional China: An Anthology of Poetry and Criticism*. Stanford: Stanford University Press, 1999.

Chang, Léon Long-yien, and Peter Miller. *Four Thousand Years of Chinese Calligraphy*. Chicago: University of Chicago Press, 1990.

Chang, Michael G. *A Court on Horseback: Imperial Touring and the Construction of Qing Rule, 1680–1789*. Cambridge: Harvard University Asia Center, 2007.

Changzhou shi wenhua ju 常州市文化局 et al., eds. *Changzhou cipai erbainian jinian shi wen ji* 常州词派二百年纪念诗文集 (Collected poems and essays in honor of the two-hundredth anniversary of the founding of the Changzhou school of lyric poetry). Changzhou: privately printed, 1997.

Chao, Chia-ying Yeh [Ye Jiaying]. "The Ch'ang-chou School of *Tz'u* Criticism." In Adele Austin Rickett, ed., *Chinese Approaches to Literature from Confucius to Liang Ch'i-ch'ao*. Princeton: Princeton University Press, 1978, pp. 151–188.

Chen Dongyuan 陳東原. *Zhongguo funü shenghuo shi* 中國婦女生活史 (A history of the lives of Chinese women). Orig. publ. 1937. Repr. Taipei: Taiwan shangwu yinshuguan, 1994.

Chen Kangqi 陳康祺. *Langqian jiwen* 郎潛紀聞 (A record of what I have heard). Orig. publ. 1880. Repr. Beijing: Zhonghua shuju, 1997.

Chen Weizhao 陈维昭. *Dai xue de wange: Qingdai wenren xintai shi* 带血的挽歌—清代文人心态史 (Blood-smeared elegy: A history of the mentality of Qing literati). Shijiazhuang: Hebei jiaoyu chubanshe, 2001.

Chin, Annping. *Four Sisters of Hofei: A History.* New York: Scribner, 2002.

Chŏng Hu-su 鄭後洙. "Chang Yo-son kwa t'aep'yŏng ch'ŏnguk ŭi nan: 'Haerin ch'ŏktok' sojae kisa rŭl chungsimuro" (Zhang Yuesun and the Taiping Rebellion: Evidence from "Letters to Yi Sang-jŏk" [Studio of the neighbor across the seas]). *Tongyang kojŏn hakhoe hwibo* 東洋古典學會彙報 7.1 (2001)–6.30 (2002): 299–333.

———. *Chosŏn hugi chungin munhak yŏn'gu* 朝鮮後期中人文學研究 (The literary movement of the professional class during the late Chosŏn period). Seoul: Kip'ŭn saem, 1990.

Chongxiu Chang Shao hezhi 重修常昭合志 (New edition of the combined gazetteer for Changshu and Shaowen counties). Printed 1904.

Chow, Kai-wing. "Discourse, Examination, and Local Elite: The Invention of the T'ung-ch'eng School in Ch'ing China." In Benjamin A. Elman and Alexander Woodside, eds., *Education and Society in Late Imperial China, 1600–1900.* Berkeley: University of California Press, 1994, pp. 183–219.

———. *Publishing, Culture, and Power in Early Modern China.* Stanford: Stanford University Press, 2004.

Ch'ü, T'ung-tsu. *Law and Society in Traditional China.* Paris: Mouton, 1961.

Cohen, Myron L. *House United, House Divided: The Chinese Family in Taiwan.* New York: Columbia University Press, 1976.

Cole, James H. *Shaohsing: Competition and Cooperation in Nineteenth-Century China.* Tucson: University of Arizona Press, 1986.

Deng Zhicheng 鄧之誠. *Gudong suo ji* 骨董瑣記 (Antiquarian fragments). Prefaces dated 1926. Facsimile reprint of edition of 1933, Minguo congshu, series 5, vol. 84. Shanghai: Shanghai shudian, 1996.

DMB. Dictionary of Ming Biography, 1368–1644. Ed. L. Carrington Goodrich. 2 vols. New York: Columbia University Press, 1976.

Dodgen, Randall A. *Controlling the Dragon: Confucian Engineers and the Yellow River in Late Imperial China.* Honolulu: University of Hawaii Press, 2001.

Dooling, Amy D., and Kristina M. Torgeson, eds. *Writing Women in Modern China: An Anthology of Women's Literature from the Early Twentieth Century.* New York: Columbia University Press, 1998.

Doolittle, Rev. Justus. Social Life of the Chinese. 2 vols. New York: Harper and Bros., 1867.

Drake, Fred W. *China Charts the World: Hsu Chi-yü and His Geography of 1848.* Cambridge: Harvard University Press, 1975.

Ebrey, Patricia Buckley, trans. and annot. *Family and Property in Sung China: Yüan Ts'ai's* Precepts for Social Life. Princeton: Princeton University Press, 1984.

EC. Eminent Chinese of the Ch'ing Period (1644–1912). Ed. Arthur W. Hummel. 2 vols. Washington, D.C.: United States Government Printing Office, 1943.

Egan, Ronald C. "The Problem of the Repute of *Tz'u* During the Northern Sung." In Pauline Yu, ed., *Voices of the Song Lyric in China.* Berkeley: University of California Press, 1994, pp. 191–225.

Elliott, Mark. "Bannerman and Townsman: Ethnic Tension in Nineteenth-Century Jiangnan." *Late Imperial China* 11.1 (1990): 36–74.

Elman, Benjamin A. *Classicism, Politics, and Kinship: The Ch'ang-chou School of New Text Confucianism in Late Imperial China.* Berkeley: University of California Press, 1990.

———. *A Cultural History of Civil Examinations in Late Imperial China.* Berkeley: University of California Press, 2000.

———. "The Social Roles of Literati in Early to Mid-Ch'ing." In Willard J. Peterson, ed., *The Cambridge History of China,* vol. 9: *The Ch'ing Empire to 1800,* part 1. Cambridge: Cambridge University Press, 2002, pp. 260–427.

Esherick, Joseph W. *The Origins of the Boxer Uprising.* Berkeley: University of California Press, 1987.

Fa shi jiasheng 法氏家乘 (Genealogy of the Fa lineage). Shanghai Library. Printed 1900.

Fairbank, John K., and Ssu-yü Teng. *Ch'ing Administration: Three Studies.* Cambridge: Harvard University Press, 1960.

Fairbank, John King, and Ssu-yü Teng. "On the Transmission of Ch'ing Documents." In Fairbank and Teng, *Ch'ing Administration: Three Studies.* Cambridge: Harvard University Press, 1960.

Fan Jinmin 范金民 and Xia Weizhong 夏维中. *Suzhou diqu shehui jingjishi (Ming-Qing juan)* 苏州地区社会经济史 (明清卷) (A social and economic history of the Suzhou region: Ming and Qing periods). Ed. Luo Lun 罗仑. Nanjing: Nanjing daxue chubanshe, 1993.

Fang Junmo 方骏謨 (fl. 1861). "Zhangjun qi Bao ruren cuozhi" 張君妻包孺人厝誌 (Mortuary inscription for Lady Bao, late wife of Master Zhang). In Zhao Zhen 趙震, comp., *Piling wen lu* 毘陵文錄 (Record of writings from Changzhou), 5/11b-12b. Shanghai: Huaxin shushe, 1931.

Fei Hsiao-tung. *Peasant Life in China: A Field Study of Country Life in the Yangtze Valley.* London: Routledge and Kegan Paul, 1939.

Feuerwerker, Albert. *China's Early Industrialization: Sheng Hsuan-huai (1844–1916) and Mandarin Enterprise.* Cambridge: Harvard University Press, 1958.

Folsom, Kenneth E. *Friends, Guests, and Colleagues: The* Mu-fu *System in the Late Ch'ing Period.* Berkeley: University of California Press, 1968.

Fong, Grace S. "Alternative Modernities, or a Classical Woman of Modern China: The Challenging Trajectory of Lü Bicheng's (1883–1943) Life and Song Lyrics." *Nan Nü: Men, Women and Gender in Early and Imperial China* 6.1 (2004): 12–59.

———. "Engendering the Lyric: Her Image and Voice in Song." In Pauline Yu, ed., *Voices of the Song Lyric in China*. Berkeley: University of California Press, 1994, pp. 107–144.

———. "Female Hands: Embroidery as a Knowledge Field in Women's Everyday Life in Late Imperial and Early Republican China." *Late Imperial China* 25.1 (2004): 1–58.

———. "Shen Shan-pao." In *ICTCL*, vol. 2 (1998), pp. 138–140.

———. "Writing Self and Writing Lives: Shen Shanbao's (1808–1862) Gendered Auto/Biographical Practices." *Nan Nü: Men, Women and Gender in Early and Imperial China* 2.2 (2000): 259–303.

Frankel, Hans H. *The Flowering Plum and the Palace Lady: Interpretations of Chinese Poetry*. New Haven: Yale University Press, 1976.

Furth, Charlotte. *A Flourishing Yin: Gender in China's Medical History, 960–1665*. Berkeley: University of California Press, 1999.

Granet, Marcel. *La polygynie sororale et le sororat dans la Chine féodale: Etude sur les formes anciennes de la polygamie chinoise*. Paris: Editions Ernest Leroux, 1920.

Guangxu Wujin Yanghu xian zhi 光緒武進陽湖縣志 (Guangxu edition of the gazetteer for Wujin and Yanghu counties [Changzhou]). Printed 1879.

Guantao xian zhi 館陶縣志 (Gazetteer of Guantao county [Shandong]). Edition of 1936.

Guo Songyi 郭松义. *Lunli yu shenghuo: Qingdai de hunyin guanxi* 伦理与生活—清代的婚姻关系 (Social ethics and daily life: Marital relations during the Qing dynasty). Beijing: Shangwu yinshuguan, 2000.

Guochao qixian lei zheng chu bian 國朝耆獻類徵初編 (Eminent elderly persons of the reigning dynasty, classified, first edition). Comp. Li Huan 李桓. Repr. Taipei: Wenhai chubanshe, 1966.

Guy, R. Kent. *The Emperor's Four Treasuries: Scholars and the State in the Late Ch'ien-lung Era*. Cambridge: Harvard University Council on East Asian Studies, 1987.

Handlin, Joanna F. *Action in Late Ming Thought: The Reorientation of Lü K'un and Other Scholar-Officials*. Berkeley: University of California Press, 1983.

———. "Lü K'un's New Audience: The Influence of Women's Literacy on Sixteenth-Century Thought." In Margery Wolf and Roxane Witke, eds., *Women in Chinese Society*. Stanford: Stanford University Press, 1975, pp. 13–38.

Hanson, Marta. "Robust Northerners and Delicate Southerners: The Nineteenth-Century Invention of a Southern Medical Tradition." *positions: east asia cultures critique* 6.3 (1998): 515–550.

Hawkes, David, trans. *Ch'u Tz'u: The Songs of the South*. Boston: Beacon Press, 1959.

Hawkes, David, and John Minford, trans. *The Story of the Stone*. 5 vols. New York: Penguin Books, 1973–1986.

Hershatter, Gail. *Women in China's Long Twentieth Century.* Berkeley: University of California International and Area Studies Project, in conjunction with the University of California Press and the California Digital Library, 2006.

Hinton, David, trans. *The Late Poems of Meng Chiao.* Princeton: Princeton University Press, 1996.

———. *The Selected Poems of Tu Fu.* New York: New Directions, 1989.

Hinton, Harold C. *The Grain Tribute System of China (1845–1911).* Chinese Economic and Political Studies, Harvard University. Cambridge: Harvard University Press, 1956.

Ho, Clara Wing-chung. "Encouragement from the Opposite Gender: Male Scholars' Interests in Women's Publications in Ch'ing China—A Bibliographical Study." In Harriet Zurndorfer, ed. *Chinese Women in the Imperial Past: New Perspectives.* Leiden: Brill, 1999, pp. 308–353.

Ho, Clara Wing-chung, ed. *Biographical Dictionary of Chinese Women: The Qing Period, 1644–1911.* Armonk, N.Y.: M. E. Sharpe, 1998.

Hŏ, Kyŏng-jin. *Chosŏn wihang munhak sa* (Literary figures among the professional class of the Chosŏn period). Seoul: T'aehaksa, 1997.

Hou, Sharon Shih-jiuan. "Women's Literature." In *ICTCL,* vol. 1 (1986), pp. 175–194.

Hsiung, Ping-chen. "Constructed Emotions: The Bond between Mothers and Sons in Late Imperial China." *Late Imperial China* 15.1 (1994): 87–117.

———. *A Tender Voyage: Children and Childhood in Late Imperial China.* Stanford: Stanford University Press, 2005.

Hu Siao-chen [Hu Xiaozhen] 胡曉真. "Wen yuan, duoluo yu huaman—Wang Yunzhang zhubian shiqi (1915–1920)" 文苑，多羅與華鬘—王蘊章主編時期 (1915–1920) (The writer's garden, the toilette case, and the *Kasuman:* Theory and practice of women's literature in the *Ladies' Journal* of the 1910s, under the editorship of Wang Yunzhang). *Jindai Zhongguo funü shi yanjiu* 12 (2004): 169–193.

Hu Wenkai 胡文楷. *Lidai funü zhuzuo kao* 歷代婦女著作考 (A survey of women writers arranged by dynasty). Orig. publ. 1957. Reprinted Shanghai: Shanghai guji chubanshe, 1985.

Hu Wenkai 胡文楷 and Wang Xiuqin 王秀琴, comp. *Lidai mingyuan shu jian* 歷代名媛書簡 (Selected letters of noted women writers arranged by dynasty). Changsha: Shangwu yinshuguan, 1941.

Hu, Ying. "Naming the First 'New Woman.'" In Rebecca E. Karl and Peter Zarrow, eds. *Rethinking the 1898 Reform Period: Political and Cultural Change in Late Qing China.* Cambridge: Harvard University Asia Center, 2002, pp. 180–211.

———. *Tales of Translation: Composing the New Woman in China, 1899–1918.* Stanford: Stanford University Press, 2000.

———. "Writing Qiu Jin's Life: Wu Zhiying and Her Family Learning." *Late Imperial China* 25.2 (2004): 119–160.

Hua Rende. "The History and Revival of Northern Wei Stele-style Calligraphy."

In Cary Y. Liu, Dora C. Y. Ching, and Judith G. Smith, eds., *Character and Context in Chinese Calligraphy.* Princeton: Princeton Art Museum, 1999, pp. 104–131.

Huang Yanli 黃嫣梨. *Qingdai si da nü ciren: Zhuanxingzhong de Qingdai zhishi nüxing* 清代四大女词人：转型中的清代知识女性 (Four great female song lyricists of the Qing period: Qing female intellectuals in transition). Shanghai: Hanyu da cidian chubanshe, 2002.

Hunter, Jane. *The Gospel of Gentility: American Women Missionaries in Turn-of-the-Century China.* New Haven: Yale University Press, 1984.

Hwang, Kyung Moon. *Beyond Birth: Social Status in the Emergence of Modern Korea.* Cambridge: Harvard University Asia Center, 2004.

HYDCD. Hanyu da cidian 汉语大词典 (Great dictionary of the Chinese language). Hanyu dacidian bianji weiyuan hui, comp. 12 vols. Shanghai: Shangwu yin-shuguan, 1994.

ICTCL. The Indiana Companion to Traditional Chinese Literature. 2 vols. Ed. and comp. William H. Nienhauser, Jr. Bloomington: Indiana University Press, 1986, 1998.

Idema, Wilt, and Beata Grant, eds. *The Red Brush: Writing Women of Imperial China.* Cambridge: Harvard University Asia Center, 2004.

Jen, Yu-wen. *The Taiping Revolutionary Movement.* New Haven: Yale University Press, 1973.

Ji Ling 季靈. *Qiangu juechang: Lidai cainü shici* 千古絕唱—歷代才女詩詞 (Utterly superb songs through the ages: Poems and lyrics by talented women arranged by dynasty). Taipei: Xingguang chubanshe, 1978.

Jiang Qingbo 江庆柏. *Ming Qing Su'nan wangzu wenhua yanjiu* 明清苏南望族文化研究 (A study of the culture of the great families of the Lower Yangzi region in the Ming and Qing periods). Nanjing: Nanjing shifan daxue chuban-she, 1999.

Jiang Tong 蔣彤. *Li Shenqi (Zhaoluo) nianpu* 李申耆 (兆洛) 年譜 (A chronological biography of Li Zhaoluo). Orig. publ. 1913. Repr. Shen Yunlong 沈雲龍, ed., *Jindai Zhongguo shiliao congkan* 近代中國史料叢刊, no. 392. Taipei: Wenhai chubanshe, 1969.

Jin shu 晉書 (History of the Jin dynasty). Comp. Fang Xuanling 房玄齡 et al. Repr. Beijing: Zhonghua shuju, 1974.

Jin Wuxiang 金武祥. *Suxiang suibi* 粟香隨筆, *Suxiang er bi* 粟香二筆, *Suxiang san bi* 粟香三筆, *Suxiang si bi* 粟香四筆, *Suxiang wu bi* 粟香五筆 (Random notes from the Studio of Millet Fragrance, vols. 1–5). Printed 1881–1894. Saoye shanfang edition.

Jing Su and Luo Lun. *Landlord and Labor in Late Imperial China: Case Studies from Shandong, by Jing Su and Luo Lun.* Trans. and intro., Endymion Wilkinson. Council on East Asian Studies, Harvard University. Distributed by Harvard University Press, 1978.

Johnson, David G. *The Medieval Chinese Oligarchy*. Boulder, Colo.: Westview Press, 1977.

Jones, Susan Mann. "Hung Liang-chi (1746–1809): The Perception and Articulation of Political Problems in Late Eighteenth-Century China." Ph.D. diss., Stanford University, 1972.

Jones, Susan Mann, and Philip A. Kuhn. "Dynastic Decline and the Roots of Rebellion." In John K. Fairbank, ed. *The Cambridge History of China*, vol. 10, *Late Ch'ing, 1800–1911*, part 1. Cambridge: Cambridge University Press, 1978, pp. 107–162.

Judge, Joan. "Reforming the Feminine: Female Literacy and the Legacy of 1898." In Rebecca E. Karl and Peter Zarrow, eds., *Rethinking the 1898 Reform Period: Political and Cultural Change in Late Qing China*. Cambridge: Harvard University Asia Center, 2002, pp. 158–179.

———. "Talent, Virtue, and the Nation: Chinese Nationalisms and Female Subjectivities in the Early Twentieth Century." *American Historical Review* 106.2 (June 2001): 765–803.

———. "Three Images of Qiu Jin: Reassessing a Chinese Cultural Icon in Light of Japanese Sources." Paper presented at the Thirteenth Berkshire Conference on the History of Women, Claremont, Calif., 2005.

Kangxi zidian 康熙字典 (The Kangxi dictionary). Orig. publ. 1716. Repr. Taipei: Qiming shuju, 1959.

Kennedy, Thomas L., trans. and annot. *Testimony of a Confucian Woman: The Autobiography of Mrs. Nie Zeng Jifen, 1852–1942*. Athens: University of Georgia Press, 1993.

Klein, Donald W., and Anne B. Clark, eds. *Biographic Dictionary of Chinese Communism, 1921–1965*. 2 vols. Cambridge: Harvard University Press, 1971.

Ko, Dorothy. *Cinderella's Sisters: A Revisionist History of Footbinding*. Berkeley: University of California Press, 2005.

———. *Every Step a Lotus: Shoes for Bound Feet*. Catalogue for the Bata Shoe Museum. Berkeley: University of California Press, 2001.

———. *Teachers of the Inner Chambers: Women and Culture in China, 1573–1722*. Stanford: Stanford University Press, 1994.

———. "The Written Word and the Bound Foot: A History of the Courtesan's Aura." In Ellen Widmer and Kang-i Sun Chang, eds., *Writing Women in Late Imperial China*. Stanford: Stanford University Press, 1997, pp. 74–100.

Ku Sui [Gu Sui] 顧隨. "Interpretation of Su Tung-p'o's Tz'u." Translation of Chia-ying Yeh's notes on a lecture by Professor Gu, by Huang Kuo-pin and Teresa Yee-wha Yü. In Stephen C. Soong, ed., *Song without Music: Chinese Tz'u Poetry*. Hong Kong: Chinese University of Hong Kong Press, 1980, pp. 157–176.

Kuhn, Philip A. "The Taiping Rebellion." In John K. Fairbank, ed., *The Cambridge History of China*, vol. 10, *Late Ch'ing, 1800–1911*, part 1. Cambridge: Cambridge University Press, 1978, pp. 264–317.

Kwok, Pui-lan. "Chinese Women and Protestant Christianity at the Turn of the Twentieth Century." In Daniel H. Bays, ed., *Christianity in China: From the Eighteenth Century to the Present.* Stanford: Stanford University Press, 1996, pp. 194–208.

Lee, Lily Xiao Hong, ed. *Biographical Dictionary of Chinese Women: The Twentieth Century, 1912–2000.* Armonk, N.Y.: M. E. Sharpe, 2003.

Legge, James, trans. *The Chinese Classics.* Vol. 1, *Confucian Analects, The Great Learning, The Doctrine of the Mean;* vol. 2, *The Works of Mencius;* vol. 4, *The She King;* vol. 5, *The Ch'un Ts'ew with the Tso Chuen.* Oxford: Oxford University Press, 1893–1895. Repr. Taipei: SMC Publishing, 1991.

Lei Jin 雷 瑨, comp. *Guixiu shihua* 閨 秀 詩 話 (Notes on poems by cultivated ladies). N.p., 1922.

Leonard, Jane Kate. *Controlling from Afar: The Daoguang Emperor's Management of the Grand Canal Crisis, 1824–1826.* Ann Arbor: Center for Chinese Studies, University of Michigan, 1996.

Leung, Angela Ki Che. "Organized Medicine in Ming-Qing China: State and Private Institutions in the Lower Yangzi Region." *Late Imperial China* 8.1 (1987): 134–166.

———. "To Chasten Society: The Development of Widow Homes in the Qing, 1773–1911." *Late Imperial China* 14.2 (1993): 1–32.

Li Junzhi 李 浚之, comp. *Qing huajia shi shi* 清 畫 家 詩 史 (History and poetry of Qing dynasty painters). Preface dated 1929; orig. printed 1930. Repr. Beijing: Zhongguo shudian, 1990.

Li Lan 李 瀾. *Shufa: Nanjing bowuyuan zhencang xilie* 書 法: 南 京 博 物 院 珍 藏 系 列 (Calligraphy: Treasures from the collections of the Nanjing Museum). Shanghai: Shanghai guji chubanshe, 1999.

Li Wai-yee. "Women Writers and Gender Boundaries during the Ming-Qing Transition." Unpublished paper presented at the conference "Traditional Chinese Women through a Modern Lens." Harvard University, June 18, 2006.

Li Xiaorong. "Engendering Heroism: Ming-Qing Women's Song Lyrics to the Tune *Man Jiang Hong.*" *Nan Nü: Men, Women and Gender in Early and Imperial China* 7.1 (2005): 1–39.

Li Zhaoluo 李 兆 洛. *Yangyi zhai quan ji* 養 一 齋 全 集 (The complete works from the Yangyi Studio). Preface dated 1852, reprinted 1878 [*wen* (prose)]–1882 [*shi* (poetry)]. University of California, Berkeley, East Asiatic Library.

Liang Qichao 梁 啟 超. "Lun nü xue" 論女學 (On women's learning). In *Bianfa tong yi* 變法通議 (Comprehensive program for reform), *Yinbing shi wen ji* 飲冰室文集 (Collected prose from the Ice-Drinker's Studio), vol. 1, pp. 37–44. Taipei: Taiwan Zhonghua shuju, 1978.

Liang Yizhen 梁乙真. *Qingdai funü wenxue shi* 清代婦女文學史 (A history of women's literature in the Qing dynasty). Orig. publ. 1925. Repr. Taipei: Zhonghua shuju, 1968.

Liu Guangjing 劉廣京. "Shijiu shiji chuye Zhongguo zhishifenzi: Bao Shichen yu Wei Yuan" 十九世紀初葉中國知識份子: 包世臣 與魏源 (Early nineteenth-century Chinese intellectuals: Bao Shichen and Wei Yuan). In *Zhongyang yan-jiuyuan guoji Hanxue huiyi lunwen ji* 中央研究院國際漢學會議論文集 (Collected papers from the International Sinological Conference of the Academic Sinica), vol. 3, part 2, pp. 995–1030. Taipei: Academia Sinica, 1981.

Liu, Hui-chen Wang. *The Traditional Chinese Clan Rules.* Locust Valley, N.Y.: J. J. Austin, 1959.

Liu, James J. Y. *The Art of Chinese Poetry.* Chicago: University of Chicago Press, 1962.

Liu, Kwang-Ching [Liu Guangjing]. "The Ch'ing Restoration: The Nien War and Its Repercussions." In John K. Fairbank, ed., *The Cambridge History of China,* vol. 10, *Late Ch'ing, 1800–1911,* part 1. Cambridge: Cambridge University Press, 1978, pp. 409–490.

———. "The Confucian as Patriot and Pragmatist: Li Hung-chang's Formative Years, 1823–1866." *Harvard Journal of Asiatic Studies* 30 (1970): 14–22.

Liu Wanlang 刘万朗. *Zhongguo shu hua cidian* 中国书画辞典 (A dictionary of Chinese calligraphy and painting). Beijing: Huawen chubanshe, 1990.

Liu Xiang 劉向. *Gu lienü zhuan* 古列女傳 (The original biographies of exemplary women). Congshu jicheng edition. Shanghai: Shangwu yinshuguan, 1936.

Liu Yongcong 劉詠聰. See Ho, Clara Wing-chung.

Lo, Irving Yucheng, and William Schultz, eds. *Waiting for the Unicorn: Poems and Lyrics of China's Last Dynasty, 1644–1911.* Bloomington: Indiana University Press, 1986.

Louie, Kam, and Louise Edwards. "Chinese Masculinity: Theorizing *Wen* and *Wu.*" *East Asian History* 8 (1994): 135–148.

Lu, Weijing. *True to Their Word: Faithful Maidens in the Qing Period.* Stanford: Stanford University Press, forthcoming.

———. "Uxorilocal Marriage among Qing Literati." *Late Imperial China* 19.2 (December 1998): 64–110.

Lufrano, Richard John. *Honorable Merchants: Commerce and Self-Cultivation in Late Imperial China.* Honolulu: University of Hawaii Press, 1997.

Luo Jianqiu 罗检秋. *Jiaqing yilai Hanxue chuantong de yanbian yu chuancheng* 嘉庆以来汉学传统的演变与传承 (The transformation and transmission of Han learning from the Jiaqing reign onward). Beijing: Zhongguo renmin daxue chubanshe, 2006.

Luo Wobai 罗我白, Shi Hong 史洪, et al. *Changzhou shi hua* 常州史话 (Stories from the history of Changzhou). Nanjing: Jiangsu renmin chubanshe, 1984.

Macauley, Melissa. *Social Power and Legal Culture: Litigation Masters in Late Imperial China.* Stanford: Stanford University Press, 1998.

Mann, Susan. "Classical Revival and the Woman Question: China's First Querelle des Femmes." In *Family Process and Political Process in Modern Chinese History,* vol. 1. Taipei: Institute of Modern History, Academia Sinica, Taiwan, 1992a, pp. 377–411.

————. "'Fuxue' [Women's Learning] by Zhang Xuecheng (1738–1801): China's First History of Women's Culture." *Late Imperial China* 13.1 (1992b): 40–62.

————. *Precious Records: Women in China's Long Eighteenth Century.* Stanford: Stanford University Press, 1997.

————. "The Virtue of Travel for Women in Late Imperial China." In Bryna Goodman and Wendy Larson, eds., *Gender in Motion: Divisions of Labor and Cultural Change in Late Imperial and Modern China.* Lanham, Md.: Rowman and Littlefield, 2005, pp. 55–74.

————. "Womanly Sentiments and Political Crises: Zhang Qieying's Poetic Voice in the Mid-Nineteenth Century." In Lü Fangshang, ed., *Voices Amid Silence: Women and the Nation in Modern China (1600–1950)*, vol. 1. Taipei: Institute of Modern History, Academia Sinica, 2003, pp. 198–222.

Mather, Richard B., trans. and annot. *Shih-shuo hsin-yü: A New Account of Tales of the World, by Liu I-ch'ing with commentary by Liu Chün.* Minneapolis: University of Minnesota Press, 1976.

Mayers, William Frederick. *The Chinese Government: A Manual of Chinese Titles, Categorically Arranged and Explained, with an Appendix.* 3rd ed. Orig. publ. 1897. Repr. Taipei: Ch'eng-wen, 1966.

McDermott, Joseph P. "The Chinese Domestic Bursar." *Ajia bunka kenkyū* (November 1990): 15–32.

Meyer-Fong, Tobie. "Packaging the Men of Our Times: Literary Anthologies, Friendship Networks, and Political Accommodation in the Early Qing." *Harvard Journal of Asiatic Studies* 64.1 (June 2004): 5–56.

Miao Quansun 繆荃孫. *Guochao Changzhou ci lu* 國朝常州詞錄 (An anthology of Changzhou song lyrics from the reigning dynasty). Yun zi zai kan 雲自在龕 edition of 1896. Harvard-Yenching Library.

Miles, Steven Bradley. *The Sea of Learning: Mobility and Identity in Nineteenth-Century Guangzhou.* Cambridge: Harvard University Asia Center, 2006.

Miller, Lucien. "Children of the Dream: The Adolescent World in Cao Xueqin's *Honglou meng.*" In Anne Behnke Kinney, ed., *Chinese Views of Childhood.* Honolulu: University of Hawaii Press, 1995, pp. 219–247.

Millward, James A. *Beyond the Pass: Economy, Ethnicity, and Empire in Qing Central Asia, 1759–1864.* Stanford: Stanford University Press, 1998.

Minford, John, and Joseph S. M. Lau, eds. *Classical Chinese Literature: An Anthology of Translations*, vol. 1, *From Antiquity to the Tang Dynasty.* New York: Columbia University Press; Hong Kong: Chinese University Press, 2002.

Mirsky, Jeannette, ed. *The Great Chinese Travelers.* Chicago: University of Chicago Press, 1964.

Morohashi Tetsuji 諸橋轍次. *Dai Kan-Wa jiten* 大漢和辭典 (Comprehensive Chinese-Japanese dictionary). Tokyo: Taishukan shoten, 1955–1960.

Nakata, Yūjirō, ed. *Chinese Calligraphy.* Trans. and adapt., Jeffrey Hunter. New York and Kyoto: Weatherhill/Tankosha, 1982. [Orig. publ. in Japanese under the title *Chūgoku no bijutsu: shoseki*].

Naquin, Susan. *Shantung Rebellion: The Wang Lun Uprising of 1774.* New Haven: Yale University Press, 1981.

Needham, Joseph. *Science and Civilisation in China,* vol. 3, *Mathematics and the Sciences of the Heavens and the Earth* (Cambridge: Cambridge University Press, 1959).

Ocko, Jonathan K. "Women, Property, and Law in the People's Republic of China." In Rubie S. Watson and Patricia Buckley Ebrey, eds., *Marriage and Inequality in Chinese Society.* Berkeley: University of California Press, 1991, pp. 313–346.

O'Hara, Rev. Albert R. *The Position of Woman in Early China According to the Lieh Nü Chuan, "The Biographies of Eminent Chinese Women."* Washington, D.C.: Catholic University of America Press, 1945.

Owen, Stephen. *The Poetry of Meng Chiao and Han Yü.* New Haven: Yale University Press, 1975.

Pastreich, Emanuel. "The Reception of Chinese Vernacular Narrative in Korea and Japan." Ph.D. diss., Harvard University, 1997.

Perry, Elizabeth J. *Rebels and Revolutionaries in North China, 1845–1945.* Stanford: Stanford University Press, 1980.

Peterson, Barbara Bennett, ed. *Notable Women of China: Shang Dynasty to the Early Twentieth Century.* Armonk, N.Y.: M. E. Sharpe, 2000.

Polachek, James M. *The Inner Opium War.* Cambridge: Harvard University Press, 1992.

Pomeranz, Kenneth. *The Making of a Hinterland: State, Society, and Economy in Inland North China, 1853–1934.* Berkeley: University of California Press, 1993.

Perry, Elizabeth J. *Rebels and Revolutionaries in North China, 1845–1945.* Stanford: Stanford University Press, 1980.

Qi Sihe 齐思和. *Zhong wai lishi nianbiao* 中外历史年表 (A chronology of the history of China and the world). Beijing: Sanlian shudian, 1958.

Qing shi gao jiao zhu 清史稿校註 (Annotated edition of the Draft History of the Qing Dynasty). Qingshigao jiaozhu bianzuan xiaozu, ed. Taipei: Guoshi guan, 1986.

Qingdai Piling shu mu 清代毗陵書目 (Bibliography of works from Changzhou [Piling] in the Qing dynasty). Comp. Changzhou lü Hu tongxianghui. Shanghai: Changzhou lü Hu tongxianghui, 1944.

Rankin, Mary Backus. *Elite Activism and Political Transformation in China: Zhejiang Province, 1865–1911.* Stanford: Stanford University Press, 1986.

Raphals, Lisa. *Sharing the Light: Representations of Women and Virtue in Early China.* Albany: State University of New York Press, 1998.

Ren Yidu 任以都 [E-tu Zen Sun]. *Ren Yidu xiansheng fangwen jilu* 任以都先生訪問紀錄 (The reminiscences of Professor E-tu Zen Sun). Zhongyang yanjiuyuan jindaishi yanjiusuo, Koushu lishi congshu 50. Taipei: Zhongyang yanjiuyuan jindaishi yanjiusuo, 1993.

Rengui zhi gao 壬癸志稿 (Draft gazetteer of Taicang for the year *rengui* [1833]). Printed 1880.

Rickett, Adele Austin. *Wang Kuo-wei's Jen-chien tz'u-hua: A Study in Literary Criticism.* Hong Kong: Hong Kong University Press, 1977.

Robertson, Maureen. "Changing the Subject: Gender and Self-Inscription in Authors' Prefaces and *Shi* Poetry." In Ellen Widmer and Kang-i Sun Chang, eds., *Writing Women in Late Imperial China.* Stanford: Stanford University Press, 1997, pp. 171–217.

Ross, Heidi A. "'Cradle of Female Talent': The McTyeire Home and School for Girls, 1892–1936." In Daniel H. Bays, ed., *Christianity in China: From the Eighteenth Century to the Present.* Stanford: Stanford University Press, 1996, pp. 209–227.

Rowe, William T. *Saving the World: Chen Hongmou and Elite Consciousness in Eighteenth-Century China.* Stanford: Stanford University Press, 2001.

———. "Women and the Family in Mid-Qing Social Thought: The Case of Chen Hongmou." *Late Imperial China* 13.2 (1992): 1–41.

Saussy, Haun. "Women's Writing Before and Within the *Hong lou meng.*" In Ellen Widmer and Kang-i Sun Chang, eds., *Writing Women in Late Imperial China.* Stanford: Stanford University Press, 1997, pp. 285–305.

She xian zhi 歙縣志 (Gazetteer of She county, Anhui). Edition of 1937.

Shen, Chuang. "Archaeology in Late Qing Dynasty Painting." *Ars Orientalis* 24 (1994): 83–104.

Shen Lidong 沈立东 and Ge Rutong 葛汝桐, eds. *Lidai funü shici jianshang cidian* 历代妇女诗词鉴赏辞典 (Critical dictionary of women's poetry and song lyrics through the ages). Beijing: Zhongguo funü chubanshe, 1992.

Shen Shanbao 沈善寶, comp. *Mingyuan shi hua* 名媛詩話 (Notes on the poetry of illustrious ladies). Edition of 1846. Repr. 1863. Shanghai Library.

Shi Mei 史梅. "Qingdai Jiangsu funü wenxian de jiazhi he yiyi" 清代江苏妇女文献的价值和意义 (The value and significance of women's writings in Jiangsu during the Qing period). *Wenxue pinglun congkan* 文学评论丛刊 4.1 (2001): 66–85.

Shi Shuyi 施淑仪. *Qingdai guige shiren zhenglüe* 清代闺阁诗人征略 (An overview of Qing dynasty female poets). Orig. publ. 1922. Shanghai: Shanghai shudian, 1987.

Shi Yihui 施义慧. "Taiping tianguo funü wenti yanjiu" 太平天国妇女问题研究 (A study of the woman question under the Taiping Kingdom of Heavenly Peace). M.A. thesis, Yangzhou Normal College (Yangzhou shifan xueyuan), 1995.

Silber, Cathy. "From Daughter to Daughter-in-Law in the Women's Script of Southern Hunan." In Christina K. Gilmartin, Gail Hershatter, Lisa Rofel, and Tyrene White, eds., *Engendering China: Women, Culture, and the State.* Cambridge: Harvard University Press, 1994, pp. 47–68.

Skinner, G. William. "Cities and the Hierarchy of Local Systems." In Skinner, ed., *The City in Late Imperial China.* Stanford: Stanford University Press, 1977, pp. 275–351.

———. "Regional Urbanization in Nineteenth-Century China." In Skinner, ed., *The City in Late Imperial China.* Stanford: Stanford University Press, 1977, pp. 211–249.

———. "'Seek a Loyal Subject in a Filial Son': Family Roots of Political Orientation in Chinese Society." In Institute of Modern History, Academia Sinica, ed., *Family Process and Political Process in Modern Chinese History,* vol. 2. Taipei: Institute of Modern History, Academia Sinica, 1992, pp. 943–979.

Spector, Stanley. *Li Hung-chang and the Huai Army.* Seattle: University of Washington Press, 1964.

Spence, Jonathan D. *God's Chinese Son: The Taiping Heavenly Kingdom of Hong Xiuquan.* New York: W.W. Norton, 1996.

Su Zhecong 苏者聪. *Lidai nüzi ci xuan* 历代女子词选 (Anthology of song lyrics by women arranged by dynasty). Chengdu: Ba Shu shudian, 1988.

———. *Zhongguo lidai funü zuopin xuan* 中国历代妇女作品选 (Anthology of women's writings in Chinese history). Shanghai: Guji chubanshe, 1987.

Sun Dianqi 孫殿起. *Fan shu ou ji xu bian* 販書偶記續編 (A bookseller's random list, continued). Shanghai: Guji chubanshe, 1980.

Sun Yuanxiang 孫原湘. *Tian zhen ge ji* 天真閣集 (Collection from the Pavilion of True Nature). Edition of 1812. East Asiatic Library, University of California, Berkeley.

Sutton, Donald S. "Shamanism in the Eyes of Ming and Qing Elites." In Kwang-Ching Liu and Richard Shek, eds., *Heterodoxy in Late Imperial China.* Honolulu: University of Hawai'i Press, 2004, pp. 209–237.

Taicang zhou Zhenyang xian zhi 太倉州鎮洋縣志 (Gazetteer of Taicang department and Zhenyang county). Edition of 1919.

Tang shi jiasheng 湯氏家乘 (Genealogy of the Tang lineage). Comp. Tang Chenglie 湯誠烈. Edition of 1874.

Tang Yaoqing 湯瑤卿. *Peng shi ou yin* 蓬室偶吟 (Casual rhymes from a modest cottage). In Zhang Qi 張琦, *Wanlin shi wen* 宛鄰詩文 (Poetry and prose from the Wanlin Studio). Orig. printing 1840. Repr. 1891.

Tao, Chia-lin Pao. "Chaste Widows and Institutions to Support Them in Late-Ch'ing China." *Asia Major,* 3rd ser., vol. 4, part 1 (1991): 101–119.

Teng, Emma Jinhua. *Taiwan's Imagined Geography: Chinese Colonial Travel Writing and Pictures, 1683–1895.* Cambridge: Harvard University Asia Center, 2004.

Theiss, Janet M. *Disgraceful Matters: The Politics of Chastity in Eighteenth-Century China.* Berkeley: University of California Press, 2004.

T'ien Ju-k'ang. *Male Anxiety and Female Chastity: A Comparative Study of Chinese Ethical Values in Ming-Ch'ing Times.* Leiden: E. J. Brill, 1988.

Tong Jun 童寯. *Dongnan yuan shu* 东南园墅 (Gardens and villas of southeastern China). Beijing: Zhongguo jianzhu gongye chubanshe, 1997.

Unschuld, Paul U. *Huang Di Nei Jing Su Wen: Nature, Knowledge, Imagery in an Ancient Chinese Medical Text.* Berkeley: University of California Press, 2003.

————. *Medical Ethics in Imperial China.* Berkeley: University of California Press, 1979.

————. *Medicine in China: A History of Ideas.* Berkeley: University of California Press, 1985.

————. *Medicine in China: A History of Pharmaceutics.* Berkeley: University of California Press, 1986.

Vittinghoff, Natascha. "Social Actors in the Field of New Learning in Nineteenth Century China." In Michael Lackner and Natascha Vittinghoff, eds., *Mapping Meanings: The Field of New Learning in Late Qing China.* Leiden: Brill, 2004, pp. 75–118.

Wagner, Rudolph G. *Reenacting the Heavenly Vision: The Role of Religion in the Taiping Rebellion.* Berkeley: Institute of East Asian Studies, University of California, 1982.

Wakeman, Frederic, Jr. "The Canton Trade and the Opium War." In John K. Fairbank, ed., *The Cambridge History of China,* vol. 10, *Late Ch'ing, 1800–1911,* part 1. Cambridge: Cambridge University Press, 1978, pp. 163–212.

Waley, Arthur. *The Opium War through Chinese Eyes.* London: George Allen and Unwin, 1958.

Waley-Cohen, Joanna. *Exile in Mid-Qing China: Banishment to Xinjiang, 1758–1820.* New Haven: Yale University Press, 1991.

Waltner, Ann. *Getting an Heir: Adoption and the Construction of Kinship in Late Imperial China.* Honolulu: University of Hawaii Press, 1990.

————. "The Moral Status of the Child in Late Imperial China: Childhood in Ritual and Law." *Social Research* 55.4 (1986): 667–687.

Wang Caipin 王采蘋. *Duxuan lou shi gao* 讀選樓詩稿 (Collected poems of Wang Caipin). Edition of 1894.

Wang Jingxian 王靖憲, ed. *Zhongguo meishu quan ji: Shufa zhuanke bian 2: Wei Jin Nan Bei chao shufa* 中國美術全集；書法篆刻編 2: 魏晉南北朝書法 (Complete collection of the art of China: Calligraphy carved in stone, vol. 2: Calligraphy from the Wei-Jin and Northern and Southern Dynasties era). Beijing: Xinhua shudian, 1986.

Wang, Lingzhen. *Personal Matters: Women's Autobiographical Practice in Twentieth-Century China.* Stanford: Stanford University Press, 2004.

Wang, Ping. *Aching for Beauty: Footbinding in China.* Minneapolis: University of Minnesota Press, 2000.

Wang Wenqiang 王文强. "Shengming xuyao daohang" 生命需要导航 (Life requires steering toward a goal). In Chen Su 陈肃, comp., *Changzhou mingshi xieying ji* 常州名士擷英集 (Legends of Changzhou notables). Nanjing: Jiangsu wenyi chubanshe, 2000.

Watson, Burton, trans. and annot. *The Tso Chuan: Selections from China's Oldest Narrative History.* New York: Columbia University Press, 1989.

Watson, Rubie S. "Afterword: Marriage and Gender Inequality." In Rubie S. Watson and Patricia Buckley Ebrey, eds., *Marriage and Inequality in Chinese Society.* Berkeley: University of California Press, 1991, pp. 347–368.

———. "Wives, Concubines, and Maids: Servitude and Kinship in the Hong Kong Region, 1900–1940." In Rubie S. Watson and Patricia Buckley Ebrey, eds., *Marriage and Inequality in Chinese Society.* Berkeley: University of California Press, 1991, pp. 231–255.

West, Stephen H. "Chilly Seas and East-Flowing Rivers: Yuan Hao-wen's Poems of Death and Disorder, 1233–1235." In Hoyt Cleveland Tillman and Stephen H. West, eds., *China under Jurchen Rule: Essays on Chin Intellectual and Cultural History.* Albany: State University of New York Press, 1995, pp. 281–304.

———. "Shih Kuo-ch'i's Commentary on the Poetry of Yüan Hao-wen." *Tsinghua hsueh pao* 10.2 (July 1974): 142–169.

Widmer, Ellen. *The Beauty and the Book: Women and Fiction in Nineteenth Century China.* Cambridge: Harvard University Asia Center, 2006.

———. "Considering a Coincidence: The 'Female Reading Public' Circa 1828." In Judith T. Zeitlin and Lydia H. Liu, eds., *Writing and Materiality in China: Essays in Honor of Patrick Hanan.* Cambridge: Harvard University Asia Center, 2003, pp. 273–314.

———. "The Huanduzhai of Hangzhou and Suzhou: A Study in Seventeenth-Century Publishing." *Harvard Journal of Asiatic Studies* 56.1 (1996): 77–122.

Wilkinson, Endymion. *Chinese History: A Manual.* Cambridge: Harvard University Asia Center, 1998.

Williams, S. Wells. *The Middle Kingdom.* 2 vols. New York: Charles Scribner's Sons, 1900.

Wolf, Margery. *Women and the Family in Rural Taiwan.* Stanford: Stanford University Press, 1972.

Wright, Mary Clabaugh. *The Last Stand of Chinese Conservatism: The T'ung-chih Restoration, 1862–1874.* Stanford: Stanford University Press, 1957.

Wu Hongyi 吳宏一. *Changzhou pai cixue yanjiu* 常州派詞學研究 (Song lyrics of the Changzhou school). Taipei: Jiaxin shuini gongsi wenhua jijin hui, 1970.

Wu Lanwan 吳蘭畹. *Guanxiangcao tang shi gao* 灌香草堂詩稿 (Collected poems of Wu Lanwan). Edition of 1866.

Wu Lanze 吳蘭澤. *Zhisi jugu cun cao* 職思居姑存草 (Poetry manuscripts of Wu Lanze). Manuscript copy. Preface dated 1863. Shanghai Library.

Wu Pei-yi. "Childhood Remembered: Parents and Children in China, 800–1700." In Anne Behnke Kinney, ed., *Chinese Views of Childhood.* Honolulu: University of Hawaii Press, 1995, pp. 129–156.

Wu Ren'an 吳仁安. *Ming Qing Jiangnan wangzu yu shehui jingji wenhua* 明清江南望族与社会经济文化 (Notable families in the society, economy and culture of the Lower Yangzi region during the Ming and Qing dynasties). Shanghai: Renmin chubanshe, 2001.

Wu Xiuhua 吳秀华 and Lin Yan 林岩. *Feng leng luan hong diao: Ye shi san jiemei zhuan* 枫冷乱红凋—叶氏三姐妹传 (Variations on the theme of dazzling red maple leaves in frost: A biography of the three Ye sisters). Shijiazhuang: Xinhua shu dian, 2001.

Wu Yang zhi yu 武陽志餘 (Addenda to the gazetteer of Wujin and Yanghu counties). Printed 1887.

Wujin Yanghu xian hezhi 武進陽湖縣合志 (Combined gazetteer of Wujin and Yanghu counties [Changzhou]). Edition of 1842.

Xin Tang shu 新唐書 (New history of the Tang dynasty). Comp. Ouyang Xiu 歐陽修. Beijing: Zhonghua shuju, 1975.

Xu bei zhuan ji 續碑傳集. (Collected eulogies from stele inscriptions, continued). Comp. Miao Quansun 繆荃孫. First printed 1893. Repr. Taipei: Wenhai chubanshe, 1973.

Xu Dingyi 許定一 [Juxue zi 咀雪子], ed. *Zuguo nüjie wenhao pu* 祖國女界文豪譜 (A guide to great women writers of our country). Beijing: Jinghua yinshuguan, 1909.

Xu Shichang 徐世昌. *Qing shi hui* 清詩匯 (Treasury of Qing poetry). 3 vols. 1929. Repr. Beijing: Beijing chubanshe, 1996.

Xu Zhenyi 許振禕. *Cai diao ji* 才調集 (Collected works). Yanghong wen shuju 洋鴻文書局. Edition of 1894.

———. *Yiwei ji* 詒煒集 (Collected works). Edition of 1897.

Yang Hsien-yi and Gladys Yang, trans. *Old Tales Retold*. Beijing: Foreign Languages Press, 1972.

Yao, Ping. "Women's Epitaphs in Tang China (618–907)." Unpublished paper presented at the Conference on Women's Biography and Gender Politics in China, University of California, Irvine, March 3–5, 2006.

Yi Sang-jŏk 李尚迪. "Haerin ch'ŏktok" 海鄰尺牘 (Letters to Yi Sang-jŏk [Studio of the Neighbor across the Seas]). N.d. Manuscript copy in the Harvard-Yenching Library.

———. *Ŭnsong dang chip* 恩松堂集 (Collection from the Hall of the Benevolent Pine). 4 vols. Printed 1847–1862.

Yu, Pauline. "Song Lyrics and the Canon: A Look at Anthologies of *Tz'u.*" In Yu, ed., *Voices of the Song Lyric in China*. Berkeley: University of California Press, 1994, pp. 70–103.

Yu, Pauline, ed. *Voices of the Song Lyric in China*. Berkeley: University of California Press, 1994.

Yu Xinzhong 余新忠. *Qingdai Jiangnan de wenyi yu shehui: Yixiang yiliao shehui shi de yanjiu* 清代江南的瘟疫与社会：一项医疗社会史的研究 (Epidemics and society in Qing dynasty Jiangnan: A study in the social history of medicine). Beijing: Zhongguo renmin daxue chubanshe, 2003.

Zhang Fuqing 张福清. *Nü jie* 女诫 (Admonitions for women). Beijing: Zhongyang minzu daxue chubanshe, 1996.

Zhang Guanying 張紃英. *Weiqing yigao* 緯青遺稿 (Surviving poems of Zhang

Guanying). Wanlin shuwu congshu edition. Preface dated 1829. Reprinted in *Jiangyin congshu* 江陰叢書, comp. Jin Wuxiang 金武祥. Suxiang shi 粟香室 edition of 1907. Held in the Fu Sinian Library, Nankang, Taipei, Taiwan.

Zhang Hongsheng 張宏生. *Qingdai cixue de jiangou* 清代词学的建构 (The construction of song lyric studies in the Qing period). Nanjing: Jiangsu guji chubanshe, 1998.

Zhang Huiyan 張惠言. *Mingke wen er bian* 茗柯文二編 (Collected prose, second fascicle). Preface dated 1869.

Zhang Lunying 張綸英. *Lühuai shuwu shi gao* 綠槐書屋詩稿 (Collected poems from the Green Scholar Tree Studio). 2 *juan.* Wanlin shuwu keben 宛鄰書屋刻本 1845. Beijing University Library. *Fu lu* 附錄 5 *juan.* N.d., Shanghai Library. Repr. Lü shi keben 呂氏刻本, 1868. 3 *juan.*

Zhang Qi 張琦. *Ming fa lu* 明發錄 (Record of illumination). Edition of 1840. In *Wanlin shi wen,* vol. 5.

———. *Wanlin shi wen* 宛鄰詩文 (Poetry and prose from the Wanlin Studio). Orig. printing 1840. Repr. 1891.

Zhang Qieying 張繻英. *Danju xuan chugao* 澹菊軒初稿 (Early poems from the Pale Chrysanthemum Studio). Edition of 1840.

Zhang shi zong pu 張氏宗譜 (Genealogy of the Zhang lineage). 42 *juan.* Comp. Zhang Yuyu 張瑀玉. Revised and reprinted 1947. Shanghai Library no. 920035-76. Also Changzhou Library. Paginations differ.

Zhang Wanying 張紈英. *Canfeng guan wenji chubian* 餐楓館文集初編 (Collected early prose of Zhang Wanying). Wanlin shuwu 宛鄰書屋 edition of 1850. 2 *juan.* Shanghai Library.

———. *Linyun youyue zhi ju shi chugao* 鄰雲友月之居詩初稿 (Collected early poems of Zhang Wanying). Guanshu Dihua guan 官署棣華館 edition. Printed in Wuchang, 1849. 4 *juan.* Also Fu Sinian Library, Institute of History and Philology, Academia Sinica, Taipei.

Zhang Weixiang 張維驤, ed. *Qingdai Piling mingren xiao zhuan gao* 清代毗陵名人小傳稿 (Short biographies of famous people of Changzhou in the Qing dynasty). Orig. ed. 1944. Repr. Hong Kong: Zhongshan tushu gongsi, 1972.

Zhang Yuesun 張曜孫. *Chanyun ji* 產孕集 (Collected writings on pregnancy and childbirth). First printed in Suzhou, 1845; reprinted Fujian, 1871. Reprint of 1871 edition, with preface dated 1898, in Qiu Jisheng 裘吉生, ed., *Zhenben yishu jicheng* 珍本醫書集成 (Comprehensive collection of rare medical texts), vol. 8. Shanghai: Shijie shu ju, 1936.

———. "Chu kou jilüe" 楚寇紀略 (A brief account of the Taiping Rebellion in Hubei and Hunan). N.d., n.p. Manuscript copy, Nanjing Library.

———. *Jinyan shenhao zhi ju shiji* 謹言慎好之居詩集 (Collected poems of Zhang Yuesun). 18 *juan.* Edition of 1904.

———. *Tongsheng ji* 同聲集 (Collected song lyrics in a common voice). Edition of 1844.

———. *Xu Honglou meng* 續紅樓夢 (Sequel to *Dream of the Red Chamber*). N.d. Reprinted under the title *Xu Honglou meng gao* 稿. Beijing: Beijing daxue chubanshe, 1990.

Zhang Yuesun 張曜孫, comp. *Dihua guan shi ke* 棣華館詩課 (Poems from the Studio of Sibling Affection). Printed 1850.

Zhang Yunhe 张允和. *Zuihou de guixiu* 最后的闺秀 (The last of the *guixiu*). Beijing: Sanlian shudian, 1999.

Zhang Zhenhuai 張珍懷, ed. *Qingdai nü ciren xuan ji* 清代女詞人選集 (Anthology of Qing women's song lyrics). Taipei: Wen shi zhe chubanshe, 1997.

Zhang Zhongxing 张中行. *Guanyu funü* 关于妇女 (With reference to women). Beijing: Xinhua shudian, 1995.

Zhao Zhen 趙震, comp. *Piling shi lu* 毘陵詩錄 (Record of poems from Piling [Changzhou]). Preface dated 1922. Copy in the Harvard-Yenching Library.

Zheng Hecheng 鄭合成. "Anguo xian yao shi diaocha" 安國縣藥市調查 (A survey of the Anguo county pharmaceutical market). *Shehui kexue zazhi* 3.1 (March 1932): 94–124.

Zhongguo renmin gongheguo diming cidian: Jiangsu sheng 中华人民共和国地名词典：江苏省 (Dictionary of place-names in the People's Republic of China: Jiangsu province). Comp. Shan Shumo 单树模. Beijing: Shangwu yinshuguan, 1987.

Zhongguo yuanlin jianshang cidian 中国园林鉴赏辞典 (An appreciative dictionary of Chinese gardens). Comp. Chen Congzhou 陈从周. Shanghai: Huadong shifan daxue chubanshe, 2000.

Zhuang Shouqi 莊受祺. *Fengnan shan'guan yiji* 楓南山館遺集 (Surviving writings of Zhuang Shouqi). Ed. Zhuang Yisun 莊怡孫. Edition of 1875.

Zong Jichen 宗績辰. *Gongchi zhai wen chao* 躬恥齋文鈔 (Collected prose of Zong Jichen). Preface dated 1856.

ACKNOWLEDGMENTS

My first thanks go to Liu Yongcong (Clara Wing-chung Ho), who introduced me to the Zhang family many years ago when she invited me to write biographies of Lunying and Wanying for her *Biographical Dictionary of Chinese Women: The Qing Period, 1644–1911* (Armonk, N.Y.: M. E. Sharpe, 1998). Several scholars in libraries in China graciously expedited my research for this book: in the classics section of the Changzhou Library, Zhu Jun and his supervisors; in the classics section of the Nanjing University Library, Shi Mei; and in the classics section of the Nanjing Library, Xu Yinong. I am also grateful for the help of Professor Zhang Yufan, director of the Rare Book Room at the Beijing University Library, and the staff in the classics and genealogy reading rooms at the Shanghai Library. At Nanjing University, my host Fan Jinmin made possible a period of uninterrupted research and writing during a sabbatical year supported in part by the National Endowment for the Humanities (FA-36959-02) and a University of California President's Fellowship in the Humanities. For a generous contribution to the publication costs, I thank the Office of the Dean of Social Sciences, University of California, Davis. In Nanjing and Shanghai, Luo Suwen, Shi Mei, Zhang Hongsheng, Mei Mei, Shi Yihui, Wang Yun, Wu Yulian, Xu Caili, Zhang Yan, and (long distance) Tobie Meyer-Fong—an honorary Nanjing native—all made my work easier and much more interesting. In November 2002, I was present at the special conference of the Changzhou Song Lyric Society marking the two-hundredth anniversary of the death of Zhang Huiyan, the founder of the Changzhou song lyric school. I am indebted to Professor Xie Chen and Wang Qinan *nüshi* for making it possible for me to attend and benefit from this meeting. In Beijing on earlier visits, Zang Jian, Deng Xiaonan, and Ding Yizhuang came to my assistance. At the Academia Sinica in Taiwan, Hsiung Ping-chen, Lin Man-houng, and Angela Ki Che Leung have given me invaluable help over the years.

In the United States, various librarians and library staff members have helped me locate sources I was seeking and directed me to some I had not known existed: at Princeton's Gest Library, Martin Heijdra; at the Library of Congress, Chü Mi; at the Harvard Yenching Library, Timothy Connor and James Cheng; at the University of California Berkeley's East Asia Library, Bruce Williams and other members of the wonderful staff. My own home library, the East Asia Collection in Shields Library, University of California, Davis, has been a bedrock resource throughout the writing of this book, for which I thank Phyllis Wang and Annie Lin. Wang Zheng, Lu Weijing, Li Guotong, and Wang Yan took precious time away from their own research to help me locate valuable materials, and Li Guotong's research assistance in the final preparation of the manuscript was particularly helpful. Ja Hyun Kim Haboush, Gowoon Noh, Sunmin Park, Li Haihong, and Kyu Hyun Kim assisted me with Korean sources. Steven West, Ellen Widmer, and Grace Fong repeatedly trampled disciplinary boundaries to come to my aid.

The chapters of this book contain ideas developed over years, during which I benefited from the criticism of many more people than I can name here. I am grateful to Lü Fangshang and Yu Chien-ming for an opportunity to present an early part of this project at a conference on women's history at the Institute of Modern History, Academia Sinica; to Susan Naquin for inviting me to discuss the project at Princeton's East Asian Studies colloquium; to Wang Zheng and the Center for Chinese Studies at the University of Michigan, where I tested some of the book's arguments; and to the Center for Chinese Studies at the University of California, Los Angeles, which afforded me several opportunities to discuss problems explored in this book. I am indebted to countless conversations with Lu Weijing and Ye Baomin, and students in my senior seminar on the Taiping Rebellion helped in more ways than they know. Judy Moores directed me to Erie Vitiello, who became my tutor in new ways to write history; no matter how short this book falls of her own standards, Erie will have to take some credit for the results. Cathy Kudlick was particularly helpful in some last-minute decisions about the organization of the manuscript. I owe a great debt to the reviewers of the manuscript for the University of California Press, and to the staff at the Press, especially Sheila Levine, for their faith in this project. For cheers from afar as well as feedback close to home I thank Beverly Bossler, Cathy Kudlick, Gail Hershatter, Mary Lou Wilson, and G. William Skinner. Gail Hershatter's comments after a close reading of a final draft gave me insights that would have otherwise remained buried. And to the late K. C. Liu, who was for years a fount of scholarly inspiration and generous counsel, I owe heartfelt thanks for balancing appreciative encouragement with thoroughgoing criticism and the sharpest of editorial advice.

The contemporary *cainü* Hong Zhang re-created the painting that now graces this volume, breathing life into a visual image of adjoining lives that captures one of the major themes of this book. Although Hong herself is one of three talented sisters, and she shares a surname with the Zhang, to the best of our knowledge she is not related to the women in her painting.

My final thanks are to my subjects, the talented women of the Zhang family, who have *not* returned to haunt me as vengeful ghosts. They know that my encounter with their lives has been challenging enough.

INDEX

"Chang di" (in *Book of Odes*), 116, 268n66

Changshu: guild, 99, 250n72; malaria treatment, 184; Wu Zan relatives, 48, 68, 118, 250n72; Zhang Qieying, 118, 160

Changzhou, 44–46, 238n102; cultural center for talented women, 13, 44–46, 87, 127–28, 178, 181–82, 263n23; De'an Neighborhood, 37, 239n112; elite families, 13, 44–45, 127, 176–77, 239n112; Fa family, 9, 24, 30, 173; famine, 49, 201, 231n32; *guixiu* (genteel ladies), 13, 67, 181–82; Lotus Day, 105; marriage customs, 47, 176–77; Miss Fa, 90–92, 95, 109, 120, 171, 173, 208, 271n14; song lyric school, 103, 123, 124, 125–26, 185, 202; Taiping Rebellion, 120, 192, 193, 194–95, 208, 256n128; Tang Yaoqing, 13, 17, 23–37, 44–49, 59, 66, 89; Wang Caipin, 130–42; Wang Xi burial trip through, 114; Zhang family "Near Garden" residence, 27–37, 58, 59, 68, 72, 203, 234n58; Zhang family return from Huizhou, 22–23, 202; Zhang family return from Jiaxing, 25, 203; Zhang family school taught by Sun Jie, 95, 130–35, 261n6; Zhang Huiyan, 22–23, 49–51, 231n31; Zhang Lunying, 130, 131–32, 155, 206; Zhang Qi, 50–51, 89, 231n31; Zhang Qieying, 68, 71–72; Zhang Yuesun as family head, 89–90, 95, 98, 108, 130–31, 177–78, 180, 206

Chanyun ji (Zhang Yuesun), 141, 206, 207, 208, 241n138, 248n50

Chen Hengzhe, 182, 273n51

Chen Hongmou, 12, 134–35, 230n14

Cheng Peiyuan, 157, 207

childbirth: mother's death in, 183, 274n54; Zhang Yuesun's *Chanyun ji* (on childbirth and infant care), 141, 206, 207, 208, 241n138, 248n50. *See also* motherhood

Chin, Annping, 228n13

Christians, 6, 116–17, 196, 276n87

ci (song lyrics), 123–29, 257–59; Chang-

zhou school, 103, 123, 124, 125–26, 185, 202, 204; *Ci xuan* anthology, 125, 202, 205, 246n40, 258n150; *haofang* (heroic) style, 101, 127, 251n81, 259nn152,161; moralistic, 125–26; Su Shi, 101, 103, 105, 123, 126, 259n152; Tongcheng *xuepai*, 258n144; Wang Xi, 70, 71, 111, 204, 207, 253–54n105; Wang Yun, 127; *wanyue* (feminine) styles, 127; "Western Zhejiang" (Zhexi) group, 258n148; women as object of male poet's gaze, 126–27; women writers, 126–29, 259–60n165; Wu Zan, 70, 71, 92, 204, 236n83, 244n10; Xuannan *ci she*, 257n143; Yangxian group, 258n148; Zhang Huiyan, 88, 102–3, 124, 125–26, 185, 259nn152–54; Zhang Qi, 51, 70, 71, 88, 102–3, 124, 125–26, 185, 204; Zhang Qieying, 75, 101–6, 116, 121, 123, 126, 250n71; Zhang Yuesun's *Tongsheng ji* collection, 111, 125, 207, 236n83, 244n10, 258n151; Zhou Ji, 126

"class": "managerial landlords," 37, 236n79; "new official class" *(xin shihuan jieji)*, 48–49. *See also* status, of concubines

classics: *Analects*, 9, 11, 18; *Book of Changes*, 52; *Book of Rites*, 10; *Four Books (Analects/Mencius/Great Learning/Doctrine of the Mean)*, 11, 229n1; *Four Books for Women*, 11; *Four Treasuries (Siku quanshu)*, 52; medical, 56–57, 205, 241n137; *Three Character Classic*, 11; for women, 11–12, 230n11; *Zuo zhuan*, 100, 143–44, 149–50, 263n23. *See also Book of Odes (Shi jing)*

clinic *(huimin ju)*, Zhang Qi opening, 40, 186

commercial markets: elite women and, 186, 198; *lijin* commercial tax, 5–6; publishing, 174. *See also* sales, noncommercial

concubines, 187–89, 274–75n68; Wang Xi's, 111, 188–89, 254n106, 260n1; Xu Zhenyi's, 2, 163, 270n89; Zhang Jinli's, 122–23; Zhang Yuesun's, 109–10, 120, 141, 187–89, 205, 207, 238n98, 253101, 253n101, 274n68

Confucianism: Changzhou, 45; *guixiu*
studies, 228n13; Korean, 119; on
poverty, 154; scholarly heritage, 50;
Taiping Rebellion and, 6; Wanyan
Yun Zhu anthologizing, 106, 128, 181;
womanly virtues, 11–12, 198, 199,
276n93. *See also* classics
cooking: Tang Yaoqing, 18; Zhang Qieying
and sisters, 25–26, 27, 63, 67

Daoguang Emperor, 116, 136, 205
de yan rong gong (four womanly virtues), 12
death, 183–85; Bao Mengyi, 109, 140–41,
171–72, 207, 271n14, 274n54; Bao
Shichen, 118, 183, 208; in childbirth,
183, 274n54; Daoguang Emperor,
116; He Guiqing execution, 275n75;
inquiry ritual, 73; Jin Bang, 202; Lady
Bai, 201; Lady Jiang, 19, 36, 202; Li
Zhaoluo, 206; Lin Zexu, 207, 252n86;
Miss Fa, 120, 171, 233n45, 248n47,
271nn14,17; Qianlong Emperor, 21,
103–4, 126, 202; *sangluan* ("death and
destruction") poems, 257n137; Shen
Shanbao's father, 100; Sun Jie, 110,
140–41, 153, 207; Sun Jie's father, 89,
180, 205; Tang Dashen, 201; Tang
Xiuye, 202; Tang Yaoqing, 43–44,
59, 89, 180, 205, 238n100; Tang Yaoqing's great-uncle and uncle, 202;
Tang Yifen, 118, 183, 231n22; Wang
Cailan/Sun Sihui, 176; Wang Caipin,
6, 163, 208; Wang Caipin's husband,
3, 118, 161, 208; Wang Ding, 103,
252nn86,90; Wang Xi, 113, 153, 207,
268n72; Wei Ji, 270n87; Wu Zan,
116, 148, 207; Zhang Chanbin, 201;
Zhang Guanying, 37, 61, 72–75, 170,
204, 244n12, 274n54; Zhang Huiyan,
22, 203, 232n41; Zhang Jindi, 201;
Zhang Jinli, 121, 122, 189, 208, 248n47;
Zhang Juesun, 24, 25, 30, 57, 62, 64,
173, 183, 184, 203, 243n2; Zhang Qi,
61, 89, 97, 137, 205; Zhang Qieying,
120; Zhang Wanying, 120; Zhang
Yuesun, 120, 121, 131, 189, 193, 208.
See also burial; mourning rituals;
suicide; widows

Deng Shiru, 20, 54, 201, 232n35,
241nn133,134
"Dihua guan" ("Studio Where Sibling
Affection Flowers"), 116, 188, 207,
267n49
diseases, 36, 184, 274n56; cholera, 184,
274nn55,56; diphtheria, 184; malaria,
184; plague, 22, 232n41; scarlet fever,
184; smallpox, 39, 77, 92, 204, 205,
245n23, 249n60, 274n56
Dong Dingyuan, 201, 231n31
Dong Sicheng, 205, 246n40
Dong Wanzhen, 249n65, 262n17
Double Seven festival, 161, 268n73, 269n76
dowry, 61, 174–75, 196, 242nn154,155;
calligraphic works in, 85; poetry
collections in, 75; Tang Yaoqing, 25,
26–27, 58–60, 175; Zhang Qieying,
75, 85
Dream of the Red Chamber (Cao Xueqin),
28, 144, 230n18; Zhang Yuesun sequel,
174, 179, 272n24
Du Fu, 166, 251n82, 269nn77,80
Duan Yucai, 44, 52

economics. *See* commercial markets; employment; family economics; taxes
education. *See* learning; patronage
elite status, 50; Changzhou families, 13,
44–45, 127, 176–77, 239n112; men,
185; Ming dynasty landed elite, 46–
47, 48; *wangzu* (leading families),
176–77; women, 185–90, 197–98,
235n43. *See also guixiu* (genteel
ladies); literary culture
Elliott, Mark, 194–95
Elman, Benjamin, 194
embroidery, 132–33; sales/exchanges,
26, 67, 174, 234n54, 274n62; Tang
Yaoqing, 14, 26, 67, 107–8, 174
employment: Wang Caipin as governess,
1–5, 130, 163, 190, 193, 270n88,
275n78. *See also* family economics;
household duties; men's employment
"Er nan" (in *Book of Odes*), 135, 261n6
eulogies: for Bao Mengyi, 171–73, 174; for
Tang Yaoqing, 171, 229n7, 234n54,
235n70, 236n77, 238n100; for Zhang

Qi, 137, 235–36nn68,72, 242n148; for Zhang Yuesun, 186, 240n112, 253n98. *See also* memoirs

"examination culture," 46, 59, 175; Changshu guild, 250n72; Changzhou, 182; marriage arrangements and, 176; verse writing restored to examinations, 258n147; Wu Zan, 79; Zhang Huiyan and, 50, 125–26; Zhang Yuesun, 108. See also *jinshi* degree; *juren* degree; literary culture; teaching positions

Fa, 173; physician family, 9, 24, 30, 54, 62, 173, 242n2. *See also* Miss Fa
Fa Ding, 24, 233n45
Fa Qianyi, 9, 229n3
Fa Zhenglin, 24
faithful widows, 20, 202, 239n110. See also *zhennü* ("faithful maiden")
family, 176–90; Changzhou elite, 13, 44–45, 127, 176–77, 239n112; child socialization, 177, 179; father as sentimental and emotional, 244n12; Han customs, 7; incest taboo, 176; Lower Yangzi region, 179; networks, 176–82, 276n76; patrilineal, xv, 47, 181, 189–90, 273n46; ritual hierarchies, 91, 172, 178, 180–81; sibling influence, 177–80; Taiping Rebellion and, 7, 117, 118, 160, 268n73; uterine, 276n76. *See also* adoption; affinal kin; ancestors; concubines; gender; *jiaxue* ("family learning"); marriage; motherhood
family economics, 175; elite status, 186–87, 198; embroidery sales/exchanges, 26, 67, 174, 234n54, 274n62; market for women's writing, 174; men's travels, 128; Miss Fa, 152; Shen Shanbao, 100; Sun Jie, 82–83, 85–86, 95, 154; Tang Yaoqing, 25–27, 34–37, 42, 58–61, 67, 71, 174, 175, 198, 235n70, 236n77; by virtuous women, 174–75, 198–99, 276n93; Wang Caipin, 1, 130–32, 190, 193; Wang Xi, 131–32; in women's learning, 197–99; women's roles and networks, 176–78, 196, 198–99,

274n62, 276n93; Wu Zan, 116; Zhang Guanying, 61, 67, 70, 244n9; Zhang Lunying, 83–85, 90, 120, 131–32, 155, 174, 186, 193, 272n23; Zhang Qi, 18, 34–35, 40, 42, 89, 237n93; Zhang Qieying, 43, 63, 67, 72, 175; Zhang Yuesun, 89, 92, 130–31, 175, 272n23. *See also* dowry; employment; patronage; sales, noncommercial
famine: Changzhou, 49, 201, 231n32; Jiangnan, 202; Shandong, 34, 40, 204
Fan Pang, 4, 228n10
Fang Bao, 258n144
Fang Junmo, 171–72, 174
Feng Guifen, 51, 183, 185, 192, 206, 208
Feng Xuan of Qi, 267–68n61
finances. *See* commercial markets; employment; family economics
"Five Phases" *(wu xing)* in nature, 56
flooding: Yellow River, 158, 228n7, 252n86; Zhang Yuesun's flood relief program, 253n98
Fong, Grace, 127, 259n161
footbinding, 7, 24–25, 117, 166–67, 233n47, 271n4
foreigners, 145–50; Boxer Uprising against, 45, 58–59, 195; Canton, 6, 137–38, 146, 205, 250n71, 251n86, 263n20; Christians, 6, 116–17, 196, 276n87; Li Zhaoluo studies, 136–39, 146, 191–92, 203, 206. *See also* British; Opium War; Taiping Rebellion
Four Books (Analects/Mencius/Great Learning/Doctrine of the Mean), 11, 229n1. *See also* classics
Four Books for Women, 11
"four quintessential attributes" (womanly virtues), 12
Four Treasuries (Siku quanshu), 52
fu dao ("wifely way"), 172

gan shi (poems on politics), 103, 250–51n81. *See also* politics
gender: household segregation by, 7, 10, 66, 117, 132, 133, 185–86; sex ratios at birth, 47; and time for writing prose, 126. *See also* men; women
God-Worshippers, 117. *See also* Christians

Japan: calligraphy buyers, 246n31; Sino-Japanese war, 5, 163–64
Jiangnan: diseases, 184; famine, 202; medical learning center, 57
Jiangyin: stone for Lady Jiang memorial, 36, 244n9; Tang Yaoqing burial, 238n100; Zhang Guanying's marital family, 36, 48, 61, 74, 154, 238n100, 244n9
Jiaonü yigui (Chen Hongmou), 12, 134–35, 230n14
Jiaqing Emperor, 21, 49, 50, 104, 251n84
Jiaxing, Zhang family, 25, 62–65, 203
jiaxue ("family learning"), 228n11; elite status, 187; Li Luan, 141–42; *mujiao* (maternal instruction), 23–24, 47, 67, 128, 255n121; sex education, 16; Sun Jie teaching Changzhou family school, 95, 130–35, 261n6; Tang family, 9–13, 106; Tang Yaoqing, 9–13, 48, 229n1, 230n11; Wang Caipin, 2, 3, 5, 6, 93, 130–35, 261n6; Zhang family reputation, 17, 48–49, 123; Zhang Guanying, 23–24, 26, 64; Zhang Juesun, 23, 24, 63; Zhang Lunying, 26, 66; Zhang Qieying, 23–24, 26, 63–67, 70–71, 99–100, 122; Zhang Wanying, 23–24, 26, 66; Zhang Yuesun, 23, 28–29, 50, 66, 67, 179–80
Jin: Anhui compound, 19–22, 49, 64, 65, 201, 241n133, 259n154, 275n71; family, 231nn32,33
Jin Bang, 19–20, 49, 201, 202, 232n35, 241n133, 259n154
Jin Wuxiang, 194
Jin Yunhuai, 19–20, 201, 231n32
Jinan, 76; Zhang family, 38, 77, 94, 204; Zhang Qi and Bao Shichen, 203
Jingzhou, 255n121, 256n131, 257n133; Taiping Rebellion, 120, 121
Jining, Xu Zhenyi, 2
jinshi degree, 59; Wang line, 112; Wu Zan, 70, 79, 154, 204; Xu Zhenyi, 228n4; Zhang Huiyan, 16, 21, 33, 49–50, 202, 240n122
juren degree, 58; Cheng Peiyuan, 157;

Zhang Huiyan, 15, 49, 202; Zhang Qi, 33, 70, 203; Zhang Yuesun, 141, 206

Kaifeng, 158; Wang Caipin, 118, 207, 208
Kang Shaoyong, 204
Kang Tongwei, 197
Kang Youwei, 45, 197, 240n128, 264n27
Kangxi zidian (dictionary), 66, 243n6
Koreans: calligraphy buyers, 83, 90, 246n32; Chinese networks, 119–20, 181, 272n24. *See also* Yi Sang-jŏk

labor: gender division of, 126. *See also* employment; family economics; household duties
Lan Dingyuan, 12, 230n14
land tenure: dowries, 59; "managerial landlords," 37, 236n79; Ming transformation of, 46–47, 48
Langui baolu (Wanyan Yun Zhu), 128
learning: Changzhou scholars, 45; elite status and, 185, 186–87; Han learning movement, 56, 57; practical learning *(shixue)*, 52, 128; Qing values, 175, 181, 199; Western learning *(yangxue)*, 5–6, 182, 185, 206, 228n13, 276n87; women's learning *(nüxue)*, 12, 197–99; women's learning denigrated, 13, 48, 87, 135, 181, 197, 230n18, 246nn36,37. See also *cainü* ("talented woman"); calligraphy; classics; "examination culture"; *jiaxue* ("family learning"); literary culture; medicine; studios; teaching positions
li (clerical script) calligraphy, 93, 232n35, 241n134
Li Bin, 109–10
Li Ciming, 256n130
Li Hongzhang, 120, 121, 192–93, 208, 257n135; Wang Caipin as governess with (unverified), 270n88, 275n78
Li Luan: birth, 205, 238n98; concubine for Zhang Yuesun, 109–10, 120, 141, 187–89, 205, 207, 238n98, 253n101, 274n68; learning, 141–42; status, 187–88, 189, 190; Wang Caipin's poetry club, 144, 157, 207

116, 203, 205, 233n49, 234n53, 236n73, 245nn18,19; Zhang Juesun, 24; Zhang Lunying, 65, 81–83, 95–97, 110, 116, 120, 128, 135–36, 140, 141, 155, 204, 207, 208, 270n90; Zhang Qi studies and teachings, 24, 122, 202; Zhang Wanying, 75, 81, 95, 98, 112, 114, 116, 131, 135–36, 140, 149–50, 155, 179, 189, 207, 263n23; Zhang Yin, 128; Zhang Yuesun, 120, 135–36; Zuo Fen, 264n28. See also *ci* (song lyrics); *gan shi* (poems on politics); publishing; Shen Shanbao; Zhang Qieying poetry

Polachek, James, 125, 128, 256n125, 257n143, 258n147

politics, 263n21; anti-Manchu, 194–95; Bao Shichen, 40, 103, 146, 185, 251n83, 263n20; Beijing, 115, 145–46; in poetry and song lyrics, 103, 124, 125–26, 128, 149, 195, 250–51n81; women and, 12, 230n13, 261n3, 264n25; Zhang Huiyan, 125–26, 191; Zhang Qieying, 103–4, 115–16, 126, 145–47, 150, 195, 250n71, 251n83, 252n93, 263n21; Zhang Wanying, 149–50. See also Daoguang Emperor; foreigners; Jiaqing Emperor; Ming dynasty; Qianlong Emperor; Qing dynasty; Taiping Rebellion

prose: *guwen* style, 116, 124, 202; parallel style *(pianwen)*, 124, 125; prose-poems, 11, 155; women's, 126; Zhang Huiyan's collection, 203, 234n56; Zhang Wanying, 106, 114, 116, 126, 155, 206, 207, 235n59, 253n94, 255n116. See also biographies of women; eulogies; literature; memoirs

publishing, 46, 126, 165–69, 174; calligraphy, 52; *Chanyun ji* reprint, 208, 241n138; commercial, 174; by Li Zhaoluo, 136, 138–39, 146, 191–92, 203, 206; Liang Qichao's "General Discussion on Reform" ("Bianfa tong yi"), 197; male sponsors of women's writing, 169, 270–71n3; production assistants, 165–66, 167 *fig;* by Shen Shanbao, 100–101, 105–6, 107; song lyric collections, 88, 125, 202, 205,

246n40, 258n150; Wang Caipin's poems, 1, 5, 159, 163, 168, 196, 208; women's poetry anthologies, 100–101, 105–6, 107, 123, 243n3, 253n94, 255n116; Wu Lanwan poems, 121; Xu Zhenyi imprint, 1, 5, 163, 165, 208; Zhang Huiyan prose collection, 203, 234n56; Zhang Lunying reprinted poems, 120, 270n90; by Zhang Qi, 33, 34, 56, 88, 203, 205, 233n49, 235n71; Zhang Qi collected works printed after death, 206, 208, 270n90; Zhang Qieying poetry not published by Yuesun, 105, 121, 208. See also literature; medical books; studios; Zhang Yuesun's publishing projects

Qian Mengdian, 168, 239n110
Qian Weicheng, 46, 239n110
Qian Zizhen, 28, 38, 43, 189
"Qian-Jia" era, 45
Qianlong Emperor, 49, 202; death, 21, 103–4, 126, 202; Hong Liangji and, 239n105; Southern Tours, 46; Tang family honors from, 9
Qin Liangyu, 167, 263–64n24
Qing dynasty, 175; calligraphy, 241n135; dowry, 242nn154,155; fall, 195; learning values, 175, 181, 199; Li Zhaoluo atlas of, 205; medicine, 56–57; monograph on the arts, 126; reforms, 45, 197, 202; song lyrics, 124, 126–29, 259–60; Wanyan Yun Zhu anthologizing, 106, 128, 181. See also Manchus; politics; Restoration/ "self-strengthening" movement
Qing shi hui poetry anthology, 128
Qiu Jin, 129, 199, 246n31, 259n161
Qu Qiubai, 44
Qu Yuan, 156, 265n38; *Li sao*, 125
"Quan shui" (in *Book of Odes*), 266n41

Rankin, Mary, 195
Ren Daorong, 122
republic, Chinese, 164
Restoration/"self-strengthening" movement, 2–3, 228n5; leaders, 2, 5, 7–8, 51, 121, 183, 208

Caipin's poetry club, 144, 157, 207; Wang Caipin's sister, 135, 144, 147; Zhang Wanying's daughter, 266n45

Wang Chenbi: birth, 92, 206, 254n106; capping, 207, 248n53; marriage to Zhang Xiangzhen, 177, 179, 189, 207, 272n28; Wang Caipin's brother, 134, 148, 158; Zhang Wanying's son, 92, 111, 113, 266n45

Wang Ding, 103–4, 251n84, 252nn86,90

Wang Hui, 234n58

Wang Qi, 56

Wang Shizhen, 257n142

Wang Xi, 111–13, 177; burial, xvi, 113–15, 147–49, 180, 207; concubine of, 111, 188–89, 254n106, 260n1; death, 113, 153, 207, 268n72; *Donghai ji* printing, 205; employment, 39, 90, 95, 98, 111, 131–32, 154, 189, 206, 253–54n105; Hangzhou, 90, 131, 206; mourning for, 148, 152, 153, 207; in painting, xx *plate*, 5, 140; poetry, 112, 131; Shandong, 40, 71; song lyrics, 70, 71, 111, 204, 207, 253–54n105; Taicang kinsmen, xvi, 113–15, 148, 149, 176, 207, 254n109; Wang Caipin's father, 5, 131, 135–36, 147–48, 158; Zhang Wanying's husband, 43, 70, 71, 80, 81, 90, 98, 111–13, 131, 153, 154, 155, 176, 206, 207

Wang Xijue, 112, 254n109

Wang Yuanqi, 112

Wang Yun, 127

wangzu (leading families), 176–77

Wanlin studio, 73, 108, 121, 136, 206, 231n20

Wanyan Yun Zhu, 181, 236n80; *Guochao guixiu zheng shi ji,* 106, 128; *Langui baolu,* 128; Zhang Qieying and, 106, 123, 127–28, 250n75

wanyue ("feminine") style of song lyrics, 127

Wei Ji, 163, 270n87

wenbing ("warm factor") school of medicine, 242n149

Weng Fanggang, 232n35, 241n133, 251n81

Western learning *(yangxue),* 5–6, 182, 185, 206, 228n13, 276n87

White Lotus rebels, 58, 117

Widmer, Ellen, 174

widows, 183; chaste widow arch for Lady Jiang, 36, 37, 72, 204, 244n9; faithful, 20, 202, 239n110; girls whose fiancé has died, 30–31; homes for, 1, 164, 190, 253n100, 271n14; Lady Bai, 17, 237n96, 239n110; remarriage refused by, 20–21; suicide of, 20–21, 237n96; Wang Caipin, 1, 182

"woman problem" *(funü wenti),* 196–97

women: advice books, 12, 134–35, 230n14; beauty in, 14; calligraphic style, 83; classics for, 11–12; death causes, 183; elite status, 185–90, 197–98, 235n43; footbinding, 7, 24–25, 117, 166–67, 233n47, 271n4; "four quintessential attributes," 12; *fu dao* (wifely way), 172; Han customs, 7; household segregation, 7, 10, 66, 117, 132, 133, 185–86; learning *(nüxue),* 12, 197–99; learning denigrated in, 13, 48, 87, 135, 181, 197–98, 230n18, 246nn36,37; *lienü* (exemplary women), 127–28; networks, 176–78, 181–82, 196, 198–99, 274n62, 276n76; "new women," 8, 182, 196, 199–200, 228n13; object of a male poet's gaze, 126–27; patronage for poets, 100, 123, 128, 143, 168, 195, 260n167; poetry anthologies, 100–101, 105–6, 107, 123, 243n3, 253n94, 255n116; poetry styles, 101, 103, 122, 127; and politics, 12, 230n13, 261n3, 264n25; published by men, 168–69; during republic, 164; ritual hierarchies in household, 91, 172, 180–81; self-censorship in writing, 166, 270–71n3; "self-strengthening" program, 8, 183; "sister influence," 177–78; song lyric writers, 126–29, 259–60n165; suicide, 18, 20–21, 31, 169–70, 237n96; Taiping, 7, 117, 229n14; uterine family, 276n76; in uxorilocal marriage, 177, 180, 188, 190; virtues, 11–12, 174–75, 197–99, 276n93; warriors, 117; women's quarters, 7, 10, 66, 132, 133, 185; *zui nenggan,* 169. *See also* affinal kin; biographies of women; *cainü* ("talented woman"); concubines; family economics; *guixiu*

women (continued)
  (genteel ladies); household duties;
  needlework; voices, women's; widows;
  zhennü ("faithful maiden")
Women's Journal (Funü zazhi), 196
Women's Learning (Lan Dingyuan), 12,
  230n14
wooden fish (muyu), 81, 245n26
writing. See calligraphy; literature; poetry;
  prose; publishing
wu guige qi ("no trace of the boudoir"),
  168. See also poetry; women
Wu Lanwan, 121, 122, 257n137
Wu Lanze, 257n137
Wu Ren'an, 48, 239n112
wu xing ("Five Phases" in nature), 56
Wu Zan, 243n8; Beijing, 39, 68, 70, 87–
  88, 92, 99, 206; birth, 201; Changshu
  native place, 48, 68, 118, 250n72;
  death, 116, 148, 207; jinshi degree, 70,
  79, 154, 204; song lyrics, 70, 71, 92,
  204, 236n83, 244n10; son Zonghan,
  68–69, 88, 92, 203, 243–44n8; Zhang
  Qieying's husband, 43, 48, 68–71,
  79–80, 92, 103, 116, 148, 154, 203,
  204
Wu Zhiying, 246n31
Wu Zonghan: copyeditor of Zhang Qieying collection, 167 fig, 244n8; son
  of Wu Zan, 68–69, 88, 92, 203, 243–
  44n8; wife, 107
Wuchang, 142–43; dialect, 143–44; Taiping
  Rebellion, 118–19, 120–21, 163, 192;
  Zhang family, 108–13, 117–18, 120,
  142–57, 163, 193, 207–8, 271n14

Xi Peilan, 93, 249n60
Xiang Rong, 118
Xie Daoyun, 245n16
Xie Lingyun, 82
Xie Qinggao, 138
Xiefang ji, 106
Xin Chang, 156, 265n39
Xin Xianying, 156, 265n39
Xu Dachun, 57
Xu Zhenyi: concubine of, 2, 163, 270n89;
  employment, 1, 3, 186, 227–28nn1,4;
  publishing imprint, 1, 5, 163, 165, 208;

Wang Caipin's employer, xvi, 1–5,
  8, 122, 163, 193, 227n1, 228n10
Xuannan ci she, 257n143
Xue Ziheng, 168
Xuehai Academy, Ruan Yuan, 40, 137

yamen, defined, 237n88
Yan Yuan, 57
Yang Fang, 263n20
Yanghu pai, 202
Yangzhou: Bao Shichen, 89, 203, 206, 208;
  Taiping Rebellion, 192, 208
Ye Gui, 57
Ye Shaoyuan, 178
Yellow Emperor's Inner Classic (Huang Di
  nei jing su wen), 56, 57, 241n137
Yellow River, flooding, 158, 228n7, 252n86
Yi Kezhong, 237n87
Yi Sang-jök, 208, 247n43, 248n51, 272n23;
  friendship with Zhang Yuesun, 92,
  98, 118–20, 191, 192, 206, 237n89,
  249n66, 255n121
Yin Hao, 252n88
Yingjili (England), 138–39, 145–46. See also
  British
yong yi ("quacks"), 57, 62, 242–43n2
yongwu ci ("poem on a thing," "poem in
  praise of an object"), 102, 128–29
youth culture, siblings, 179–80
Yu Xinzhong, 184, 274n56
Yuan dynasty: social system, 47; song
  lyrics, 124
Yuan Haowen, 103, 166, 250–51n81
Yuan Mei, 87
Yuezhou, Taiping Rebellion in, 117–18, 195
Yun Jing, 45, 202, 239–40n112
Yun Shouping, 122, 234n58
Yun Zhu. See Wanyan Yun Zhu
Yuzhou, 158–59; Wang Caipin, 156–64, 175

Zeng Guofan, 230n14, 255n121; daughter,
  276n93; Restoration, 2, 5, 7, 51, 121,
  183; Taiping Rebellion, 2, 7, 120,
  192, 227n4, 268n63; Tongcheng
  school, 258n144; Xu Zhenyi and,
  5–6, 227nn1,4; Zhang Yuesun and,
  227n1, 257n135
Zeng Jifen, 276n93

TEXT:
11/13.5 Adobe Garamond
DISPLAY:
Adobe Garamond, Perpetua
COMPOSITOR:
Integrated Composition Systems
INDEXER:
Barbara Roos
PRINTER AND BINDER:
Thomson-Shore, Inc.